D1536272

POSTMODERN IMPERIALISM
Geopolitics and the Great Games

Eric with protesters in Tahrir Square at the statue of General Abdul Munim Riad who died in the War of Attrition 1967--1970 (*photo*: Mahmoud Shaban)

POSTMODERN IMPERIALISM

Geopolitics and the
Great Games

ERIC WALBERG

CLARITY PRESS, INC.

© 2011 Eric Walberg
ISBN: 0-9833539-3-X
       978-0-9833539-3-5

In-house editor: Diana G. Collier
Cover: R. Jordan P. Santos

Library of Congress Cataloging-in-Publication Data

Walberg, Eric.
  Postmodern imperialism : geopolitics and the great games / by Eric Walberg.
  p. cm.
  ISBN-13: 978-0-9833539-3-5
  ISBN-10: 0-9833539-3-X
  1. Imperialism--History--20th century. 2. Imperialism--History--21st century.
3. Geopolitics--20th century. 4. Geopolitics--21st century. 5. Game theory. I.
Title.
  JC359.W18 2011
  325'.32--dc23
                              2011017873

Clarity Press, Inc.
Ste. 469, 3277 Roswell Rd. NE
Atlanta, GA. 30305 , USA
http://www.claritypress.com

TABLE OF CONTENTS

ILLUSTRATIONS

ABBREVIATIONS

ADL   Anti-Defamation League (1913)
AIPAC American Israel Public Affairs Committee (1963)
AJC   American Jewish Committee (1906)
ASEAN Association of Southeast Asian Nations (1967), members
       Indonesia, Malaysia, the Philippines, Singapore, Thailand,
       Brunei, Myanmar, Cambodia, Laos, and Vietnam
BCCI   Bank of Credit and Commerce International (1972-99)
BRIC   Informal economic bloc (2008), members Brazil, Russia, India,
       China, as of 2010 including South Africa, making it BRICS
CFR   Council on Foreign Relations, New York-based think tank
       (1921)
CSTO   Collective Security Treaty Organization (2002), members
       Armenia, Belarus, Kazakhstan, Kyrgyzstan, Russia, Tajikistan,
       Uzbekistan
CIS   Commonwealth of Independent States (1991), successor
       to the Soviet Union, members Armenia, Azerbaijan,
       Kazakhstan, Kyrgyzstan, Moldova, Turkmenistan, Tajikistan,
       and Uzbekistan
GATT   General Agreement on Tariffs and Trade (1949–93), replaced
       by the World Trade Organization (WTO) in 1995
GCC   Gulf Cooperation Council (1981), members Bahrain, Kuwait,

	Oman, Qatar, Saudi Arabia and the United Arab Emirates
IDF	Israeli Defense Force
IAEA	International Atomic Energy Agency (1957)
ISAF	International Security Assistance Force (2003), NATO forces in Afghanistan
ISI	Inter-Services Intelligence, Pakistan's umbrella intelligence agency (1948)
NPT	Nuclear Non-Proliferation Treaty (1970), 189 members including the US, Russia, Britain, France, and China
OPEC	Organisation of Petroleum Exporting Countries (1960)
OSCE	Organization for Security and Cooperation in Europe (1973), 56 members in Europe, the Caucasus, Central Asia and North America
PNAC	Project for a New American Century, Washington-based neoconservative think tank (1997–2005)
RIC	Informal economic bloc (2001), member Russia, India, China
RIIA	Royal Institute of International Affairs (1920), London-based think tank
SAARC	South Asian Association for Regional Cooperation (1985), members Bangladesh, Bhutan, India, the Maldives, Nepal, Pakistan and Sri Lanka, with Afghanistan joining in 2005 and Mauritius in 2008
SCO	Shanghai Cooperation Organization (1996), members China, Kazakhstan, Kyrgyzstan, Russia, Tajikistan, and Uzbekistan
UAE	United Arab Emirates, members Abu Dhabi, Dubai, Sharjah, Ajman, Umm al-Quwain, Ras al-Khaimah and Fujairah (1971)
ZOA	Zionist Organization of America (1897)

ACKNOWLEDGMENTS

In the first place, I would like to thank Diana Collier at Clarity Press for her careful and thoughtful work in editing my MS.

There are many people who contributed indirectly to this work, both in assembling key information from the huge flow of facts and in sharing their ideas; in particular, Peter Myers, Rick Rozoff, Gilad Atzmon and Israel Shamir.

The internet has created a radically new virtual resource that gives access to information on an unprecedented scale, requiring much hard work to master, and at the same time providing new vistas for those who want to understand what is happening around them. Most of the people who helped me digest facts and formulate my ideas, including the above-mentioned writers, I have met only online. WikiLeaks, which may be defined as an anonymous collective of truthseekers around the world, provided confirmation of many elements in the chilling games now being played out in the world, and I salute Julian Assange for his courage and brilliance.

Thanks go to Mike Lucas for helping me get to Moscow during the Cold War so that I could experience the Soviet reality first hand, to my editors at *Al-Ahram Weekly*, who gave me the opportunity to write uncensored about the many burning topics of world politics and economics confronting us, to graphics designer Ahmed Sultan, and to my sister Carol, who provided a necessary retreat to collect my thoughts during my periods of relaxation from the pressures of newspaper deadlines.

Finally, I would like to thank my parents Alf and Betty who set an example for me to follow by making their faith central to their lives, and for supporting my efforts to take advantage of the many opportunities that western 'civilization' presents, which culminated in this work.

PREFACE

To young people today, the world as a global village appears as a given, a ready-made order, as if human evolution all along was logically moving towards our high-tech, market-driven society, dominated by the wealthy United States. To bring the world to order, the US must bear the burden of oversize defense spending, capture terrorists, eliminate dictators, and warn ungrateful nations like China and Russia to adjust their policies so as not to hinder the US in its altruistic *mission civilatrice*.

The reality is something else entirely, the only truth in the above characterization being the overwhelming military dominance of the US in the world today. The US itself is the source of much of the world's terrorism, its 1.6 million troops in over a thousand bases around the world the most egregious terrorists, leaving the Osama bin Ladens in the shade, and other lesser critics of US policies worried about their job prospects.

My own realization of the true nature of the world order began with my journey to England to study economics at Cambridge University in September 1973. I decided to take the luxury SS France ocean liner which offered a student rate of a few hundred dollars (and unlimited luggage), where I met American students on Marshall and Rhodes scholarships (I had the less prestigious Mackenzie King scholarship), and used my wiles to enjoy the perks of first class. The ship was a microcosm of society, a benign one. The world was my oyster and I wanted to share my joy with everyone.

But I was in for a shock. Cambridge was also a microcosm of society, but a very different one. My friends at Cambridge included many Latin Americans, and the tragic events of that September 11—the US-orchestrated coup against Salvador Allende in Chile—were what I was to cut my political teeth on. The look of despair on the face of a Chilean friend, suddenly a refugee whose friends and family were now in peril, was etched in my memory. That began my path of study and activism, and drove home to me the essence of the world political and economic system. Imperialism was not an abstraction, but a devastating force that destroyed good, idealistic people, whole peoples. Enemies of imperialism must be reconsidered, in the first place, the Soviet Union, which until then I had accepted as a dangerous and evil force in the world.

I immediately began studying Russian and was determined to experience Soviet reality from the inside. The "Soviet threat" was the pretext for Nixon's undermining the Chilean revolution. It was the pretext for the blockade of Cuba. It was the pretext for the horrors the US was inflicting on the Vietnamese. Was it really the evil empire which I had been indoctrinated into fearing and loathing my entire life? I had to find out for myself.

Looking back on this turning point in my life, I can only marvel at the few slight breathing spaces in the Cold War that allowed people to reject the capitalist paradigm, to realize who the real enemy is. As opposed to Thatcher's TINA (There Is No Alternative) —There Was An Alternative (TWAA)! Fear of this 'enemy' quickly evaporated among intelligent mainstream people in the West during the periods of detente (1941–48, 1963–68, 1973–79). These brief respites were tactical retreats in the long-term fight by imperialism, biding its time.

My studies were framed by the coup in Chile in September 1973 and the liberation of Saigon in the spring of 1975. Celebrating the latter moment with my friends in the university cafeteria is also etched in my mind. The world belonged to us. The low point for US imperialism, the high point (the last, it turned out) for the Soviet Union. I studied with Marxists such as Maurice Dobb, and neo-Ricardians such as Piero Sraffa, Luigi Pasinetti, and Joan Robinson, and suddenly saw the twentieth century through new lenses.

Upon my return to Toronto, I sought out what I learned were called "fellow travelers". There weren't so many as I expected. In desperation, I looked in the phone book under USSR, but there was not even a Soviet Consulate in Canada's largest city (though there was a Bulgarian, a Czech, even a Cuban one). I eventually stumbled across the Canada-USSR Friendship Society, a motley collection of primarily Slavic and east European immigrants, Jews, with a smattering of WASP peaceniks. A friendly if doctrinaire group, with no sign of any super spies like Kim Philby. In retrospect, I see that the peacenik contingent was more conspicuous in its absence.

With great difficulty, I got to Moscow in 1979 to study Russian at Moscow State University (MGU) through the Friendship Society, a bizarre and memorable experience to say the least. I fell sick and became sicker after a short stay in a filthy hospital, but managed to stick it out till we were peremptorily shunted to unfinished Olympic accommodations in order to make room for newly revolutionary Ethiopian students at MGU.

The Soviet invasion of Afghanistan took place as we trudged through the freezing mud to our new residence in December, the subsequent collapse of détente playing out on an international stage my own frustrations with "real existing socialism", a system that left no room for criticism or doubt in the face of much nonsense and cruelty.

My former enthusiasm for Soviet-style communism* was gone; however, on returning to North America, I was faced with the mindless propaganda and belligerence of Reagan America, and I realized that my love affair with the ornery Soviet beast was not over—TWAA. When Gorbachev dismantled censorship (*glasnost*) and began his ill-fated economic reforms (*perestroika*), I landed a job at *Moscow News*. My sense of urgency in getting there ASAP was not ill-founded, as it turned out.

The brief respites from the Cold War and this final crazy attempt to create a 'nice' socialism were indeed remarkable. The US actually feared and respected another country, and that country held out its diplomatic hand in friendship, only to find itself subverted by its new 'friend'. The Bushes and now Obama have all vowed since never to let another country challenge the US militarily again. How ironic, now that conventional military superiority has lost all meaning in an age of dirty bombs and anthrax.

The Soviet Union produced environmental disasters, notably the death of the Aral Sea. Collective farming enforced at gunpoint destroyed a vibrant peasant tradition. The gulags and Stalinist repression were a terrible tragedy. But colonialism and fascism killed far more innocent people, and both were aggressive, starting wars with other countries. The Soviet Union was a one-party system, a dictatorship, but not an aggressively expanding empire, contrary to what we were and are indoctrinated into believing.

For all its political flaws, it showed the viability of a non-capitalist way of organizing technologically advanced urban society. Its economic flaws—inefficiency, sloppiness, low standards, ecological disregard—were countered by its pluses—guaranteed employment, free public services, encouragement of modest material needs, broad access to culture, security for the individual, a less competitive more egalitarian lifestyle. This is how it was understood in the third world, where its passing is still mourned.

Until the collapse of the Soviet Union, the main foe of Israel, I hadn't paid special attention to the Middle East, assuming that as the anti-imperialist forces grew, Israel would be pressured to make peace. The assassination of Yitzak Rabin in 1994 and the ascendancy of the neocons made it clear that this was not going to happen.

The defeat of communism meant that the only remaining anti-imperialist cultural force was Islam, and I was drawn to Uzbekistan in Central Asia, with a vibrant Muslim heritage. This culminated in another major turning point for me—watching the twin towers collapse 28 years after the "9/11" coup in Chile, on that more familiar "9/11" of 2001, in bleak post-Soviet Tashkent.

My immediate reaction was that their collapse simply could not be the work of a band of poorly trained Muslims orchestrated by someone in a cave in neighboring Afghanistan. Subsequent study has confirmed to me that the events of 2001 had far more to do with US imperialism—and Israel—than Islam.

I am fortunate to have lived my life on both sides of the "Iron Curtain" and now in the heart of the supposed enemy today—the Islamic world. This has given me the opportunity to experience alternative realities, to step back from my western heritage and see more clearly how the western world confronts and plays with other countries and cultures. There are many such journeys of discovery by people coming of age politically. I hope my reflections provide readers the opportunity to step back from their frame of reference, and help them understand the games we are forced to play.

*A note on the use of the terms communism, capitalism and imperialism: communism refers to both the theory as proposed by Marx and the attempts to realize the theory as embodied in the social formations of post-1917 Russia and post-WWII eastern Europe. While the latter strayed far from the theory, they were nonetheless inspired by Marx. Critics may replace "communism" with "failed workers' state" or "state capitalism" as they like. This does not undermine the overall thesis about communism made here. I treat the terms capitalism and imperialism as scientific terms as used by Marx and Lenin. The Soviet Union became a ruthless dictatorship under Stalin, but the logic of it and its relations with eastern Europe were not imperialist. To use such terms cavalierly to refer to noncapitalist social formations would reduce any analysis to rubble—a kind of intellectual 9/11, an apt metaphor for how US capitalist mind-control prevents any real opposition from taking root.

INTRODUCTION
GEOPOLITICS AND THE GREAT GAMES

Turkestan, Afghanistan, Transcaspia, Persia—
to many these names breathe only a sense of utter remoteness or
a memory of strange vicissitudes and of moribund romance. To me,
I confess, they are the pieces on a chessboard upon which is being
played out a game for the dominion of the world.
Lord Curzon, viceroy of India (1898)[1]

Who rules East Europe commands the Heartland;
Who rules the Heartland commands the World-Island;
Who rules the World-Island commands the World.
Halford Mackinder (1919)

Geopolitics of Central Asia and Middle East

The term "Great Game" was coined in the nineteenth century to describe the rivalry between Russia and Britain. Britain sent spies disguised as surveyors and traders to Afghanistan and Turkestan and, several times, armies to keep the Russians at bay. The ill-fated Anglo-Afghan war of 1839–42 was precipitated by fears that the Russians were encroaching on British interests in India after Russia established a diplomatic and trade presence in Afghanistan. Already by the nineteenth century there was no such thing as neutral territory. The entire world was now a gigantic playing field for the major industrial powers, and Eurasia was the center of this playing field.

The game motif is useful to describe the broader rivalry between nations and economic systems with the rise of imperialism and the pursuit of world power. This game goes beyond UK rivalry with Russia over Afghanistan, for the heart of Eurasia really encompasses both Central Asia and the Middle East, what was once Turkestan, the

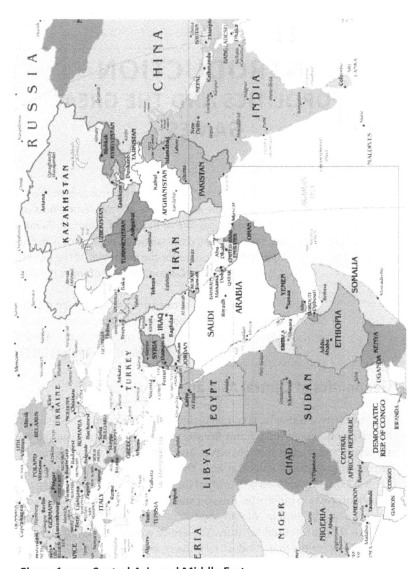

Figure 1 map Central Asia and Middle East

Persian empire and the Ottoman Caliphate, comprising the Persian, Turkic and Arab worlds, peoples that are mostly Muslim.

Eurasia contrasts geopolitically with the north-south American hemisphere which since the days of the Monroe Doctrine[2] has been securely under the hegemony of the US. The Monroe Doctrine is the most enduring of geopolitical declarations, promoting the idea of national and continental self-sufficiency and the drive for hegemony by the dominant power as much for supremacy as for economic interest. America's geography prevents any rival from challenging this state of affairs, unlike the much vaster Eurasia, stretching both east-west and north-south, containing more than 80 per cent of the world's population, with many rivals contending for hegemony.

This study of the geopolitics of Eurasia begins with the US joining in the competition in the early twentieth century, when Britain, as the dominant world power, was laying out its colonial game plan for the region at the expense of the other imperial powers.

The term geopolitics refers to the use of politics in controlling territories, where certain geographical positions are more strategic than others, for resources, historical and socio-political reasons. It is usually associated with the early twentieth century geographer and politician, Halford Mackinder, though he thought the term misleading, too romantic, and leading to false comparisons.[3] Munich professor Karl Haushofer was more enthusiastic about manipulating "territorial competition and cooperation" in the "heartland" to provide "a place in the sun" for a New European Order and eventually a Eurasian Order,[4] one dominated not by Britain but by Germany in cooperation with Russia, and opposed to Anglo-American power. The "rimland" Britain relied on naval power to contain the heartland powers, namely Germany.

Friedrich Ratzel noted in *Lebensraum* (1901) that Eurasian land borders in the massive expanse of Eurasia are arbitrary and can be changed to meet the increasing needs of the (in the view of Haushofer and Ratzel, German) population and industry. Ratzel theorized that states are organic and growing, artificial constructs, that the land and people form a spiritual bond, and that a healthy nation's borders are bound to expand. This was the Monroe Doctrine and the concurrent Manifest Destiny writ large for the Eurasian continent.

The two components of Eurasia which are the focus here— the Middle East and Central Asia—constitute the legendary Silk Road, composed of various routes for cultural, commercial and technological exchange between traders, merchants, pilgrims, missionaries, soldiers and nomads from China, India, Tibet, Persia and Mediterranean countries, dating from the third century BC and deriving its name from the lucrative Chinese silk trade.

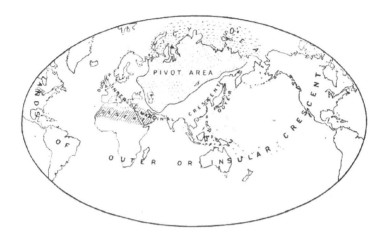

Figure 2 map Heartland

With the rise of Islam in the seventh century, its central routes, apart from China, were united in opposition to the Christian/ pagan/ Jewish West as the Islamic Caliphate of the Ummayads, centered in Damascus, and later the Abbasids in Baghdad, uniting the vast distances under the banner of Islam. The Mongols, originally shamanists who later converted to Islam, swept down through Eurasia in the 13th–14th centuries, briefly uniting it with China. The Muslim Temurids again united it in the 14th-15th centuries. Over time these proto-empires disintegrated into tribal fiefdoms in the east and the Ottoman Caliphate in the west, but without developing the western-style ethnic nationalisms, nation states or the economic system of capitalism.

The Middle East was united under the Ottomans starting in the fourteenth century, while Turkestan (Central Asia) and the Silk Route went into decline after the Temurids, due to the rise of western seafaring commerce and thereafter of western empires linked to the East by ocean transport.

Russia annexed most of Turkestan through the 17th–19th centuries, beginning with Kazakhstan and the Caucasus. British rivalry in what became known as the Great Game resulted in several attempts by Britain to subdue Afghanistan in the nineteenth century, culminating in an agreement with Russia in the 1890s where Afghanistan would remain neutral territory. "In 1907 Russian foreign minister Count Alexander Izvolsky and British ambassador Sir Arthur Nicholson signed a secret treaty in St Petersburg in which both countries defined their imperial interests in Central Asia. The Russian government accepted that Afghanistan lay in the British sphere of influence. In turn, London pledged never to challenge the Tsar's rule over the rest of Central Asia."[5] China asserted its claim over east Turkestan (Xinjiang province) in 1877. This established the spheres of influence that have endured more or less until today.

The decline in the Middle East was slower, linked as it was more directly with the West through commerce. During the nineteenth century imperial game, what I call here **Great Game I** (GGI), Britain kept Afghanistan, Iran and the Ottoman Caliphate as nominally independent political formations, though in compliance with British interests. The former were carefully monitored by Britain, while in the latter, the weakened Ottoman rule had turned the caliphate into a useful neutral actor allowing the various imperial powers to pursue trade in the region without resorting to war.

This situation changed radically with WWI. The war was a disaster for all the European imperial powers, and the Russian revolution in 1917 was a declaration of war against the imperialist system itself. This marked the beginning of what is called here **Great Game II** (GGII)—the Cold War between imperialism and communism, where the US united its former imperial rivals, Britain, Germany, France, et al to fight the anti-empire forces, though this game did not take center stage till the end of WWII. The period from 1917 to WWII can be called the **endgame of GGI.**

In the Middle East, cynical British plans to carve up the Ottoman Caliphate after WWI were exposed when the Russian communists immediately published British diplomatic correspondence with Tsar Nicholas II, much as WikiLeaks exposed diplomatic mendacity in 2010. Britain went ahead anyway in 1918 to carve up the caliphate, as a political compromise in the region with rival interests of France, Germany and imperial Russia was no longer necessary. Apart from the Turkish Anatolian heartland, the caliphate was divided into quasi-colonies—"mandates"—with a radical plan to create a Jewish state in the Palestinian heartland.

Turkestan was now part of the new communist politico-economic formation. Until the end of GGII, with the collapse of the Soviet Union, it remained off bounds to imperialism, a backwater, an integral part of a kind of secular caliphate, where borders meant little and people were united around a stern communist faith rather than nationalism or religion. In the 1920s the USSR divided it up roughly according to ethnicity into *pro forma* administrative divisions Uzbekistan, Kazakhstan, Tajikistan, Kyrgyzstan and Turkmenistan (in order of population), the 'stans', plus Azerbaijan. These were developed in accordance with Soviet central plans, achieving a high standard of living compared to nonsocialist neighbors Afghanistan, Iran and colonial Pakistan, but at the expense of Islam, which was largely repressed.[6]

As the Soviet Union was not viewed then as an imperial threat to British India, Afghanistan, a weak monarchy, lost its geopolitical importance as a Russian gateway to India during the GGI endgame. Iran, which straddles the Middle East and Central Asia, was also a weak monarchy, but by the late nineteenth century was becoming far more important than Afghanistan, as vast oil reserves had been discovered there, and coal was being replaced by the much more practical oil as the fuel to run the growing empires. Iran was occupied by Britain and imperial Russia during WWI, and again by Britain and the Soviet Union in WWII, during the GGI endgame, to keep it from siding with Germany and to ensure access to its oil. It became vital to the support of the empire in GGII but took on a radically different role as GGIII got underway.

The Great Game II endgame—the embrace of Islamists by Reagan and the collapse of the Soviet Union is a page turner. Truth is indeed stranger than fiction.

With the collapse of the Soviet Union and the socialist bloc in 1989–91 and the beginning of what is called here **Great Game III** (GGIII), the two regions—the Middle East and Central Asia—once again came together as a new Silk Road, stretching as it did a millennium ago from Italy to China. It is once again accessible to all comers and takes in at least seventeen new political entities: the former Yugoslav republics of Bosnia, Croatia, Macedonia, Montenegro, Serbia, Slovenia, and Kosovo in the Balkans; Armenia, Azerbaijan and Georgia in the South Caucasus; Kazakhstan, Kyrgyzstan, Tajikistan, Turkmenistan and Uzbekistan in Central Asia; with Moldova and Ukraine in eastern Europe.

But instead of being united under Islam or the Mongols, today it is largely under the sway of the US and its multilateral military arm—the North Atlantic Treaty Organization (NATO). The way stations on NATO's twenty-first century caravan route from the Atlantic Ocean to the Chinese frontier reveal the nature of the current game. All the above new countries have official ties with NATO, and two former Yugoslav republics, Slovenia and Croatia, are now full members. Most have provided troops for US wars in Afghanistan and Iraq. The US has military bases in Kosovo, Kyrgyzstan, and Tajikistan, is directly arming and training Georgia's military forces, occupies Iraq, and is waging war in Afghanistan from Pakistan.

The region, from the Balkans to the borders of China, has been one of intrigue and war for a century, more so now than ever. US-NATO interest in this vital crossroads is keen. The region is important in geopolitical-strategic terms: US control there means containing Russia, China and Iran, the dream of British strategists in GGI and of American strategists in GGII&III. It is also the location of most of the world's petrochemical resources, from Saudi Arabia and the Persian Gulf in the south to Kazakhstan in the north and Iran in the east. This, of course, might explain why the US is so keen to take and keep control of it and has gambled its all in pursuit of this goal over the past decade. The three major wars conducted by the US in the past decade—Yugoslavia (1999), Afghanistan (2001) and Iraq (2003)—all lie on this legendary Silk Road.

Britain, the US and NATO have no business invading any of these countries. Rather, in any peaceful scenario for the region, it is local powers that must come together to promote their regional economic well being and security. Further wars would be a tragedy for all concerned. But such wars are far from Washington, and are increasingly being fought from computer control panels in such unassuming suburban locations as MacDill Air Force Base Florida, home of the US Central Command, rather than by ground troops in the region's hostile deserts and mountains. And the forces abetting war are not rational in any meaningful sense of the word.[7]

After all, it was perfectly 'rational' in the mind of Robert Gates, a National Security Council adviser to President Carter in 1979, to help finance and arm Islamists in Afghanistan to defeat the Soviet Union. The planners in the Pentagon or NATO HQs argue 'rationally' in 2010 that their current deadly surge and bombings in Afghanistan will bring peace to the region. If such plans fail, at least the chaos they engender is far away. The only peace the US has brought to the region so far in GGII&III is the peace of the dead.

After seven centuries, the fates of both the Middle East and Central Asia have once again converged. But today, the vast region, with its dozens of ethnic groups, tribes, and clans, is composed of largely artificial states, the result of imperial divide-and-rule, inciting friction between peoples who had not experienced such brutal wars and invasions since the fourteenth century. The vast region is once again discovering common roots in Islam, now the chief catalyst of dissent and resistance to the imperial players, the US and Israel, bent as they are on further dismembering the region.

The games as variants of imperialism

Goals
The goal of empire, and of all the games described here, is some variation on economic growth, the pursuit of profit, and (for public consumption)

improving the well-being of the backward peoples—the latter infamously dubbed "the white man's burden" by Rudyard Kipling, though surprisingly not in reference to the British empire, but to the US war against the Philippines, justified as a noble enterprise:

> Go bind your sons to exile
> To serve your captives' need;... [in]
> The savage wars of peace.[8]

This underlying goal is much more hardnosed than sending "sons" to serve "captives' need" in "wars of peace". It is to expropriate the wealth—surplus[9]—of weaker countries—the periphery, their incorporation into the economy of the empire—the center—in a subordinate and profitable way, and to ensure that other competing imperial powers are kept at a disadvantage. Lenin defines imperialism as,

> capitalism in that stage of development in which the dominance of monopolies and finance capital has established itself; in which the export of capital has acquired pronounced importance; in which the division of the world among the international trusts has begun; in which the division of all territories of the globe among the biggest capitalist powers has been completed.[10]

The flowering of imperialism in the late nineteenth century, with all its pomp and cynical manipulation of the masses, was a remarkable development, as J.A. Hobson marveled in 1902:

> Imperialism is only beginning to realize its full resources, to develop into a fine art of the management of nations: the broad bestowal of a franchise, wielded by a people whose education has reached the stage of an uncritical ability to read printed matter, favours immensely the designs of keen business politicians, who, by controlling the press, the schools, and where necessary the churches, impose Imperialism upon the masses under the attractive guise of sensational patriotism.[11]

He saw how capitalism was setting the stage for the first time in history for complete world control, the increasingly conscious goal of GGI imperialists, making innocent Joe Sixpacks their accomplices in murder and theft.

In the span of fewer than two centuries, the struggle to achieve this mastery has gone through distinct stages, with world control the goal. The current game, GGIII, is very different from the previous ones, though there are parallels with the earlier games:

- The great financial houses of GGI, in the first place, the Rothschilds, now have their modern equivalent in the International Monetary Fund (IMF) and other international financial institutions.

- The playing field, the geopolitical context, as in GGI, once again includes both the Middle East and Central Asia, with the fiercest battle once again in Afghanistan.

- As in GGI, there is geopolitical rivalry, but now the rivalry is not only between major powers, but within the imperial team itself, between the US and Israel, rather than the more straightforward GGI rivalry between the likes of Britain, Germany, France and the US and the more complex rivalry of the US and the Soviet Union in GGII.

- The GGII defense treaty against communism, NATO, has been transformed in GGIII to justify the global reach of a US imperialism still in denial.

- As in GGII, there is a common enemy but a very different kind of enemy, one which can never be defeated.

The players use strategies developed and honed over the past century in the earlier games, adding new stratagems, employing ever new technology, though locked into the age-old quest for power and control of resources.

But now the entire region is experiencing unprecedented conflict and upheaval, and the teams in the game of extracting surplus now include all the major world powers in shifting alliances, including Turkey, Iran, Pakistan, India and China, all with their own historical and cultural ties and their own aims and "niches of influence"[12] which must be considered in light of their center/ periphery status. The existence of Israel is an anomaly which lies at the heart of all three games—as a specter in GGI, as an imperial outpost in the Middle East in GGII, and as an independent world player in GGIII, a sometime US ally but actually a rival to all the major players.

The geopolitical and economic objectives in both GGI (competing empires) and GGII (the empire vs communism) were 1. not to lose influence and 2. to gain the most wealth, a zero-sum game. In GGIII, the aims are more complex, as the many players are hardly united into clear camps, and the striving for world control by the empire is occurring all over the world, creating many variations on the underlying game, which is no longer zero-sum.

Strategies

To extract surplus requires direct or indirect political control of the periphery. The colonial powers of GGI and neo-colonial powers of GGII&III preferred to rely on trade and financial means, but if necessary pursued their goals through outright war.

This control is brought about in various ways. The foundations or pillars of imperial hegemony are financial and military-political, to ensure control of world labor power and raw materials. The financial mechanisms include "terms of trade" which benefit the center and money-lending at interest. The private international financiers of GGI have been supplemented by international institutions such as the IMF in guaranteeing the extraction of surplus. The latter are just as much the creation of the center, controlled by the center, to front and facilitate this process. Periphery actors must follow their dictates, which are really just the center's dictates once-removed. Trade in humans (slavery), the backbone of GGI surplus extraction, is replaced by "guest workers" and a vast, largely illegal, stream of migrant labor from the periphery to the now more diffused center,[13] desperate for any work, no matter where and under what conditions.

The political mechanisms of imperialism include creating colonial and—in GGII&III—neocolonial structures which are dependent on the center. The periphery, today's third world, went through a completely different process of nation formation from the center. These countries either resulted from bloody wars of independence as in Latin America and Asia, or were carved into being by imperial powers with borders which were intended to provide the basis for future ethnic and sectarian conflict, and hence external manipulation.

This was the fate of most of the colonies in the Middle East, and was to a large extent intentional. As the main victor of GGI, Britain pursued a divide-and-rule strategy in the Middle East aimed at creating a string of weak, subservient Arab states and a European imperial outpost in a region now vital to the Anglo-American empire.[14] The British occupation and then nightmarish partition of India created festering problems which have become the centerpiece of GGIII conflict in Central Asia.

In keeping with Clausewitz's "War is a mere continuation of politics by other means,"[15] there is 'hard power', and just as important, the many 'soft power' strategies and tactics used in lieu of or in addition to war as part of politics' arsenal. This soft power is called "parapolitics"— the exercise of political power by covert means, which can metastasize into "deep politics"—the interplay of unacknowledged forces over which the original parapolitical agent no longer has control.[16]

Besides the formal institutions of empire, there are informal ones, include piracy and privateering (piracy authorized by the state) a traditional means used by the center to expropriate the periphery's wealth (usually gold and slaves), now romanticized in such legendary figures as Francis Drake. Piracy was transformed by capitalism into various mafia groupings in GGI&II&III, the latest and most powerful being the Russian mafia or Kosher Nostra. Privateers—mercenaries—key players in GGI, are now once again crucial to the success of GGIII.

The US has never admitted to being an empire, despite the Manifest Destiny of colonial America, the Monroe Doctrine, the war with imperial Spain for the Philippines and Cuba, the wars in Korea and Vietnam, and the current wars, despite the fact that it has benefited the most throughout all the games from the process of surplus extraction from the periphery.[17] True, in comparison to European imperial powers in GGI, it was relatively innocent, certainly with respect to the Middle East.

Admitting the obvious, British mainstream analysts such as Robert Cooper, an EU counselor and adviser to British Prime Minister Tony Blair, called for a "new kind of imperialism" where western states "take political responsibility for zones of disorder ... We are all, it seems, imperialists now."[18] But Lenin's old-fashioned definition of imperialism as "the latest stage of capitalism", characterized by the hegemony of financial capital and monopolies, requiring foreign markets to keep expanding and increasing profits, is all that is necessary—we are merely living through yet a further permutation of international capitalism as described by Hobson and Lenin in GGI.

The logic is simple, if deadly. Center exploits peripheries. Heartland contrasts geopolitically with rimlands. This process is the very reason the center is rich.[19] The different centers actually acquired their very identities as nations through domination of the periphery, Hobson's "sensational patriotism".

There are different tools to analyze current developments, including "premodern states" which co-exist with "modern" and "postmodern"[20] in a confusing smorgasbord. The subsequent chapters describe and trace the progress of the imperial games of the past century, the developments in financial and military-political strategies to ensure control over the world's resources, and the distinctive features of each of the Great Games, culminating in the current world order.

ENDNOTES

1   Quoted in Ahmed Rashid, *Taliban: Militant Islam, Oil and Fundamentalism in Central Asia*, New York: Yale Nota Bene, 2000, 146.

2   President James Monroe stated in 1823 that further efforts by European countries to colonize land or interfere with states in the Americas would be viewed as acts of aggression requiring US intervention.

3   Halford Mackinder, *Geographical Journal*, Volume 23, 1904.

4   Johannes Mattern, *Geopolitik: Doctrine of National Self-Sufficiency and Empire*, Baltimore: Johns Hopkins Press, 1942, 17.

5   Lutz Kleveman, *The New Great Game: Blood and Oil in Central Asia*, New York: Grove Press, 2004, 263.

6   Stalin had approved an Islamic Directorate for Central Asia and Kazakhstan during WWII to mobilize Central Asian Muslims against the Nazi invasion and from the 1960s madrassahs in Tashkent and Bukhara were allowed to function, but observing the faith was severely restricted.

7   That is, given the knowledge available, to maximize the beneficial outcome of any activity, as opposed to irrational acts which undermine the agent's activity or purpose.

8   "The white man's burden", poem in *McClure's*, 1899.

9   Surplus is the wealth expropriated by the ruling class. Surplus value is a more scientific term, associated with capitalism, referring to value created by production appropriated by the owners of the means of production after wages have been paid.

10   Vladimir Lenin, *Imperialism, the Highest Stage of Capitalism*, Peking: Foreign Languages Press, [1917] 1970, 106.

11   J.A. Hobson, *Imperialism: A Study*, 3d ed., London: Allen and Unwin, [1902] 1938, 361.

12   Matthew Edwards, "The New Great Game and the new great gamers: disciples of Kipling and Mackinder", *Central Asian Survey*, March 2003.

13   "Center" in GGIII refers to the West as a whole which is complicit in the US-Israeli empire, benefiting through the international financial institutions and condoning US-Israeli wars. It's a diffused center, unlike the clearer GGI empires, which were centers. China, Russia, etc. are reluctant members and could scuttle it.

14   In fact it is an American empire, with Britain a junior partner by GGII, but this phrase still is used, indicating the commonality of culture, language, imperial legacy and the intimate bonds linking British and American capital.

15   Carl von Clausewitz (1780–1831), German military theorist, author of *On War*.

16   Peter Dale Scott, *Drugs Oil and War: The United States in Afghanistan, Colombia, and Indochina*, New York: Rowman and Littlefield, 2003, xiii.

17   "A historian once remarked that Britain acquired its empire in 'a fit of absence of mind'. If Americans have an empire, they have acquired it in a state of deep denial." Michael Ignatieff, "The American Empire: The Burden", *New York Times Magazine*, 5 January 2003.

18   Allen Murray, "Manifesto Warns of Dangers Associated With an Empire", *Wall Street Journal*, 15 July 2003.
19   In the eighteenth century, there was no difference in living standards around the world, no 'third world'. By 1880, per capita income in the 'developed world' was twice that of the colonial world, by 1913—three times, by 1950—five times, and by 1970 seven times. E.J. Hobsbawm, *Age of Empire: 1875--1914*, London: Wedenfeld and Nicolson, 1987, 15.
20   See Chapter 3. The term was coined by Robert Cooper in "Why we still need empires", *Guardian,* 7 April 2002.

CHAPTER ONE
GGI:
COMPETING EMPIRES

To think of these stars that you see overhead at night,
these vast worlds which we can never reach.
I would annex the planets if I could; I often think of that.
It makes me sad to see them so clear and yet so far.
Cecil Rhodes[1]

Pure philanthropy is very well in its way but
philanthropy plus five per cent is a good deal better.
Cecil Rhodes[2]

Beginnings of GGI and goals

Great Game I was the classical imperialism as described by Marx and Lenin,[3] with competing empires vying for territory and resources, the professed goal being to bring the benefits of western civilization—especially Christianity—to the 'backward' peoples. The real goal was: "Which side can capture the most land/ colonies?" GGI in the nineteenth century pits Britain against seven main rivals:

- Spain, Portugal and Holland the earliest but already in decline,
- France having lost much of its empire due to the revolution and its defeat in the Napoleonic wars,
- Russia already having expanded through Asia to its limit as predominantly a land-based Eurasian power,
- Germany very much on the make, having united in the nineteenth century and become an economic powerhouse, and finally
- the US, a newly liberated settler-colony which denied being an empire but was acquiring colonies and extracting surplus from the periphery like the others.

Between 1870–1900, the heyday of imperialism, there was a rash of imperial grabs, with Britain acquiring by far the most (30 territories covering 4.8 million square miles with a population of 88 million).[4]

The plan for the complete triumph of the British Empire was formulated and implemented at that time—as far as the real world allowed—by Cecil Rhodes. He had made his fortune exploiting southern Africa's mineral and resource wealth. The model was based

- financially on the British government assuming the role of guarantor of the pound as international reserve currency backed by gold, ensuring free trade through conquest and/or treaty, and

- militarily on the British government building the necessary institutional infrastructure (railways, ports, local administration, including courts, schools, medical facilities) and providing a military force to protect it all

while Rhodes and his London bankers would assume all the gains, a model that has become the template for subsequent international business practice.

In the first draft of his will in 1877, Rhodes planned to give his considerable fortune to found an elite society to further the aim of reunifying Britain and the US, to colonize

> the entire Continent of Africa, the Holy Land, the Valley of the Euphrates [and more, inaugurating] a system of Colonial representation in the Imperial Parliament which may tend to weld together the disjointed members of the Empire and, finally, the foundation of so great a Power as to render wars impossible, and promote the best interests of humanity with the British empire as the prototype of a world imperial government.[5]

At the time of his death in 1902 his secret society was functioning, chaired by his protégé, Lord Milner. His board of trustees included Lord Rosebery (son-in-law of Leopold Rothschild) and Jewish financier Alfred Beit, who proceeded to set up the ambitious Rhodes Scholarship fund to train the elite of the US and British empire(s).[6]

His plan for world empire *in perpetuum* was put into effect via the creation of the Rhodes-Milner Round Table with affiliates throughout the empire, and eventually the Royal Institute for International Affairs (RIIA) in Britain and the Council on Foreign Relations (CFR) in the US.

The British Empire represented an evolution of the path to global dominance: a single hegemonic power playing off other powers against one another, a global financial and economic order, an imperial mindset nurtured through an increasingly global media, intelligence operations involving covert intervention and diplomacy, and when all else fails, the exercise of military power. Britain was a rimland power with control of the oceans and the ability to contain the heartland rivals Germany and Russia.

Mackinder, also a Round Table member, proposed a less formal empire to be called the British Commonwealth of Nations, with supporters including liberals such as H.G. Wells. The global empire, with a "Jewish-dominated Palestine, beholden to England for its tenuous survival, surrounded by a balkanised group of squabbling Arab states"[7] was foreseen by Mackinder as a key linchpin: "If Arabia, as the passage-land from Europe to the Indies and from the Northern to the Southern Heartland, be central to the World-Island, then the hill citadel of Jerusalem has a strategical position."[8] He was a realist in foreseeing that the new "Crusade" to capture the Holy Land would be a political and economic quest rather than the supposedly spiritual and in fact military quest that the original Crusades were (and the new Zionist version would become). Mackinder realized that this one last formal colony was necessary to complete the empire geopolitically. Though Zionism already had its following in the British political elite,[9] his inspiration was not Zionist but rather imperial, and by putting Jews in a Palestinian homeland, he was assembling the pieces in today's imperial order, but for a different "World-Island" and with a very different "hill citadel" at the heart of the world-island empire.

However there was something less obvious and more ominous lurking behind Rhodes' pompous fantasies of Rule Britannia. As capitalism advances, writes Hilferding,

> a steadily increasing proportion of capital in industry ceases to belong to the industrialists who employ it. They obtain the use of it only through the medium of the banks which, in relation to them, represent the owners of the capital. On the other hand, the bank is forced to sink an increasing share of its funds in industry. Thus, to an ever greater degree the banker is being transformed into an industrial capitalist. This bank capital, i.e., capital in money form, which is thus actually transformed into industrial capital, I call 'finance capital'. Finance capital is capital controlled by banks and employed by industrialists.[10]

Imperialism as the "advanced stage of capitalism", characterized by banks controlling industrial monopolies relying on the export of capital and colonialism for increasing profits, becomes a project of world control not so much by a nation state, but by the international banking establishment. The exploitation of the periphery with the connivance of the center's working class is hidden behind the innocent-looking balance sheets of these faceless financial corporations.

Ideology

The ideology that acted as a screen for this was liberalism, which emphasized private property and the market as the supreme regulators of economic activity. Liberalism focuses on the individual, arguing that the state should not infringe on individual rights. This program (plus Christianity) was imposed on periphery countries, and justified the center intervening and disrupting traditional structures to lay the foundations for the eventual transformation of those countries.

This theory was flawed from the start, since to bring about an economy based entirely on market relations required the state using a great deal of force, as the colonies would soon find out. In the imperial centers of the West, this had required dismantling the feudal order, creating a legal infrastructure for the commoditization of land and labor, and forcing land and labor 'owners' to accept market dictates, a process that was fiercely resisted as unnatural and exploitative.[11] Liberalism ignores the fact that some individuals are 'more equal' than others due to birthright, and that market prices can reflect many factors other than producers industriously pursuing efficiency. The market in fact negates the more noble characteristics associated with liberalism, as devastatingly illustrated by the historic liberal victory—the repeal of the Corn Laws in 1846 (ironically, by Tory prime minister Robert Peel)—where a freed market economy was a major factor in the mass starvation and emigration of Irish peasants.[12]

The nascent US empire claimed a Manifest Destiny (coined in 1845 and understood as belonging to the "Anglo-Saxon race") to expand across the North American continent to the Pacific Ocean and even farther, updated by President Wilson in a message to Congress in 1920 to refer to an American mission to promote and defend democracy throughout the world.

In terms of the Middle East and Central Asia another key ideological element was provided by the British academic discipline of Orientalism, which recognized Islam as a variant of Christianity but still defined it as "un-culture" seeking to understand and interpret it for the purposes of empire.[13] This was critiqued by (Christian) Palestinian-American Edward Said (1979) who argued that Islam and Muslims are engrained in the western mind as "the other", oriental, a negative inversion of western culture opposite to the Christian and European Jewish experience. Missionaries saw Islam as a Christian heresy, embedded in the lives of Muslims in way it is not for Christians or Jews, requiring "reforming" to make it compatible with the ways of the modern world. This mindset justified and still justifies the invasion and even colonization of Muslim lands in order to modernize them in line with the imperial agenda.

The role of ideology in the games is subtle. It is the water we swim in, the air we breathe, without fully realizing what we are doing, the thought-equivalent of the autonomic functioning of the nervous system. How else to explain the willingness of politicians to condone and even take responsibility for mass killings (Clive and Churchill in India and Africa in GGI, McNamara and Kissinger in Vietnam in GGII, Bush and Obama in Afghanistan and Iraq in GGIII)? How else to explain Zbigniew Brzezinski's rhetorical: "What is most important to the history of the world? The Taliban or the collapse of the Soviet empire? Some stirred-up Moslems or the liberation of Central Europe and the end of the Cold War?"[14]

The ideology that shapes each game creates a mindset that captures the players' thinking processes, makes them for the most part willing handmaidens to the game logic, losing their moral compass.[15] It must be embraced by all the players, big and small. The peasants in a filthy rural village in Egypt, with the stink of sewage from open canals ever-present, scraping a miserable existence, must believe that the global market system is the only one there is, that their US-backed dictatorship was doing the best it can for them,[16] and continue to work diligently and accept their fate as their leaders play the high stakes political game supporting the 'free world'.

Rules of the game and Strategies

Rules which formed the basis of GGI included 1) free trade, 2) the center's right to obtain colonies, and 3) empire exceptionalism (the right of competing empires to do whatever is necessary to ensure 1) and 2)).

A neutral observer can step back from the complex interactions of the players and posit the underlying rules of GGI and with variations all the games:

1. Free trade is really a means of forcing underdeveloped countries to compete as 'equals' in an alien monetized world market

controlled by a competitively stronger center, which acts to keep them underdeveloped and dependent on the rich countries through trade and currency blackmail.

2. Wars by powerfully armed, technologically advanced countries are condoned against innocent natives, who are unaware of concepts of private property, and have neither standing armies nor advanced armaments.

3. Exceptionalism means that Britons, Americans and those serving the empire are not accountable for their actions, including murder and theft.

In each case, the underlying rule is effectively 'might makes right'.

German military theorist Carl von Clausewitz argued that strategy (a plan of action designed to achieve a particular goal) belongs primarily to the realm of art, while tactics (the actions taken to execute the strategy) belong primarily to the realm of science. The Round Table's strategy of achieving world hegemony through control of Eurasia with a strategic citadel in the Middle East is very much in the realm of art. Already by the great surge of imperial expansion in GGI after 1870, the strategy/ tactics which would be used in all the games were largely developed.

In 1756, Robert Clive wrote to historian Robert Orme describing his methods in conquering Bengal: "Fighting, tricks, chicanery, intrigues, politics and the Lord knows what; in short there will be a fine Field for you to display your genius in."[17] Clive befriended and lavished gifts on the Nawob (ruler) of Bengal, working *with* him against the French. At the same time he plotted with a pretender to the throne *against* the Nawob and, conspiring with the leading Hindu merchant, deposed the Nawob, securing first Bengal and then further territories for the East India Company and indirectly for the British government. He promptly instituted a tax system on the natives to pay for the export of their textiles to England (essentially free of charge). Such legal-financial and military-political strategies and tactics and variations on them have been used in all the games, always draped in humanitarian and civilizing garb.

Britain was the main empire in GGI and its strategy was, as rimland, to contain the heartland German and Russian empires, and keep the other major rimland power—the budding US empire—in alliance with it. The US in GGI was more modest in its ambitions, more concerned with keeping the other imperial powers out of the American continent, considering any interference there to be an act of aggression as expressed in the Monroe Doctrine, though this did not preclude the US from seizing faraway south Asian islands, especially Hawaii and the Philippines and importing slaves from Africa and indentured labor from China.

Financial Strategies
Traditional imperialism was based on the gold standard and mercantilism—the center amassing gold from the periphery either through direct theft or trade. London was the banking center that ensured the pound as international reserve currency based on gold. Hobson defines imperialism as the quest for markets and "outlets for the investment of our surplus capital and for the energies of the adventurous surplus of our population".[18] By the beginning of the twentieth century the financial system of GGI had developed rapidly, with the advent of the telegraph, steamships and even oil-fueled ships facilitating secure and rapid international financial transactions throughout the various empires. The decline of piracy and the improvement in ocean safety which the British navy provided, plus the gold standard, allowed trade and production (and thus surplus extraction) around the world to expand rapidly. The period up to WWI was indeed a halcyon one for the European and US empires.

The system of national banks regulated by independent central banks[19]—a GGI innovation by the now powerful international banking elite—allowed effective coordination among all the financial elites of various empires through their central bankers. As the national empires grew and economic relations became ever more cross-border, reliance on international banks, acting independently of governments, became greater.

Evelyn Baring (later Lord Cromer) gave the following explanation of his mission when he came to Egypt in 1877 as "the British Commissioner of the Public Debt": "The origin of the Egyptian Question in its present phase was financial."[20] Egypt's public debt had jumped from 3.2 million pounds in 1863 to 94 million pounds in 1876, 16 million for building the canal and most of rest to pay interest on debt to European financiers. Britain occupied Egypt in 1882 purportedly to protect bond-holders, bringing back Cromer in 1883 as "British Agent and Consul-General" to advise the Khedive.

The reality was much different—an important example of parapolitics: the British government, in league with France, used usurious banking practice to provide a pretext to seize the strategic Suez Canal, financed by international loans and built by Egyptian forced labor, a standard for later GGII&III moves involving the IMF. Britain did not bother to invade many other less strategic countries, especially in South America, to protect private bondholders. The British also used the opportunity to route a rebellion by Colonel Ahmed Arabi, a forerunner of Major Gamal Abdel-Nasser in GGII, who wanted to assert a national politics independent of imperial intrigues. Cromer's modest title of consul-general upon his return belies the fact that he was all but absolute ruler of Egypt for the next 24 years.

By the outbreak of WWI, though Britain may still have ruled the waves, its loss of financial hegemony[21] was ultimately more telling than maintaining a superior military might and even control of the known sources of oil. The international bankers, who enjoyed the protection of the British crown around the world, were well aware that the British government was virtually bankrupt by the outbreak of WWI. They were already focusing on the US and were able to pressure President Woodrow Wilson to sign the US Federal Reserve Act in 1913, putting money creation in the US in the hands of private bankers rather than of government,[22] as it was already in Britain, France and Germany. These GGI central banks were already moving towards the financial endgame of imperialism—the creation of a world system of financial control in private hands, coordinated by them.

The creation of the Bank for International Settlements in Basel, Switzerland, in 1930, ostensibly to manage German reparations payments, marked a new stage in the globalization of financial capital, with the BIS a "coordinator of the operations of central banks around the world", intended

> to create a world system of financial control in private hands able to dominate the political system of each country and the economy of the world as a whole. This system was to be controlled in a feudalist fashion by the central banks of the world acting in concert, by secret agreements arrived at in frequent private meetings and conferences. The apex of the system was to be the Bank for International Settlements in Basel, Switzerland, a private bank owned and controlled by the world's central banks which were themselves private corporations.[23]

The capital flows in GGI originally consisted of the import from the periphery of gold and other valuables as part of the looting of the colonies during the early stages of colonization. But this could not continue forever. Clausewitz's epithet about war and politics translates under imperialism as "*trade* is a continuation of war by other means". Also *rent*. Colonies were reformed via European settlement and ethnic cleansing or land reform to allow for extraction of rent to the colonial administration, in the case of the East India Company in Bengal, financing this 'trade', which amounted to legal looting.

As this money capital amassed in the center, these flows eventually reversed, funding the building of transport and other infrastructure in the periphery which then further accelerated the exploitation of the colonies' raw materials by the center. The resulting infrastructure, owned nominally by the, say, British, investors was actually being built on the expropriated surplus of the periphery recirculated via international banks, and of course by cheap periphery labor.

The positive side of this is that, in many cases, there was substantial development during GGI in the colonies. Furthermore, being a British colony (especially a dominion, where the economy was directly administered by British officials) made loans cheaper and provided preferential tariffs. Given sufficient capital investment, access to new technology, migration (and ethnic cleansing of the natives), responsible administration (even if tilted to imperial interests) meant low corruption, and a colony could truly develop as did Canada and Australia, for example.

Under the influence of British-Russian intrigues, from the 1890s on, both Central Asia and the Middle East, too, modernized somewhat. Reforms came from the top—the westernized Young Turks achieved a constitutional monarchy in the Ottoman Caliphate and introduced educational reforms. Under British occupation, Egypt experienced much improved administration and rapid economic development despite the need to pay off the excessive national debt. Under Russian and subsequent Soviet rule, Turkestan got railways, established a modern education system, and developed large-scale farming. Under British prompting, Afghan emirs and King Amanullah Khan attempted minimal reforms and improved relations with the West. The latter faced fierce resistance, and he was deposed in 1929 by Nadir Khan with British support, leaving Afghanistan largely untouched by western influence until the 1960s.

The British gamble in WWI was that it would win quickly and make up any losses by seizing German colonies and most of the Ottoman territories. But the war dragged on, and by the end Britain and France were in hock to US banks, with JP Morgan Britain's official financial representative in the US, and the war debt guaranteed by the

US government. The world currency was already no longer the pound, and the financial center for the world was already no longer London, despite the British victory. Whichever side 'won' WWI, the international bankers were guaranteed to emerge the true victors, with both warring parties deeply in debt to the international banking elite. Morgan and other US bankers were present at Versailles on a special Commission for Reparations, thus effectively controlling key elements of the world's post-WWI finances, another important example of parapolitics on the part of the financial elite.

The rules of the gold standard (bank notes must be redeemable by an equivalent amount of gold) prevented Britain from continuing to maintain the global military force necessary to 'protect' its empire simply by printing money, once it was bankrupt after WWI. When it was finally forced to abandon the gold standard in 1930, it effectively ceded its imperial status to the US, which by then controlled more gold and had far fewer military expenses. It is no wonder that even as the Round Table circle was organizing RIIA in London in 1919, the CFR was established in New York, financed by Morgan money, which would be the mouthpiece of the American branch of the now Anglo-American empire. The US was not an active international player in the post-WWI GGI endgame; however, as WWII approached, it became more and more the world financial refuge, preparing the way for the post-WWII US empire.

Military-political strategies
Hard Power
The two strands of pre-WWI British imperial military-political strategy as it expanded in the Middle East and Central Asia were:

- backing Ottoman Turkey, necessary to block expansion of Russia into the Balkans, which would give it control of Dardanelles. Britain and France nursed the "sick man of Europe", propping it up as they chipped away at its caliphate (seizing Algeria, Tunisia, Libya, Egypt). The bankrupt caliphate was a useful cover for the British imperial advance into Egypt in 1882; officially, it was there not as an occupying power, but merely to support the local government and ensure compliance with international financial obligations.

- gaining control over Afghanistan to block Russian expansion south in its supposed quest for access to the Indian Ocean. Britain invaded Afghanistan twice during the nineteenth century, giving rise to the term Great Game. The Russian army had subdued Central Asia, or Turkestan, including the Emirate of Bukhara, and the khanates of Khiva and Kokand in 1865–73, exploiting differences between them, driving Persia out of the region. After a half century of war and intrigue, the British prevailed in Afghanistan, with Russia acknowledging Britain's sphere of influence there by 1880, signing a series of agreements on borders and influence without regard to Afghan leadership.

However, in the Levant, now called the Middle East, Britain faced increasing problems. In the nineteenth century, without any significant empire, but with a national economic protectionist policy supporting its industry, Germany quickly outpaced Britain in economic growth. This prompted Germany to seek its own empire—and source of oil—via the German-financed and German-built Berlin-Baghdad railway, the first leg of which opened in 1896, reaching Konia in Anatolia. Oil deposits had been discovered near Baghdad, and Germany had no oil of its own.

Though Germany tried to convince Britain and France to join in the ambitious project, which was beyond the financial resources of Germany alone, it was seen as a threat to British hegemony in the region, in particular, to the Suez Canal as the chief transport corridor to the empire in India and southeast Asia and Persian oil. Instead of reaching a *modus vivendi* with Germany and creating a peaceful win-win situation, Britain pursued a policy of containment of Germany and intrigue. There simply was no room for two dominant world empires in British strategists' minds. Referring to the German railway, British military adviser R.G.D. Laffan warned that "Russia would be cut off by this barrier from her western friends, Great Britain and France. German and Turkish armies would be within easy striking distance of our Egyptian interests, and from the Persian Gulf, our Indian Empire would be threatened."[24]

The build-up to WWI set the stage for British strategists to secure their world empire. Britain had managed to cow its 'friends', Russia and France. After Russia's drubbing in the Russo-Japanese War in 1905, where Britain allied with Japan against Russia, the Tsar's chief of the Council of Ministers, the nationalist and industrializer, Count Witte, resigned and his successor gave in to British imperial designs, acceding to its fiat in both Afghanistan and Persia.

Britain established the Triple Entente by 1907, and used the next seven years to prepare to destroy its only real threat at that time on the continent. This included the so-called First Balkan War of 1912, with "Serbia, Bulgaria and Greece, secretly backed by England" waging war against the weak Ottoman Turkey, and the Second Balkan War in 1913, caused by disagreements on dividing the spoils of the previous war.[25]

By the time of the outbreak of WWI, Britain controlled the Suez Canal, strategic ports in Kuwait, Oman, Bahrain, and both the Atlantic and Pacific oceans. The Round Table plan of conquest, which the "war to end all wars" was supposed to realize, was to link the Rhodes-Rothschild South African gold fields northward, through a predominantly British colonial Africa, through the Suez Canal to Mesopotamia, Kuwait and Persia into India, based at each stage on divide-and-rule. With this solid imperial core, the rest of the world would come into line either as friend or subordinate. British bases and colonies around the world were to ensure its control of trade, natural resources and labor power in its vast world colonial network. To some extent this was realized by 1919 when Britain presided over a new League of Nations.

Soft Power
Compared to GGII, the mechanisms of soft power were in their infancy in GGI. As was the case in pre-capitalist empires, in addition to co-opting local elites to rule on the center's behalf (and deposing them if they strayed too far from British interests or failed to command sufficient authority), the pre-eminent instrument of soft power was the export of the center's culture. In the case of GGI, this meant both sending thousands of Christian missionaries to the periphery to indoctrinate locals with subservience to Jesus and empire, and bringing promising colonials to the center to study and return as a privileged caste to administer the empire—in the center's *lingua franca,* English—firmly entrenching the 'superiority' of the West.

After WWI, rather than turning the Ottoman territories into fully fledged colonies, the soft power strategy of co-opting local elites was used. Pro-British monarchies similar to Egypt's were created in the "mandates" to govern on behalf of the imperial center, in Jordan, Saudi Arabia and Iraq.[26] Britain similarly supported a puppet monarchy in Persia,[27] giving it control of the oil in both Iraq and Persia. France was given Syria, Lebanon and the Maghreb. Yugoslavia was created at Versailles as a pro-British "southern Slav" kingdom from the Serbian, Croatian and Slovenian kingdoms after the collapse of Habsburg Austria-Hungary.

In the Middle East, the British government was at the same time grooming Islamists,[28] attempting to create a pro-British pan-Islamic movement as part of its plans to control the region. From 1879–90, it supported Persian-Afghan Islamic activist (and Freemason) Jamal

Uddine al-Afghani, credited with laying the intellectual foundation for conservative quietist political Islam. In 1885 he organized a pan-Islamic alliance of Egypt, Turkey, Persia and Afghanistan against Tsarist Russia and in opposition to the decadent Ottoman Caliphate.[29] His collaborator, Abduh (also a Freemason), was promoted by the British in Egypt and eventually became chief mufti of Al-Azhar, the leading Islamic religious school in the Muslim world. The Muslim Brotherhood, founded by Hassan al-Banna in Egypt in 1928, was supported by the nascent British-backed Saudi state and the Suez Canal Company.

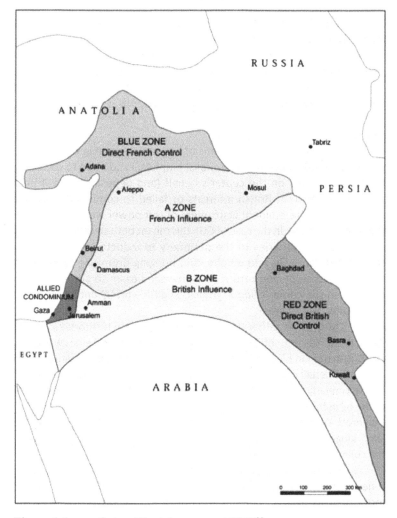

Figure 1.1 map Sykes-Picot Agreement 1916[30]

The British simultaneously encouraged both main Middle East rivals—the Hashemites of Mecca who claimed descent from the Prophet and the Wahhabi fundamentalist forces of Ibn Saud. Colonel T.E. Lawrence incited the former to blow up the German-Turkish railroad during WWI with the promise of liberation of the Levant from the Turks, which was betrayed in the infamous Sykes–Picot Agreement of 1916.

When the Hashemites were overpowered by the Saudis in Arabia, the British offered them the consolation prize of the kingdoms of Jordan and Iraq, keeping both sides happy, and at the same time enemies—win-win for the British. 'Lawrence of Arabia' wrote, "If properly handled they would remain in a state of political mosaic, a tissue of small jealous principalities incapable of cohesion."[31]

The Americans were introduced to the Saudi monarch Ibn Saud by British secret agent Jack Philby, who was Ibn Saud's close friend, and who clinched a long-term deal for Standard Oil with the monarch in 1936, thereby easing the US into GGI Middle East politics and its own use of Islamists.

Control of world resources

Even as Britain preened itself as master of the world following WWI, the prize of GGI—control of world resources—was already slipping from its hands. Even as the British General Strike tore the country apart in 1926, its economic elite was planning for the new American ascendancy. Behind-the-scenes jockeying over oil, now the most important strategic resource, came to an end in 1927 with the creation of an Anglo-American oil cartel, later dubbed the Seven Sisters, which by 1932 included the British government's Anglo-Persian Oil Company (BP), Royal Dutch Shell, Standard Oil (ExxonMobil, Esso, Chevron), Gulf, and Texaco, whereby the major oil companies would henceforth cooperate in dividing up the world's oil resources without precipitating war, at least among themselves.[32]

Endgame 1914–45

The culmination of GGI, WWI, was a Pyrrhic victory for the winners, who were not much better off than the losers. Britain and France were left bankrupt and their youth dead, maimed or traumatized. The real victors were Britain's unruly offspring, America, which had benefited financially and economically, and the international bankers, who held the massive war debts of victors and defeated alike, and had no intention of forgiving them.

A semblance of British imperial glory remained through the 1930s due to inertia, but the war had turned the common people against the empire. Several short-lived Labour governments began the long process of moving towards a post-imperial order. In Russia, this happened even before WWI had ended, in a much more dramatic way. The war led to the overthrow of the Russian empire by the communists, who electrified the world, inspiring a strong socialist movement bent on dismantling empire everywhere, sowing the seeds of GGII—the fight against communism. Germany was reduced to a humiliated periphery country, which barely escaped communist revolution.

WWI also sowed the seeds of GGIII, with the Balfour Declaration promising the Zionists a Jewish state in Palestine and creating a new Islamic enemy once communism was defeated.

The competing empires Britain, France, would-be Germany and the would-not-be US, and their financial and industrial elites, together played a cruel and cynical game of brinkmanship through the 1930s. While the German Nazis crushed their communist foes, British and French ruling circles couldn't decide whether the Nazis or communists were the bigger threat. A French-Soviet mutual assistance pact in 1935 and a short-lived socialist government in France in 1936 briefly entertained the idea of a military alliance with the Soviet Union against Germany, but this unraveled quickly under British pressure. The Conservative British government pushed Hitler to turn against the Soviet Union with craven concessions of European territory, culminating in the 1938 Munich agreement to cede part of Czechoslovakia to Germany, encouraged by Hitler's avowals that his ultimate goal was to destroy communism.[33]

Though some European and American politicians were more worried by the Nazi threat, business, especially US business interests such as General Motors, Ford, Standard Oil, Du Pont, Union Carbide, Westinghouse and General Electric, and American banks such as JP Morgan, invested in Hitler's industrious Reich. A major backer of Hitler was Union Bank, managed by Prescott Bush, father of President Bush senior and grandfather of Bush junior. Many western enterprises were doing business with the Soviet Union as well. Their concern was not so much to support any political ideology, but to make profit and promote their own interests in these rising powers, no matter who emerged on top. For western big business, neither fascism nor communism was a problem.

The long term goals of American politicians and capitalists, however, did coincide on other important issues. They sought to finish off the British empire, open new markets to US investment, and encourage Germany and the Soviet Union to destroy each other, just as Britain, France and Germany had destroyed each other in WWI to the benefit of the US. This cynical parapolitics was hinted at by many at the time: congressman and future president Harry Truman famously stated when the Germans invaded Russia 22 June 1941: "If we see that Germany is winning we ought to help Russia and if Russia is winning we ought to help Germany, and that way let them kill as many as possible."[34] Just as it hung back from WWI until Britain and France had exhausted themselves, so the US astutely waited until a desperate Britain was on the brink of defeat in WWII, had racked up a large debt and was ready to cede its empire after the war, reducing it to the role of grateful junior partner.

The glorious pomp hiding the cruelty and inhumanity of GGI is best epitomized by the figure of Winston Churchill, a swashbuckling romantic who saw military action in British India, participating in the slaughter of Afghan Pashtuns, who were angry that Britain had stolen half of their lands as part of its Great Game with Russia. He earned a comfortable living as a war correspondent there, in the Sudan, and during the second Boer War, using the new mass media 'soft power' to promote the imperial cause and, first and foremost, himself. He gained fame and notoriety as an adventurer, rhetorician, adventurer and sybarite, and eventually during WWII murderer on a mass scale, who never had second thoughts about the imperial project until it collapsed under his feet.

As mentioned above, GGII actually dates from the beginning of the GGI endgame, rather than from Churchill's notorious Iron Curtain flourish in 1946, when the Soviet Union was at its peak of prestige and authority. The 1917 Russian revolution was the logical outcome of the imperialism of competing empires, bankrupting themselves in senseless wars and exploiting the periphery countries, creating famine and horrors too numerous to list here. Churchill knew what the score was, who the enemy of empire was, and demanded that Bolshevism, a "conspiracy [of] ... atheistic Jews", be "strangled in its cradle".[35] The imperial powers, led by Britain and the US, invaded the new Russia in 1918 to try to defeat the communists GGI-style and failed, though they left a trail of devastation and were, over the next few decades, able to cripple the new state and eventually bring it down.

Imperial greed at the WWI peace conference in Versailles and throughout the post-WWI period both created the Nazi monster and unwittingly gave succor to the Soviet attempt at spearheading a post-imperial order, resulting in a totally new Great Game, GGII—united empires against communism. The term Great Game took on a new meaning, used by the Nazis to refer to the war against the communists and their plan to sign a separate peace with Britain and the US. That it was the logical extension of the original Great Game is confirmed by the fact that most of the top Nazis were employed by the US after the war, especially those who already had experience in this new Great Game.[36]

The GGI endgame culminated in the forced alliance of the anti-Nazi imperialists with the hated Soviet Union. The imperialists provided arms and food aid to the communists and more or less sat back and watched as the communists defeated fascism, ending the Nazi dream of a thousand-year German Reich. The US once again emerged stronger than ever from a world war, and was able to discard its communist ally without a thought, and dictate the rules for the former empires against the anti-empire in the new game GGII.

ENDNOTES

1   S. Gertrude Millin, *Rhodes*, London: Simon Publications, 1933, 138.

2   J.C. Johari, *Voices of Indian Freedom Movement*, New Delhi: Anmol Publications, 1993, 207.

3   Marx did not use the term, referring only to world capitalism. It was coined in the 1870s and popularized by Hobson and later Lenin. Rhodes referred to "social imperialism". See E.J. Hobsbawm, *Age of Empire: 1875—1914*, London, Weidenfeld & Nicolson, 1987, 69.

4   Table of British territorial acquisitions in J.A. Hobson, *Imperialism*, 3d ed., London: Allen and Unwin, [1902] 1938, 369. By 1935 Britian governed 458 million subjects, France 65 million, the Netherlands 70 million, and the US 15 million. Ibid., 17.

5   Available at: <http://mailstar.net/rhodes-will.html>.

6   Carroll Quigley, *Tragedy and Hope*, Georgetown: University Press, 1996, 68, available at: <http://mailstar.net/quigley.html>.

7   Quoted in William Engdahl, *A Century of War: Anglo-American Oil Politics and the New World Order*, revised ed., London: Pluto, [1992] 2004, 47.

8   Mackinder, *Democratic Ideals and Reality*, 89.

9   What came to be known as "Christian Zionism" emerged in England in the early 1800s. In 1839 the evangelical Anthony Ashley-Cooper called on parliament to support creation of a Jewish state in Palestine, prompting Lord Palmerston to appoint the first British Consul to Jerusalem, supporting the idea of a "Jewish entity" allied to the Ottoman Empire as a counterweight to Egypt "to blend the biblical interest in Jews and their ancient homeland with the cold realities of [British imperial] foreign policy". Yves Engler, *Canada and Israel: Building Apartheid*, Vancouver: Fernwood Publishing, 2010, 12.

10   R. Hilferding, *Finance Capital*, Moscow, 1912 (in Russian), 338–39, quoted by V. Lenin, *Imperialism, the Highest Stage of Capitalism*, Peking: Foreign Languages Press, [1917] 1970, 52.

11   This is admitted today by so-called liberals: "The hidden hand of the market will never work without a hidden fist. McDonald's cannot flourish without McDonnell-Douglas, the designer of the F-15, and the hidden fist that keeps the world safe for Silicon Valley's technology is called the US Army, Air Force, Navy

and Marine Corps." in Thomas Friedman, "A Manifesto for the Fast World", *The New York Times*, 28 March 1999.

12   The repeal marked, also ironically, the beginning of the gutting of the British economy, both agriculturally and industrially, as imports began to take the place of local production. In this respect, the logic of liberalism and empire follows a similar path for both British and US empires in all phases of the Great Games— the zealous promotion of free trade led in both cases to deindustrialization of the domestic economy and bankruptcy of the government as production shifted to cheaper offshore colonies (outsources) and as the expenses of military control of the empire increased beyond sustainable limits.

13   Reinhard Schulze, "Mass Culture and Islamic Cultural Production in the 19th Century Middle East", in Stauth, Georg and Zubaida, Sami eds, *Mass Culture, Popular Culture and Social Life in the Middle East*, Boulder, USA: Westview Press, 1987, 190.

14   Zbigniew Brzezinski, Interview in *Le Nouvel Observateur*, 15–21 January 1998.

15   "Are they themselves deceived by shadowy forces who use the veneer of spreading democracy to conceal a more base purpose? Or is it instead that imperialism, once in motion, exerts a momentum of its own?" in Jonathan Freedland, "Bush's Amazing Achievement", *New York Review of Books*, 14 June 2007.

16   As this work was going to press, Egyptian president Hosni Mubarak, in power for 30 years, was overthrown in a popular uprising, showing how tenuous the imperial order is, despite its appearance of invincibility.

17   John Stratchey, *The End of Empire*, New York: Praeger, 1959, 24.

18   J.A. Hobson, *Imperialism: A Study*, 71.

19   A central bank controls currency issue, and is run independent of government, usually owned by a consortium of large private banks, with a chairman appointed by the national government from among nominees put forward by the board of governors, who are the owners and/or leading business and banking figures in the country. It is a profit-making enterprise accountable—at least in theory—to the country's legislature. It is different from a "national bank" like China's, which controls currency issue and is directly controlled by the government.

20   Earl of Cromer, *Modern Egypt*, New York: Macmillan, 1908.

21   William Engdahl, *A Century of War*, 35.

22   FR owners include the Rockefellers, JPMorgan, the Rothschilds, Warburg and other leading European bankers.

23   Carroll Quigley, *Tragedy and Hope: A History of the World in Our Time*, Chapter 20, 1966. < http://www.archive.org/stream/TragedyAndHope/TH_djvu.txt >. There are only 5 nations without a Rothschild model central bank: North Korea, Iran, Sudan, Cuba and Libya. Until recently, there were two others: Afghanistan and Iraq. Felicity Arbuthnot, "Libya: Oil, Banks, the United Nations and America's Holy Crusade", *www.globalresearch.ca*, 5 April 2011.

24   Engdahl, *A Century of War*, 23.

25   Engdahl, *A Century of War*, 34.

26   The British Mandate of Mesopotamia was established in present-day Iraq by the League of Nations following WWI when Britain imposed the Hashemite monarchy of Faisal I on Iraq in 1921 and defined its territorial limits without taking into account the politics of the different ethnic and religious groups in the country. During the British occupation, the Shia and Kurds fought for independence. Nominal independence was only achieved in 1932, when the

British Mandate officially ended, but it had been created according to divide-and-conquer, from 3 disparate *vilayets* (Sunni, Shia and Kurd), and unpopular King Faisal, with no legitimate claim, was made nominal head of state.

27   Iran was also part of GGI between Russia and Britain, though again Britain retained the upper hand in the Anglo-Russian Convention of 1907, which divided Persia into spheres of influence, regardless of its nominal 'independence', a relative term in classical GGI imperialism. British prospectors discovered oil in 1908. Churchill personally managed negotiations to retain majority British government control of the new Anglo-Iranian Oil Company (now BP). During World War I, the country was occupied by British and Russian forces but was essentially neutral. In 1919, after the Russian revolution and withdrawal, Britain attempted to establish a protectorate in Iran, which was unsuccessful. Persian nationalism had achieved a *bona fide* Constitution in 1906. An ambitious officer, Reza Khan, carried out a coup in 1921 and crowned himself Shah, establishing the Pahlavi dynasty and ruled until deposed by the British in 1941 when the British and Soviets occupied Iran, suspecting the Shah of German sympathies and anxious to secure oil supplies. The British put his 22-yrear-old son Reza Shah Pahlavi on the throne.

28   The designation "Islamist" formally means a supporter of a strict or "fundamentalist" interpretation and practice of Islam (or alternatively a scholar of Islam), though many of those described as Islamists oppose use of the term, arguing: "If Islam is a way of life, how can we say that those who want to live by its principles in legal, social, political, economic, and political spheres of life are not Muslims, but Islamists and believe in Islamism, not [just] Islam?"(Al-Jazeerah Op-Ed, 27 February 2006). As popular understanding has evolved in the West, however, it has become a synonym for terrorist or anti-American. The term here is used to indicate a politicized Islam, a process that, while it indeed was actively encouraged by British politicians and later American ones to serve their imperial aims, was taken up by Muslims who were not mere imperial satraps but rather pursuing their own agenda, seeking to remove foreign occupations from Muslim lands and re-institute Islamic politico-legal institutions to fully restore the Islamic way of life. The confusion arises in and is perhaps intentionally generated by application of the term "fundamentalism", which in Christianity and Islam has different connotations, in the former referring narrowly to a rightwing Protestant movement emanating from what are derisively viewed in the West as the more ignorant elements of the Christian population. In the Islamic world, the term is open to a range of interpretations, and has been applicable to intellectuals and professionals as well as the popular masses. There are radically different tendencies among "Islamists", as the political systems in Saudi Arabia and Iran show, in keeping with their collaborationist or revolutionary anti-imperialist orientations. A quietist non-political Islam financially endowed by the government of Saudi Arabia (as opposed to private Saudi support for its nemesis, Osama Bin Laden) competes with and seeks to counter among Muslim populations the inspiration of the anti-imperial Islamic revolution emanating from Iran. The quietist/non-political 'innovation' of Islam by the Wahhabis can be seen as a direct result of Saudi protection by first the British and then American empires. It vied with the budding secular Arab nationalisms from the 1930s on. When nationalists came to power in Egypt, Syria and Iraq, Islam was in varying degrees suppressed, but with the failure, elimination or discrediting of the leaderships of these nationalisms, Islamic movements have sprung up

everywhere as the bedrock of last resistance to increasing Western/Zionist attacks and domination.

29   Al-Afghani seems to have envisioned Islam as primarily a means of social control. He also collaborated with the French and Russians on various political schemes.

30   With thanks to Mahmoud Abu Rumieleh, Webmaster. <http://www.passia.org>.

31   Waïl Hassan, "Lawrence, T.E." *The Oxford Encyclopedia of British Literature,* Oxford: Oxford University Press 2005. At Versailles, the British also forged agreement between the Zionists and the Hashemites (which survives today in the Jordan-Israel relationship).

32   Engdahl, *A Century of War,* 75.

33   On 11 August 1939, when Hitler told Jacob Burkhardt, commissioner of the League of Nations: "Everything I undertake is directed against Russia; if the West is too stupid and blind to grasp this, I shall be compelled to come to an agreement with the Russians, beat the West and then, after their defeat, turn against the Soviet Union with all my forces. I need the Ukraine so that they cannot starve me out as happened in the last war." quoted in Roy Dennan, *Missed Chances,* London: Indigo, 1997, 65.

34   Cited in *Time,* 2 July 1951 available at: <http://www.time.com/time/magazine/article/0,9171,815031,00.html>.

35   Winston Churchill, "Zionism vs Bolshevism: the struggle for the soul of the Jewish people", *Illustrated Sunday Herald,* 8 February 1920, and Jeffrey Wallin and Juan Williams, "Churchill's Greatness", *Fox News,* September 2001. <http://web.archive.org/web/20031216033237/http://www.winstonchurchill.org/i4a/pages/index.cfm?pageid=282, *Fox News,* September 2001>.

36   This is documented by the greatest spy of WWII, Leopold Trepper, a Polish Jewish communist who ran the so-called Red Orchestra in occupied Europe, the network of communist sympathizers who informed Soviet military intelligence of Nazi plans. The Germans eventually captured Trepper and he pretended to be a double agent, convincing the Germans that he could negotiate a separate peace between the Soviet Union and Germany at the very time the Germans were desperately seeking a separate peace with the US and Britain. This Great Game was code-named Operation Bear. See Leopold Trepper, *The Great Game: Memoirs of the Spy Hitler Couldn't Silence,* New York: McGraw-Hill, 1977.

CHAPTER TWO

GGII:
EMPIRE AGAINST
COMMUNISM

Whenever we want to subvert any place,
we find the British own an island within easy reach.
US spy[1]

The genius of you Americans is that you never make
clear cut stupid moves, only complicated stupid moves
which make us wonder at the possibility that
there must be something we are missing.
Gamal Abdel-Nasser (1957)[2]

This empire, unlike any other in the history of the world,
has been built primarily through economic manipulation, through
cheating, through fraud, through seducing people
into our way of life, through the economic hit men.
I was very much a part of that.
John Perkins (2010)[3]

Beginnings of GGII and goals

What is dubbed Great Game II here is called super-imperialism by Michael Hudson, referring to the unique role of the US dollar. The professed goal in GGII was still to bring the benefits of western civilization—be they the fruits of capitalism or communism—to the undeveloped nations and to improve the well-being of the 'backward' peoples. Christian missionaries were as visible as in GGI, acting as handmaidens of imperialism. But they were now competing with third world communist and socialist idealists and, for those ex-colonies able to achieve some genuine independence, advisers from behind the 'Iron Curtain' dividing Europe.

The underlying goal of the formerly competing western empires of GGI, now united under US hegemony, was to align ex-colonies against communism and capture the most market control in competition with the now Soviet-Chinese heartland and the anti-colonial movement, while the Soviet Union and its allies tried to encourage the emerging nations to follow a more independent course, to build balanced, self-reliant economies that meet basic social needs, while avoiding tying themselves to the traditional colonial role of supplying raw materials to a capricious world market, where prices can rise or fall wildly, alternately providing windfall profits or threatening bankruptcy.

This playing field was very different from GGI, providing a modicum of hope that the dependency model of imperialism could be broken through anti-imperialist alliances and farsighted planning. This hope derived from the fact that the western nations had been forced to ally with the Soviet Union from 1941–45 and adopt its anti-imperialist rhetoric as GGII got underway. As a consequence, the period from 1945–1980, though officially one of peace, was really one of unremitting upheaval, with imperialism on the defensive, especially in the 1950–60s, during the heyday of anti-imperial struggle, when socialist and communist revolutionary fervor was sweeping the globe. Even western Europe, occupied by US forces, witnessed communists holding important cabinet posts in coalition governments after the war. Britain elected a Labour government in 1945, intent on socialist reforms, despite the prestige of wartime leader Winston Churchill.

For a few years, it looked like communism might triumph around the world. The experience of the US during the war as a planned economy had shown the viability and advantages of socialism—full employment and extensive social welfare—policies the allies were compelled to follow during the war to ensure a compliant working class remained united with their capitalist elites to defeat Nazism. Ghana's Kwame Nkrumah was once of several charismatic African leaders versed in western politics and economics who led their nations to independence in the 1950s, fully intending to build socialism. As president, Nkrumah, still considered the "greatest African", penned GGII's seminal *Neocolonialism: The Last Stage of Imperialism* (1965).

But even as the alliance with the communists was transforming the nation's, even the world's consciousness, the imperial establishment was preparing to reverse the process and, failing to incorporate the Soviet Union into the imperial post-war world order, to launch a Cold War to defeat it. When the likes of Nkrumah failed to embrace capitalism, they would be deposed, as indeed he was in a CIA-inspired coup in 1966.

The days following WWI had been halcyon ones for British foreign policy strategists. Britain was able to divide up the Middle East according to its GGI plans, with the League of Nations as a legitimizing cover. Following WWII, an exhausted and bankrupt Britain and France quickly shed their Middle East colonies, and the US, stronger than ever, set up new international organizations even before the end of the war—the International Monetary Fund and World Bank (founded in Bretton Woods, New Hampshire in 1944) and the United Nations (founded in San Francisco in 1945).

But there were storm clouds already on the horizon, as the US and Britain were forced to compromise with the Soviet Union on a division of Europe, and had to struggle to re-establish western control over the colonies which Japan had seized and to make sure the newly independent British "mandates" in the Middle East remained onside. Ironically, the blatantly colonial scheming following both WWI&II was justified in the first case by President Wilson's Fourteen Points and in the second by Roosevelt and Churchill's 1941 Atlantic Charter between the US and Britain, later agreed to by the Soviet Union, which asserted that self-determination was a right of all people, implying that colonies would become independent sovereign states, when adequately 'prepared' by their colonial occupiers.

The architect of what came to be the post-1945 imperial strategy consensus for Central Asia was, curiously enough, the same Mackinder who so captured the imagination of British imperialists prior to WWI. He published his strategy for the now US empire, appropriately not in the RIIA's *International Affairs*, but in the US-based CFR's *Foreign Affairs*, as the CFR had by then become the mouthpiece of US foreign policy and the US was now clearly in charge of any post-WWII imperial agenda. "The Round World and the Winning of the Peace" outlines how US strategists planned to dominate the post-WWII world. "If the Soviet Union emerges from this war as the conqueror of Germany, she must rank as the greatest land power on the globe ... the power in the strategically strongest defensive position. The Heartland is the greatest natural fortress on earth."[4]

The situation was dire for US strategists. With the overwhelmingly pro-communist world sentiment following the defeat—primarily by the Soviet Union—of the Nazis, it was very much touch and go. But Mackinder was not so worried, and anticipated the Cold War as not such a bad thing for the long term interests of the empire. He was more worried about a resurgent western Europe with the now reformed Germans as the engine of prosperity. He had read his Haushofer, remembered Rapallo[5] and saw the real threat to the Anglo-American empire not from a now devastated Russia, with a crude planned economy and a ruthless dictatorship, but from an independent Europe, which unless tied carefully to the US, could become the post-imperial social democratic alternative to empire and come to terms with the Soviet Union, opening the Eurasian heartland to itself. He argued that western Europe, above all a resurgent Germany, would be the main challenge to post-war Anglo-American hegemony. It did not matter whether the Soviet Union was still friendly to Washington or a Cold War foe. What was important was to contain western Europe and keep it solidly in the US sphere of influence after 1945.[6]

Ideology

The ideologies motivating the western players in GGII were a confusing mix of liberalism and socialism, but above all—anticommunism. The alliance with the Soviet Union in WWII had inspired the western public with the ideas of socialism, especially after the widespread suffering during the protracted depression of the GGI endgame in the 1930s, when the experiment in socialist planning in the Soviet Union was much admired. The wartime planned economies in the US and Canada quickly ended unemployment and resulted in rapid economic development, further inspiring popular support for a post-war socialist order, especially in Europe, where imperial dreams had already largely faded, and where communist partisans had been the most visible and principled actors in liberating Nazi-occupied lands. Despite deeply engrained anticommunism in North America, communists were elected there. This frightened the western establishment, caught between the Nazi devil and the deep blue sea of world socialist revolution.

The US government's answer—after offering Stalin extensive post-war reconstruction aid in exchange for acquiescence to a subordinate role in an imperial post-war world—was the Cold War. This still required considerable domestic compromise, forcing western governments to provide a minimum level of social welfare to the people to dampen enthusiasm for socialism, though the socialist measures were never explicitly acknowledged as 'socialist'.

This work can only deal peripherally with the nature of the Soviet Union, its ideology and strategies against the imperialists during the GGI endgame and GGII. During its existence, it faced constant hostility, subversion and two invasions (1918 and 1941), as the imperial powers attempted to destroy it, realizing it was indeed the enemy of imperialism. The resulting harsh, paranoid rule of Stalin proved a useful foil for the imperialists, and the later decline in Soviet economic performance, combined with unremitting pressure from the West, finally led to its collapse. Its ideology of equality on the personal level and between states internationally, of the importance of the collective, plus its disapproval of private property and commodity fetishism were ascetic and idealistic. It faced an uphill battle competing with the subtler ideology of market equality, individualism, private property and the lure of unlimited personal wealth.

The chief ideological mantra of GGII, anticommunism, was Goebbels' "big lie", that is, people will believe a big lie sooner than a little one; and if you repeat it frequently enough people will sooner or later believe it. The Soviet Union was not responsible for any of the dozens of third world revolutions against imperialism and never threatened to invade western Europe or attack America. On the contrary, its foreign policy was cautious to the extreme—Stalin supported the Kuomintang in China, not Mao's communists; he failed to come to the aid of the powerful Greek communists and watched as they were murdered by the British and Americans after the war, sticking to the wartime agreement with Churchill and intent on avoiding further war. The only real communist threat that the West faced was from the progressive elements in the West's own population who hoped to end capitalism and imperialism and the incessant wars and havoc that they lead to.

The geopolitical version of the ideology of anticommunism was the domino theory, warning that if one country came under the influence of communism, then the surrounding countries would follow. In reality this is what Chomsky calls the Mafia doctrine,

> one of the few pervasive principles of imperial domination—the dedication to ensure 'global equilibrium' or 'stability', in the preferred euphemism ... The Godfather sends his goons, not just to collect the money, which he wouldn't even notice, but to beat [the rebel] to a pulp, so that others do not get the idea that disobedience is permissible.[7]

Kissinger, inspired by the Monroe Doctrine, said "If we cannot manage Central America, it will be impossible to convince threatened nations in the Persian Gulf and in other places that we know how to manage the global equilibrium."[8]

Rules of the Game and Strategies

While Britain was the rimland in GGI, the Anglo-American rimland has led to a much grander empire in GGII&III. The rules of the game remain the same in GGII, except for 2)—the center's acquisition of colonies. Now, colonies had the right to, and were to be given (in some cases only after they had won it) their independence, subject to the domino theory. No country was to be allowed to "go communist", where communist was intentionally ill-defined. Instead, they were expected to continue to abide by the rules set down by the ex-imperial mother country, to respect private property and the market, to follow western practices of electoral democracy and later to observe "human rights". Any sign of challenge to US hegemony, as in the case of Iran and many other countries in the 1950–60s, however, did not permit invasion and colonization as in GGI, but it did legitimize 3)—empire exceptionalism, permitting the US to employ all necessary means short of invasion to bring into line and if necessary overthrow the offending government and install an acceptable one, preferably later legitimized in US-monitored elections—using the new soft power techniques.

In GGI, the goals of empire could be pursued without much concern about how—might and the interests of the empire were enough. GGII required more subterfuge, since all nations were, at least theoretically, sovereign and there was no empire, at least not officially. The imperial strategy in GGII was to cover up the real age-old imperial objectives with both liberal and anticommunist cant, and, taking this logic a step further, to 'create the problem, provide the solution'. When a sovereign Guatemala elected a leftwing government bent on land reform, stories were planted in the media about communist subversion and a Soviet threat of invasion which justified a CIA-orchestrated coup d'etat to restore 'freedom'. This strategy became the standard for GGII, both using financial, political and other pretexts to justify intervention by the center.

GGII was really two games: one directed against the Soviet Union and its European socialist allies, and the other against the nations struggling for independence from imperial control. While the Soviet Union supported the latter against the US, these countries were rarely subservient to Soviet demands and all could have been seduced by a more benign US to stay neutral or even pro-US. However, the US was obsessed with destroying communism, and sacrificed all other options in pursuit of this one phantom.

Financial Strategies
As GGII got underway following WWII, Britain and France were saddled with huge war debts, while losers Germany and Japan were allowed to rebuild with a blank slate, allowing the US to level the second-tier imperial playing field. This hardnosed approach by the US was necessary

to ensure that the British and French empires would be destroyed, at the same time as the losers—Germany and Japan—would be rebuilt under US control, all now beholden to the US, as faithful allies. It was vital to avoid the disastrous blowback which followed the Versailles Treaty, which had victimized the loser, prepared the way for the Nazis and strengthened the communists.

Under the specter of communism, now a very real internal threat to capitalism, this world order was more equitable than the one Britain tried to create following WWI. As Europe recovered after the war, trade grew rapidly, working class living standards rose spurred on by full employment, Germany was integrated peacefully into the fabric of a subdued Europe, and Japan and South Korea became thriving developed economies. "By 1957, for the first time ever, world trade in manufactured goods exceeded that in primary goods."[9]

In chess, a pawn reaching the opponent's rear is promoted, usually to the most powerful figure, a queen, changing the fundamental dynamics of the game. In real life, the American empire achieved two such coups as GGII got underway, creating a new playing field and rules of the game. What became the cornerstone to the US GGII game plan was the ascendancy of the US dollar as world reserve currency. By 1948, the US possessed 72 per cent of the world's gold, and the gold exchange system of the new IMF pegged each country's national currency to the dollar. The real financial pillar was in fact the dollar, with the US having effective veto power in the IMF (whose head is chosen, at least officially, by an obedient Europe) and the World Bank (whose head is chosen by the US). Britain was bankrupt and the pound on life-support. The US GGI game against the British empire ended with the US crowning its dollar as the new financial queen.[10]

Initially the post-war world followed Hobson's imperial dynamic, with huge US reserves—financial and material—first amassed prior to and during the war and now exported to a devastated Europe as well as to Africa, Latin America and Asia. A prostrate Europe was saved from communist revolutions by the US Marshall Plan begun in 1948, and its ex-colonies, upon achieving independence, were drawn into the US orbit.

But as empires expand and reach their zenith, eventually capital flows in reverse again, with the outsourcing of jobs, and with financial resources accumulated in the periphery eventually flowing back to the center as profits and to cover growing trade deficits. This happened in the past in the Roman and British empires, and started in the US from 1971 on, during the Vietnam war, when the US became a net debtor and US gold reserves almost disappeared, forcing President

Richard Nixon to suspend the last pretense of the gold standard. US creditors now had to accept US debt, no longer backed by gold, as part of their countries' reserves, as the US suspended gold payments, and forced currencies to "float", supervised by the IMF.

By removing the last trace of the gold standard, countries would get only promissory notes to pay promissory notes. As US foreign debt continued to increase, this effectively wiped out US obligations overnight while seemingly increasing them, completing the global transition to total reliance on the US dollar—now with no gold backing— as the world's reserve currency. This was the parapolitical equivalent of recrowning the already threadbare dollar queen, since the rest of the world would now fund US wars and prop up the declining US economy even as its balance of trade deficit grew exponentially.

The irony of this is that, as a bankrupt on the international account, a strong industrial nation can exert even greater force in the world of nations than a solvent creditor can. All the capitalist world "has become a guarantor of America's credit."[11] The US holds its creditors at ransom: if the US dollar collapses, other countries' US dollar reserves are worthless and their economies will collapse, too. This exposes the US dollar-based monetary system as the real domino, not the supposed communist one. Surplus is now extracted from not only the periphery but from the other first world countries by the US on the basis of this subterfuge.

The goal, then, becomes to protect the US dollar at all costs. Combined with the other crucial goal—to ensure oil supplies, now mostly imported—this led to the strategy of manipulating oil prices. The oil cartel OPEC was set up in 1960 by US Middle East allies led by Saudi Arabia, Iran and Venezuela.[12] It was designed to keep world oil prices well above production costs to the benefit of the handful of oil producing nations but more importantly to US-British Big Oil, the banks, and indirectly, the dollar. Such a blatant cartel would be illegal if undertaken by the oil companies, but was fine if done by sovereign nations acting on their own.

Following the 1967 invasion of Sinai and all of Palestine by Israel, the pressure to establish some kind of equilibrium in the Middle East built up to a breaking point. When Israel refused to return Sinai to Egypt, it was clear that Egypt would have to launch a war, a war which it could hardly be expected to win, but which could endanger US access to Middle East oil.

The Egyptian move in 1973 to regain Sinai and push Israel towards a genuine settlement of the Palestinian problem was supported by Saudi King Faisal, who effected the oil embargo in protest against US support for Israel in the war. The embargo resulted in oil prices jumping from $3 to $12 per barrel, targeting those countries supporting Israel, the only time OPEC appeared to act in defiance of the US.[13] It was soon lifted—despite the refusal of Israel to withdraw from Sinai and the occupied territories—though oil prices remained at the new price. Only US consumers were inconvenienced, with oil producers reaping huge profits, and US and British banks the beneficiaries of the flood of dollars.

The fortuitous result was a new standard for the dollar, replacing gold—an oil standard, dubbed "petrodollars". The Saudis, Iraqis and Iranians, mollified by a vague promise by Israel to negotiate the return of Sinai, and awash in dollars, acquiesced to continued US world financial *diktat* and the recycling of their new wealth denominated in dollars, reinforcing the power of Anglo-American financial interests.

> We have to remember that the two key governments that pushed for the 1973 oil rise were Saudi Arabia and Iran, then under the Shah of Iran, the most pro-American government in the whole of OPEC. The major consequence of that oil rise and price rise, the first one, was in fact to shift money to the oil-producing countries, which was immediately placed in US banks. It was harder for Europe and for Japan to deal with this than it was for the United States.[14]

Engdahl, Wallerstein and others argue that Kissinger actually precipitated the 1973 war between Egypt and Israel, using the crisis to keep Israel in line and at the same time to provide the oil shock desired by Big Oil, making the Arab oil-producing nations the scapegoats, while the major beneficiaries, "the Anglo-American interests responsible, stood quietly in the background".[15] Kissinger was killing two birds with one stone, as Israel's intention to keep Sinai would precipitate a war in any case, and a small war which the US would mediate was the only way to push Israel to the negotiating table, something that was very much in US interests, but already diverging from Israel's more open goal of colonizing all of Palestine. Israel was already out of control and direct appeals were pointless. If so, this was a master stroke by Kissinger, a classic case of 'create the problem, provide the solution'.[16]

Kissinger hinted that the US was and is in control of oil prices —or else—in a 1975 article, "Seizing Arab Oil," in *Harper's*. To quell any fears in the US political elite that OPEC represented a threat to US world hegemony, Kissinger, who used the pseudonym Miles Ignotus, outlined how we could "solve all our economic and political problems by taking over the Arab oil fields [and] bringing in Texans and Oklahomans to operate them." In an interview with *Business Week* a few months later, Kissinger (anticipating the neocons in GGIII) mused about bringing oil prices down through "massive political warfare against countries like Saudi Arabia and Iran to make them risk their political stability and maybe their security if they did not cooperate".[17]

The continuity of financial strategy from Nixon's 1971 discarding of the gold standard through to the new post-embargo scenario with high oil prices is suggested by the secret Saudi Arabian Monetary Agency (SAMA) accord initiated by Nixon's assistant treasury secretary Jack Bennett (who later became a director of Exxon) and finalized in 1975 in a memo to Kissinger whereby the Saudi revenues were used to finance the growing US government deficits.[18] This is further confirmed by "economic hit man" John Perkins.[19] OPEC remained safely wedded to payments in US dollars only—not German marks, Japanese yen or Swiss francs.

The consequence of the recycling of petrodollars into London and New York banks was the emergence of US and British banks (Chase Manhattan, Citibank, Manufacturers Hanover, Bank of America, Barclays, Lloyds, Midland) as the giants of world banking, paralleling the emergence of their clients, the Big Oil Seven Sisters, then Standard Oil of New Jersey and Standard Oil Company of New York (now ExxonMobil); Standard Oil of California, Gulf Oil and Texaco (now Chevron); Royal Dutch Shell; and Anglo-Persian Oil Company (now BP) as the giants of world industry.[20] This created a world economic crisis, one where the banks lent petrodollars to impoverished nations to finance the 4x higher cost of oil imports. By 1979, the hegemony of the American-Anglo financial establishment over the world's economic and industrial potential had been reasserted, with continued control of world oil flows, in dollars, through primarily US banks.[21]

Perkins documents the role he played in keeping the Saudis onboard the imperial wagon, ensuring the oil price manipulation did not backfire and deprive the US of its vital energy imports. A young idealist, he was recruited by the National Security Agency and given a job with a private consulting firm in the early 1970s after completing a stint with the Peace Corps. There, he learned to manipulate statistics to produce conclusions which served US corporate and government purposes, that is, to justify huge loans that would funnel money back to his consulting firm and other US companies, paying US contractors and enriching a few already wealthy families in those countries, but bankrupting the country "so they would present easy targets when we needed favors, including military bases, UN votes, or access to oil and other natural resources."[22] Perkins personally was key to establishing the United States-Saudi Arabian Joint Economic Commission after the 1973 oil crisis, which funneled billions of petrodollars back to the US, entrenching "the US deeply in the Kingdom, fortifying the concept of mutual interdependence"[23] at the same time as the US turned a blind eye to Saudi financing—both official and private—of Islamists, outside of American purview.

The outcome of this and Federal Reserve Chairman Paul Volker's extreme hike in interest rates following the oil embargo has been to deepen periphery debt over time (via the interest on repayment)—a vicious circle, a variation on the classical imperialist mechanism of using financial structures to drain surplus, monetized as profit and interest, from the periphery. This happened starkly in Mexico in the 1980s, followed by Argentina, Brazil, Peru, Venezuela, Zambia, Zaire, and Egypt and much of Asia through the 1990s. World Bank figures show that between 1980–86, for a group of 109 debtor countries, $326 billion was paid in interest, $332 billion on the debt principal, and yet the principal still more than doubled from $430 billion to $882 billion, with the repaid or newly lent money never even leaving New York or London, but merely transferred from one column to another in bank ledgers.[24] While bank profits soared, the real effects in, say, Zambia, Brazil or Egypt were disintegration of the economy and starvation. The pious campaign by first world countries in the 1990s to "forgive" third world debt masks the reality that this debt is largely a result of creative accounting dreamed up in offices in Manhattan and London in the first place.

The few attempts by Europeans to break the Big Oil mould were nipped in the bud. Italian ENI oil magnate Enrico Mattei tried to break the oligopoly of the Seven Sisters (a term he coined), initiating agreements with Iran, Egypt and other Middle East countries. In 1960, after concluding an agreement with the Soviet Union and while negotiating with China, Mattei publicly declared that the American monopoly was over. He died in 1962 in a mysterious plane crash. In 1977 France and Germany unsuccessfully proposed a barter deal with OPEC. Only de Gaulle dared to dream of an independent Europe, refusing to cow to NATO, but a subservient Germany prevented any alternative to the Anglo-American empire from taking shape in Europe.[25]

Financial moves in GGII endgame
In a remarkable example of parapolitics – remarkable particularly in that it was revealed to the world because of bank fraud investigations by the US government—the international banking sector was mobilized

as a conduit for financing of Islamic jihadists. The Bank of Credit and Commerce International (BCCI) was founded in 1972 by Agha Hasan Abedi, a Pakistani financier, based in Karachi. It was transformed by the head of Saudi intelligence and then-CIA director G.H.W. Bush into "the biggest clandestine money network in history."[26] By the mid-1980s it was the seventh largest private bank in the world by assets. The bank's transformation was guided by the head of Saudi intelligence with a view to enabling it to finance covert intelligence operations when American intelligence agencies were hampered by the fallout from the Watergate scandal that toppled Nixon. The CIA held numerous accounts at BCCI, according to former US Commissioner of Customs William von Raab, which were used in arming and financing the Afghan mujahideen and to launder proceeds from trafficking heroin grown in the Pakistan-Afghanistan borderlands.[27] *Time* described "a clandestine division of the bank called the 'black network' which functions as a global intelligence operation and a Mafia-like enforcement squad."[28]

Reagan was able to make devastating political use of the oil manipulation strategy in reverse as OPEC let the price of oil fall below $10 a barrel by 1986 from a high of $26 in 1980. This produced a foreign trade crisis for the oil-exporting Soviet Union, just as Reagan was conducting a new Cold War to consign communism to the "ash heap of history".[29] Combined with US support for the mujahideen in Afghanistan, this quickly led to the collapse of the Soviet Union (see GGII endgame).

Military-political Strategies

As GGII got underway, the crudest strategy to achieve the prize of Eurasia would have been of course straightforward invasion of the Soviet Union. Churchill contemplated an immediate war against the Soviet Union when Germany surrendered—Operation Unthinkable.[30] Only Britain's own prostration and US government reluctance prevented it. To keep the Anglo-American imperial project on course, he officially launched the Cold War in sleepy Fulton, Missouri in 1946, as a second-best strategy to ensure the US did not make a post-war deal with the Soviet Union, pushing Britain aside. The term "special relationship between the British Commonwealth and Empire and the United States" was coined there (along with "Iron Curtain"), though unlike the "special relationship" between the US and Israel, this one required the British to accept complete political subservience to the US.

The Cold War was really just the "North-South conflict writ large",[31] the post-1917 invasion of Russia by the US, Britain and Japan the precursor of GGII's struggles again communism. The Cold War became the ideological cornerstone of US geopolitical strategy to dominate the postwar global order, using the Russian and Chinese communists as the pretext for US military dominance of "the free world" both directly, as well as through NATO and various Asian defense pacts. With the heartland out of reach for the moment, the rimland West had to use "containment of communism" as its geopolitical strategy. Contrary to Cold War mythology, the Soviet Union had no plans to invade the West, never threatened to attack the West, nor did it even engage in acts of sabotage.[32] On the contrary, the West invaded Russia in 1918 and again in 1941, and after WWII, constantly threatened to 'liberate' the socialist bloc, engaging in countless acts of sabotage to bring the anti-imperialist rival system down.

In a 1978 Joint Chiefs of Staff memorandum, the three strategic objectives for the US in the Middle East were

- to assure continuous access to petroleum resources,

- to prevent an inimical power or combination of powers from establishing hegemony, and

- to assure the survival of Israel as an independent state in a stable relationship with contiguous Arab states.[33]

This is a mix of professed and real motives. The US indeed needed assured oil access, but this does not require geopolitical hegemony, as this could have been accomplished via the world market system. Just which powers threatened to impose their own hegemony in the region other than the US and Israel is not stated. Of course what was implied was that independent Arab states could threaten the other two objectives. But the US would only have to fear for its access to oil if it was tied to an Israel making war on its Arab neighbors, which had nothing to do with the Soviet Union. Israel needed a stable relationship with its neighbors, but this was not something the US could guarantee, as from the start it was not part of the Zionist agenda (see Chapter 4). The Soviet threat was really code for "nationalist Arab regimes", independent regional actors beholden to their own people, opposed to Israel and therefore to its patron, the US.

Because the Soviet Union could not be portrayed as just another empire,[34] it was portrayed as a civilizational threat, a threat to western ideals of "democracy and freedom". Samuel Huntington admitted that this professed Soviet threat in the case of the Middle East was merely a cover for the actual objectives of oil and Israel in 1981, arguing "selling" intervention abroad might require creating "the misimpression that it is the Soviet Union you are fighting".[35] The professed fear of the communist domino effect was really fear of the possibility that "successful independent development and steps towards democracy, out of US control, might well have a domino effect, inspiring others who face similar problems to pursue the same course, thus eroding the global system of domination."[36]

The British imperial establishment, which continued to formulate foreign policy under the post-war Labour government, did not fully appreciate the implications of its alliance with the newly internationalist US government. But the British imperial 'domino' was falling everywhere. In 1949, in line with the rest of Europe, Britain allowed the US to establish permanent military bases on British soil, a revolution in British foreign policy, formally acknowledging Britain's junior role in the new GGII. Suave British diplomats still couch the new subordinate role of Britain in the US empire in terms of British influence and restraint over the brash US; however, the British had no say in the use of nuclear weapons in Japan, and have no veto over even those on hair-trigger notice on UK bases. Only de Gaulle dared protest US military plans, closing all US bases in France and withdrawing from NATO command structures in 1966 in what was really a token gesture.

There was no serious attempt to achieve a *modus vivendi* with the Soviet Union in the post-WWII world, despite the wartime alliance and goodwill, as this would have allowed the emerging ex-colonies to opt for socialism as opposed to incorporation into the US empire. The main international organs created at the time to regulate international economic matters—the World Bank, the IMF, GATT[37]—and the Marshall Plan for European reconstruction were rejected by the Soviet Union as part of US imperial plans. Which of course they were, since it is only rational that the US as chief architect of the post-war international system would set rules which would allow it to win. The US Senate rejected US participation in the British-designed League of Nations, rightly seeing it as an infringement on US sovereignty, but voted 89–2 for membership in the clearly US-controlled UN in 1945.

Decolonization
The very existence of certain players requires a move on the part of the imperial team. For instance, Britain and France carved up the Ottoman Middle East at the end of WWI to ensure control of the region and the oil reserves of Iraq through a calculated policy of divide-and-rule. They fashioned the kingdoms of Yugoslavia and Albania in the Balkans to be friendly to the British monarchy. Similarly, the US and its Cold War allies tried to control the process of decolonization at the end of WWII, the

beginning of GGII, to give them an advantage over their communist rivals.

The platform for doing this was the UN, which began in 1945 with 51 members and reached 192 by 2007, with well over a hundred of the new members being ex-colonies which achieved independence during GGII.

Just as the British added the German colonies and Ottoman territories to their empire after WWI, the US now was building its world order on the ruins of the British and other GGI empires. Attempts to reinstate British, Dutch and French imperial rule in Malaysia, Indonesia and Vietnam to 'prepare' them for independence met with stiff resistance, and US plans to replace the Japanese in the strategic Korean peninsula led to the outbreak of war in 1950. The division of Europe was also a perilous process and, together with southeast Asia, soon became the focus of GGII military-political scheming which lasted more than four decades and laid the foundations for the even more lethal GGIII. In the Middle East, the British-French mandates were effectively deposited on the US doorstep in 1945, and it was left to the US to sort out how best to promote imperial interests there and on the Indian subcontinent given the bankruptcy of Britain.

The general pattern of decolonization followed the scenario of **India/Pakistan**. Britain's most pressing problem following the war was trying to control the march to independence in India. The division of India into Hindu and Muslim nations in August 1947 was in the tradition of divide-and-rule. A united socialist, secular India, along with communist Russia and China, would have tipped the Eurasian balance fatally against the imperial powers. The Muslim League's call for a Muslim state was not a popular demand among Muslims (let alone the Congress Party), just as the Zionists' demand for a Jewish state was not popular among the world's Jews prior to the creation of Israel (let alone the native Arabs).

It was only the support of the Indian Muslim League for Britain during the war—in sharp contrast to Congress's Quit India campaign—that allowed the British to proceed with partition. The sympathy of British leaders for the Muslim League parallels their sympathy for the Zionists, who loudly supported the British in WWII, while Arabs, like Congress in India, were hostile towards their imperial master and even to some extent supported Germany. In both cases, the Muslim nationalists in India and the Jewish nationalists in Palestine and Europe used a desperate British imperialism on its last legs to get their otherwise unattainable goals, goals which conveniently served the long term imperial interests. The partition of India left up to 2 million dead and

11 million refugees, transforming the once peaceful united South Asian subcontinent into a weak, divided one plagued by unending ethnic and religious conflict.

Intense Zionist lobbying and finally outright terrorism leading up to the 1948 UN vote forced a beleaguered Britain to accede to the demand to create a Jewish state in Palestine—**Israel**—recapping the horror of the partition of India. A united Palestine would have required resolute support for the indigenous Arabs in the face of international Zionist hostility, not something Britain, the US or the Soviet Union had any interest in or the ability to enforce. The partition of Palestine was an even worse disaster for the native Palestinians than partition was for the Indians, but like the division of India, eventually proved to be a geostrategic coup for the US in its geopolitical divide-and-rule strategy for the Middle East, the equivalent of a second queen promotion,[38] providing the US with Mackinder's "hill citadel", a western outpost promising imperial control over the Middle East and a stepping stone to control over Eurasia. A much greater prize than Pakistan, and one which quickly came to play an outsize role in imperial plans.

Originally the Zionists were courted by both the US and the Soviet Union, the two rivals hoping, based on very different reasoning, that the creation of a Jewish state in Palestine would be an opportunity to gain influence in the Middle East after Britain pulled out. Prior to WWII, the religious convictions of Muslim society gave the atheist communists little hope for allies among the emerging Arab nations, whereas Jews were the very backbone of communism and revolution in Europe and America. The Soviets saw in Israel a potential pro-communist junior partner, and provided weapons at the time of independence, ensuring its survival in the face of Arab hostility. However, American and European Zionist lobbyists representing powerful financial and business interests had assured British and US political leaders for decades that the Jewish state would remain onside. Jewish elites have through the centuries been prominent in finance and banking in western society (see Chapter 4), unlike Muslims, and the Zionists used this ace to their advantage in 1948.

Many new Middle East states emerged from the ruins of GGI. The last French troops withdrew from newly independent **Syria** and **Lebanon** in 1946. **Transjordan** was granted independence from Britain in 1946. (All of them were soon swamped by hundreds of thousands of Palestinian refugees, with the ethnic cleansing of Palestine following the creation of Israel in 1948.) Among north African states, it was not till 1951 that the British protectorate of **Libya**, taken over from Italy in 1943, achieved independence after a brutal occupation, the British ceding power to weak, pro-British 'King' Idris. The French ceded **Tunisia** to the anticommunist, pro-French president Habib Bourguiba in 1956, **Morocco** also extricated itself from France and Spain in 1956 as a solidly pro-western kingdom, but **Algeria** only achieved independence from France in 1962 after a million Algerians died in the liberation struggle. Throughout the war of independence, the Soviet Union provided military, technical and material assistance to Algeria and *de facto* recognized the provisional government in 1960. Contrary to US fears, Algeria did not come under Soviet influence (unlike neighboring Morocco, Tunisia and Libya with regard to the US), though, crippled by the long struggle for independence and the departure of the French colons who had largely run the economy, it was not to play a major role in regional politics.

As GGII began, Soviet and British troops were still occupying **Iran**. Pro-Soviet elements tried to seize power in the Soviet-occupied north and the Soviet Union hoped that this movement would spread and bring Iran into the anti-colonial camp. The Azerbaijan People's Government and the Republic of Kurdistan were declared in late 1945 but collapsed when the Soviet forces retreated in 1946. However, the Iranians had had enough of imperial intrigues by the end of WWII and nationalized the British-owned Anglo-Iranian Oil Company in 1951. The Labour government, infected by the imperial virus, considered GGI-style military intervention to overthrow the nationalist prime minister, Mossadegh. British minister of defense Emanuel Shinwell warned that if tough action was not taken, "Egypt and other Middle Eastern countries would be encouraged to think they could try things on; the next thing might be an attempt to nationalize the Suez Canal."[39] Eventually, using the GGII game move, the CIA overthrew the Mossadegh government in 1953 in a coup supported by the British.

The weakness of Britain did not escape the notice of Colonel Abdel-Nasser, who forced them out of **Egypt** in 1954 and nationalized the Suez Canal in 1956, in a rare win for a periphery player in GGII. Prime Minister Anthony Eden believed that a British-French-Israeli attack on Egypt would not only remove Nasser, getting back the canal, but would also strengthen the British position vis-à-vis the United States. As early as 1954 he had complained that the Americans "want to replace us in Egypt," indeed, "they want to run the world."[40] The ruse—Israel acting on its own with Britain and France coming in to mediate—fooled nobody and the Eisenhower administration forced a humiliating withdrawal on all parties, including—for the first and last time—Israel.

In 1961, **Kuwait**, a British protectorate carved from the Ottoman caliphate in 1899, was granted independence by Britain, though Iraq immediately claimed sovereignty over it. **Iraq** had achieved nominal independence in 1932 at the same time as Saudi Arabia, but British influence ended only in 1958 when Brigadier Abd al-Karim Qasim overthrew the British-installed Hashemite monarchy and annulled the British-US sponsored Baghdad Pact. In 1963, the Baath Party took power and after a period of instability General Saddam Hussein became *de facto* leader of Iraq in 1976 and president in 1979. Though he created the most advanced Arab nation and managed to become an important geopolitical player in GGII, his fatal misjudgments—the war against Iran and the invasion of Kuwait—led to his isolation and the destruction of his country by the end of GGII.

Yemen was formed from a collection of British protectorates, patched together in 1963 to form the Federation and Protectorate of South Arabia, with a British promise of total independence in 1968. Inspired by Egypt's Nasser, nationalist groups immediately began an armed struggle. With the temporary closure of the Suez Canal in 1967, the British forces were cut off and southern Yemen became independent as the People's Republic of South Yemen, and in 1970, the People's Democratic Republic of Yemen. This was the closest the Soviets ever came to having a reliable ally in the Middle East. Socialist Yemen unraveled in 1990 along with its sponsor, and was forced to join the north.[41] **Bahrain, Qatar, Oman** and the sheikhdoms comprising the **United Arab Emirates** were British protectorates and bases until they were granted nominal independence in 1970–71, when the US took over guaranteeing their security within the western camp.

Libya was an active player in GGII after Muammar al-Gaddafi came to power in a coup in 1969, soon betraying his CIA backers[42] and declaring his own version of socialism, nationalizing the oil industry and supporting the Palestinian struggle. He focused on African and Arab unity, remaining aloof from the Soviet Union. However, when Libya intervened in Chad in 1980 it was wrongly perceived by the American authorities as a Soviet proxy, and Reagan began a campaign to undermine al-Gaddafi, whose sin was compounded by his defiant support for Islamic Iran in the 1980–88 war with Iraq. Reagan decided to actively work to overthrow this thorn in the imperial side and broke off relations with Libya in 1981, shooting down 2 Libyan military aircraft, and arming neighbours Tunisia, Egypt and Sudan to contain the "mad dog of the Middle East". Reagan even ordered the bombing Tripoli and Benghazi in 1986, attempting to assassinate al-Gaddafi, though the bombing of al-Gaddafi's tent only managed to kill his daughter. Al-Gaddafi continued to provide financial support and even token weapons support to the Palestinian Liberation Organization (PLO), the Irish Republican Army and other groups he deemed anti-imperialist, and remained the most outspoken Arab critic of the US empire and Israel, a lightning rod for western anti-Arab sentiment, but an eccentric, ineffectual leader for Arab nationalists.

The **Palestinians** were left out in the cold in GGII, unprepared to confront the highly organized, determined Zionists, who were able, unlike the Palestinians, to count on powerful allies around the world in addition to Zionist troops trained primarily by the British and armed by the Soviets during and after WWII. The British made no effort to prepare the Palestinians to form a government after the occupier's hurried departure. The Arab Liberation Army was hastily put together in 1948 by the fledgling Arab states, but untrained, without proper weapons, it was routed by the Zionists, and most of the Palestinians forced into exile in refugee camps.

The Palestinians remained without a unifying secular political organization until Fatah was founded in late 1950s and the PLO was sponsored by Egypt in 1964. PLO head Yasser Arafat was recognized as the *de facto* leader of Palestine, which gained observer status at the UN in 1974. These moves were important to legitimizing the Palestinian cause in the West, but from the start, for Arab regimes intent on maintaining their neocolonial power and intimidated by the fierce commitment and powerful backing of Israel, the PLO was more about finding a way "to co-opt and restrain the Palestinian resistance movement" to prevent them from drawing Arab states inadvertently into war.[43] Only the Soviet Union—after Stalin had recognized his fatal misjudgement of recognizing Israel in 1948—was a firm supporter of the Palestinian cause throughout GGII, and it too was ineffectual, concerned in the first place with its own survival in the face of the overwhelming economic and military might of the US empire.[44]

While the major moves in the game, the major victories and defeats, were in the first place the work of the US and the Soviet Union, there were a few cases of emerging nations using the Cold War to further their own ends. The few victories against the US empire are the stuff of legend: China in 1949, Ghana, Egypt and Cuba in the 1950s, Vietnam and Libya in the 1960–70s. But the victories were at best achieved with horrendous suffering, and were temporary or Pyrrhic.

The repercussions of this Anglo-American devil's pact resound today.

Many of the world's most intractable conflicts are in former British colonies or protectorates: from the West Bank and Gaza, Iraq, Kurdistan, Yemen and Somalia to Pakistan, Sri Lanka, Afghanistan, Cyprus and Sudan—with the reflex imperial resort to partition a recurrent theme. The failure in modern Britain to recognise the empire for what it was—an avowedly racist despotism, built on ethnic cleansing and ruthless exploitation, which undeveloped vast areas and oversaw famines that killed tens of millions—is a dangerous encouragement to ignore its lessons and repeat its crimes in a modern form.[45]

The use of military might to destroy potential threats to the imperial status quo achieved the desired result, even when the states concerned seemingly defeated the US. The US is popularly thought of as losing in Vietnam, but by destroying its economy, killing millions of its people and devastating its land, it prevented the successful development of a strong socialist country which could have been a catalyst in the non-imperial transformation of southeast Asia. The only holdouts from GGII today—Cuba and North Korea—remain impoverished, besieged by the empire.

Institutions
The **United Nations** was set up along with the Bretton Woods financial institutions at the end of WWII. Though the Soviet Union opted out of the latter, it fulfilled its wartime pledge of cooperation by co-founding the UN and taking part in the only forum available for pursuing world peace after the war. The UN's first moves, which have haunted it ever since, were the partition of Palestine and recognition of Israel in 1948, and the Korean War (1950–53).[46] With a very few exceptions, the UN has been effectively undermined in its political role as peacekeeper and harbinger of collective security ever since.

The Arab-Israeli war that followed the declaration of a Jewish state in Palestine by the UN meant it had to immediately deal with the problem it had created. Swedish Count Folke Bernadotte of Wisborg was agreed as mediator, but was promptly assassinated by the Zionist Stern Gang. After more than a year of painstaking negotiations, his assistant, African-American Ralph Bunche, managed to secure separate armistice agreements between Israel and Egypt, Lebanon, Transjordan and Syria, which left Israel with all the territory it had conquered, hundreds of thousands of Palestinian refugees in neighboring Jordan and Syrian, and no state of Palestine—a template for all future Israeli 'compromises', for which Bunche was awarded the Nobel Peace Prize in 1950.

From GGII to the present, there have been three UN peacekeeping missions protecting Israel at UN expense, and Israel has killed dozens of UN peacekeepers over the years with impunity. The first fully fledged UN peacekeeping effort was covering the withdrawal of British, French and Israeli forces from Egypt in 1956, following their invasion in the wake of the nationalization of the Suez Canal. UN troops were stationed in Sinai afterwards as part of a deal to get Israel to withdraw, and when Egypt finally ordered them to leave in 1967 to reassert its sovereignty, Israel invaded and re-occupied Sinai and all of Palestine.

Despite its inauspicious beginnings, the UN provided a forum for world dialogue to a much greater degree than GGI's League of Nations. As long as the Soviet Union existed, it provided a platform for socialism and helped protect countries such as Cuba from overt invasion, though it could do nothing to help Vietnam in the face of US determination to work outside the international community. Empire exceptionalism—imperial *diktat*—trumped international law.

The **European Coal and Steel Community** was set up in 1950 with the intent of promoting European integration, approved by Truman and Eisenhower as a Cold War anti-domino measure. Later GGII US administrations came to view it ambivalently, fearful that an independent unified Europe could forge a separate détente with the Soviet Union, combining Europe's technology and industrial capacity with Soviet natural resources, manpower and ideology, gaining access to the Eurasian heartland and creating a continent-sized competitor able to 'threaten' North America (that is, threaten US world hegemony).

At the same time, and as the military adjunct to the nascent European Union, the **North Atlantic Treaty Organization** (NATO) was set up in 1949, ostensibly to counter the Soviet threat. In 1952, the first major NATO maritime exercises began, in defense of Denmark and Norway (threatened by no country), a prelude to a flood of exercises by NATO members ever since, clearly intended to intimidate any country contemplating neutrality. The Eisenhower Doctrine, first articulated with respect to the need to "protect" the Middle East from communism, was at work in Europe too, creating a new playing field out of the rubble of WWII, pushing the players into the US-backed Cold War line-up, demonizing and excluding European communists as the enemy within, denying Europe any possibility of finding a third way to develop, just as in the Middle East, countries were forced to choose sides and then join the appropriate Cold War regional alliance.

Strategic Concepts were issued in 1949, 1952, 1957 and 1968, all based on NATO's purported mission to keep the Soviets at bay, despite the fact that the Soviet Union was in ruins after WWII, received no help in reconstruction, and, both before and after the death of Stalin, made many clear overtures for peace and disarmament. The real rationale for NATO was to bind Europe militarily and thus politically to the US and

NATO & THE WARSAW PACT: COLD WAR ERA

Figure 2.1 map[47]

to threaten the Soviet Union. "What other reason is there for NATO to exist except to control the Europeans?"[48]

The US military remained in Europe after the war and lived at European expense, with the US repeatedly refusing to negotiate a mutual withdrawal of US and Soviet forces from Europe. In 1954, Khrushchev launched a peace offensive and even proposed that the Soviet Union should join NATO to preserve peace in Europe. This was brusquely dismissed, as a western Europe without US troops would very likely have elected communist governments in the 1950s, leading to the collapse of

NATO and even the end of US empire.[49] Instead West Germany was invited to join NATO, abrogating the post-war understanding that Germany would remain disarmed. This provocation of the Soviet Union took place on 9 May 1955—on the 10th anniversary of the Soviet celebration of the end of WWII. A slap in the face, it prompted Khrushchev to move—sensibly—to create the Warsaw Pact[50] a few days later.

In GGII, NATO conducted no open military engagement as an organization, never once invoking Article 5 on collective defense, but it played an important role in initiating the GGII endgame against the Soviet Union. In May 1978, at perhaps the low point for the imperialists in GGII following the US defeat in Vietnam and with a still vigorous Soviet Union, NATO officially defined two aims of the Alliance: to maintain security and pursue détente, that is, protect Europe from the Warsaw Pact's supposed offensive capabilities while facilitating moves towards peace. However, on 12 December 1979, it nonetheless approved the deployment of US cruise missiles and Pershing III theatre nuclear weapons in Europe—offensive weapons—in the face of overwhelming public opposition in western Europe.

This move by the US to threaten the Soviet Union in Europe using NATO as a cover was taken at the same time that the US was pouring millions of dollars of arms into Afghanistan to fight the socialist regime that had taken power the previous year. Two weeks later, on 27 December 1979, the clearly spooked Soviet Union, observing the new aggressive US-NATO move, took the fateful decision to send troops into Afghanistan to support the failing regime. This can hardly have been a coincidence: Brzezinski, Gates and others involved in convincing Carter to begin funding the Afghan jihadists in July 1979 now admit their intent was to draw the Soviet Union into a Vietnam-type quagmire.[51]

NATO strategists called the simultaneous arms build-up, while supposedly proposing détente, a "dual track" policy. The nuclear weapons in Europe were supposedly to strike targets on the battlefield if the Soviets invaded West Germany—something they never threatened to do. The real dual track was this new geopolitical game: continuing to mouth words about détente while in fact threatening war both in Europe and in Afghanistan, arming the Taliban mujahideen against the pro-Soviet government. The strong peace movement at the time was threatening to topple European governments, and the US plot to draw the Soviet Union into Afghanistan as proof of its expansionist threat provided the propaganda coup necessary to overcome Euro-skepticism. NATO played its most important role in 1979 as a very useful decoy at this critical point in GGII.

The US organized other regional military blocs as part of the

Truman Doctrine in order to counter nationalist movements fighting against the restoration of Europe's colonial empires in southeast Asia and Africa. In the early 1950s (a period known as pactomania), the US formalized a series of alliances:

- ANZUS in 1951 with Australia, New Zealand;

- Middle East Defense Organization (MEDO) in 1952–53 and Central Treaty Organization (CENTO) in 1955–79 with Pakistan, Iran, Iraq, Turkey and Britain (Iraq withdrew in 1959);

- Southeast Asian Treaty Organization (SEATO) in 1954 with Australia, New Zealand, Thailand, Philippines, Taiwan, East Pakistan, France, Britain, with South Korea and South Vietnam "dialogue partners";

- Association of Southeast Asian Nations (ASEAN) in 1967 with Indonesia, Malaysia, the Philippines, Singapore, Thailand, and later Brunei, Myanmar, Cambodia, Laos, and Vietnam.

Neither NATO nor any of these regional mini-NATOs has had to protect its members from external threats; however, they fulfilled their goal of forcing countries to line up with the US against its foes, and allowed US intelligence operatives greater freedom to both gather information and conduct subversion.

There are three important institutions which are unofficial forums for developing imperial strategy:

- The Council on Foreign Relations, founded as a forum for the imperial leaders in 1921, has been a central fixture in US politics since the 1930s, with its *Foreign Relations* journal a barometer of imperial thinking. Though apparently not a member himself, President Franklin Roosevelt set the precedent of filling his cabinet with CFR members in 1940. Besides Treasury Secretary Morgenthau, other CFR members included Secretary of State Edward Stettinus, Secretary of State Henry Stimson, and Assistant Secretary of State Sumner Wells. Subsequent administrations have followed suit, in effect concretizing global governance by committee for the first time in history. With the exception of Johnson, Reagan and George W. Bush, all presidents have been members since FDR (Johnson, Reagan and George W. Bush were surrounded by CFR members, including their vice presidents).

- The Bilderberg Group, a secretive organization founded in

1954 by Prince Bernhard of the Netherlands, represented a European elite now resigned to US world hegemony which realized the best way to convince the US of policies favorable to Europeans was to seduce US leaders with Euro-snobbism. As opposed to forums where leaders must publicly profess pious political and economic goals, it is one where actual goals are discussed openly, at least among participants. Although no proceedings are published, an observer at the first meeting wrote,

> The intention behind the Bilderberg meetings was about how to create an "aristocracy of purpose" between Europe and the US, and how to come to agreement on questions of policy, economics, and strategy in jointly ruling the world. The NATO alliance was their crucial base of operation and subversion because it afforded them the backdrop for the plans of "perpetual war", or at least for their "nuclear blackmail" policy.[52]

Critic Daniel Estulin argues the group aims "to subjugate all free nations to their rule through international laws, which they manipulate and have the UN administer."[53] They and their proxies control the central banks in the US and Europe and can wield this power to make governments conform, at the same time as they make fortunes for themselves through insider knowledge. "The Bilderbergers are too powerful and omnipresent to be exposed," writes French broadcaster Thierry de Segonzac. The group is behind many moves such as oil price manipulations.[54]

- The Trilateral Commission was founded in 1973 as a complement to the CFR and Bilderberg Group by David Rockefeller, with Zbigniew Brzezinski, future national security adviser to Carter and patron of Obama, as the first chairman, to control the rising Asian economy.

Hard Power
Despite the formal agreement with the Soviet Union that GGI colonialism (and the wars it gave rise to) was over, GGII witnessed

unending **war**. However, apart from Israel's wars against its neighbors, they were undeclared and conducted using proxies, local agents who opposed the liberation forces, assisted by the rapidly expanding and well-financed CIA and other secret services. US-inspired **black-ops** were also used to undermine the existing socialist regimes, that is 'behind the Iron Curtain', using pro-western local agents and émigrés who could be parachuted back and blend in locally to conduct sabotage operations.[55]

The best known such operation in the Middle East was the 1953 overthrow of the Iranian Prime Minister Mossadegh. In a 'create the problem, provide the solution' scenario that was the pattern for more than 80 such black-ops during GGIII,[56] the CIA organized and paid anti-Mossadegh protesters and street thugs to riot, loot and burn mosques and newspapers, leaving almost 300 dead. The CIA team, led by retired army general and Mossadegh's former interior minister Fazlollah Zahedi, mobilized a few pro-Shah tank regiments to storm the capital and arrest Mossadegh on the pretext that he was a communist. Mossadegh was an avowed anticommunist and thus unable and unwilling to turn to the Soviet Union for help. The Shah, who had previously 'fled' on CIA instructions, came back and was re-installed.

But Iranians never forgot this and finally it was the Shah's turn. Several commentators argue that even the overthrow of the Shah and facilitation of the return of Ayatollah Khomeini to Iran in 1979 was orchestrated in the final act by a US working on the principle that when a rupture is imminent, it is best to try to control the outcome,[57] to create a grateful (and hence, hopefully loyal) new proxy in the GGII war against communism. There were such attempts to control Nasser after the 1952 revolution in Egypt, Castro after the 1959 revolution in Cuba, al-Gaddafi in Libya and Saddam Hussein in Iraq after their coups in 1968, and the Taliban in the 1990s, despite their avowed anti-colonialism, but these all failed. Whether CIA planners were naive enough to think they could control Ayatollah Khomeini is impossible to verify, though it is true the Iranian clergy had turned against Mossadegh at the end in 1953, allowing the CIA to mobilize effectively against him. The apparent conspiracy between the Republicans and the Iranian government during the 1980 presidential elections[58] and the subsequent Iran-Contra scandal demonstrate the ability and willingness of the imperialists to use even the staunchly anti-American Islamist regime in Tehran at its most fervently anti-American to further their GII aims.

Following the failed Bay of Pigs invasion of Cuba in 1961, the US Joint Chiefs of Staff had even drawn up and approved plans for

launching a secret and bloody war of terrorism *against*

their own country in order to trick the American public into supporting an ill-conceived war they intended to launch against Cuba. ... Codenamed Operation Northwoods, the plan . . . called for innocent people to be shot on American streets; for boats carrying refugees fleeing Cuba to be sunk on the high seas; for a wave of violent terrorism to be launched in Washington DC, Miami, and elsewhere. People would be framed for bombings they did not commit; planes would be hijacked. Using phony evidence, all of it would be blamed on Castro, [for] "public and international backing they needed to launch their war.[59]

New accidents and provocations were to be used to advance US interests. The Gulf of Tonkin false-flag operation justified the escalation of the only full-blown (but still undeclared) war by the US in GGII, in Vietnam.

The CIA used NATO as a cover for black-op operations in GGII run jointly with European secret services, supposedly in preparation for a Soviet invasion, but in fact to prevent the European left, in particular, the communists, from taking power. Named Gladio (Latin for double-edged sword), "NATO's secret armies" included the Clandestine Committee of the Western Union and in 1957, a second secret army called the Allied Clandestine Committee. An Italian parliamentary investigation in 2000 concluded that CIA operatives were involved in bombings, massacres, and other terrorist attacks as part of a campaign against the left. In 2001, General Giandelio Maletti, former Italian counterintelligence head, confirmed the CIA's involvement to "do anything to stop Italy from sliding to the left".[60]

After a brief post-war reduction in military spending with the demobilization of the US fighting army, the Truman administration quadrupled the 1951-52 US defense budget,[61] and though Eisenhower again reduced military spending, war expenditures eventually crept up to WWII levels by 1968. The hold on the US economy by the military-industrial complex was condemned by Eisenhower in his famous farewell speech to the American people in 1960, but to no avail. Massive military spending under Reagan would become one of the key factors in bankrupting the Soviet Union.

The shaping of US industrial might around **arms production**, dwarfing all other countries, is an important indirect game strategy, purportedly to defend freedom, but implicitly to tie countries to it economically and politically. The US strives to arm both sides in the Middle East. Already in May 1950, it issued the Tripartite Declaration with France and Britain allowing them to sell arms to both Arab states and Israel. By then, the Soviet Union was eager to support the Arab cause, including with arms. Better the arms be western, with the balance of course in Israel's favor, using friendly European proxies to support Israel to keep a semblance of neutrality and Arab goodwill.[62]

GGII military strategy is best remembered by the acronym **MAD** (mutually assured destruction)—referring to the strategy which evolved thanks to the Soviet acquisition of nuclear weapons. Because of the overwhelming destructive force of nuclear, especially fusion weapons and the long term radioactive fallout, neither side dared to use them. Their only use in battle was by the US in 1945 against Japan, which did not have nuclear weapons. Only twice did the US actually contemplate unleashing nuclear war (the Soviets never did), when DEFCON (defense condition) was raised from the usual 4 to 3 ("Increase in force readiness above that required for normal readiness"): during the Cuban missile crisis in 1962 and during the Egypt-Israel war in 1973, when Egyptian President Anwar Sadat requested Soviet military assistance faced with a potential massacre of Egyptian troops by the Israelis. In the 1973 Egypt-Israel war, the defense condition level was raised to 3 by Kissinger, Defense Secretary James Schlesinger, CIA Director William Colby, and White House Chief of Staff Alexander Haig (Nixon was asleep), indicating mobilization for war if the Soviets acted unilaterally to defend Egypt. The Soviet leader, Leonid Brezhnev, delayed action and Sadat agreed to negotiate directly with Israel, satisfying the US. "It is not reasonable to become engaged in a war with the United States because of Egypt and Syria," said Premier Alexei Kosygin. KGB chief Yuri Andropov said, "We shall not unleash the Third World War."[63] In both cases, the US threatened to launch nuclear war and the Soviet Union acceded to US fiat.

Soft Power
The chief method of promoting compliance with the US-sponsored post-war order was through provision of **aid**. The Marshall Plan was the vehicle for Europe. US aid was provided *ad hoc* until USAID (Agency for International Development) was set up in 1961 along with Peace Corps. Aid was tied to the purchase of US goods and services, effectively subsidizing the US balance of payments.

The CIA was founded in 1947, based on the wartime anti-Nazi Office of Strategic Services and British MI6, which in turn was modeled on the Secret Service Bureau founded in 1909 at the height of GGI. Given the new rules of GGII, the secret services became important actors, in theory answerable to the chief executive, a kind of Praetorian Guard, but increasingly a law unto themselves. They were occupied not only in spying and subversion, but propaganda and the promotion of US cultural hegemony.

In GGII the CIA turned to **culture**, especially the mass media, using more than 400 journalists internationally for intelligence gathering, as go-betweens with spies, and to give US government propaganda credibility.[64] It began a secret program of experimenting with mind-control techniques—MKULTRA—in the early 1950s which was officially investigated in 1975 by the Church Committee (though all the files relating to it were destroyed in 1973).

The FBI, founded in 1908, had an extensive project to disrupt civil rights organizations through infiltration, disinformation, legal harassment and assassination—COINTELPRO—which officially operated from 1956–71, though such tactics can be seen in FBI activities from WWI on. After the program was exposed,[65] FBI director Herbert Hoover unapologetically announced that operations would be conducted on a "case-by-case basis".

European culture was still being exported along with Christian missionaries and technology, and colonial subjects still brought to the center to be educated in the imperial establishment, but now the broader cultural role became much more important in GGII. The imperial cultural image of GGI was of privilege and elitism; the cultural image of neo-imperialism had to be one of personal freedom and the American Dream of unlimited personal wealth. This was necessary to counter the more prosaic socialist promises of mass health care, free education, social welfare and guaranteed employment. Hollywood entertainment and mass culture spread around the world, promoting the simplistic but alluring vision of a carefree, rich New World.

The mainstream media everywhere was used to "manufacture consent". The CIA paid and helped periphery journalists and newspapers which toed the line. But just as important, the CIA and their allies worked to manufacture dissent, the acceptable boundaries for liberal, socialist and even rightwing political criticism.[66] The Congress for Cultural Freedom (CCF), "a kind of cultural NATO"[67] founded in 1950 and funded by the CIA, using the Ford Foundation as a conduit for funds, was at its height active in 35 countries. Its stated purpose was to find ways to counter the view that communism better served to raise the level of culture than liberal democracy, and its founders included John Dewey, Bertrand Russell, Benedetto Croce, Arthur

Koestler, Tennessee Williams and Sidney Hook—both conservatives and anti-Stalinist left-wingers such as a young Irving Kristol. In May 1967 Thomas Braden, head of the CCF's parent body the International Organizations Division, published "I'm Glad the CIA is Immoral" in the *Saturday Evening Post*, admitting that for more than 10 years, the CIA had subsidized the literary magazine *Encounter*, founded in 1953 by poet Stephen Spender, through the CCF, and that one of its staff was a CIA agent.

In Europe, the CIA was particularly interested in and promoted the anticommunist social democratic left and ex-leftists, including Stephen Spender, Arthur Koestler, Raymond Aron, Anthony Crosland and George Orwell. It even funded symphonies, art exhibits, ballet, theatre groups, and well-known jazz and opera performers with the explicit aim of neutralizing anti-imperialist sentiment in Europe and creating an appreciation of US culture and government. The CIA was especially keen on sending black artists to Europe—singers such as Marion Anderson, writers, and musicians such as Louis Armstrong—to neutralize European hostility toward US racist domestic policies.

At the same time as the US was building up Israel as its chief ally in the Middle East, it was nurturing its alliance with the Saudi monarchy begun in the 1930s, confirmed by FDR's meeting with Saudi King Abdulaziz in 1945 in Cairo. This courting of the most conservative Wahhabi Muslims, taking over from the bankrupt British empire, morphed into a strategy of arming **Islamists** as proxies to fight the communists. (see GGII Endgame below).

Just as Britain used the opium trade and the Triads of Malaysia in GGI to weaken and open up China, the US has used the drug trade as a weapon in its practice of parapolitics. The US strategy of opposing third world countries breaking away from the imperial system pushed the US into alliances with drug-traffickers like the Sicilian Mafia and the Triads in southeast Asia, a strategy which became more important in GGIII with US support of the Contras in Nicaragua, the Kosovo Liberation Army in Europe, the death squads in Colombia and the Northern Alliance in Afghanistan. President Johnson's secretary of state Dean Rusk said the USA "should employ whatever means ... arms here, opium there."[68]

The US first started to copy the British in 1949, when it armed the defeated Kuomintang's drug networks in Burma and Laos, after the victorious Chinese revolution began to eliminate Chinese opium, then the source of 85 per cent of the world's heroin. The US state encouraged its allies to enrich themselves through **drugs**, while blaming the communist enemy for the evils that its allies were committing. From 1949 until at least 1964, the US told the UN Narcotics Commission that

China was responsible for drug imports into the US. In fact, the drugs were trafficked from Burma and Thailand, under the protection of Kuomintang troops backed by the CIA.

The US state assaulted the whole region of southeast Asia between 1950 and 1975, just as it is attacking the Middle East and Central Asia today. Regime change in Laos in 1959–60 put drug traffickers in power, a case of parapolitics metastasizing into deep politics as the military facilitated the trade, making alliances with local producers and international distributors, and large banks facilitated the transfer and laundering of drug proceeds. Supporting the drug trade involved the CIA in money laundering and people smuggling and unleashed forces over which it no longer had control. "Covert operations such as drug smuggling, when they generate or reinforce autonomous political power, almost always outlast the specific purpose for which they were designed, enlarge and become part of the hostile forces the US has to address,"[69] resulting in blowback (the CIA's own term). Opium production soared during the years of US intervention in the 1950s and 1960s, and plummeted in 1975 after the Vietnamese forced the US out of the region. US military interventions have invariably led to increased production of drugs and a greater flow of them into the US, as Afghanistan proves today.

If there is one person who epitomized the use of GGII soft power in all its financial, military and political intricacies before the neocon ascendancy and the start of GGIII, it is Kissinger. Kissinger's foreign politics are *realpolitik*, balance of power, shuttle diplomacy. As a secular Jewish refugee from Nazi Germany, he was a grateful, assimilated American, and 'soft' Zionist, a strong supporter of Israel as a useful ally of the US. In his memoirs he downplays Israel's private agenda, depicting its obstinacy as a useful wild card,[70] a variation on the Nixon/Kissinger 'madman' doctrine from Vietnam disengagement days intended to keep the enemy off-balance. A self-made man, he served in the US army in occupied Germany and earned his PhD in history from Harvard, where he initiated a series of International Seminars which gave him a platform to meet budding political figures from around the world, a goldmine for his future career as statesman. (He acted as an unofficial informer to the FBI for these seminars.)

His career is contradictory, with his views ranging from advocating limited nuclear war when massive first strike was the rage in the early 1950s, to a condemnation of limited nuclear war when later advocated by Nitze and Teller, from active engagement with the Soviets via détente, to covert subversion of such policies, including the 'madman' strategy. His most prominent legacy is perhaps his enduring belief in negotiations, mediation, striving for stability in international relations, maintenance of the status quo. He believed in traditional nineteenth century diplomacy, saw himself as a great statesmen shaping policies to protect the balance of power of nation states without resort to outright war. One of his favorite quotes is Goethe's: "If I had to choose between justice and disorder, and injustice and order, I would always choose the latter."

An obsessive anticommunist, he saw all events as proxies for the Cold War, justifying to him what can only be called crimes against humanity (the bombing of North Vietnam and Cambodia, the overthrow of the Socialist government in Chile, the betrayal of East Timor to Sukarno's Indonesia, a myriad of covert and not so covert operations in dozens of other countries). This despite knowing deep down (at least in his last days in power) that this was wrong. For instance, in a speech in Missouri in 1975, he reflected: "We must outgrow the notion that every setback is a Soviet gain or every problem is caused by Soviet action." Of course, if he hadn't been a militant anticommunist, he would never have reached the pinnacle of power in the US; he would have been pushed aside, like Henry Wallace in 1944, who was replaced as vice presidential candidate, as the alliance with the Soviet Union was drawing to a close, by the anticommunist Harry Truman. Kissinger was an astute GGII handmaiden. The eclipse of Kissinger and his *realpolitik*, and the arrival of upstart Reagan marked the end of an era, the transition from GGII to GGIII.

Control of world resources

The international institutions set up by the US after WWII secured the US dollar as world reserve currency, even without gold backing. This period marks the high point of the US both in terms of prestige and wealth, with rising incomes among all classes, unfettered access to the non-communist world's resources, and control of the world political agenda, focused on preventing further victories of the communists. Successful manipulation of oil prices and financial moves by Nixon ensured that surplus—both raw materials and in monetary form—continued to flow from periphery to center.

Apart from the threat of communism to the imperial project in GGII, the most notable threat from the point of view of the economic hegemons, Big Oil and the big banks, were two developments in the 1960s which they identified and were able to manipulate to secure their agenda of an oil-based future: nuclear power and the ecological movement with its demands for renewable energy.

Their logic was to discourage widespread use of nuclear power to replace high cost oil energy. Nuclear power (at the time, at least) had a strong ecological argument in its favor as compared to hydrocarbon-based electrical production and transport fuel, so it was necessary to forestall any movement to replace oil with nuclear energy, which would not be in their control, requiring by definition major government involvement and regulation of the industry. Its widespread use would leave Big Oil with falling profits, and would mean the end of Big Oil's economic hegemony.

From the start, the US goal for control of nuclear technology (the Baruch Plan, 1946) has been and remains to keep monopoly control through a neocolonial-type institution, the International Atomic Energy Agency (IAEA, 1957), where the US maintains effective control. But the concern for Big Oil, rather than to simply prevent countries from building bombs—the intent of the Nuclear Non-Proliferation Treaty (1970)—is to limit the use of nuclear power in general.

Thus, the manipulation of the growing ecological movement by oil-funded foundations made sure that an anti-nuclear energy focus was at the top of ecological activists' agenda. This is confirmed by analysis of the green movement from the 1960s on. Leading green or ecology organizations such as Greenpeace, Nature Conservancy, Sierra Club and others have all received backing from the oil industry, notably BP (formerly the Anglo-Iranian Oil Company, now employing greenwash by marketing itself as "Beyond Petroleum").[71]

Big Oil had a firm stranglehold on US government, despite the possibility of the US nuclear industry expanding sales around the world. The post-oil embargo period was particularly crucial, as many countries decided to opt for nuclear energy given the high cost of oil. But in the US no new nuclear reactors were ordered and scores of half-built or planned nuclear projects were cancelled after 1979.[72] Plans by oil-poor Brazil (prior to Petrobras) and Germany to undertake nuclear programs in the 1970s were cancelled. Pakistani Prime Minister Zulfikar Ali Bhutto was planning a major nuclear power program but was overthrown in a US-approved coup in 1977 as too close to the Soviet Union, and his successor, General Zia, cancelled Bhutto's plans. Iran started a nuclear power program in the mid-1970s in conjunction with France and Germany; however, the nuclear energy program was shelved after Ayatollah Khomeini's return from France.

As for the growing chorus for renewable energy technologies, which do not have the long term storage dangers of nuclear power, oil companies (especially BP and Shell) depict themselves as being on the forefront of research and buy up patents as they are developed, which will allow a controlled transition to non-oil energy—if necessary—but still in their hands.

Big Oil, the dollar and Israel—these were not issues for political debate in GGII. Intentions by President John F. Kennedy to rein in Israel, break the stranglehold of the Federal Reserve on money creation, and end the Cold War were undermined. Carter's efforts at weaning the US from oil, promoting peace with the Soviet Union, China and in the Middle East were subverted by his military advisers and the CIA with their "two-track policy" of funding jihadists in Afghanistan.

Endgame 1979–91

1979 changed everything in the Middle East, Central Asia and in US-Soviet relations. In the first place, having been dragged to the negotiating table by Carter, Israel finally made peace with its main protagonist—Egypt—and could explore new ways to achieve Greater Israel and regional hegemony. Israel had won *its own* GGII, so to speak, early, by neutralizng its most important enemy Egypt, and could now move ahead unimpeded to consolidate its 1967 gains, keeping the US onside by helping it defeat *their common* GGII enemy—the Soviet Union. This battle was very much in Israel's interests too, a win-win, as it would free Soviet Jews to emigrate to Israel and eliminate the Arabs' main support.

But 1979 was even more fateful as a result of developments in Central Asia, where the reluctant Soviet occupation of Afghanistan created a new situation, at one and the same time the endgame of GGII and the beginning of a new game on a new playing field. The jittery Soviets, worried about a renewed arms race in Europe and a newly militant Islamic state next door in Iran had taken the Brzezinski/ Gates bait, and occupied Afghanistan to shore up a failing pro-Soviet regime. Though India for one recognized the Afghan government, seeing no GGI geopolitical *redux* in Russia's move, it was used by the US as proof of Soviet plans to take over the world, justifying all possible reactions to resist it. Thus the US misguided notion that it could use Islamic fundamentalists as proxies in Afghanistan and simply discard them later, as if they had no agenda of their own. Instead, having driven out one empire, the Afghan mujahideen were to turn on the other.

The other earth-shattering event of that fateful year was the Islamic revolution in Iran, which like the Egypt-Israeli peace accord and the war in Afghanistan would impact the global political climate throughout the end of the twentieth century and on into the twenty-first.

The promotion of Islamists was not new as a strategy, as during GGI, the British had promoted conservative Islamists. It would be a misunderstanding, however, to regard the Muslim Brotherhood as having been co-opted by British imperialism. In its profile of the Muslim Brotherhood, the BBC notes: "The movement initially aimed simply to spread Islamic morals and good works, but soon became involved in politics, particularly the fight to rid Egypt of British colonial control and cleanse it of all Western influence."[73]

The US, taking its lead from Saudi Arabia, also tried supporting the new Muslim Brotherhood, which opposed Arab nationalists and socialists and had no pretensions to political power. In 1953, Eisenhower met Said Ramadan, who until his death in 1995, would be the Brotherhood's chief international organizer, and was considered an asset by US intelligence. (But then, the CIA had considered the Taliban an asset too.) Hamas grew out of Ramadan's organization set up in Jerusalem in 1945. He worked with other Arab fundamentalists to create Hizb ut-Tahrir (Party of Liberation) in 1953, which called for re-establishing the Muslim Caliphate, and would become a popular 'terrorist' group among Muslims in Europe and, after the collapse of the Soviet Union, in Central Asia.

This superficial, pragmatic US approval of conservative Islam meant that by the 1950s, the whole political establishment in the US had became captive to an erroneous understanding of Islam, seeing in the Wahhabis and the Muslim Brotherhood a harmless, even passive, reactionary ideology, a bulwark against the atheistic communists, that could be manipulated and would never be a real danger to Israel or the pro-US regimes in the Middle East. In 1947 Princeton University set up the first Near East Center in the US. Partly sponsored by the government, centers for Middle Eastern affairs sprang up around the country. Hollywood created a romanticized fantasy of Arab life, at the same time disdaining their primitive and exotic ways. Orientalism, really a British project, entailed serious academic study of languages, anthropology, etc., albeit again at the service of empire; in America it was different, less academic, and metamorphosed into Islamophobia in GGIII.[74] It never dawned on Americans interested in the Middle East that the Islamists were qualitatively different from the comprador Christian clerical establishment they were used to in the West.

For those who knew little about the religion and culture of Islam, in search of strategic allies who would not interfere with the US agenda, fundamentalist Islam seemed the best bet to undermine communism. Arab nationalists and socialists posed a threat to US-Israeli hegemony in the region at the time, and thus to growing US energy needs. Egypt's Nasser took over in 1952 when the entire Arab world was in disarray and symbolized Arab revolution, independence, and self-determination. In quick succession, Lebanon, Iraq, and Jordan were rocked by rebellions and Syria even joined Egypt in the United Arab Republic (1958–61). In 1969 Libya's king was overthrown and Sudan's rightwing regime swept away by pro-Nasser officers. From Guatemala to Indonesia, the CIA was busy trying to overthrow such leaders not because they were communist, but because they tried to be independent. Nasser inspired Arabs in Saudi Arabia with republican ideals, threatening the oil/petrodollar needs of a US tied to the Arabs' implacable foe Israel. Between 1954 and 1970, Nasser's secular, modernizing vision competed with the tribal/feudal monarchies subservient to the US everywhere in the Middle East.

CIA covert operations specialist Robert Baer states, "The White House looked on the Brothers as a silent ally ... the Dulles brothers approved Saudi funding of Egypt's Brothers against Nasser."[75] Bernard Lewis explained how "Naqshbandi Sufis living in the Caucasus region might be used as a fifth column inside the Soviet empire."[76] Islamic fundamentalism, even in the 1950s, was pushed onto the international stage thanks to US anticommunist policies. Mark Curtis documents how the Brotherhood was used by Britain and France from 1953 on to try to undermine Nasser in *Secret Affairs: Britain's Collusion with Radical Islam*.

Saudi Arabia's system of higher education began with the creation of the Islamic University of Madina in 1961 (Maulana Maududi was a trustee) and King Abdul Aziz University in 1967. Pakistani fundamentalist Abu Alaa Maududi, the Brotherhood and Wahhabis . convinced the king that Al-Azhar in Cairo was too close to Nasser, so the Islamic University was lavishly funded in competition to promote Wahhabi-style apolitical Islam. Eighty-five per cent of students were foreign, expanding from 3,265 students in 1965 to more than 113,000 in 1986, so the Wahhabis could spread their quietist ideology everywhere, now with the assistance of the CIA. The anticommunist Muslim World League was founded in 1962 with 22 members. Charles Freeman, a veteran US foreign service officer and ambassador to Saudi Arabia, stated, "[Saudi King] Faisal made a deliberate decision that Islam was the antidote to Nasser."

The Arab defeat in 1967 led to a worldwide surge of fundamentalism among Muslims, though between 1967–71 Syria, Libya, Iraq and Sudan nonetheless established left-leaning regimes, and the Palestinians came close to toppling the king in Jordan (stymied by Israel and the Brotherhood). From 1976 until its suppression by Syrian president Hafez al-Assad in 1982, the Brotherhood in Syria led an armed insurgency against the secular Baath socialist regime, with Israel funneling support through proxies in Lebanon.[77] Their defeat was the end of the Brotherhood in Syria, but overall, the struggle of Muslim peoples to live under an Islamic system—Islamism, as the West termed it—prevailed. CIA analyst Martha Kessler regarded the 1973 war as a turning point: "The war was fought under the banner of Islam. The period marks the disillusionment of the Arab world with European ideas. It marks the rise of political Islam."[78]

Many of the radicals were followers of Sayyid Qutb, who was executed by Nasser in 1966. Egyptian President Anwar Sadat, close to the Brotherhood up until the end of WWII, made an alliance with Saudi Arabia following the 1973 war, brought the Brotherhood triumphantly back to Cairo, and realigned Egypt with the US. In 1974, the Brotherhood issued a formal declaration to support Sadat's pro-IMF policies. Islamists, throughout their history have been pro-capitalist[79] and have opposed class struggle. In Egypt they engaged in strike- and union-breaking as Sadat's *infitah* (opening) undermined Nasser's welfare state. Sadat was able to consolidate his weak hold on power and consolidate his new pro-US regime by using the Islamic anticommunists and generous funding by Saudi Arabia.

The Islamic movement became increasingly radicalized, while the secular nationalist left was gutted, especially after Sadat visited Jerusalem in 1977. Meanwhile, the Saudis were afloat on a sea of petrodollars, and the increasing prominence of Islamic banks after the 1973 oil embargo (especially BCCI) was enthusiastically welcomed by US banks, which handled their vast fund of petrodollars. The economic preferences of the Saudi elite were all-American— in favor of capitalism, with no room (or need) for social welfare, land reform, state ownership—given their fantastic dollar wealth. Saudi Prince Mohammad al-Faisal brought all the banks together in a multi-billion dollar network, organized and controlled by Brotherhood activists. Practicing its own parapolitics, Saudi Arabia offered aid to poor Muslim countries in exchange for a political shift to the right. Egypt became a part of the US alliance of Saudi Arabia, Iran, Turkey and Israel.

The center of this new parapolitics was the Safari Club, a secret network of western intelligence agencies set up in 1976—more than three years before the Soviet intervention in Afghanistan—with Saudi, Pakistani, Iranian and Egyptian intelligence agencies, as part of the war against communism. Then-CIA director George H.W. Bush, a close friend of the Saudi royals, intended the Club to "allow for a more covert and discreet network of intelligence operations, with no oversight"[80] in the post-Watergate period when Congress was trying to rein in covert operations. BCCI became its conduit for funds.

The Islamic revolution in Iran in 1979 should have awakened the US and Israel to the change in the Islamic fundamentalists from grudging but passive supporters of rightwing regimes against socialism and secularism to anti-Israeli/western militants ready to act on their beliefs. It never entered CIA strategists' minds that for these strict Muslims, the US is just as much the Great Satan as the Soviet Union and Israel. The Iranian revolution catalyzed a fundamental change in the Islamic right. Just as western intelligence services overestimated the strength of the Soviet Union at the time, they failed to see the potency of Islam as a truly worldwide movement linked by fraternal bonds, radicalized by Israel's continued expansion and oppression of the Palestinians. Brzezinski and then-CIA director William Casey continued to regard political Islam as just another pawn on the former's "grand chessboard".

Islam in Afghanistan too was becoming politicized and militantly anticommunist due to communism's atheism, under the influence of the Brotherhood and Pakistan's Jamaat e-Islami (Party of Islam). Among the leaders in the 1960s were Burhanuddin Rabbani and Gulbuddin Hikmatyar. After King Zahir Shah's cousin Daoud, with the help of communists, toppled the king and established a republic in 1973, the CIA stepped up its subversion working together with Pakistan, first under Zulfikar Bhutto, later under General Zia, and with the Shah of Iran to try to control the new Afghan government. According to Soviet archives, "Beginning in 1974, the Shah of Iran launched a determined effort to draw Kabul into the security sphere embracing India, Pakistan and Persian Gulf states" actively encouraged by the US. "SAVAK and the CIA worked hand in hand with Afghan fundamentalists, who were linked with the Brothers and the Muslim World League, while Pakistan's Inter-Services Intelligence (ISI) helped coordinate raids on Afghanistan."[81]

Now Afghanistan's president, Daoud, under pressure from the US, Iran and Pakistan began to tilt to the right, met the Shah and Bhutto, and started installing rightwing officers in key posts. His power base was reduced to a small ultraconservative clique, the real power behind the scene wielded by SAVAK, the Brotherhood, and the World Muslim League. The situation became critical, and as Daoud moved closer to the US, in April 1978, Noor Mohammad Taraki staged a leftwing coup and appealed to the Soviet Union for support.

Events moved rapidly, as the Islamists, supported by the ISI and the US, launched an all-out campaign of terror, assassinating hundreds of teachers and civil servants. Brzezinski told *La Nouvel Observateur* in 1998 that US arms began flowing to the Islamists by 3 July 1979. But the Islamists were supported by Pakistan's ISI, the Shah and the CIA through the Safari Club much earlier, US geopolitical strategists seeing a window of opportunity where the Afghan government led by Daoud was weak and not widely supported.

This new strategy followed the GGI&II policy of cultivating Islamists against communism, but was qualitatively different and can be called a third queen promotion, as important in the game being played as the earlier ascendancy of the US dollar as reserve currency and the creation of Israel, changing both the players and playing field. Despite the fact that the superpowers were engaging in a policy of détente and that it was in the rational interests of both sides to keep Afghanistan on a secular road of development as opposed to a militant Islamic one, the US was locked in its zero-sum game strategy against communism.

Thus began an unprecedented campaign to recruit, train, transport and pay tens of thousands of Islamic fighters—terrorists by any definition—to fight what were, from the Muslims' perspective, the occupying Soviets in Afghanistan, eventually bringing together communist China, Islamic Iran, Iranophobes Saudi Arabia and Egypt, and many more incongruous 'allies'. This policy went into high gear after 1979—in secret and illegally, coordinated through the Safari Club.

By 1979, Egypt was a close ally of the US, Sadat having turned on his long-time Soviet allies and concluded a peace treaty with Israel, brokered solely with the US. On US urging, Sadat too sponsored local Islamic fundamentalists al-Tabligh Islami (Spreading Islam) and al-Nahda (Renaissance),[82] allowing a base in Upper Egypt for training and an airport for transporting them to Afghanistan. At the same time, he was persecuting moderate Brotherhood members who wished to work within the system and participate in elections, and who were not interested in working for the US and the Egyptian government in their jihad in Afghanistan.

Fundamentalists were recruited from Tunisia, Algeria, Morocco, Lebanon, Syria, Jordan and of course Saudi Arabia. Charismatic 22-year-old Osama bin Laden joined what he may at least initially have been unaware was a US-sponsored jihad, following his own agenda to liberate Muslim lands from foreign occupation, personally recruiting "4,000 volunteers from his own country and developing close relations with the most radical mujahideen leaders". The US was careful not to be directly involved in the project, channeling all funds and arms through Pakistan's ISI despite Reagan's loud support and famous meeting in the White House in 1983. The CIA insists "they had no direct link to bin Laden."[83] The number of CIA-Saudi sponsored religious schools (madrassahs) increased from 2,500 in 1980 to over 39,000.

Relations between the CIA and the ISI had grown increasingly warm following Zia's ouster of Bhutto and the advent of the military regime ... During most of the Afghan war, Pakistan was more aggressively anti-Soviet than even the United States. Soon after the Soviet military invaded Afghanistan in 1980, Zia sent his ISI chief to destabilize the Soviet Central Asian states. The CIA only agreed to this plan in October 1984.[85]

Figure 2.2 Reagan meets mujahideen in White House 1983[84]

Funds were raised through front organizations (charities and foundations), drug smuggling and other illegal activities, with active support of the Saudis, who guaranteed to match the US dollar-for-dollar (in fact the Saudis provided most of the funding). It was coordinated by Saudi intelligence, headed by Prince Turki al-Faisal, in close liaison with the CIA. Drug smuggling was a major source of funding as documented by Cockburn, McCoy[86] and Scott. "By 1982, [governor of the North West Frontier Province Lieutenant General Fazle] Haq is listed with Interpol as an international drug trafficker. But Haq also becomes known as a CIA asset."[87]

Once the operation got going, Pakistan became the conduit for virtually all the money, arms and fighters. Pakistani President General Zia, eager to be in control of a future Islamist government in Afghanistan, was delighted to have the millions of dollars and advanced arms, a chance to upstage India. In December 1984, *sharia* law was established in Pakistan and a few months later, in March 1985, Reagan issued the secret National Security Decision Directive (NSDD) 166, which authorized "stepped-up covert military aid to the Mujahideen" as well as support for religious indoctrination in cooperation with the ISI operations. The supply of arms increased from 10,000 tons in 1983 to 65,000 tons annually by 1987. As director of the CIA (1981-87) William Casey was responsible for delivering over $1 billion worth of arms to Afghanistan. NSDD 166 was the largest covert operation in US history:

> The most important contribution of the US was to ... bring in men and material from around the Arab world and beyond. The most hardened and ideologically dedicated men were sought on the logic that they would be the best fighters. Advertisements, paid for from CIA funds, were placed in newspapers and newsletters around the world offering inducements and motivations to join the Jihad.[89]

Figure 2.3 ISI, CIA, mujahideen 1987 (Front row, from left: Major Gen. Hamid Gul, director general of Pakistan's ISI, CIA director Willian Webster; deputy director for operations Clair George; an ISI colonel; and senior CIA official Milt Bearden at a mujahideen training camp in North-West Frontier Province of Pakistan in 1987.)[88]

The US plan for jihad was a Saudi dream-come-true. The Saudis were eager to see a Saudi-groomed Sunni Islamic state beside Pakistan as a counterweight to Shia Iran. The US showed no concern for the long term implications of destroying the fragile Afghan state, satisfied with creating a Vietnam-like quagmire for the Soviet Union in order to destroy it.

Islamic Iran was mobilized by the "Great Satan", having its own agenda of arming the Afghan Shia. But the finishing touch was the new US ally China, as of 1 January 1979, recognized by the US and also eager to undermine the Soviet Union. It became a vital member of the coalition supplying arms and training jihadis, despite the obvious danger from its own restive Muslims in east Turkestan (Xinjiang).

All scruples were tossed aside by the US, as it forged truly bizarre alliances with its real enemies against a Soviet Union eager for détente, funding atrocities by Islamists (this is not to say there were no Soviet atrocities), abetting China, Iran and Pakistan in their separate agendas—all of which conflicted with long run US geopolitical interests. Gulbuddin Hekmatyar, founder of Hezb e-Islami (Party of Islam), was particularly notorious for his cruelty and murders, yet Charles Wilson, a Texas Republican who was the leading congressional advocate for the Afghan jihad, approvingly noted that Zia was "totally committed to Hekmatyar, because Zia saw the world as a conflict between Muslims and Hindus, and he thought he could count on Hekmatyar to work for a pan-Islamic entity that could stand up to India."[90]

As the horrors inflicted by both sides mounted, the Soviets retreated and the Soviet Union imploded. The jihadis returned to their homelands to foment terror and revolution there. Thus the GGII denouement—'victory' for the US. On the surface, the result was the collapse of the core opponent, the Soviet Union and the co-opting of Chinese communism, with China now a sort-of ally moving rapidly (perhaps too rapidly) towards capitalism. As GGIII began, strategists in Washington were preparing for a game where the US superpower now controlled the entire world.

But the GGII endgame had also empowered political Islam and created a battle-hardened cadre of skilled guerilla fighters. The US-led campaign to use them strengthened the international bonds between Islamists all over the world, laying the foundation for al-Qaeda, energizing what had till the 1980s been a pipedream of restoring Islamic rule in the territories populated by Muslims. Even before GGII was over, GGIII had begun, unleashing the anti-imperialist struggles of Islamists on the world stage.

ENDNOTES

1   Cited in Roger Cohen, "As US Mumbles, Britain Speaks Out", *New York Times*, 22 November 2010.

2   Quoted in Miles Copeland, *The Game of Nations*, New York: Simon and Schuster, 1970, 216.

3   John Perkins, conversation with Amy Goodman, "Confessions of an Economic Hit Man", *www.informationclearinghouse.info*, 2010.

4   Halford Mackinder, "The Round World and the Winning of the Peace", *Foreign Affairs*, Washington: CFR, Volume 21, Number 4, July 1943.

5   The 1922 Soviet-German treaty of cooperation under which each renounced all territorial and financial claims against the other angered Britain and France, anxious to keep both Germany and Russia weak and isolated.

6   US provoking of intra-European dissent today and hostility to Russia demonstrates how this policy continues today.

7   In the case of Cuba, the State Department understood that Castro "rejects the concept that hemisphere defense under US leadership is necessary". The State Department argued, "The simple fact is that Castro represents a successful defiance of the US, a negation of our whole hemispheric policy of almost a century and a half", that is, the Monroe Doctrine. Bolender documents the US obsession with Cuba, that the CIA convinced the White House that overthrow of the Castro regime "was the key to all of Latin America; if Cuba succeeds, we can expect most of Latin America to fall." in Chomsky, Introduction to *Voices from the other side: An oral history of Terrorism against Cuba*, London: Pluto Press, 2010.

8   Henry Kissinger, in support of Reagan's policy of supporting Central American death squads. Ibid.

9   William Engdahl, *A Century of War: Anglo-American Oil Politics and the New World Order*, revised ed., London: Pluto, [1992] 2004, 105.

10   This put paid to the debate between Kautsky and Lenin about whether the imperial order would easily be united or would consist of competing rivals and lead to war. Kautsky posited a kind of truce among empires, allowing them to exploit their colonies without going to war. Lenin dismissed this, as the empires were at different stages of development, some older and others more aggressive, which would inevitably lead to war between them. Lenin was correct: In GGI the British, German and US empires competed and went to war twice, exhausting the former two, resulting in the triumph of Kautsky's "ultra imperialism" but as a result of one empire setting itself above the others rather than a truce among empires. This is the US-dominated 'peaceful' world order of so-called postmodern states united around the US dollar which began to take shape during GGII and came to fruition in GGIII. Michael Hudson calls this new super-imperialist order "as revolutionary as the Bolshevik revolution itself". Michael Hudson *Super Imperialism: Economic Strategy of the American Empire*, London: Pluto Press, [1972] 2003, 7.

11   Hudson, *Superimperialism*, xi.

12   OPEC founders were Saudi Arabia, Iran, Venezuela, Iraq, Kuwait, with Qatar, Libya and Algeria joining later.

13   Here was an attempt at an oil embargo of countries supporting Israel following the 1967 war but it was a failure and effectively ended 1 September 1967 with

the Khartoum Resolution.

14   Immanuel Wallerstein interviewed by Jae-Jung Suh, "Capitalism's Demise?" *hnn.us*, 12 January 2009.

15   Matti Golan, *Secret Conversations of Henry Kissinger,* New York: Quadrangle, 1976, quoted in Engdahl, *A Century of War,* 136. Engdahl provides the minutes of the Bilderberg meeting just prior to the embargo in May 1973 (attended by Kissinger) showing this was in fact Bilderberg policy, that the whole point was to use the embargo to force a dramatic increase in world oil prices. American participant Walter Levy predicted the imminent rise of the price of oil, suggesting that the possible "unprecedented foreign exchange accumulations of countries such as Saudi Arabia and Abu Dhabi" would require creative accounting. He referred to the change "underway in the political, strategic and power relationships between the oil producing, importing and home countries of international oil companies and national oil companies of producing and importing countries." Quoted in William Engdahl, *A Century of War,* 131. The 1973 Bilderberg guest list included BP and other oil corporations. As a result of the embargo, Exxon surpassed GM as the largest US corporation in gross revenues in 1974.

16   The oil embargo and the inability to defeat the Egyptians in their war to liberate Sinai in 1973 forced Israel to undertake its only serious negotiations with the Arabs, resulting in the 1979 Israel-Egypt Peace Treaty, whereby Israel returned Sinai to Egypt in 1982, evacuating the 4,500 civilian Israelis already living there, in exchange for recognition, peace and a guaranteed $3 billion a year from the US.

17   Miles Ignotus, "Seizing Arab oil", *Harper's,* March 1975, quoted in Paul Atwood, *War and Empire: The American Way of Life,* London: Pluto Press, 2010, 215. Whether or not the embargo was implicitly supported by Kissinger in the interests of Big Oil, Saudi King Faisal was assassinated in 1975 by his half-brother's son, Faisal bin Musaid, who interestingly had just come back from studies in the US, and replaced by the more compliant King Fahd, who went as far as accepting a permanent US military presence on Saudi territory.

18   Engdahl, *A Century of War,* 137.

19   See endnote 1.

20   Engdahl, *A Century of War,* 154. Though the original Seven Sisters remain powerful in terms of the empire's financial, economic and political policies, the world's seven largest oil firms today are: "Saudi Aramco, Russia's Gazprom, CNPC of China, NIOC of Iran, Venezuela's PDVSA, Brazil's Petrobras and Petronas of Malaysia". From Carola Hoyos "The new Seven Sisters: oil and gas giants dwarf western rivals", *Financial Times,* 11 March 2007.

21   According to Morgan Guaranty Trust eurodollar offshore markets accounted for 57 per cent of the entire domestic US money supply by 1979. Quoted in Engdahl, *A Century of War,* 175.

22   John Perkins, *Confessions of an Economic Hit Man,* San Francisco: Berret-Koehler, 2004, 15.

23   Ibid., 84.

24   According to former Peruvian oil minister Pedro Kuczinski only 8.4 per cent of loans cashed by Latin American countries left New York. Cited in Engdahl, *A Century of War,* 196.

25   William Engdahl, *A Century of War,* 106, 169–70.

26   Joseph Trento, *Prelude to Terror: Edwin P Wilson and the Legacy of America's*

Private Intelligence Network, New York: Carroll and Graf, 2005, 104.

27   Michel Chossudovsky, "The Spoils of War: Afghanistan's Multibillion Dollar Heroin Trade", *www.globalresearch.ca*, 5 April 2004.

28   "BCCI: The Dirtiest Bank of All", *Time*, 29 July 1991. The legendary Abu Nidal link man for the BCCI accounts was Samir Najmeddin based in Iraq. Throughout the 1980s, BCCI had set up millions of dollars worth of letters of credit for Najmeddin, largely for arms deals with Iraq. BCCI employee Ghassan Qassem testified that Najmeddin was often accompanied by an American, whom Qassem subsequently identified as the financier Marc Rich. Rich was indicted in the US for tax evasion and racketeering in an unrelated case and fled the country but was later pardoned by Bill Clinton.

29   In a speech to the British House of Commons on 8 June 1982, Reagan used the term, coined by Leon Trotsky according to Harrison Salisbury, letter to *The New York Times* 13 February 2007.

30   "Operation Unthinkable (Churchill's Plan for War with the Soviet Union)", *www.freerepublic.com*, 16 November 2001.

31   Noam Chomsky, *Hegemony or Survival*, New York: Holt, 2003, 70–1.

32   Proof of this is found in the so-called Mitrokhin Archives. KGB Major Vasili Mitrokhin was for 30 years KGB archivist in foreign intelligence, and brought every conceivable secret when he defected to Britain in 1992. Christopher Andrew's *Sword and the Shield* (1992) and *The KGB and the Battle for the Third World* (2005), based on the archives show pathetically little in terms of subversion and no overarching plan to invade anywhere. Despite his anticommunist bias, Andrew shows that the KGB did little with the information it collected, which mostly involved technology acquisition, and which shows the reactive nature of Soviet undercover work—attempts to uncover sabotage by the West, use of blackmail to protect Soviet sources.

33   Quoted in Jonathan Cook, *Israel and the Clash of Civilisations: Iraq, Iran and the Plan to Remake the Middle East*, London: Pluto, 2010, 10.

34   Third world leaders were too savvy to believe this western propaganda. It is still conventional wisdom in the post-Soviet period to refer to the Soviet empire, but in fact the Soviet Union was tied to the West in a quasi-periphery role as exporter of raw materials, and its relations with the non-Russian constituent republics and eastern Europe were the reverse of the economic imperial logic of surplus extracted in the periphery and sent to or used by the center. The Soviet Union's so-called empire was in fact a drain on it. The standard of living was virtually the same throughout the Soviet Union and much higher in eastern Europe. After the 1973 oil embargo, when international oil prices quadrupled, they remain unchanged for Soviet allies.

35   Quoted in Cook, *Israel and the Clash of Civilisations*, 10.

36   Noam Chomsky, *Failed States: The Abuse of Power and the Assault on Democracy*, New York: Metropolitan Books, *2006*, 120.

37   General Agreement on Tariffs and Trade

38   The first queen being the crowning of the US dollar as world reserve currency

39   William Roger Louis, *The British Empire in the Middle East*, Oxford: Oxford University Press, 1984, 673.

40   Evelyn Shuckburgh, *Descent to Suez: Diaries 1951–1956*, London: Weidefeld and Nicolson, 1986, 167.

41   It was bad timing, as oil had been discovered in the mid-1980s and it could have become a socialist success story similar to Venezuela.

42   The British prepared to overthrow al-Gaddafi and restore the monarchy but the US felt that Gaddafi was sufficiently anti-Marxist and nixed the operation. Tony Geraghty, *Who Dares Wins, The Story of the SAS 1950–1982*, London: Fontana Books, 2002, 1–7.

43   Mark Tessler, *A History of the Israeli-Palestinian Conflict*, Bloomington IN: Indiana University Press, 1994, 374.

44   In 1948, communism had no following among the Arab masses, while the creation of a Jewish state was a leftwing and liberal *cause célébre* in the West. *The New York Times* reported in 1948 a 10,000 strong demonstration in support of Progressive Party presidential candidate Henry Wallace composed of communists and Leftist labor leaders that marched under the banner of the United Committee to Save the Jewish State and the United Nations. The combination of new Israeli communists, Arab conservatism, and the rising Cold War prompted Stalin to recognize Israel as a means of ensuring imperial instability in the Middle East with his own strategic ally there. The failure of this strategy led to a reversion to Soviet anticolonial policy and support for the Palestinians and Israel's other neighbors. The Soviet Union continued to support the Arab states, even when it got little in return. It was the first country to recognize Saudi Arabia in 1932 but the Saudis broke relations in 1938. Its influence was never strong and by 1972, not only were the Soviets unceremoniously expelled from Egypt, but soon all the Arab countries would be at least implicitly backing the mujahideen to wage war on the Soviet Union, financed by the US and egged on by Israel.

45   Seumas Milne, "Ignoring its imperial history licences the west to repeat it", *Guardian*, 6 April 2011. <http://www.guardian.co.uk/commentisfree/2011/apr/06/ignoring-imperial-history-licence-west>.

46   The US was able to get UN backing for the Korean war only because the Soviet Union was boycotting the UN over China's lack of representation in the UN. The Soviet Union came to its senses and the Russian veto subsequently became a powerful tool to defy US imperialism in GGII.

47   Courtesy of *Stratfor* <http://web.stratfor.com/images/europe/map/NATO_v2_800.jpg?fn=9117341898>.

48   Tariq Ali, *The Clash of Fundamentalisms: Crusades, Jihads and Modernity*, New York: Verso, 2002, 276.

49   Novelist Hugh Thomas imagines the horror experienced by American and British negotiators when a Soviet delegation accepts their proposal for a settlement in Europe in *The World's Game,* London: Eyre & Spottiswoode, 1957.

50   The Soviet Union, Hungary, Czechoslovakia, Poland, Bulgaria, Romania, Albania, and East Germany

51   Then-CIA director Robert Gates (later defense secretary under both George W. Bush and Barack Obama) in his memoir *From the Shadows: The Ultimate Insider's Story of Five Presidents and How They Won the Cold War,* New York: Simon & Schuster, 1997, revealed that Carter himself approved a secret $500 million aid program designed to counter the Soviet support to the socialist regime that had overthrown the dictator Mohamed Dawoud Khan (who had just overthrown his cousin, King Mohamed Nadir Shah). According to Gates, at a meeting on 30 March 1979, Under-Secretary of Defense Walter Slocombe suggested "there was value in keeping the Afghan insurgency going, 'sucking the Soviets into a Vietnamese quagmire'." Carter, who authorized the covert

program on 3 July 1979, today explains that it was definitely "not my intention" to inspire a Soviet invasion.

52   Pierre Beaudry, *The Mennevee Documents on the Synarchy,* Book 4, chapter 3, Leesburg VA: ICLC, 2005, 97. <http://www.tuks.nl/docs/SYNARCHY_ MOVEMENT_ OF_EMPIRE_BOOK_04.PDF>.

53   Daniel Estulin, *The True Story of the Bilderberg Group,* Oregon: TrineDay LLC, 2007, 22.

54   See endnote 15.

55   The US government protected and employed many Nazi war criminals to use in its GGII subversion of the Soviet Union. For example, the CIA funded Ukrainian fascist leader Mykola Lebed, who collaborated with the Nazis in the murder of the Jews of the western Ukraine and killed thousands of Poles, from 1949–91 to carry out black ops against the Soviet Union from his front organization Prolog in New York. According to CIA director Allen Dulles, he was "of inestimable value to this Agency and its operations." Prolog published journals, newspapers, beamed radio programs into Soviet Ukraine, as the sole "vehicle for CIA's operations directed at the Ukrainian Soviet Socialist Republic and [its] forty million Ukrainian citizens." Richard Breitman and Norman Goda, "Hitler's Shadow: Nazi War Criminals, US Intelligence, and the Cold War", Washington: National Archives, 2010, 87–89. 2010. <http://www.archives. gov/iwg/reports/hitlers-shadow.pdf >.
The most spectacular GGII endgame black-op against the Soviet Union is described in Chapter 3.

56   See William Blum's *Killing Hope: US Military and CIA Interventons Since WWII* and *Rogue State: A Guide to the World's Only Superpower*, New York: Common Courage Press, 2004.

57   Engdahl, *A Century of War,* 171.

58   What is now called the "October Surprise" refers to Carter's attempt to rescue the 52 American hostages in the US embassy in Tehran in October 1980, which would have assured him victory in the November presidential elections. This was prevented by the apparent conspiracy arranged between Iran's Islamist government and the Reagan election team, allowing Reagan to trounce Carter. That it was a conspiracy is confirmed by secret meetings at the time confirmed by key officials, the fact that 20 minutes after Reagan concluded his inaugural address in January 1981 the hostages were released, and the subsequent Iran-Contra affair.

59   James Bamford, *Body of Secrets: Anatomy of the Ultra-Secret National Security Agency from the Cold War Through the Dawn of a New Century*, New York: Doubleday, 2001, 82.

60   Stephen Lendman, "Nato's Secret Armies", *www.rebelnews.org,* 16 September 2010.

61   The Korean war (1950–53) provided the necessary pretext to consolidate the US economy as a "military-industrial complex".

62   Gregory Harms, *Straight Power Concepts in the Middle East*, London: Pluto, 2010, 79.

63   Abraham Rabinovich, *The Yom Kippur War: The Epic Encounter That Transformed the Middle East*, New York: Schocken Books, 2004, 484.

64   According to Bernstein, quoted in Jesse Ventura, *American Conspiracy*, New York: Skyhorse, 2010, 42.

65   The Citizens' Committee to Investigate the FBI broke into the FBI field office in

Media, Pennsylvania and stole incriminating documents which they passed on to the media, which initially refused to publicize the evidence.

66   Rightwing dissent too is increasingly monitored and manipulated, particularly by Zionists, from the 1930s on. See Michael Collins Piper, *Judas Goat,* Washington D.C.: AFP, 2006.

67   James Petras, "The CIA and the Cultural Cold War Revisited", *Monthly Review,* November 1999. Saunders (1999) documents the ways in which the CIA penetrated and influenced cultural organizations through front groups and philanthropic organizations like the Ford and Rockefeller Foundations.

68   Peter Dale Scott, *Drugs, Oil and War: The United States in Afghanistan, Colombia, and Indochina,* New York: Rowman and Littlefield, 2003, 64.

69   Ibid., 29.

70   In his second volume of memoirs in 1982, Kissinger tries to square the circle of this developing rift: "Israel is dependent on the US as no other country is on a friendly power... Israel's obstinacy, maddening as it can be, serves the purposes of both our countries best. A subservient client would soon face an accumulation of ever-growing pressures. It would tempt Israel's neighbors to escalate their demands. It would saddle us with the opprobrium for every deadlock." in Henry Kissinger, *Years of Upheaval,* Boston: Little Brown, 1982, 483–4.

71   For example, Nature Conservancy awarded BP a seat on its International Leadership Council after the oil company gave the organization more than $10 million. Conservation International accepted $2 million in donations from BP and from 2000 to 2006, John Browne, then BP's chief executive, sat on the Conservation International board. The Environmental Defense Fund joined with BP, Shell and other major corporations to form a Partnership for Climate Action, to promote a market-based mechanism to reduce greenhouse gas emissions. Robert Anderson's Atlantic Richfield Oil funneled millions of dollars through their Atlantic Richfield Foundation into organizations targeting nuclear energy, in particular Friends of the Earth, aimed in the first place at the budding German nuclear industry in the 1970s. Anti-nuclear actions at the Brockdorf site in Germany were led by Friends of the Earth head, Hoger Strohm. In Engdahl, *A Century of War,* 143–7. Also see Joe Stephens, "Nature Conservancy faces potential backlash from ties with BP", *Washington Post,* 24 May 2010.

72   The pretext was the Three Mile Island nuclear station, where radioactive gases were emitted following a partial core meltdown, though epidemiological studies in the years since have supported the conclusion that radiation releases from the accident had no perceptible effect on cancer incidence in residents near the plant.

73   "Profile: Egypt's Muslim Brotherhood", BBC News Middle East, February 9, 2011.

74   See Stephen Sheehi, *Islamophobia: The Ideological Campaign Against Muslims,* Atlanta, USA: Clarity Press, 2011.

75   Robert Dreyfuss, *Devil's Game: How the United States Helped Unleash Fundamentalist Islam,* New York: Owl Books, 2006, 102.

76   From NSC Staff papers at the Eisenhower library, in Dreyfuss, *Devil's Game,* 124.

77   Ibid., 201.

78   Ibid., 156.

79   Islam approves of private property, promotes entrepreneurship and calls for fair wages, much as did medieval Christianity. The system of capitalism only came into being in the eighteenth century and is critiqued in Islamic literature as being based on usury and leading to monopoly and extreme exploitation. Socialism is also criticized as unrealistic and, like capitalism, without a spiritual basis. Publicly, Muslim leaders and scholars side with capitalism with the above caveats. See Yousuf Kamal, *The Principles of the Islamic Economic System*, Cairo: Dar Al-Nashr for Universities, 1996, 39–70.

80   Andrew Gavin Marshall, "Wikileaks and the Worldwide Information War Power, Propaganda, and the Global Political Awakening", *www.globalresearch.ca*, 6 December 2010.

81   Diego Cordovez and Selig Harrison, *Out of Afghanistan: The Inside Story of the Soviet Withdrawal*, Oxford: Oxford University Press, 1995, 16, 19, 23.

82   Cook, *Israel and the Clash of Civilisations*, 68.

83   Phil Gasper, "Afghanistan, the CIA, bin Laden, and the Taliban", *International Socialist Review*, November-December 2001.

84   Photo Reagan meets mujahideen in White House 1983 courtesy of <http://www.reagan.utexas.edu/archives/photographs/atwork.html.>

85   Gasper, "Afghanistan, the CIA, bin Laden, and the Taliban".

86   "1982-1989: US Turns Blind Eye to BCCI and Pakistani Government Involvement in Heroin Trade" *www.historycommons*. <http://www.historycommons.org/context.jsp?item=a82blindeyedrugs>. Also Alfred Mccoy, *The Politics of Heroin: CIA Complicity in the Global Drug Trade*, revised ed., Chicago, USA: Lawrence Hill, [1991] 2003, 477–81.

87   Pervez Hoodbhoy, "Afghanistan and the Genesis of the Global Jihad", *Peace Research*, 1 May 2005.

88   Photo source RAWA at Ahmed, Nafeez Mosaddeq, "Our terrorists", *New Internationalist*, 426, 25 October 2010.

89   Hoodbhoy, "Afghanistan and the Genesis of the Global Jihad".

90   Robert Dreyfuss, *Devil's Game,* Chapter 10.

CHAPTER THREE

GGIII:
US-ISRAEL—
POSTMODERN IMPERIALISM

*A degree of 'controlled dis-integration' in the
world economy is a legitimate objective for the 1980s.*
New York CFR director Cyrus Vance
in his policy blueprints for the 1980s (1975)[1]

*We have before us the opportunity to forge for ourselves
and for future generations a new world order—
a world where the rule of law, not the law of the jungle,
governs the conduct of nations.*
US president George H.W. Bush (1991)[2]

The struggle to establish the new GGIII goals

The collapse of the Soviet Union in 1991 had a profound effect on the
world order, inaugurating a completely new game. Bush I,[3] US president
at the time, professed the goal to be "a new world order—a world where
the rule of law, not the law of the jungle, governs the conduct of nations
... an order in which a credible United Nations can use its peacekeeping
role to fulfill the promise and vision of the UN's founders."

The US and European Union would help the ex-socialist bloc,
including the ex-Soviet Union and its energy-rich Central Asian republics,
rebuild their economies and political structures along western capitalist,
democratic lines, fashioning weak, "postmodern states" out of them
and out of the other GGII "modern states" (see below). This process
began in Europe with the creation of the EU after WWII and accelerated
as GGIII got underway in North America with the North American Free
Trade Agreement (NAFTA) in 1994. Such alliances, with NATO under
US guidance, would lay the foundations for a united, peaceful world,

a "postmodern imperialism",[4] devoid of messy competitive wars for colonies, neocolonies or a life-or-death defense of western civilization. In the Middle East, the 1991 invasion of Iraq was a warning to that vital geopolitical region that the US called the shots. It was a stern master and must be heeded—by all. Thus the Iraqi dictator was bloodied but left in place, despite Israeli frustration, as the lessons of GGI&II were clear: overt colonialism is too expensive; a game that relies on neocolonialism, the market, and the magical US dollar is preferable.

There was the sense in these early GGIII days that a benevolent US empire, like the Roman empire, could last forever, or, given the environmental crisis, at least as long as the earth holds out. The socialist alternative was gone, leaving no inspiration for potential rebels in the periphery. They would be kept subservient to the empire using carrots and sticks—soft and hard power. It looked in 1991 like "the end of history" which Francis Fukuyama proclaimed the next year. True, there was the pesky "clash of civilizations" and the simmering problem of "Islamic fundamentalism"[5] with Israel at its heart. The US had won GGII, providing Israel with a gift of 1 million Soviet Jews in 1991, and trounced Israel's major enemy in the Middle East. If these two very expensive gifts had been rewarded by an obedient Israel willing, at long last, to make peace with the Palestinians, the threat from the Arab and Muslim world would abate, ushering in Bush I's neoliberal new world order, a *pax americana,* a postmodern imperial order.

The underlying goal had not changed: to complete Mackinder's plan—a renewed energetic thrust by the US for world economic and political hegemony, now active on the whole Silk Road, from the Balkans to China's frontiers. In its present reincarnation, the Mackinder plan required the securing of oil supplies in both the Middle East and the newly opened Central Asia.

The fly in the ointment was the fundamentally anachronistic nature of Zionist plans. They had not changed either. Israel was still a settler colonial regime in a neocolonial era—a recipe for permanent war. When Bush I tried to end Israel's colonial mentality, force it to stop building new settlements, his new game plan unraveled, and a struggle to define the new GGIII game plan began. Eisenhower had made Israel bend to the US game plan in 1956. Ford/ Kissinger/ Carter had too, though just barely in the 1970s, curbing somewhat Israel's colonial ambitions. Both, ironically, relied on the Soviet threat to the neocolonial order. But 'in victory, defeat'. The Soviet threat was no more, and in the meantime, the Israel lobby in Washington had become too powerful for a president to counter. The Zionists were in no mood to swallow their pride and obey a newly holier-than-thou imperial Washington. Bush found he had no allies for his plan to bring Israel into line and in the face of the now powerful Israel lobby lost his re-election bid.

But it was not only the Zionists who were at fault. The unprincipled endgame played by the US in GGII could hardly evolve into a peaceful postmodern imperial world order. The effort to exploit Islamists was just as fraught with contradictions as Israel's colonial mission, and could not be dismissed and forgotten. Though primarily a US-sponsored effort, Israel had done its bit to encourage Islamists as a counter to the PLO, as part of its plans for Greater Israel and regional hegemony (see Chapter 4), and this joint US-Israeli genie could not be put back into its lamp.

The ideologues in Washington fashioning the new game plan were the neoconservatives, devotees of Israel's game plan. Even as Bush I fought the Israel lobby in the final months of his presidency, his defense secretary Dick Cheney, Lewis Scooter Libby and Paul Wolfowitz, who would become respectively vice president, vice presidential chief of staff and deputy defense secretary under Bush II, wrote a position paper "Defense Strategy for the 1990s" outlining their expansionist post-Soviet US agenda. It was necessary to "extend the zone of peace to include the newly independent nations of eastern Europe and the former Soviet Union ... and work to build an international environment conducive to our values." So far, so good. However, not only "US leadership", but "forces ready to protect our critical interests" are necessary, where "collective efforts" are not enough.[6] Under the neocon game plan, "forces" would include Israeli forces acting on their own, defining "our" critical interests in the Middle East. Within a decade, extending "the zone of peace to include the newly independent nations" would mean expanding NATO. Together, these strategies would mean replacing any shreds of the "rule of law" and reliance on the UN with a US-led world war on terror using NATO, leaving the Middle East to be shaped by the ever evolving plans of the Zionists in Israel.

Bush I's defeat and the advent of Clinton was a watershed in this process. While Bush I had no Jewish cabinet secretaries, Clinton had a record five out of the top seven and appointed two Supreme Court judges, both Jewish. The election to the presidency of Bill Clinton led to what an Israeli journalist described as a "Judaization of the State Department", a situation that has grown more pronounced with each successive administration.[7] This penetration of the American Jewish elite into the highest political offices continued under Bush II with Wolfowitz and Douglas Feith, as under secretary of defense for policy, even setting up an Office of Special Plans[8] headed by Abram Shulsky in the Pentagon, using Israeli officers as consultants, and bypassing established protocol. There are now "structural continuities over time and place: the long-term, large-scale presence of unconditional Israel-firsters across administrations especially over the past two decades."[9]

A corollary to the Cheney thesis was a return to the GGI rule of invasion or open subversion by those "forces ready to protect our critical interests". Cheney's vision inspired the founding of the Project for a New American Century (PNAC) think tank (1997–2006) by veteran neoconservatives William Kristol and Robert Kagan. PNAC's "Rebuilding America's Defenses: Strategy, Forces and Resources for a New Century" in 2000 called for a "new Pearl Harbor" which would justify launching pre-emptive wars against suspect nations. The US "must discourage advanced industrial nations from challenging our leadership, or even aspiring to a larger regional or global role" as "the US is the world's only superpower... America's grand strategy should aim to preserve and extend this advantageous position as far into the future as possible."[10] It also called for renewing Reagan's Star Wars project, now called "missile defense", control of cyberspace, and biological weapons "that can target specific genotypes and may transform biological warfare from the realm of terror to a politically useful tool."[11] It targeted Bush II's future "Axis of Evil"—North Korea, Iran and Iraq, called for the US to "play a more permanent role in Gulf regional security",[12] and would become the blueprint for Bush II's foreign policy. All the instruments of power were refashioned with US world hegemony, "full spectrum dominance",[13] in mind.

9/11 did not change the underlying aim, but merely added a new-old professed goal of winning the "war on terror", a phrase coined by Reagan during the Lebanon war in 1983, and merely dusted off to allow Bush II to pursue his more aggressive imperial agenda. The irony in pursuing this will-o-the-wisp is that "the 'war on terror' can't be won" by definition.[14]

Mackinder's vision of the empire (now the American empire), complete with a Jewish Middle East outpost, didn't target Islam openly, though this is a corollary of his concern to incorporate the Middle East via such an ally. His GGI mentality was colonial (racist): the Arabs were not white and would need supervision. Jewish financiers were at the heart of the British empire, and as the Zionist project was well underway by the early twentieth century, what better colonial masters, able to call on history to justify an imperial citadel, the last colonial brick necessary to complete the empire's edifice?

In GGIII the fundamentally anti-imperial nature of Islam had to be dealt with at last. The British and US had coddled and allied with conservative, nonpolitical Islam in GGI&II to pursue their empires. The Arab nationalists' cause was weakened mortally when their only friend, the Soviet Union, was defeated. It was time to abandon the Islamists and put them in their place now that the Arab Muslims had no ally left, to reform Islam and incorporate it a la Christianity into a secular, democratic order modeled on the West. This neocon goal in GGIII was necessary in the Middle East to pacify Israel's immediate Muslim neighbors. It was also necessary to extend the empire's reach along the Silk Road—the Eurasian region of the Caucasus through to Afghanistan—newly opened for business, and which is dominated by Muslim countries.

But what looked relatively simply in the early 1990s, over the decade became much more difficult. The Islamists had not lost any of their fervor, and were continuing to fight in Afghanistan among themselves. The Islamic Salvation Front, denied the fruits of their electoral victory, took up arms to fight for power in Algeria; a similar refusal of a democratic avenue to power elsewhere was leading Islamists to conduct terrorist operations in various countries, now targeting their former allies, the US and its compliant Middle East regimes. Iran's Islamic regime remained vigorous, the only reliable anti-imperialist power in the region.

Russia, also, was no longer showing the US gratitude for destroying communism. In fact, the transition to the market economy in the former Soviet Union produced a "demographic collapse", a dramatic drop in life expectancy among Russian men to 58 years.[15] The communists narrowly lost a crucial election in 1996 only because of massive US interference. Russian President Boris Yeltsin (1991–99) and his successor Vladimir Putin (2000–08) became increasingly assertive in Russia's "near abroad", especially the Central Asian part of the Silk Road.

Even more daunting has been the rapid rise of China, at the eastern end of the Silk Road and Eurasia, now forecast to overshadow the US as the world's largest economy by 2027 if not sooner. Hobson foresaw China as the ultimate prize for the British empire in the nineteenth century. The century that has elapsed since he wrote transformed China in ways Hobson could not imagine, but his political instincts were right. After the battle with Islam, the battle to cow Russia and China would be the main task of the US in GGIII.

Ideology

To understand the current game, we must look at the major ideological shift that took place in the endgame of GGII. Just as the realpoliticker Kissinger embodies GGII, so the Hollywood icon Ronald Reagan embodies its endgame (1979–91) and can be called the inspiration of GGIII itself. Originally a New Deal Democrat, he drifted to the anticommunist establishment in the late 1930s–40s and became a Republican. His political career thrived and finally brought him the supreme political prize. Kissinger despised him as "shallow"[16] though in many ways Reagan was a worthy successor to the master politician, with his anticommunist obsession, lack of concern for the many victims of his bombings and campaigns of subversion, his concern for Israel, and ability to lie and get away with it.

Until Reagan's presidency (1981–88), the Cold War dynamic was the pursuit of a balance of power for the US in its crusade against communism. All previous presidents, though avowed anticommunists one and all, negotiated treaties, ceasefires, even during WWII allied with the Soviet Union. Reagan refused to accept this paradigm, even contemplating nuclear war, as his threat to consign the Soviet Union to the "ash heap of history" chillingly hints.

With his domestic supply-side economics and rejection of the social role of government, Reagan emulated Prime Minister Margaret Thatcher in Britain (1979–90), who dismantled much of the post-war welfare state. This quasi-socialism was the price the British ruling class had paid for its enforced alliance with communism against Britain's GGI German enemy, and for the need to rebuild its economy after the war, which required a pact between labor and industry mediated by the state. The US had also been forced to make such a pact to beat the GGI foe, but time had passed, communism was the enemy and as its track record was not so impressive anymore, Thatcher and Reagan found it possible to undo the social pact with promises of greater personal wealth and freedom.

Thatcher was following the philosophy of neoliberalism, where in theory the state should be radically reduced in power, allowing the market to regulate all of economic life, transforming society into a market-based collection of individuals (who now include corporations). GGI was based on liberalism, which was concerned with human individuals rather than corporations; GGIII neoliberalism, apart from deviously expanding the definition of individuals, required the state once again enforce compliance with the market, just as it had in the 18th–19th cc, only this time to dismantle social welfare provisions built up during the twentieth century. The pretense is of a return to a previous order when the state was weaker, but the reality is the emergence of a Hobbesian state, as powerful as ever, and using force to maintain order in the absence of the cohesive role of social welfare.[17]

Reagan also embraced neoliberalism—"Government is not the solution to our problem; government is the problem!"[18]—adding an aggressive foreign policy, including a strategy to bankrupt the Soviet Union through an arms race and a rejection of the Kissinger *realpolitik*, which had sought accommodation with the Soviet Union as a legitimate if flawed member of the Westphalian political order of competing nation states. This new combination—market deregulation, jettisoning the welfare state, rejecting *realpolitik* in favour of military intervention, and appealing to religion and nationalism—eventually came to be known as neoconservativism, a movement associated with Irving Kristol (father of William Kristol) and Norman Podhoretz, which gained momentum in the 1960s.

Though associated with the Republicans, the neocons are a bipartisan group, including Dixiecrats, opposed to the openly anti-imperialist Democratic presidential nominee in 1972 George McGovern, who instead supported Nixon. They rallied behind Democratic Senator Henry Jackson, whose protégés include Richard Perle, Paul Wolfowitz, Elliott Abrams and Douglas Feith.

Inspired by Irving Kristol, a former Trotskyist, they all were admirers of Israel's aggressive stance in the Middle East, calling for the US to emulate it in the broader quest for world hegemony, which of course meant emulating Israel's strategy of permanent war (see Chapter 4). With the military-industrial complex in place by the 1960s, and this new ideology, the interests of business, the financial sector, the Pentagon and the White House were more in sync than at any time in American history—and never so tied to the interests of Israel, as exemplified by the many powerful Israeli and Jewish lobbies working together across the US with a clear agenda tying US world hegemony and Israeli Middle East hegemony together. PNAC, founded "to promote American global leadership.. [which] is both good for America and good for the world" and to support "a Reaganite policy of military strength and moral clarity", merely gave voice to this reality. It was the charismatic Reagan that put his own simplistic and importantly—non-Jewish—stamp on the movement.

Their best-known vehicles are rightwing think tanks such as the American Enterprise Institute (AEI), the Jewish Institute for National Security Affairs (JINSA), later PNAC, the Center for Security Policy, and the powerful lobby group American Israel Public Affairs Committee (AIPAC), as well as the Committee on the Present Danger. "The basic and generally agreed plan is unilateral world domination through absolute military superiority ... since the collapse of the Soviet Union in the early 1990s."[19]

The neocon program is merely the American version of the political process in Israel/ Palestine, where the victory in 1967 and peace agreement with Egypt in 1979 did not lead towards a *realpolitik* peace with Israel's neighbors, at a time when Israel was strong and could have dictated favorable terms, but on the contrary, to more Israeli aggression. Neither did US maximalism as practiced from Reagan on lead to a peaceful world. This underlying logic, the logic of Lenin's imperialism, is at the very heart of US and Israeli strategies.

Though not isomorphic, imperialism and Zionism came together with the ascendancy of the neocons in Washington under Bush II. The logical new enemy for both was Islam, the underlying ideology being the "clash of civilizations", refashioning the atavistic anti-Muslim Crusades for the new era, complete with an evangelical religious flavor to pander to the now strong Christian fundamentalists, and an updated version of the legendary Muslim suicide Assassins.[20] The ideological offensive is to try to weaken Islam, using Israel as a Trojan Horse in the Middle East and Iran as the scapegoat, though the elephant in the room is US ally and client Saudi Arabia.

While on the one hand the Saudi government promotes its conservative de-politicized Islam (seeking to co-opt pre-empt political Islam), and at the same time funds (through official and/or private sources) jihadist movements to complement the interests of US empire, on the other hand, it faces privately Saudi-funded anti-government attacks by Sunni Islamists such as Osama bin Laden, critical of its role as a proxy for the US, and seeking to liberate Muslim lands—including Saudi Arabia—from what they view as foreign occupation. In one way or another, Saudi Arabia has remained a focal point in all the struggles, both anti-imperial and anti-communist, throughout all the games, starting with the anti-colonial struggle of the then-militant Muslim Brotherhood in GGI, reaching a peak in the GGII endgame.

The ideological dispute that arose after 9/11 between Fukuyama's "end of history" and Samuel Huntington's "clash of civilizations" is really just a disagreement over sound bytes. The former trumpeted the victory of the West as ushering in a new era based on western market/ political principles, in keeping with the triumphalism of the winners of the Cold War. That no such new era has consolidated itself is supposedly due to unfortunate cultural anachronisms. In a post-geopolitical world, it is "cultural conflict ... with alien civilizations" that leads to "confrontation".[21] This "cultural resistance to capitalism and modernity"[22] divides the world. "Civilizations unite and divide mankind ... blood and belief are what people identify with and what they will fight and die for."[23] Only the West, it is contended, values individualism, liberalism, constitutionalism, human rights, the rule of law, democracy, free markets.

The two most menacing cultural throwbacks are Islam and Confucianism (read: oil and Chinese exports) and if they unite, "they would pose a threat to the existence of the core civilization."[24] Disdain for Islam has been part of the western cultural discourse for over a century now, as Said made clear in *Orientalism* and elsewhere.[25] We can add Confucianism as the other main oriental frame of mind. The end of history thus still involves some residual "confrontation".

Ideological contempt for Islam turned into a reckless use of Islamists throughout all the games, culminating in the GGII endgame. The communist knights and rooks were defeated in the mountains of Afghanistan, the bishops—the communist ideologues—discredited, and the communist pawns in revolt. Finally the king was checkmated, swept from the board, and the team disbanded. The world expected a new era free of the threat of war, a peace dividend that would improve the lot of people everywhere, ensuring that the material imperative behind war was eliminated. But the triumph of empire has never led to an end to empire, and strengthening empire has never led to improving the lot of the periphery. This was clear in both GGI&II, where the periphery was impoverished at the expense of the center.[26] There is no reason to believe GGIII could be any different, even Bush I's postmodern variant, and indeed, the impoverishment of all who are not part of the center/periphery elite has only accelerated.[27]

Meanwhile, the new enemy had been prepared and was loudly decried. Stephen Sheehi documents the "unprecedented mainstreaming of Islamophobia since 9/11"[28] and argues it is an "ideological formation" that runs across the spectrum of political and cultural discourse in the US. The "enemy within" is the essential component of the empire's war to subdue the most resilient force opposing it in GGIII. The clash of civilizations began, though Tariq Ali counters in response to the "civilization-mongers" that there were a range of political possibilities in Muslim countries, that western civilization itself had prevented the exercise of western-style democracy, leading their citizens to find political expression through Islam:

> After WWII, the US backed the most reactionary elements as a bulwark against communism or progressive/ secular nationalism. [In Iran] the secular opposition which first got rid of the shah was outfoxed by British Intelligence and the CIA. The vacuum was later occupied by the clerics who rule the country today. ... The 70-year war between US imperialism and the Soviet Union affected every single 'civilization'.[29]

We are all victims of imperialism, all losers in GGIII, our cultures distorted and perverted rather than merely anachronistic, including American culture and Islam.

Rules of the game and Strategies

The collapse of the Soviet enemy meant the empire could set the rules itself, even to some extent shed its pretense of not being an empire.[30] The image projected under Bush I and Clinton in the GGIII opening gambit was of the US as the sole superpower, at worst a grudging, benign "empire lite" pursuing a "liberal imperialism". These are terms coined by Harvard professor, currently Canadian Liberal Party leader Michael Ignatieff. "Empire lite [is] a global hegemony whose grace notes are free markets, human rights and democracy, enforced by the most awesome power the world has ever known." Given these virtues, "the empire's interest has a right to trump the sovereignty of a state."[31] Ignatieff's use of 'liberal' and the 'liberal' faction of the imperial establishment here refers to the Democrats' approach to empire, supposedly concerned with individual rights, with a preference for soft power over hard power, in contrast to the neoconservative 'hawks', promoters of 'might is right', though Stephen Walt argues

> The only important intellectual difference between neoconservatives and liberal interventionists is that the former have disdain for international institutions (which they see as constraints on US power), and the latter see them as a useful way to legitimate American dominance.[32]

The professed rules once again include:

1. Free trade, now regulated more rigorously by the World Trade Organization (1995),

2. Wars and direct occupation of countries considered of strategic importance, even though they are not called colonies as in GGI. They are seized on various pretexts: the pre-emptive search for weapons of mass destruction (WMDs), the need to nurture democracy, defend human rights, prevent terrorism, and most recently, the responsibility to protect civilians from purported crimes of genocide, war crimes, crimes against humanity and ethnic cleansing, so-called Responsibility to Protect (R2P).

3. Empire exceptionalism, though now only one empire decides when and where to break the rules. Exceptionalism means that the US can choose to ignore any international

body or ruling it disapproves of (WTO rulings, the International Criminal Court), and that the US (and those like Britain that do its bidding) are not accountable for their actions.

The domino theory no longer refers to countries 'going communist' but 'going Islamist'. This is even worse than the imperial arrogance of GGI. In each case, the underlying rule is of course 'might makes right'.

Financial Strategies
The victory over communism was a powerful psychological force reaffirming the US dollar. Freed of its nominal relationship to gold in 1971, as the world's reserve currency, its supply is now at the whim of the US government, to be increased to indirectly finance its multiple wars and outsize consumption. This control over the world's money supply serves in actuality as a means of taxing the world's resources. If used within reason, such an unprecedented imperial system could last for a long time, despite the creeping de-industrialization that empire logic eventually entails, as long as the world is willing to accept this money as reserve currency.

Since 1971, floating exchange rates for most of the world's currencies had created an ongoing atmosphere of speculation, which dramatically increased with computer technology, allowing instantaneous multiple transactions around the world. The most infamous currency speculator has been George Soros, who became known as "the Man Who Broke the Bank of England" after he made a reported $1 billion during the 1992 "Black Wednesday" British currency crisis by short-selling the pound, betting that it would be forced to quit the European Exchange Rate Mechanism (the proto-euro).

The speculative role of banks and financial intermediaries has increased dramatically during GGIII, showing distinct signs of parapolitics. The Asian financial crisis of 1997–98 was precipitated by western banks with the intent of crippling these high growth economies, which were using traditional government-supported national economic development plans to encourage stable, balanced growth, uncontrolled by international capital.[33] Enforced deregulation made it "much easier for wealthy nationals to liberate themselves from the fortunes of their country of residence and operate on a truly world scale",[34] while leaving states helpless to protect or direct their economies.

Argentina and Russia were bankrupted in 1999 as speculators transferred their money abroad (see Chapter 4 Oligarchs), leaving the countries with no reserves and huge deficits. This contributed to a massive transfer of wealth from periphery to center, and again in both instances, the US tried to force the countries to submit to the neoliberal world order via IMF structural adjustments (reduce social welfare payments, 'improve' the business environment, deregulate markets) though neither submitted fully and the IMF was forced to back off.

The repeal in 1999 of the Glass-Steagall Act (passed in the wake of the stock market crash of 1929 to separate banking from securities activities) and the Commodities Futures Modernization Act in 2000 (deregulating the derivatives markets and credit-default swaps) led to a frenzy of speculation, "casino capitalism", culminating in the world financial crisis of 2008. The Dow-Jones index dropped 34 per cent at the height of the crisis, the worst decline since 1931, as Lehman Brothers, AIG and hundreds of smaller banks declared bankruptcy, leading Bush II and Obama to authorize the Federal Reserve to create more than $2 trillion as a bailout,[35] even as bankers continued to give themselves multi-million dollar bonuses.

There were no guilty parties and no serious reforms, despite avowals and angry words from Obama. Washington had become unashamedly captive to Wall Street. The Paul-Grayson amendment to the Financial Stability Improvement Act of 2009 to audit the Federal Reserve, approved by House Financial Services Committee, was stymied by Federal Reserve Chairman Bernanke as it "would shatter the Fed's independence".[36] Bernanke realized that the dollar-denominated world financial system would collapse if its workings were exposed to light.

But it was not only Washington that was worried. Saudi Arabia, China and Russia also cannot afford to see the dollar collapse. A collapse of the dollar would wipe out much of the world's foreign currency reserves, sharply reducing the world's money supply, penalizing countries with high savings rates and trade surpluses, bringing an end to casino capitalism— the equivalent of revolution.

So the system staggers on. The process of wealth transfer from poor to rich continues, both within the US and between center and periphery. The overall banking system showed record profits by 2009 (Goldman Sachs $13.4 billion) as wages fell, official unemployment hovered at 10 per cent, and hundreds of thousands of lower-middle class Americans lost their homes.

The unification of Europe has been officially the goal of the US in both GGII&III, as long as the EU remains beholden to the US. Britain joined the EU in 1973, more as a spoiler, representing US interests. The problem with European unity for the US began in 1999 with the creation of the euro, which within a year began to rise sharply in value against the dollar, indicating that it could become an alternative world reserve currency, representing far more people than the US (500 million), a powerhouse of exports, with governments committed to balanced budgets and modest defense spending. Understandably it attracted the interest of such opponents of US empire as Iraq and Iran who wanted to use the euro for oil pricing, and understandably this was viewed with alarm by the US financial establishment.

The invasion of Iraq in 2003 was resisted by France and Germany, and their attempts to marshal a common EU foreign policy also alarmed the US, which mobilized the new pro-US eastern Europe and ex-Soviet EU members to support the war. It was already time to put Europe in its place. The financial crisis of 2008 provided the opportunity to pursue parapolitics with a vengeance.

In late 2009 and early 2010 a group of Anglo-American hedge funds launched a speculative attack against the government bonds of Greece, Spain, and Portugal, with the goal of using a crisis in the southern tier of the euro to bring on a panic flight away from the euro, supporting the dollar.[37] The EU is a hodgepodge of very different states with radically different governments and economies, with no parallel European-wide budget to allow for fast and broad stimulus measures to counter the economic crisis and a 3 per cent limit for each country on its budget deficit. The US budget deficit was 10 per cent of GDP in 2009. So it was easy for US banks to create a Euro-meltdown. And then to veto attempts by European leaders to restrict risky practices such as hedge funds at the G8 in 2010.

With the attack on Greek bonds, massive bank loans and drastic social welfare cuts were the only solution, given there was no Greek currency to devalue. Like the US, Europe poured billions into its banks and all political leaders demanded that citizens should now have social benefits slashed, shifting the burden of the crisis from those who caused it (the banking elite) to the ordinary citizen. By rescuing Greece financially, France and Germany were merely adding to their own liabilities while not reducing Greece's.[38] The process was repeated in Spain and Ireland. The very fabric of the EU was being torn asunder as the rich members turn their backs on the poor and castigate the PIIGS (Portugal, Italy, Ireland, Greece, Spain). The only European country which experienced a casino capital meltdown and survived was Iceland, which is not in the EU, still had its own krona to devalue, and refused to bow to IMF dictates.

Brzezinski writes in *The Grand Chessboard* that Europe is actually one battle ground within a geo-economic war. The 2008–10 European financial crisis precipitated by the US banks promotes greater economic integration of the EU around its poorer members, in line with the US strategy of maintaining the EU as a junior partner similar to Britain. The crisis served as the pretext to introduce a tighter federal system encompassing all 27 member states. The countries that do not manage to reduce their total national debt to less than 60 per cent of GDP will have their budgets amended by Brussels. The member states will be, vis-à-vis the EU, like the American states vis-à-vis their federal state. A weakened EU will pave the way for a grand North Atlantic common market incorporating both NAFTA and the EU, an economic union dominated by the US, with the euro, or what's left of it, now securely tied to the fate of the dollar. "Nothing can prevent the integration of Europe within a trans-Atlantic Bloc. In the end, the merging of the euro with the dollar will accelerate the union of the old world and the new world,"[39] a kind of neo-Manifest Destiny. The agreement concluded between the EU and the IMF in 2010, giving the Fund partial oversight of EU economic policies, is a first step in this direction.

In GGII the oil embargo of 1973 and the subsequent high price of oil proved to be beneficial to the US given the pricing of oil in dollars. The oil producers soaked up the accumulated dollars states were obliged to hold as foreign exchange reserves for this purpose, and recycled them via US banks. This manipulation of oil prices continues as the system is basically unchanged. In 2008, oil hit $147 a barrel, just as Bush II and Obama were acceding to banker demands to pump $2 trillion dollars into the financial system. A stable high price of oil is essential to the empire's financial health and will continue, no matter what happens in Iraq, Afghanistan and Iran, as the petrodollars either stay in the hands of US-controlled Big Oil and big banks or are held as reserves around the world.

As with Iraq, it is the continued threat to the dollar, rather than worries about WMDs, that motivates the drumbeat to invade Iran, "precisely because such an aggression would likely lead to a blocking of the Straits of Hormuz"; just the apprehension of it jerks the price upwards.[40] Following the tested model of the 1973 war and oil boycott, if deemed necessary, a disruption of oil supplies could be precipitated by an invasion of Iran. Even if the Islamists can't be dislodged, the price of oil could rise to $500 per barrel,[41] thus creating enough demand for dollars to buttress the "oil standard".

The ultimate goal of world bankers is to create a new reserve currency for the empire. WWII was a great boon to them, especially in Germany and Japan, where US-controlled post-war reconstruction was structured financially with the new IMF in mind, forcing them to transform themselves into components of a globalized private banking system that puts institutional creditworthiness and profitability as prerequisites, serving the needs of the global financial system to preserve the security and value of global private capital... The IMF and the international banks regulated by the BIS are a team: the international banks lend recklessly to borrowers in emerging economies to create a foreign currency debt crisis, the IMF arrives as a carrier of monetary virus in the name of sound monetary policy, then the international banks come as vulture investors in the name of financial rescue to acquire national banks deemed capital inadequate and insolvent by the BIS.[42]

Financial crises, arguably induced by the machinations of global financial players themselves (e.g., in 2005 in Japan and 2008 around the world) provide convenient excuses to accelerate the process, with the BIS doing nothing to address the underlying factors responsible for the crises, but rather promoting its own agenda of globalization.

The 2009 Bilderberg meeting reported on its desire to advance long-existing plans to create a global treasury or global central bank, to manage the world economy. In 2009, prior to the Bilderberg meeting, the G20 set in motion plans to make the IMF a global central bank, upgrading Special Drawing Rights (SDRs) to the status of world currency. In May 2010, IMF Managing Director Dominique Strauss-Kahn stated that "crisis is an opportunity", and while SDRs are a step in the right direction, ultimately what is needed is "a new global currency issued by a global central bank, with robust governance and institutional features".[43] What Strauss-Kahn left unsaid was: "This will only work if the US is in control and not forced to submit to IMF 'structural adjustments' like all other countries."[44] But that would merely strengthen the stranglehold international bankers already have on the world economy, effectively ceding the empire to them. It is very unlikely that US nationalists, not to mention the BRICs, would allow this, as it would truly signal the "end of history".

Military-political Strategies
GGIII Imperial Doctrines
In his February 1985 State of the Union Address, Reagan said: "We must not break faith with those who are risking their lives...on every continent, from Afghanistan to Nicaragua... to defy Soviet aggression and secure

rights which have been ours from birth. Support for freedom fighters is self-defense." This was dubbed the Reagan Doctrine by neocon columnist Charles Krauthammer in a *Time* article, and marked the rejection of containment and *realpolitik* (even as Gorbachev was hoisting a white flag). It was formulated in conjunction with the Heritage Foundation and other conservative foreign policy think tanks, which saw a political opportunity to significantly expand Carter's Afghanistan policy into a more global doctrine including US support to anticommunist resistance movements in Soviet-allied nations in Africa, Asia and Latin America. Reagan's invasion of tiny Grenada in 1983 marked his first victory in his "confrontation between good and evil",[45] just as Thatcher's war against Argentina in 1982 marked hers.

Despite the shift in foreign policy which Reagan and the neocons represented, and their disdain for Kissinger and his *realpolitik*, they made use of the fruits of Kissinger's detente efforts—the crowning item being the Helsinki accords, with their "human rights basket". Combined with Reagan's new arms race, his war in Afghanistan, and Gorbachev's ill-defined perestroika, the clever use of this accord further undermined the Soviet Union's credibility and precipitated its collapse, much to Kissinger's surprise. The first great neocon con was the winning of the Cold War, the triumph of freedom-and-democracy over tyranny-and-dictatorship.

Ironically, it was not Reagan, but the non-neocon Bush I, Brzezinski's Global Leader I, who launched the first official war of GGIII, with his (albeit limited) invasion of Iraq in 1991, and the non-neocon Clinton (Global Leader II) who launched the second, with his bombing of the remains of Yugoslavia. While rejecting the neocon label, Clinton carried out the neocon scenario for Iraq, relentlessly bombing and starving it in hopes of toppling Hussein without a messy invasion, and pursuing Israeli interests in the Middle East with the so-called Oslo Accords. He contributed the Clinton Doctrine in a speech (26 February 1999), really just a vaguer version of the Reagan Doctrine, referring to Bosnia: "Where our values and our interests are at stake, and where we can make a difference, we must be prepared to do so," justifying NATO's "out of region" intervention there, its first venture abroad.

With respect to the Middle East, his national security adviser Anthony Lake said that just as the US had taken the lead in containing the Soviet threat, it must now bear a "special responsibility" to "neutralize" and "contain" rogue states in the Middle East, including Iran, Iraq, Libya and Sudan",[46] but pointedly leaving out reference to the real rogue state. With his inability to hold Israel to a meaningful dialogue in the Oslo talks, his Israeli-inspired goal to overthrow Saddam Hussein, his war in the Balkans, and his refusal to extradite bin Laden from Sudan when he had the chance, Clinton set the stage for the neocon ascendancy. Two essentially neocon tickets vied for the presidency in 2000, Gore/ Lieberman 'fighting' Bush/ Cheney.

The neocon ascendancy was confirmed by the election of Bush II with his Bush Doctrine,[47] originally describing the unilateral withdrawal from the Anti-Ballistic Missile treaty and refusal to support ratification of the Kyoto Protocol but given a new meaning with the supposedly pre-emptive invasions of Afghanistan and Iraq against potential or perceived threats to the US. This bald imperial doctrine marked a return to the open aggression of GGI, rejecting the soft power strategies of GGII. It was the Reagan Doctrine with a punch: "Either you are with us or the terrorists. Any nation continuing to harbor or support terrorism will be regarded by the US as a hostile regime."[48] This essentially denied the legitimacy of any criticism of US policies and publicly confirmed empire exceptionalism in line with GGI&II.

However, it went too far and ended up endangering the very existence of the empire. It is now resisted by the more 'liberal' faction of the imperial establishment represented by Brzezinski and his protégé President Barack Obama, whose imperial strategy is an attempt to return to *realpolitik* and diplomacy. Obama asserted his national security strategy in a speech at West Point in 2009. The Obama Doctrine emphasized negotiation and collaboration, prompting the Nobel Peace Prize committee to award him the Peace Prize. In his acceptance speech he nonetheless warned that "force is sometimes necessary", and continued the Bush Doctrine in all but name, however unwillingly.[49]

In tandem with the Obama Doctrine is the Petraeus Doctrine, enunciated by the head of US forces in Afghanistan—the strategy of pursuing counterterrorism via the counterinsurgency long war combined with nation building, embraced by both Bush II and Obama, a replay of GGI's white man's burden and GGII's failed Cold War Vietnam policy.

While the neocons and what can be termed the neo-neocon factions (Obama) use different rhetoric and ever-so slight differences in policy, US world hegemony remains the goal. During her trips in July 2010 to Georgia and Vietnam, Secretary of State Hillary Clinton reiterated that the US recognizes no "spheres of influence" by any other nation anywhere in the world, including by Russia and China on their borders and in their immediate neighborhoods, and that Washington reserves the exclusive right to intervene in regional conflicts around the world and to "internationalize" them when and how it sees fit.

Institutions
United Nations
The UN became an albatross for the US long before Reagan excoriated it, cut funding, and withdrew from UNESCO, demanding reforms in accordance with US wishes. After 1967, it had increasingly become a mouthpiece for world disapproval of US aggression and Israel's occupation and invasions. General Assembly Resolution 3379 in 1975 equated Zionism with racism. But in GGIII the UN began to yield to the newly empowered hegemon. In 1991, with 19 new pro-US ex-socialist bloc countries, the UN General Assembly decided that Zionism was no longer racism. It carried out crippling sanctions against Iraq which resulted in up to a half million infant deaths, and allowed the partition and bombing of Iraq by the US and Britain. It provided a convenient cover for US aggression, though it was still largely vilified in the US.

The UN record continued to be mixed. It did not approve direct intervention in the Yugoslav civil war, but it did impose US-proposed sanctions against Serbia in 1992, and admit the breakaway Yugoslav republics immediately. Only a Russian Security Council veto prevented a UN blessing for the bombing of Serbia and invasion of Kosovo, and it obediently took responsibility for the "interim administration" in Kosovo (UNMIK).

Similarly in Iraq, the UN provided a platform for the 34-nation coalition that invaded Iraq in 1991 and the four-nation coalition that invaded in 2003. While the former got UN authorization for "all necessary means to uphold and implement Resolution 660" demanding withdrawal from Kuwait, no UN military action was contemplated.

In 2003, the UN Security Council refused to endorse US plans to overthrow the Iraqi government directly on the clearly trumped-up charges of harboring WMDs. Following Clinton's example in Serbia, a furious Bush II invaded anyway, claimed a quick victory, intending to leave a very reluctant UN to pick up the pieces. But the Iraqi resistance targeted the UN HQs in August 2003, killing 22 people, including UN envoy Sergio Vieira de Mello. The UN then pulled out, returning later with only a skeletal staff, meekly rubber stamping the occupation by the US "coalition of the willing" until 2008, when the US and the Iraqi government negotiated their own legality.

Even in America's 9/11 centerpiece invasion of Afghanistan, the UN extended only a limited endorsement of the US invasion in resolution 56/1 calling "for international cooperation to bring to justice the perpetrators, organizers, and sponsors of the outrages". "The cause must be pursued by all the States of the world, working together and using many different means, including political, legal, diplomatic and financial means," and UN nations must "step up our humanitarian work as soon as possible," said UN General Secretary Kofi Annan.[50] In other words, assuming Osama bin Laden was the perpetrator, capture him, withdraw, and then provide aid to Afghanistan. Nothing about occupation, building a pipeline, bases, torture prisons, etc. The invasion was already in progress at the time, with the UN scrambling to be relevant, but it still did not endorse invasion and occupation. In 2009 UN official Robert Watkins said the UN would not be involved in NATO's reconstruction plans for the province of Marjah "because we would not want to have the humanitarian activities we deliver to be linked with military activity."[51]

The UN has been more compliant with US imperial needs on the economic front. Development agencies such as the UN Development Program (UNDP) and UN International Development Organization (UNIDO) played a major role in the ex-socialist bloc, especially Central Asia, where UNDP and UNIDO quickly moved in to assist the new pro-western political elites to privatize state-owned industries. The energy sector in each case became a prime target of western capital, though with mixed success, as governments, especially Russia's, moved to secure the energy sector when it was in danger of falling into foreign hands.

The agencies now play the same role throughout the third world, as neoliberalism spreads from center to periphery. This benefits primarily the center, with its developed market infrastructure and traditions, and its comprador representatives in the periphery making clear whose interests the UN now serves. It has produced a backlash against the UN in these countries, for privatization is essentially a transfer of wealth from the broader society to the rich, radically increasing income disparity and unemployment—hardly part of the original UN mandate.[52]

NATO

The proposed goals of NATO at the beginning of GGIII are set out in its Strategic Concepts in 1991 and 1999, still emphasizing security with a Euro-Atlantic focus, but already in collaboration with strategic out-of-area states. The current Strategic Concept adopted in November 2010 confirmed the new global role of NATO, stating the alliance will protect its member nations against violent extremism, nuclear proliferation, cyber assaults and attacks on energy infrastructure and supply lines, requiring a rapid response force deployable around the world. "Defense of our territory and our citizens no longer begins at our borders. Threats can originate from Kandahar or from cyberspace ... As a consequence,

NATO must build more partnerships and engage more with the wider world."[53]

The shift from its modest GGII role to its new global role in GGIII is attributed to 9/11, the first time that NATO invoked Article 5 for collective self-defense. Reluctant though NATO members may have been, most took part in the occupation of Afghanistan and some in the Iraq occupation, and remain, at least on paper, committed to NATO's new ambitious Strategic Concept, despite the unpopularity of the wars in all countries, including in the US itself.

The enlargement of NATO took place both east (a blatant violation of the US pledge to Gorbachev in 1990)[54] and south, including:

- new members Hungary, the Czech Republic, and Poland in 1999; Bulgaria, Estonia, Latvia, Lithuania, Romania, Slovakia and Slovenia in 2004; Croatia and Albania in 2009, bringing the total to 28;

- 22 Partnerships for Peace set up with Eastern Europe and the ex-Soviet Union in 1991;

- the Mediterranean Dialogue (Egypt, Algeria, Jordan, Mauritania, Tunisia, Morocco, Israel) in 1994;

- the Euro-Atlantic Partnership Council to handle relations between NATO countries, the ex-socialist bloc and ex-Soviet "partners" in 1997;

- the Istanbul Cooperation Initiative, to try to militarize the Mediterranean Dialogue and the Gulf Cooperation Council (Bahrain, Kuwait, Oman, Qatar, Saudi Arabia and the United Arab Emirates) in 2004.

- France returning to full membership in 2009 after four decades.

With the end of the Cold War and the dissolution of the Warsaw Pact in 1991, NATO's real role in the US empire has become clearer as, instead of disbanding, it expanded to encompass, in conjunction with US military commands, most of the world, with even Russia having a special consultative relationship via the NATO-Russia Council established in 1998. It has become the centerpiece of the empire's military presence around the world, moving quickly to respond to US needs to intervene where the UN won't, as in Yugoslavia, Afghanistan, Iraq and now Libya. In April 2003 NATO agreed to take command of the International Security Assistance Force (ISAF) in Afghanistan, marking the first time in NATO's history that it took charge of a mission outside the Euro-Atlantic area.

Figure 3.1 map NATO post-1991[55]

ISAF now includes troops from 46 countries. In 2004 the NATO Training Mission—Iraq (NMT-I)—was formed to train security forces there.

This redefinition of a supposedly passive defense grouping into a kind of player in its own right in GGIII is no less significant, as game-changing, as the ascendancy of the dollar, the creation of Israel, and the alliance with Islamists—the queen promotions of GGII. "Just as the Pentagon has replaced the State Department, NATO itself is being used by the United States as a potential substitute for the United Nations," says Diana Johnstone. World conquest by the US becomes a "crusade by the world's 'democracies' to spread their enlightened political order to the rest of a recalcitrant world",[56] leaving the UN, the EU Foreign Affairs Council and NATO member governments without any say. It is perhaps what Mackinder had in mind when proposing to transform the empire into a commonwealth—a group of like-minded countries under the overwhelming political and military authority of the empire—controlling the world at the behest of the empire once-removed.

NATO, with its Rapid Response Force set up in 2003, now projects itself as an apparently neutral means for garnering support from around the world to attack any nation the US considers an enemy, something it didn't dare do so openly against the Soviet Union. The public excuse is "to defend the security on which our economic prosperity rests".[57] Less ingenuously, German President Horst Koehler defended his country's deployment in Afghanistan: "In emergencies military intervention is necessary to uphold our interests, like for example free trade routes, for example to prevent regional instabilities which could have a negative impact on our chances in terms of trade, jobs and income."[58]

The NATO missile defense system, purportedly to defend Europe from a rogue state, is also a cover for the US missile defense system, a way of spreading the cost while the US maintains effective control, as the main system is the US one and NATO's is part of it. When NATO General Secretary Anders Rasmussen argues for missile defense, he is on the surface referring to, say, Iran launching nuclear war on Europe, but what he really implies is that if the US launches a war against Iran, an interceptor system could prevent effective retaliation. Russian President Dmitri Medvedev even agreed to participate in such a 'European' missile defense system at the NATO summit in 2010—the first time a Russian president has attended the summit.

The Arab uprisings of 2011 have provided a new strategy for NATO, which was delegated the task of policing a no-fly-zone over Libya to drive out al-Gaddafi. The need to push eastward, threatening an increasingly compliant Russia concerned with maintaining its hegemony in its "near abroad", has abated, at least for the time being. The groundwork for turning the Mediterranean into a *mare nostrum* was laid by Sarkozy's 2008 EU-sponsored Mediterranean Union (MU), based on the Mediterranean Dialogue (1994). The opportunity to add a military flavor to the MU, which was only a ill-defined club, came with the pleas of the Libyan rebels. This shift makes sense for both Europe and the US. Afghanistan is a lost cause and will have to be abandoned soon. Much more rational to pour money and effort into the Mediterranean region, integrate Israel and (hopefully) pull in Iraq as this new version of GGII's MEDO gains traction. AFRICOM, the latest arm of the US military command structure (see below), will be more than glad to help out.

Premodern, modern and postmodern states
An important GGIII institutional innovation has been the shaping of a new type of state out of the traditional GGI&II nation states and the remains of the socialist bloc. The collapse of the Soviet Union and Yugoslavia resulted in the creation of 22 new states,[59] all of which were

eager to curry favor in Washington, up to and including permission to establish bases via Status of Forces agreements. These states have been dubbed postmodern as opposed to pre-modern (or failed) and modern (the traditional post-WWII nation state). "The postmodern system in which we Europeans live does not rely on balance; nor does it emphasize sovereignty or the separation of domestic and foreign affairs. The European Union has become a highly developed system for mutual interference in each other's domestic affairs, right down to beer and sausages."[60]

The political elites of the new states of the socialist bloc and ex-Soviet Union were eager to renounce whatever sovereignty necessary to join the European institutions, and welcomed NATO commissions which proceeded to restructure them militarily and politically in accordance with US-NATO requirements. Even Iraq's new army and security forces are supposedly being structured and trained in accordance with US-NATO requirements. EU President Herman Van Rompuy confirmed this when he said that "the time of the homogenous nation state is over."[61] Hence, the notion of postmodern imperialism.

Hard Power

Hard power became a major strategy once again in GGIII, now called "humanitarian intervention", dubbed by critics as the "imperialism of human rights".[62] It is also called the Annan Doctrine, asserting the loss of the traditional prerogatives of sovereignty in the face of crimes against humanity.[63] In response to Annan's call, Canada's government established an International Commission on Intervention and State Sovereignty, which issued its report "The Responsibility to Protect", recommending that military intervention could be justified where large-scale loss of life is occurring or imminent, owing to deliberate state action or the state's refusal or failure to act. R2P, as it was dubbed, was endorsed by the UN General Assembly and, with Rwanda's 1994 genocide in mind, the reconstituted African Union in 2005.

However noble in theory, R2P undermines the very nature of post-WWII international relations, based on national sovereignty. That said, it really just acknowledges the emptiness of national sovereignty as a uniform principle applicable to all nations equally, given the imperial set-up. While lesser western states—former empires—may have lost sovereignty to the now dominant imperial power and its institutions, "third world sovereignty never existed anyway."[64] In the Middle East, the policy is just an update of the GGI British promise to 'liberate' the Arab world from the Ottomans.

Wars
Yugoslavia

The three major wars in GGIII—so far—have very different origins but all have followed a similar scenario. The war in Yugoslavia was a direct result of the disintegration of the socialist bloc in the late 1980s, with the US and EU actively involved in shaping a Balkans to fit their needs. Instead of imposing an arms embargo and supporting the federal authorities to maintain the union—which had maintained peace in the Balkan cauldron through most of the twentieth century—the West backed the various civil war factions from 1991–95, unleashing the whirlwind. The pretext for subsequent western intervention was humanitarian.

The real purpose was to facilitate the break-up of a powerful anti-imperialist force, Yugoslavia, the most successful of the GGII socialist states, to support local pro-western elites to head weak ethnic states, and join the ex-communist regimes in eastern Europe as compliant postmodern members of the EU and NATO. Balkans nationalism was manipulated from outside, recapitulating GGI when British, French and Russian interests, intent on dismantling the Ottoman Empire and stopping Germany's Baghdad railway plans, had interfered there. The principal difference between GGI and GGIII was that Germany was now working *with* the Anglo-American empire through the EU, where it was now a second tier power, a postmodern state, in league with the only remaining empire.

The war in the Balkans initially involved soft power, especially the National Endowment for Democracy (NED), which arrived in 1988 and financed opposition groups and human rights NGOs, providing junkets and seminars for journalists and even trade union opposition. Its activities, monitored and controlled by the CIA, were purportedly to foster democracy. After the various local groups had become dependent on US largesse, US Congress passed the Foreign Operations Appropriations Act in 1990 that required regions to declare independence from Yugoslavia within six months or lose all US financial support, for each of the six republics to hold elections supervised by the US State Department, and for no further aid to go through the central Yugoslav government.[65]

The country descended into war, exacerbated by veteran Islamist fighters from Afghanistan, who poured into Kosovo and Bosnia, still funded by Saudi Arabia and possibly the US. This provided a pretext to quash the last socialist outpost, Serbia, still trying to hold the federation together. Bin Laden visited al-Qaeda cells in Bosnia, Kosovo and Albania in the 1990s. Even as the US bombed Serbia in 1999 and backed the Kosovo Liberation Army (KLA, on the US list of terrorist organizations),

Graham Fuller, former deputy director of the CIA's National Council on Intelligence, was still advocating using Muslim forces to further US interests in Central Asia. "The policy of guiding the evolution of Islam and of helping [Islamists] against our adversaries worked marvelously well in Afghanistan against [the Russians]. The same doctrines can still be used to destabilize what remains of Russian power, and especially to counter the Chinese influence in Central Asia."[66] After 11 weeks of bombing and over 500 civilian deaths, Serbian President Slobodan Milosevic finally accepted UN resolution 1244, allowing NATO to occupy Kosovo under a UN mandate.

The break-up of Yugoslavia in the 1990s, along with the drawn-out campaign of sanctions and "no fly zones" against Iraq from 1990, were defining moments in establishing the new GGIII. The Clinton administration 'saved' Bosnia and Kosovo from Serbia's attempts to hold the Yugoslav union together, establishing NATO-sponsored Muslim statelets Bosnia-Herzegovina and Kosovo, in an eerie reversion to GGI. Bosnia is governed by High Commissioner Valentin Inzko, an Austrian national, who wields powers similar to a colonial administrator. It is occupied by NATO forces, with the central bank governor appointed by the IMF. Kosovo is nominally independent, the site of the largest US base in Europe, Camp Bond Steel, housing 3,000 soldiers, giving the US control of the Balkans, within easy reach of the Caspian Sea and Israel.

Afghanistan

The 'liberal' Clinton era was characterized more by multilateral cooperation, free-market economic policies and corporate globalization, a projection of soft power. Clinton downplayed military spending and oil geopolitics, Yugoslavia being his "empire lite" effort. Afghanistan was invaded outright by the US, on the pretext of capturing Osama bin Laden and as an act of revenge, the assumption—tenuous at best—being that bin Laden carried out the destruction of the New York World Trade Center on 9/11.

The invasion was really the first thrust in the new neocon strategy of remaking the Middle East and capturing Central Asia in line with Mackinder and Rhodes' original GGI dream of world empire. Like the intervention in Yugoslavia, it was to extend US power along the re-emerging Silk Road, this time in areas that had been in the Soviet sphere of influence.

The immediate goal in the 1990s was to secure an ambitious oil and gas pipeline deal between UNOCAL and the Taliban (Arabic for students) to draw the Central Asian countries away from dependence on Russian pipelines and bring Caspian Sea oil and Turkmen gas south to

Pakistan for export. Despite protests from human rights groups, a State Department official told Ahmed Rashid, "the Taliban will develop like the Saudis ... no parliament, and lots of *sharia* law. We can live with that."[67] There was little likelihood of Russia regaining any influence in Afghanistan and it was very much in US interests to work with the Taliban, which it did from 1994–98 mediated by the Saudis, as the US never recognized the Taliban government.

There is considerable evidence that the US frustration with this vital geopolitical link in its plans for Eurasia, epitomized by the failure of UNOCAL's negotiations, precipitated the invasion. During the pipeline negotiations, "US representatives told the Taliban, 'Either you accept our offer of a carpet of gold, or we bury you under a carpet of bombs'."[68] Bush II's national security adviser on Afghanistan and Central Asia was UNOCAL's Zalmay Khalilzad.[69] Former Pakistani foreign secretary Niaz Naik was told by senior American officials in mid-July 2001 that military action against Afghanistan would go ahead by the middle of October.[70] The full scale invasion was launched a mere 26 days after 9/11, an improbably short notice.

The relationship between the US government and al-Qaeda is still very much an enigma. The major terrorist events in the mid-1990s were not associated with bin Laden, who decamped to Afghanistan from Sudan in 1996 after Bill Clinton refused Sudan's offer to extradite him. Instead, Clinton destroyed a pharmaceuticals plant in Sudan and dropped a few bombs in a remote Afghan valley where it was rumored bin Laden was training his jihadis the next year. The US military's Khobar Towers in Saudi Arabia were bombed in 1996, followed in 1997 by the Luxor massacre of 62 local Egyptians and tourists and the 1998 car bombings of US embassies in Kenya and Tanzania, all while bin Laden was *incommunicado.*

After 9/11, Bush II, like Clinton earlier, refused to negotiate the Taliban hand-over of bin Laden (the Taliban offered to extradite him to a third country to ensure a fair investigation and trial), instead, launching a full-scale war against an entire nation. This refusal of both the 'liberal' and neocon versions of the imperialists to nip the bin Laden myth in the bud can only be explained one way: bin Laden was a useful foil for imperial plans to invade Afghanistan and then Iraq, and was worth more as a specter than as a prisoner with potentially embarrassing facts to reveal, or as a martyr.

With 9/11 and the invasion of Afghanistan, the US made a deal with Russia. In a supreme irony, the US joined up with its defeated *rivals* in Afghanistan—Russia and the Tajik and Uzbek remnants of the Afghan communists—to defeat the erstwhile US Pashtun *allies* which had now turned against the Americans, determined to clear their lands of foreign occupation. Clearly more worried about the Islamist threat than the new US imperial threat, Russia gave the US full backing in its invasion, handing it a ring of military bases in Central Asia. The presence of al-Qaeda and bin Laden, accused of masterminding 9/11, was the pretext for invading Afghanistan, though no serious proof of bin Laden's guilt has ever been revealed.

Bush saw a virtually defenseless country, loathed in the media, as a perfect opportunity to easily insert US power into the heart of Central Asia. It was quickly overrun with a few thousand troops after a massive air attack. NATO took over in 2003 as the International Security Assistance Force but the combined military might of close to 50 nations has been unable to defeat a resurgent Taliban. Just like the search for genocide in Kosovo and WMDs in Iraq, so the search for bin Laden proved fruitless. Just as in Kosovo and Iraq, a new goal of democracy and nation building provided the pretext for US presence in this latest 'backward' Muslim country.

Iraq

The first war of GGIII was in fact the invasion of Iraq in 1991, the pretext being Iraq's seizure of Kuwait in August 1990. Saddam Hussein's invasion of Kuwait was not a surprise. Iraqi leaders have always insisted—rightly—that Kuwait was an artificial construct created as a British protectorate in 1899, a geostrategic way station between the Suez Canal and India. Iraq claimed—rightly—that Kuwait was stealing its oil by drilling under the border.

In reality, Saddam Hussein was a used-up ally, far too supportive of the Palestinians, far too unpredictable, and far too geopolitically strategically located to be left in place. He was led into a trap. As Iraqi military preparations to occupy Kuwait were under way, Saddam Hussein was told by US ambassador April Glaspie that Washington, "inspired by friendship and not by confrontation, does not have an opinion ... on the Arab-Arab conflicts."[71] Saddam Hussein interpreted this as a reward for launching the war against Islamist Iran (which he didn't win and almost lost).

Weakened after a decade of war with Iran, Iraq was easy prey for the massive invasion launched from Saudi Arabia. Operation Desert Storm was comprised of 3/4 of NATO's members, though they participated merely as a coalition of the willing, without invoking Article 5 on collective defense. The Iraqi strongman was left in place, on the clear assumption that Iraqis would overthrow him, but, incredibly, survived more than a decade of subversion, crippling sanctions and partition.

Bush II cabinet member Paul O'Neill, who was fired in 2002, revealed that ten days after Bush took office, "topic A" was Iraq.[72] The apparent quick success in Afghanistan encouraged Bush II to move ahead with an unprovoked (not even pre-emptive) war on 19 March 2003, with Bush II and British Prime Minister Tony Blair colluding to create false proofs of nonexistent WMDs.

This was the original pretext, but it was soon exposed as a lie, and a second official reason for the invasion—to topple a cruel dictator and install democracy—was fabricated. What initially appeared as another successful war encouraged Bush II to buttress this new pretext by calling for a doubling of the NED budget in his January 2004 State of the Union address to develop "free elections, free markets, free press and free labor unions in the Middle East".[73] This too was a lie.

True democratic elections, which could have been held almost immediately, would have ensured a Shia majority in the south, the demand for an immediate withdrawal of US troops and for close ties with Iran, creating a powerful Shia alliance that would effectively control the region's oil, take over leadership of the Middle East, and create a Kurdish state in the already quasi-independent north.

British diplomat Gertrude Bell pieced Iraq together as a Sunni kingdom in 1932 from three provinces of the collapsed Ottoman Empire "because otherwise we will have a theocratic state, which is the very devil."[74] Saddam Hussein's dictatorship was based on the same realities. Democracy was and is "impossible, for it required a degree of trust among the communities that make up the underlying society that did not exist. Minorities need to be assured that they will not be permanent losers, or else they will secede to set up a state of their own."[75]

Such calls for democracy in the Middle East are belied by real US-Israeli interests. For instance, in Egypt, honest elections would most likely produce a government dominated by the Muslim Brotherhood which along with Iran and Iraq would quickly bring Israel to its senses.[76]

Thus, a third pretext was invented. The war-for-oil explanation soon became a cynical but politically correct fall-back reason, given the obvious lies concerning WMDs and democracy, necessary to avoid any talk of a deeper Israel-related agenda. At the Shangri-La security conference in Singapore in June 2003 Paul Wolfowitz told delegates, "The most important difference between North Korea and Iraq is that economically, we just had no choice in Iraq. The country swims on a sea of oil."[77] Later, Greenspan was equally surprisingly frank.

But Big Oil was not lobbying for the war, as it already had access to the oil. The geopolitical-strategic argument, in line with the invasion of Afghanistan, has some merit, though again, the Iraqi regime, unlike the

Taliban in Afghanistan, was not really a problem for Washington. Saddam Hussein had proved his enmity to US-nemesis Iran and had dispensed with pretenses to produce WMDs.

There were in fact two reasons to invade. While the real reason did not involve the oil companies, it very much involved oil.[78] The tipping point in the decision to invade was Saddam Hussein's determination to end payment for oil in dollars, which he managed to do in 2000. While the Iraqi oil trade in itself was far from large enough to impact the dollar's standing, compared with the voluminous US-Europe-Japan trade conducted in dollars, its danger was the precedent it set.

At first, his demand was met with ridicule, later with neglect, but as it became clearer that he meant business, political pressure was exerted to change his mind. When other countries, like Iran, then wanted payment in other currencies, most notably the euro and yen, the danger to the dollar was clear and present, and a punitive action was in order. Bush's Shock-and-Awe in Iraq was not about Saddam's nuclear capabilities, about defending human rights, about spreading democracy, or even about seizing oil fields; it was about defending the dollar, the American empire. It was about setting an example that anyone who demanded payment in currencies other than US dollars would be likewise punished.[79]

The other reason is clear from a consideration of who the most vocal war lobbyists were in Washington. "The war in Iraq was conceived by 25 neoconservative intellectuals, most of them Jewish, who are pushing President Bush to change the course of history."[80] Israel was the inspiration and a key beneficiary of the destruction of Iraq, but was not part of the invasion, limiting its role to shadowy post-liberation advisers, especially in Kurdistan, and covert operations in an enemy state now devastated, where it could roam freely. Israel has its own interests in destabilizing the region which increasingly conflict with the overall US imperial ones, preventing the US from pursuing its pre-GGII positive relations with the Arab world. While the US had no real geopolitical problem with an Iraq run by a strongman like Saddam Hussein (if he could be convinced to keep using dollars), Israel did. Its GGIII geopolitical strategy from the 1980s on was to partition Iraq and produce weak, feuding governments in the tradition of divide-and-rule, dressed up as the Yinon Doctrine (see Chapter 4).

Carving up countries is fraught with danger. The GGI process of carving up countries by redrawing borders on maps is no longer possible. The GGII partitions of India and Palestine, and the GGIII partition of Yugoslavia may have served imperial purposes, but were a nightmarish recipe for full scale civil war. Bush I was implicitly rejecting this option, when he continued to play according to the GGII rules in 1990 and left the Iraqi strongman in place. Bush II was playing according to the GGIII neocon rules, which gave Israeli's interests pride of place.[81]

This is confirmed by a plan for restructuring the Middle East published in the *Armed Forces Journal* in July 2006 which stated "Iraq should have been divided into three smaller states immediately" creating a "Free Kurdistan, stretching from Diyarbakir through Tabriz," that is, carved out of Turkey, Iran and Iraq, which "would be the most pro-western state between Bulgaria and Japan." Saudi Arabia, Afghanistan and Pakistan would all be dismantled, and the US army "will continue to fight for security from terrorism, for the prospect of democracy and for access to oil supplies in a region that is destined to fight itself."[82] The Saban Center for Middle East Policy issued a policy recommendation in June 2007 similarly calling for the division of Iraq into sectarian and ethnic regions linked by a federal government. In May 2008, Joseph Biden, Obama's future vice president, also called for the partition of Iraq into three autonomous regions.

Israel and the neocons in Washington knew from the outset that invading Iraq and overthrowing its dictator would unleash sectarian violence on an unprecedented scale, and can only have wanted this outcome, or at best were indifferent to it. In 1996 the architects of the invasion—David Wurmser, Richard Perle and Douglas Feith—predicted the chaos that would follow an invasion. "The residual unity of the Iraqi nation is an illusion" and after Saddam Hussein's fall, Iraq would "be ripped apart by the politics of warlords, tribes, clans, sects and key families."[84] They made no mention of WMDs or terrorism as a reason to invade but did worry about Iran or Syria trying to move in. The National Intelligence Council warned in January 2003 that an "American invasion would bring about instability in Iraq that would be exploited by Iran and al-Qaeda."

The invasion and subsequent dismantling of the Iraqi army was the most obvious step in promoting sectarian violence leading to the dismantling of the country. However, evidence points to US and Israel black-ops after the invasion as inciting even greater sectarian violence (see below—Proxies). By passing control of the government to supposedly safe émigré Shia politicians, a pretense of democracy was effected, but the underlying reality was that "the Pentagon itself is destabilizing the country it is supposed to control."[85]

As in Syria, the secular Iraqi Baathists had been successful in holding the country together, controlling sectarian tensions and discouraging Islamists. It was for this very reason that Israel had long regarded Iraq, Syria and Iran to be its prime enemies—the Arab nationalism of the first two and the Persian nationalism in Iran had proved immune to Israeli intrigues (though Israel had success in courting the Kurds in all three nations as well as in Turkey).

Redrawing the Middle East map

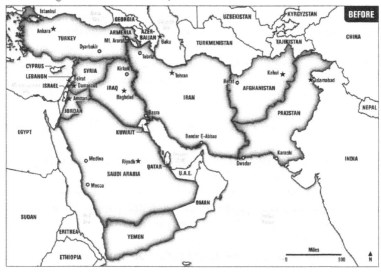

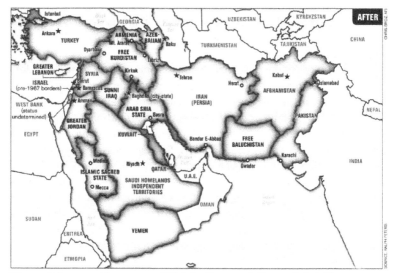

Figure 3.2 map of a neocon Middle East and Central Asia[83]

By end of his first term, Bush II had presided over the most dramatic extension of military power in US history, with bases now allowing it to control Eurasia, with the exception of Iran, at least in theory; that is, encircling Russia, China, controlling the Indian subcontinent, determining energy routes. This had come at a huge cost, however. By the mid-2000s, the US government and economy were experiencing unprecedented deficits, which should have been unacceptable, but with the dollar secure, the US was able to continue on its imperial course with no effective opposition other than the insurgents in Afghanistan and Iraq and the defiant Iranians.

All three wars have common features in consolidating the new US empire, employing divide-and-rule and regime-overthrow-and-occupation against countries strategically located, resource-rich and threatening to undermine US-Israeli goals.

Even the horrendous GGII wars in Korea and Vietnam were dressed up as civil wars, with the West defending the anticommunists against the communists. The prototype now is to *provoke* a civil war, as in the case of Yugoslavia, which was dismembered and incorporated into the new world order, or in the case of Serbia, Afghanistan and Iraq to use fabricated charges to justify invasion, with dismemberment, a long term goal in each case. The charge that the US is "pre-emptively" invading is not even true, as in each case, and in the case of the threatened war against Iran, there was/is nothing to "pre-empt".

Is it really possible that the chaos and murder by the invaders in Yugoslavia, Afghanistan and Iraq is intentional, indeed, pre-planned? Remarkably, considering the GGI Balkan tradition of ethnic strife, socialist Yugoslavia had become a peaceful, prosperous federation in GGII. Though harsh rulers, the Taliban did completely disarm the nation and wipe out the production of opium. Similarly, Saddam Hussein presided over a stable welfare state—arguably the best in the Middle East—where its many ethnic groups were not at each other's throats. But they all shared a tradition of defying the US-Israeli empire, and were situated in geopolitically strategic locations. US intervention has destroyed the state structures in these countries and turned them into arms dumps. It has managed to turn the peoples against each other, leading to civil war and disintegration.

Military bases, missile defense, cyber warfare, arms production, nuclear weapons

In GGIII the US military itself has been structured for world operations. USCENTCOM was set up in 1983 as a worldwide rapid reaction force.

In 1992, it became one of six regional commands:

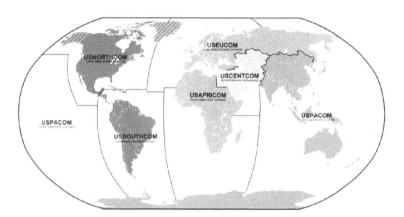

Figure 3.3 map Unified Command[86]

- USCENTCOM (1983—Middle East, Central Asian, southern Caucasus, coalition command units in Israel, Turkey, the Persian Gulf and the Diego Garcia military base)
- USNORTHCOM (2002—Mexico to the Arctic)
- USSOUTHCOM (1963—Central America to Argentina)
- USPACOM (1947—southeast Asia and Pacific)
- USAFRICOM (2007)
- USEUCOM (1947)

In GGI, one could trace the spread of imperialism by counting up colonies. America's version of the colony is the military base. New military bases have been built since 9/11 in Poland, Lithuania, Hungary, Bulgaria, Romania, Kosovo, Afghanistan, Iraq, Israel, Kyrgyzstan, Qatar and Bahrain. The US military has 737 bases in 63 countries according to the 2005 Base Structure Report, but the actual number probably exceeds 1,000. There were 38 large and medium-sized American facilities spread around the globe in 2005—mostly air and naval bases—approximately the same number as Britain's 36 naval bases and army garrisons at its imperial zenith in 1898. The Roman Empire at its height in 117 AD required 37 major bases to police its realm from Britannia to Egypt, from Hispania to Armenia.[87]

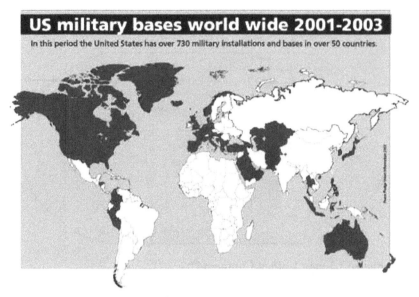

Figure 3.4 map of US bases[8]

Following the apparent success against the Taliban in 2001, in August 2002, Secretary of Defense Donald Rumsfeld unveiled his "1-4-2-1 defense strategy" to replace the Clinton era's plan for having a military capable of fighting two wars—in the Middle East and northeast Asia—simultaneously. Now, war planners would defend the US while "deterring aggression and coercion" in four "critical regions": Europe, Northeast Asia (South Korea and Japan), east Asia (the Taiwan Strait), and the Middle East. They would be able to "defeat aggression" in two of these regions simultaneously, and "win decisively" (in the sense of "regime change" and occupation) in one of those conflicts "at a time and place of our choosing".[89] Given the track record of the wars in Iraq and Afghanistan, one might be forgiven for taking these assertions with a grain of salt...

Rumsfeld's plan was to scale back the troop levels and rely increasingly on air power—a new, leaner military, possibly even cheaper. Whether the latter was ever really intended, the very opposite has occurred since. According to the Stockholm International Peace Research Institute, US military spending has almost doubled since 2001.

Still not satisfied with its present level of control of the planet, the Pentagon is now planning for future "sea-basing". Already 11 aircraft carriers circle the globe. The US Navy also patrols the Persian Gulf with missile-equipped warships. No longer just a fleet on the world's oceans, sea-bases will be "a hybrid system-of-systems consisting of operations,

Top 10 shares of world military expenditure 2010

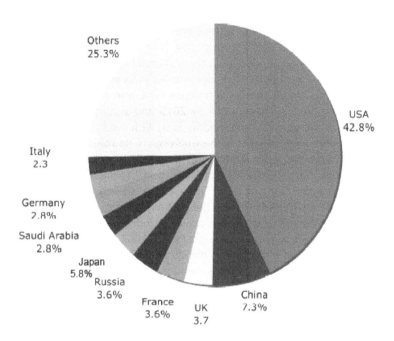

Figure 3.5[90]

ships, forces, offensive and defensive weapons, aircraft, communications and logistics". They "will help to assure access to areas where US military forces may be denied access to support land facilities". As a report by the US Defense Science Board points out: "Seabases are sovereign, not subject to alliance vagaries."[91]

There was a flurry of concern in the spring of 2010 when the Kyrgyz regime was overthrown and the new interim president Roza Okunbayeva called for closing the US air base at Manas. Riots ensued in Osh in the south as the country seemed to disintegrate. By September, she was being feted by Obama at the Millennium Goals Summit in New York and plans were being considered to open an additional US base in Osh itself. What role covert US actions may have played in this decision is impossible to prove by definition, but the rule of thumb is clear: once you accept a US base, it is very difficult to close it.

The decision by Bush II weeks after 9/11 to tear up the ABM treaty, the beginning of the Bush II Doctrine, retroactively made legal almost two decades of missile defense spending. Reagan had announced this policy in a speech in 1983 when he called for massive spending on what came to be called Star Wars (the blockbuster "Star Wars" had premiered in 1977), an impermeable anti-missile space shield, officially called the Strategic Defense Initiative. The Clinton administration gave it only modest support until the National Missile Defense Act of 1999 proposed an active missile defense "as soon as is technologically possible". The American missile defense system in eastern Europe is expected to be fully operational by 2015 and would be capable of covering all of Europe and the Middle East, with installations in Israel, Turkey and an Arab country in the Gulf region. Its role is purportedly to defend against a rogue nation's missile attack, thereby reducing the likelihood of such an attack. Its more likely role is to prevent retaliation, say, by Iran in the case of a US or Israeli attack, thereby increasing the likelihood of such an invasion on the part of US and/or Israel.

Domination of the entire planet includes outer space as well. The US Air Force Transformation Flight Plan of 2004 states: "Freedom of action in space is as important to the US as air power and sea power." Missile defense including military satellites is the final element in a first-strike global missile shield system. "It will probably soon be possible for the United States to destroy the long-range nuclear arsenals of Russia or China with a first strike."[92] Deploying short-, medium- and long-range interceptor missile batteries, mobile missile radar stations, long-range super-stealth nuclear bombers, surveillance satellites and weapons in space is "not designed to target non-existent intercontinental ballistic missile threats from Iran or Syria, or even from North Korea but to blackmail Russia and China and prepare the groundwork to 'win' in a first strike nuclear war."[93]

Computer or cyber warfare began as soon as computers became integral to industry. The most spectacular example of this was the CIA plan to sabotage the economy of the Soviet Union, which resulted in "the most monumental non-nuclear explosion and fire ever seen from space". The CIA covertly transferred computer technology containing malfunctions, including software, that later triggered a huge explosion in a Siberian natural gas pipeline in mid-1982, former air force secretary Thomas Reed revealed in his memoirs.[94] The US was trying to stop western Europe from importing Soviet natural gas. A KGB insider gained access to Russian purchase orders and the CIA slipped in the flawed software.

In time the Soviets came to understand that they had been stealing bogus technology, but now what were they to do? By implication, every cell of the Soviet leviathan might be infected. They had no way of knowing which equipment was sound, which was bogus. All was suspect, which was the intended endgame for the entire operation.[95]

In May 2010 Secretary of Defense Gates announced the activation of the world's first comprehensive multi-service Cyber Command (CYBERCOM). The pretext for cyber warfare development is to protect small countries, such as Estonia, which suffered such an attack in 2007 (attributed to Russia in revenge for the Estonians pulling down the WWII memorial to Russian troops in Estonia). China and Russia called this the start of another arms race.

The reality was hinted at by its director, Keith Alexander, who told Congress that in addition to the defense of computer systems and networks, "the cyber command would be prepared to wage offensive operations."[96] The cyber attack on Iran's Bushehr nuclear facilities in September 2010 was predicted in 2007 by Dennis Ross, special adviser for the Persian Gulf and southwest Asia to Secretary of State Hillary Clinton: such an attack would "prove very costly for the Iranians to overcome, and yet would be completely deniable."[97] This is part of a new, concerted cyberwar strategy by the US and Israel which involves planting viruses, Trojan Horses and secret codes in the energy, defense and transportation systems of hostile states. By planting these electronic "trapdoors", the US or Israel is capable of paralyzing its enemies in any war by attacking their infrastructure at sensitive points, possibly causing another Chernobyl.[98]

At the end of the Cold War, the world awaited a peace dividend, assuming that the US and the West would sharply cut military spending and increase aid, both to the newly independent countries and the third world. While official military expenditures declined from $427.7 billion (1989) to $307.8 billion (2001) they have since increased dramatically to $494.31 billion (2009) excluding the cost of Iraq and Afghanistan wars.[99]

The US is the main arms supplier to all sides in the Middle East with the exception of Iran and Syria. The parapolitical significance of the US being virtually the sole supplier of arms and military training to all the Middle East countries and increasingly in Central Asia is to tie those countries to US policy for the region.

This principle does not work, however, in the case of Israel, because the US has very little military presence there, Israel is itself a major producer of advanced weapons systems, both in cooperation with US companies and on its own, and Israel conducts espionage activities in the US to steal high tech weapon designs (see Chapter 4). Traditionally, the US has provided arms to both Israel and its enemies, on the understanding that Israel will get the superior weapons, and its enemies will get arms which they can use against each other but would not dare use against Israel.

Pakistan particularly has 'benefited' in terms of US military aid since 9/11. In the three years before 9/11, Pakistan received approximately $9 million in American military aid. In the three years after 9/11, this increased to $4.2 billion. By 2006 it was the top client for US arms producers.[100] Of course, this largesse comes at the price of national sovereignty.

Following 9/11, India too offered use of its territory to the US for bases in the war against terrorism. In 2005 Bush I announced a new Civil Nuclear Cooperation Agreement, forgiving India its refusal to sign the Non-Proliferation Treaty (NPT) and its multiple nuclear tests, clearly to pre-empt India from turning to Russia or China for nuclear cooperation. With China poised to replace the Soviet Union as the main US rival in Eurasia, containment means keeping India onside, a fine balancing act given the virtual state of war between India and Pakistan (they have fought 3 wars over Kashmir since independence), and US military aid to Pakistan. "Where Nixon had used China to balance the Soviet Union, Bush was using India to balance China."[101] Arms sales to India increased rapidly after 2001 and the US now vies with Israel for second place after Russia. The US wants to replace Russia as India's main arms supplier, further tightening an Asian NATO cordon around China. The case of India epitomizes the game strategy of GGIII well, where a weakened Russia is being pushed aside by the US and Israel, now competing between themselves for geopolitical influence.

The US has deep defense ties with both sides in other conflict areas: Armenia and Azerbaijan at war over Nagorno-Karabakh,[102] Greece and Turkey over Cyprus and the Aegean Sea, Croatia and Slovenia over the Adriatic coast. NATO and US command structures have provided the Pentagon with mechanisms for bilateral military ties with over 100 of the world's 192 nations. "By supplying arms to those nations and eliminating traditional rivals for that role, Washington is laying the groundwork for integrating most every country in the world into its military network."[103]

Concerning nuclear weapons, Gorbachev's offer to radically slash nuclear arsenals during his negotiations with Reagan in the GGII endgame—the Soviet chess king trying to negotiate a draw—was a valiant bid to try to achieve a nuclear weapons-free world. His idea was that the leading nuclear powers would set an example which other countries would then willingly follow, thereby strengthening the NPT and preventing any other countries from pursuing nuclear weapons.

This strategy failed, since the US continued to increase its military spending and update its nuclear arsenal, forcing Russia to turn once again to nuclear weapons as the bedrock of its defense strategy. NATO supports the continued deployment of 200-400 US tactical nuclear weapons stored on air bases in Britain, Belgium, Germany, Italy, the Netherlands and Turkey, all but Britain being non-nuclear states—in violation of both the 1991 promise to Gorbachev of a nuclear-free Europe, and of the NPT. Russia now faces nuclear powers the US, Britain and France to the west, Pakistan and India to the south, and China to the east. The START treaty renewal in 2010, while reducing the number of remaining bombs, did not prevent further development of nuclear weapons and in fact confirmed that nuclear weapons would remain an important part of both the US and Russian arsenals. The MAD nuclear weapons strategy of GGII continues in GGIII, but with many players now, making the game all the more deadly.

Proxies

As Kissinger quipped to the Pike Committee in 1975: "Covert action should not be confused with missionary work."[104] The use of soft power at times is not enough. Proxy military forces have been a mainstay of US empire during both GGII&III. The covert use of proxies has been dubbed the Salvador Option, as paramilitary death squads were used against opponents of the Salvadoran regime to devastating effect in 1980–92.

With respect to Iraq, the US first supported the Baath Party in the 1960s as a proxy to eliminate Iraqi communists and later Saddam Hussein, supporting him again in 1980 in the Iraq-Iran war to weaken the Iranian Islamic regime. [105] The cynicism of this was captured in another Kissinger quip: "A pity they both can't lose."[106]

The Salvador Option was used following the US invasion of Iraq in 2003 with the enthusiastic support of US-installed prime minister, Ayad Allawi.[107] US Special Forces and Pentagon-hired mercenaries like Dyncorp helped form the sectarian militias that were used to terrorize and kill Iraqis and to provoke civil war. The purpose is to target the civilian population and turn them against the resistance, a policy of state terrorism and collective punishment. US officials experienced in the dirty wars in Central America and Colombia (including John Negroponte, ambassador to Honduras 1981–85, James Steele, chief American military adviser in El Salvador 1984–86, and Steven Casteel, former Drug Enforcement Agency officer in Colombia who worked with paramilitaries) were sent to Iraq. They organized Special Police Commandos which incorporated death squads like the Badr Brigades with direct connections to the Iraqi Interior Ministry.

When extrajudicial killings and indiscriminate bombings peaked in 2006, this was blamed by Casteel on insurgents, and torture was blamed on rogue elements in the Interior Ministry. The impression created was of senseless violence initiated by the Iraqis themselves, but the "sectarian violence" that engulfed Iraq "was not an unintended consequence of the US invasion and occupation, but an integral part of it"[108] to target Iraqis who rejected the illegal invasion and occupation of their country.

Like the Kosovo Liberation Army in the Balkans, the Iranian dissident Mujahideen-e-Khalq (MeK) has operated on the Iran-Iraq border for decades with US backing, despite the fact that it too was on the official US list of terrorist organizations. The US claims it disarmed the terrorist bases in Iraq after the invasion in 2003 and there is a push by its supporters in Congress to remove MeK from the terrorist list. Their military arm continues to function and the al-Maliki government demanded their bases be closed, prompting the US to pressure Kurdish Iraq to let them set up a base there, out of reach of Baghdad.

The Iranian Sunni terrorist organization Jundullah operates in Baluchistan on both sides of the Pakistan-Iran border with the assistance of Anglo-American intelligence, according to Seymour Hersh.[109] In 2010, the Iranians, with the help of Pakistan, succeeded in capturing Jundullah leader Abdolmalek Rigi, who Iran's Intelligence Minister Heydar Moslehi claimed had been at a US base in Afghanistan 24 hours before his arrest. Jundullah is also suspected of links with al-Qaeda, which if true shows the US is still using Islamic terrorists both as enemy and ally, as it did (and quite possibly continues to do) in Afghanistan.

Friend Turkey is kept in line by covert US (and Israeli) support of Kurdish secessionists, as are rivals China and Russia by support for Chechen and Uighur separatists. If a country shows too much independence, it may find that terrorism suddenly erupts inside its borders, attributed to separatists, be they Kurd, Chechen, Uighur or others.[110] Veiled in secrecy, the funding of terrorists occasionally comes to light, as in the case of the overthrow of Mossadegh in 1953 or the BCCI and Iran-Contra scandals in the 1980s but even then only minor figures involved are held accountable. Reagan 'forgot' and was exonerated of any guilt in Iran-Contra. It has virtually become a law of US politics that no president will suffer impeachment for such illegal acts.

This is not to denigrate the struggles of oppressed minorities like the Kurds, Chechens or Uighurs who pursue their own liberation, but to note how all such struggles are monitored and manipulated according to the needs of empire. Neither Russia nor China can hope to match the US in this strategy. What is different about GGIII is that now Israel is using this and other imperial strategies to meet its own needs in countries both near and far afield.

The use of Islamic fighters as proxies (even as it is officially fighting them as "terrorists") is the centerpiece of US strategy in the GGII endgame. And the Kosovo Liberation Army, bin Laden, MeK, Jundullah, the Chechens and other documented cases are not the only current Islamists accused of being proxies for the US. The Pakistani Taliban leader Mehsud's ex-comrade, Qari Zainuddin, critical of Mehsud's policy of blowing up mosques and schools, accused Mehsud of being an American and Mossad agent. "These people are working against Islam," he said in July 2009, shortly before Mehsud was assassinated. There is little hope that the US has learned its lesson, as this policy dates from the GGI rivalry between Ibn Saud and the Hashemites over control of Mecca.

Soft Power
Culture, aid, NGOs
The use of soft power in GGI was mostly ad hoc. Then, imperial culture was exported both directly with the colons, colonial administrators and missionaries, and indirectly by bringing colonial subjects to the center for education, who on return would import the center's culture. The new comprador colonial elite became living proof of the superiority of the center.

GGII was a more complex period, as cadres for the neocolonies were also trained in the socialist bloc, with the emphasis on the superiority of socialism over capitalism. In the use of soft power by both empire and anti-empire, for the Middle East, this meant a culture of secularism, as the resilience of Islam precluded widespread conversion to Christianity for those trained in the West, and those trained in the socialist bloc were not encouraged to forge an Islamic socialism. Egypt's 1952 revolution under Nasser proceeded on a socialist path, though one with the clear stamp of Nasserism, which emphasized Arab nationalism. Similarly, Saddam Hussein's program in Iraq. Both Gamal Abdel-Nasser and Saddam Hussein alternately used and suppressed the communists. Hussein suppressed the remnants of the communists in 1978.

The CIA had an extensive soft power program of anticommunism, directed more towards US and European intellectuals and workers, but also to eradicate communists in the Middle East, providing intelligence even to anti-imperialists such as Nasser and Saddam Hussein.

The use of soft power was much bolder and sophisticated in GGIII. USAID became the official conduit for US development aid, tied to the political desirability of the regime which received it. Its 2009 budget was $40 billion. Just how politicized it was is shown by the top USAID recipients in 2004: Iraq, Israel, Egypt, Afghanistan, Colombia, Jordan and

Pakistan. While some aid has helped improve standards of living, it is used in the first place to promote the specific imperial agenda, including the promotion of US exports. In the case of Afghanistan during the US-sponsored war to defeat the Soviet Union,

> The United States spent millions of dollars to supply Afghan schoolchildren with textbooks filled with violent images and militant Islamic teachings....the primers, which were filled with talk of jihad and featured drawings of guns, bullets, soldiers and mines, have served since then as the Afghan school system's core curriculum. Even the Taliban used the American-produced books... The textbooks were developed in the early 1980s under an AID grant to the University of Nebraska and its Center for Afghanistan Studies. The agency spent $51 million on the university's education programs in Afghanistan from 1984 to 1994.[111]

The US was able to make much greater, and by now more systematic use of soft power in consolidating US empire from the 1980s on in both eastern Europe and the Soviet Union (see the war in Yugoslavia, above). NGOs—private organizations involved in charitable and humanitarian work—date from GGI, though the term came into use only in 1945, and their numbers and activities increased dramatically by the end of GGII.

Though a contradiction in terms, US government-sponsored NGOs have proliferated since GGII, primarily in democracy promotion. The most important ones for the US empire include the National Endowment for Democracy (NED, founded in 1983), its related International Republican Institute, National Democratic Institute for International Affairs, and the union affiliate American Center for International Labor Solidarity which provide funds at arms length to local groups. The other major ones are Freedom House (founded in 1941) and the US Institute for Peace (USIP, founded in 1984). All are funded directly or indirectly by Congress. According to Allen Weinstein, one of the founders of NED, "A lot of what we do today was done covertly 25 years ago by the CIA."[112] It was set up by Reagan, and its initial budget of $50 million (funded primarily by Congress and the AFL-CIO Free Trade Union Institute) reached $135.5 million by 2009 (see wars in Yugoslavia and Iraq, above).

The public aim of US Institute for Peace (USIP) is "to promote international peace and the resolution of conflicts among the nations and peoples of the world, without recourse to violence". Reagan was not enthusiastic when pushed by Congress to approve it, and warned its first board of directors in 1986, "In the real world, 'peace through strength' must be our motto." After the 1995 Dayton Accords were signed, "We took the Balkans apart and put it on the operating table, looked at it from every possible dimension, and came up with a state-of-the-art analysis on what had happened and what it would take to stitch a country back together again [sic]," said USIP chairman, 1992–94, Chester Crocker. USIP is active in Iraq now where they train local Iraqis as facilitators, assemble American conflict resolution teams, and brief Prime Minister Nouri al-Maliki. "The institute operates in the increasingly hazy no man's land between war and peace that defines twenty-first century conflicts."[113]

The other main NGO active in the ex-socialist bloc from 1984 on was George Soros's Open Society Institute (OSI), established in 1993 to encompass foundations he set up in eastern Europe to undermine communism. Though not funded by the US government, multi-billionaire Soros promotes electoral democracy and "open societies", human rights, and economic, legal, and social reform in more than 60 countries.

The real goal of the NED, USIP, OSI, Freedom House and other such democracy-promoting NGOs is indeed to bring US-style democracy to the world, if democracy is defined as polyarchy, where a small group rules "on behalf of capital, and participation in decision-making by the majority is confined to choosing between competing elites in tightly controlled electoral processes."[114]

In the Middle East, NED's activities amount to "the manipulation of liberal democratic mechanisms to create pluralistic competition that would destroy Arab unity."[115] Under their tutelage and without outside observers, the US neocon favourite Allawi won a plurality of the votes in Iraq's national elections in 2010. This manipulation of electoral politics, honed to perfection in the US over two centuries, is the basis of US soft power around the world, with NED the main vehicle.

There are NGOs and NGOs. In GGII, the best of the more well-known ones, for example Oxfam, have maintained a critical distance from imperial designs and helped empower local groups in the periphery. But increasingly in GGIII, many NGOs do not or no longer serve a genuinely supportive role to help third world locals resist the negative effects of the market and empire, but are now mobilized "to mitigate poverty and restructure from below" in a participatory partnership with local groups, acting to undermine revolutionary opposition.[116]

Oxfam and other leading, *bona fide* nongovernmental organizations, including Amnesty International, Human Rights Watch, *Medecins sans Frontieres*, Reporters without Borders, Inter Press Service, and the World Social Forum, all work through mainstream organizations such as the UN and OECD and are funded to varying extents by western government aid agencies and in many cases the World Bank, and thousands of corporate and private foundations such as the Ford, Rockefeller or Soros foundations. They claim to be nonpartisan. But they still recruit pro-western locals to study in, say London or Washington, just as did colonial administrators in GGI and neocolonial aid adiministrators in GGII.[117] This includes even 'alternative' news media on the internet. The media monitor Reporters without Borders admitted to receiving funding from NED and has been accused of having CIA links.

They all function to define the limits of dissent, target the empire's latest enemy, Iran and Islam, and provide only mild criticism of Israel. While most NGOs start out with good intentions, it only makes sense that any organization that threatens to impinge on the game players will be taken note of and if seen as hostile, either be infiltrated and controlled, or failing that, destroyed.[118]

Color revolutions
Given the neocolonial restrictions imposed in GGII, the preferred strategy to tie nations to the imperial agenda has involved promotion of western concepts of electoral democracy and human rights. The goal is to weaken central governments in newly independent states through US government financed NGOs which then act as watchdogs to keep these states on the 'straight and narrow', cementing these countries as postmodern states within the imperial order.

In GGIII, this process led to a remarkable series of coups in the ex-Soviet Union, modeled on the 2000 coup against Milosevic in Serbia, where NED, OSI and other western NGOs funded and organized local dissidents, notably *Otpor*, which disrupted a planned election run-off between Milosevic and Vojislav Kostunica, creating chaos in which Milosevic resigned to prevent further bloodshed.[119]

Georgia had its Rose Revolution replacing Eduard Sheverdnadze with Mikheil Saakashvili in 2003, Ukraine its Orange Revolution replacing Viktor Yanukovich with Viktor Yushchenko in 2004, and Kyrgyzstan its tulip revolution replacing Askar Akayev with Kurmanbek Bakiyev. Bush II hailed the overthrow of regimes with their origins in the dying days of the Soviet Union as inspired by the US during his visit to Tbilisi in 2005: "Americans respect your courageous choice for liberty, and as you build a free and democratic Georgia the American people will stand with you."[120]

The regime change in Georgia was concurrent with the construction of the Baku–Tbilisi–Ceyhan oil pipeline from Azerbaijan on the Caspian Sea to Turkey started in 2002 and completed in 2005, allowing Azerbaijan to export its oil without passing through Russia. The political

Figure 3.6[121] **Baku-Tbilisi-Ceyhan oil pipeline**

'revolution' in Georgia, really a coup by the losers in elections that year, who stormed the unguarded parliament buildings in the capital, merely reflected the new economic forces at work, abetted by the anti-Russian sentiment of the post-Soviet ruling elite (Saakashvili studied at Columbia and George Washington Universities). Saakashvili's rule has been anything but democratic and, despite launching a disastrous war against Russia in 2008, he remains entrenched in power in 2011.

The Ukrainian 'revolution' was accompanied by a concerted western media campaign, with a hysterical opposition leader claiming he was poisoned by the winner and calling on his followers to strike, forcing an unconstitutional re-election, all openly orchestrated and financed by NED and OSI. As in Serbia, Yanukovich agreed to the demand for new elections to avoid bloodshed. The pro-West Yushchenko won, but his rule plunged Ukraine into economic chaos and further exacerbated the ethnic divisions with the country.

Kyrgyzstan's coup was openly coordinated via the US embassy, overthrowing probably the most democratic of the post-Soviet leaders, with tragic consequences as the new leader Bakiyev quickly moved to plunder the treasury and create a virtual khanate with his clan in charge, leading to yet another coup in 2010, hundreds of deaths and the image of Kyrgyzstan as a failed state. A similar attempt at regime change in Uzbekistan failed due to a particularly brutal dictator heading a police state, who quickly arrested all opposition.

In Lebanon, the assassination of the former Lebanese prime minister Rafik Hariri in 2005 precipitated what has been called the

Cedar Revolution which resulted in the withdrawal of Syrian troops but otherwise left the political order untouched as evidence implicating Syria was discredited and Hezbollah leader Sheikh Hassan Nasrallah revealed evidence pointing to Israel as being behind the assassination.[122]

The waning of the neocons by 2006, with the Democrats taking control of the Congress and Senate and the subsequent election of Obama in 2008 buttressed the 'liberal' imperial strategy, which theoretically should mean less direct interference in other countries' politics, but the attempt to shape further color revolutions continues. In 2009, despite winning 49 per cent of the popular vote, the Communist Party in Moldova was beset by opposition insurrection, with demonstrations in the capital, now facilitated by westernized youth using Twitter and mobile phones, and the opposition parties forced a re-election. Strong resistance by supporters of the communists prevented a replay of the earlier coups, much as was the case in Lebanon, but the government remains unstable. The same year the western-backed Green Revolution in Iran, relying on similar use of demonstrations protesting presidential election results, failed, though it rattled the Iranian government. The greatest fear of the Islamic Republic of Iran is not direct invasion by the US/Israel but "a bloodless toppling of the regime as the result of reform and closer ties to the West".[123] An Iranian cartoon video casts Soros as the "Jewish tycoon and the mastermind of ultra-modern colonialism".[124]

2010–11 witnessed a surge of spontaneous revolutionary fervor in the Arab world which owes much to western influence, in particular pro-democracy NGO activity.[125] Tunisia's popular uprising, sparked by the self-immolation of Mohamed Bouazizi on 17 December 2010, and which overthrew the government on 15 January 2011, has even been dubbed the Jasmine revolution. However, this, Egypt's uprising[126], and subsequent protests in Yemen and Jordan came as an unwelcome surprise to western governments and have proved not as open to manipulation, being on the contrary anti-western in orientation, despite their pedigree as westernized, computer-savvy middle class youth movements. This development has transformed GGIII as it reverberates throughout the Muslim world and is dealt with Chapter 5.

These color revolutions have been inspired and advised by Gene Sharp and his Albert Einstein Institute (AEI, 1983) which promotes nonviolent tactics to overthrow autocratic governments. While by no means a direct tool of NED, AEI has received NED grants and works with groups such as *Movements.org*, which was co-founded by Jared Cohen (a CFR member, director of Google Ideas, and former State Department official under both Condoleezza Rice and Hillary Clinton), and PR executives Jason Liebman and Roman Sunder, at the first annual Alliance of Youth Movements (AYM) conference in New York in December 2008. AYM is sponsored by the United States Department of State, partnered with Facebook, Howcast, MTV, Google, YouTube, AT&T, JetBlue, Gen-Next, Access 360 Media, and Columbia Law School, in order "to launch a global network and empower young people mobilizing against violence and oppression".[127] Given this powerful corporate and US government involvement, there can be no doubt that however well-intentioned, such 'nongovernmental' organizations coordinate their activities with, or at the very least, act as willing handmaidens to the postmodern imperial project.

Co-opting regimes

The color revolutions were an innovation on the older policy of co-opting regimes. With respect to the Middle East, this has been the traditional policy from GGI&II used most successfully in the case of Saudi Arabia, where the British established good relations with both royal family-pretenders, descendants of whom rule there and in Jordan to this day, and in Egypt, where the monarchy was co-opted in the service of Britain with only a modest military presence necessary to keep control.

Today, Egypt, through dependence on the US for aid and military technology, and incorporation into the western financial and economic system following Sadat's *infitah* (opening) policy after the 1973 war and 1979 peace treaty with Israel, is irrevocably tied to US Middle East policy under a pseudo-democracy. As *de facto* leader of the Arab world, especially after the destruction of Iraq, it has acted as a reliable supporter of the US-Israeli Middle East order.[128] Just how much room for maneuver there is for Egypt in its post-revolutionary period has yet to be seen.[129]

Turkey was encouraged by the US to move into ex-Soviet Central Asia as it opened up after the collapse of the SU, with the goal of co-opting the Turkic-speaking 'stans', bringing them into the western fold by appealing to their Turkic heritage. This renewed the GGII role that the new post-WWI Turkey briefly played when Enver Pasha pursued a policy of pan-Turkic unity. Cultural and economic ties are developing with Turkey, though current efforts to mould the 'stans' into a political union tied to Turkey have had as little success as Enver Pasha's quixotic mission in the 1920s. Furthermore, Turkey is becoming a player in its own right, increasingly critical of the US and Israel.

Anti-piracy moves

The increase in incidents of piracy off the coast of Somalia since 2001 and concern over WMD smuggling prompted then-US Undersecretary of State for Arms Control and International Security John Bolton to launch the Proliferation Security Initiative (PSI) in 2003 as "a global effort that aims to stop trafficking of weapons of mass destruction, their delivery systems, and related materials to and from states and non-state actors". It allows the US to board ships on the open seas, contrary to marine law. US pressure has resulted in over 90 of the world's 148 coastal nations joining. Iran, North Korea, China, Indonesia and Malaysia have refused, viewing PSI as a vehicle for US global surveillance, as it operates without a UN mandate. In the context of UN sanctions against Iran, it encourages the US to board Iranian vessels purportedly to search for WMDs.

Drug trade
The extent to which the US government and in particular the CIA are actively involved in drug smuggling as part of its arsenal of parapolitics is, like other covert activities, the subject of speculation, backed by considerable circumstantial evidence.[130] In the case of the Iran-Contra scandal, CIA involvement in drug smuggling was revealed in US Department of Justice hearings, though this did not lead to any serious investigation.[131]

In Afghanistan and Pakistan, prior to the Soviet-Afghan war, opium production was directed to small regional markets. There was no local production of heroin.[132] No heroin came to the US from Afghanistan but already by 1980 it accounted for 60 per cent of supplies.[133] Within two years of the CIA operation in Afghanistan, "the Pakistan-Afghanistan borderlands became the world's top heroin producer."[134]

> Under CIA and ISI protection, Afghan resistance opened heroin labs on the Afghan and Pakistani border. Among the leading heroin manufacturers were Gulbuddin Hekmatyar, an Afghan leader who received about half of the covert arms that the CIA shipped to Pakistan. In 1995 the former CIA Director of this Afghan operation, Charles Cogan, admitted sacrificing the drug war to fight the Cold War. 'Our main mission was to do as much damage to the Soviets. There was fallout in terms of drugs, yes, but the main objective was accomplished. The Soviets left Afghanistan.'[135]

The same scenario was repeated with the US invasion of 2001. Though not proof of direct US government involvement in the drug trade, in the immediate wake of the US-led invasion, pressured by the CIA, the Bush administration ordered that the opium harvest not be destroyed on the pretext that this would undermine the military government of

Pervez Musharraf. Said a frustrated US official: "If they [the CIA] are in fact opposing the destruction of the Afghan opium trade, it'll only serve to perpetuate the belief that the CIA is an agency devoid of morals; off on their own program rather than that of our constitutionally elected government."[136] Since 2001, opium production has increased 33 fold from 185 tons in 2001 to 6100 tons in 2006. In 2007, Afghanistan provided approximately 93 per cent of the global supply of heroin, reaching the West via Central Asia and Pakistan.[137] Afghan President Hamid Karzai's brother, Ahmed Wali Karzai, chairman of the Kandahar provincial council, is involved in the heroin trade.

This is the result of conscious US policy, which has condoned the illegal drug trade conducted by its Afghan proxies and targeted only the Taliban's share, with is less than 10 per cent of the total. According to the Center on International Cooperation, "If counternarcotics policies are effectively targeted at pro-insurgency traffickers, they may be able to reduce insurgency *by enabling pro-government traffickers and corrupt officials to enjoy a monopoly.*" [emphasis added] Holbrooke said in 2009, "The poppy farmer is not our enemy. The Taliban are."[138] This was precisely the US policy in Vietnam. There, as in Afghanistan today, US troops' easy access to the US comprador ally's semi-legal heroin is producing a steady stream of army veteran returning as heroin addicts.

Engdahl even argues the US military is in Afghanistan first to restore and control the world's largest supply of opium for the world heroin markets and to use the drugs as a geopolitical weapon against opponents, especially Russia, similar to the GGI Opium Wars in China by Britain and the GGII cocaine wars in Colombia and Bolivia.

According to United Nations Office on Drugs and Crime Executive Director Antonio Maria Costa, even Wall Street has become 'addicted' to the Afghan drug trade: "Drug money is currently the only liquid investment capital. In the second half of 2008, liquidity was the banking system's main problem and hence liquid capital became an important factor." Costa said there were "signs that some banks were rescued in that way", referring to drug money laundering.[139]

Domestic repression
The Federal Emergency Management Agency (FEMA) was set up in 1979 by Carter (Presidential Review Memorandum PRM 32), with the mandate to maintain "the continuity of government" (COG) during a national security emergency. PRM 32 bypassed the US Constitution, awarding power to unelected officials at the National Security Council (NSC) to direct government operations by emergency decree. The leading theoreticians behind the creation of FEMA were Carter's NSC consultant

Samuel ("clash of civilizations") Huntington and Carter's national security adviser, Zbigniew Brzezinski. Carter and Huntington both belonged to Brzezinski's Trilateral Commission and the CFR. By placing FEMA under the NSC's control, Huntington, Brzezinski, et al effectively turned the NSC into a shadow technocratic dictatorship, waiting for a real or manufactured crisis to seize control of the country.

In GGIII, COG was activated during 9/11, a shadow government was put into place, and the Patriot Act was passed within a few weeks, extending FBI and executive powers. FEMA was merged into the Department of Homeland Security in 2003. There are 8,000 names on the US No Fly List (including Nelson Mandela until 2008),[140] and invasive, humiliating body searches introduced as standard airport security. The police have been militarized and US government spying has now become a regular part of American life, with the possibility of extensive files being kept on all citizens and the monitoring of their every conversation and internet transaction. Instead of Bush I's benign postmodern imperialism, Bush II introduced an imperialism based on terror abroad and fear, persecution and surveillance at home.

Control of world resources

GGIII began with a blaze of glory. The ex-socialist bloc, won over by soft power, at first basked in a *faux* sense of freedom after the plodding years of "real existing socialism", eagerly opening up to the neocolonization wave from the West. Industry was privatized, much of it to western capital, banks moved in—and capital (surplus value) moved out. This period 1991–2000 will be remembered in the West as a brief period of relative prosperity, free of the worries, however false, of MAD nuclear war and communist invasion, with a fall in military spending, and an investment bonanza for capitalists, who bought up newly privatized industry and were able to employ cheap, educated labor now flooding western Europe and North America, re-enacting the surplus flows from the periphery to center identified by Hobson and Lenin.

It was a tragic period for the vast majority of those 'freed', especially Russians and Yugoslavs, confirmed by recent opinion polls throughout the ex-socialist bloc that show 20 years later a majority of people pine to return to their once-despised socialism.[141] It was also a period of increasing poverty in the periphery, according to the UN Conference on Trade and Development 2010 report, with the number of very poor countries and the number of people living in extreme poverty having doubled since 1980, confirming the zero-sum nature of imperialism after the defeat of the GGII communist enemy, which had provided at least some incentive for development in the periphery, if only to stave off revolution.

The hard power wars in Afghanistan, Iraq and Israel to further colonize the Middle East and Central Asia also began with a sense of insuperable imperial power—"shock and awe". But both the soft power neocolonization and hard power colonization of GGIII have bogged down. Neither Afghanistan nor Iraq are stable states for business and the wars have accelerated the decline of the US economy. The various soft power color revolutions sputtered or collapsed.

The West fell into depression after 2008, and unemployment, poverty and skewed distribution of wealth have created a sense of disillusionment in the West rivaling that in the ex-socialist bloc.[142] Only the US dollar, now free of any gold-based restrictions, keeps the flow of surplus from periphery.

Appendix: Critique of 'New NATO' literature

In 2009, NATO celebrated its 60th anniversary; its new larger HQs in Brussels will open in 2015. The conventional wisdom now is that NATO will endure indefinitely. As NATO changed from Cold War defense pact to something much more ambitious, mainstream writers provided various rationales.

Because it is composed of "likeminded liberal democracies with shared interests" (Thies, 2009) and is "a community of values" (Sloan, 2010) it will endure, and expansion is justified as "a tool for democracy promotion" (Moore, 2007), the building of liberal democracy in the former communist countries, and crisis management in Europe and the world (Kaplan, 2004), responding to "new" threats of terrorism and proliferating weapons of mass destruction (Shalikashvili et al, 2002). It is an instrument of collective security with new "cooperative" security institutions, including the Partnership for Peace and the special consultative forums with Russia and Ukraine, for crisis management and peacekeeping operations beyond NATO territory. (Yost, 1999) Strengthening existing networks and developing new ones "will create a genuine global rule of law without centralized global institutions." (Slaughter, 2005)

This acceptance of the transformation of NATO from a "temporary Cold War creation to fight the Soviet Union to a strategic partnership" which "transcended the common or any other specific threat—based on common values and interests"[143] was far from certain when the Soviet Union collapsed. People just assumed NATO would disband along with the Warsaw Pact. French president François Mitterand coined the slogan "US out and Russia in", meaning, of course, Europe. Czech Foreign Minister Jiri Dienstbier in 1990 proposed replacing NATO and the Warsaw Pact with the OSCE European Security Commission but clearly the new Czech leaders were given a talking-to and in 1991 a Czech Foreign Ministry official reversed Mitterand's call: "We wanted it the other way around."[144]

Asmus, a Cold War Hungarian dissident now at the German Marshall Fund of the United States, and a so-called 'liberal' hawk ('liberal' on domestic policy and hawkish on foreign policy), was a key player under Clinton to end talk of shutting NATO down, and instead sought to expand it as quickly as possible. He set out the new program in the CFR's *Foreign Affairs*,[145] portraying the new member-hopefuls as a pro-US political elite eager and willing to do whatever the US wants, and exhorting France to "abandon its exaggerated fear of American hegemony". He predicted that future massacres such as occurred in Bosnia will be prevented by a rapid reaction force. He admits that Yeltsin was conned into agreeing on the new NATO expansion plans regarding Poland after an evening of vodka with Lech Walesa in 1993 and when Havel asked for the same deal for Czechoslovakia a few days later, Yeltsin's advisers forced him not to repeat the giveaway publicly.

There was also a split in the US establishment over expanding NATO. Unlike the Euro-split, which was really a disagreement over US world hegemony, the US debate was, on the contrary, whether being saddled with a string of poor, unprepared, untried statelets would advance or hinder this hegemony, making NATO a confused, ungovernable, fractious debating forum (like the expanded EU), or a functional alliance, bringing the new entries up to western military standards quickly and cementing them in the western alliance of nations.

Democrat defense doyen Sam Nunn was against expansion: yes, defend eastern Europe against Russia but Russia would see expansion as aimed at it. That Yelstin did not represent Russian sentiment was clear from the strong opposition in the Duma. Realists like Nunn realized that Russia would not submit and that enlargement was very expensive, that expansion was probably not really useful to US imperialism, and control of nuclear weapons was a more important objective and one that would not antagonize Russia.[146]

Republicans and 'liberal' hawk Democrats like Asmus were generally in favor of expansion,[147] and approved of the NATO bombing of the Serbian Republic of Bosnia in 1995. The slogan for the expansionist hawks popularized by Republican Senator Lugar was: "Out of the area or out of business."[148]

Russian opposition to expansion increased when Yevgeny Primakov became Yeltsin's foreign minister in 1996, finally settling on a NATO-Russia consultative committee and a Russian ambassador to NATO.[149]

This transformation of NATO in the 1990s cemented the GGIII team as a US-Euro-Israeli alliance (Israel is now in the largely European OECD and has special status both within the EU and NATO). The EU was transformed as well into a looser and hence weaker union of postmodern states, all the more easily dominated by the US politically, suiting Asmus as "America's geopolitical base in a new strategic partnership."[150] Among *post*modern states, the use of force is now unthinkable, but it is fine when dealing with *pre*modern states.

This postmodern imperialism on the surface is the voluntary, multilateral global economy, with the IMF, the World Bank, the WTO etc. The postmodern EU offers a vision of cooperative empire: "The age-old laws of international relations have been repealed. Europeans have stepped out of the Hobbesian world of anarchy into the Kantian world of perpetual peace."[151]

But this ignores US control of NATO and—so far—the EU as instruments of US imperialism, ignores the many reasons for the premodern failed states. It ignores the fact that the US and Israel remain as unapologetic *modern* nation states—foxes in the chicken coop, the elephants in the poli-sci lecture room, insistently sovereign and unilateral. Underlying this elegant reinterpretation of classical imperialism is an even more brutal, deadly politics. The transformation of countries, be it to post- or premodern status, is really a form of castration, of their subordination to the US agenda. The US, by invading the remains of Yugoslavia, Iraq and Afghanistan, and by pressuring and subverting Iran, Syria and others, is in reality trying to reduce—to carve up—these countries into similarly harmless but crippled third world versions of the more fortunate postmoderns. Israel has been hard at work trying to do this to the remains of Palestine and its neighbors. The US and Israel have parallel but increasingly separate agendas to transform the world along these lines, as argued in Chapters 4–5.

Almost nowhere in the mainstream literature is the question raised of whether NATO should have been dissolved with the dissolution of the Warsaw Pact, clearly the intent of Gorbachev, western non-hawks and ordinary citizens everywhere. One prominent mainstream US voice has been William Pfaff, who complained that "large and firmly implanted bureaucratic organizations are almost impossible to kill, even when they have no reason to continue to exist, as is the case of NATO since the Soviet Union, communism, and the Warsaw Pact all collapsed."[152] Apart from the huge and useless expense of maintaining it,[153] it is nonsensical for a military alliance to pretend to be a democracy-promotion vehicle. Worse, its continued existence and expansion has led to a new arms race and Cold War with Russia.[154] Its only justification—its real intent—is as a means to ensure uninterrupted US world hegemony.

ENDNOTES

1. Quoted in Engdahl, *A Century of War: Anglo-American Oil Politics and the New World Order*, revised ed., London: Pluto, [1992] 2004, 155.

2. Televised speech by Bush I on 16 January 1991 at the start of the Gulf war, available at <http://www.historyplace.com/speeches/bush-war.htm>.

3. Brzezinski, tongue-in-cheek, refers to the first Bush president, George Herbert Walker Bush, as Global Leader I, Bill Clinton as Global Leader II and the second Bush president George Walker Bush as Global Leader III. "Brzezinski Grades Presidents, US Foreign Policy", *www.npr.org*, 12 March 2007. He refers to Bush I and Bush II in *Second Chance: Three Presidents and the Crisis of American Superpower*, New York: Basic Books, 2007. In this spirit of US Caesarism, and for simplicity, I will refer to Bush senior as Bush I and Bush junior as Bush II.

4. Robert Cooper coined the term as a "new kind of imperialism, one acceptable to a world of human rights and cosmopolitan values ... which, like all imperialism, aims to bring order and organisation but which rests today on the voluntary principle". Periphery states must accept the international economic order and "open themselves up to the interference of international organisations and foreign states". Cooper refers to the EU as a "cooperative empire". Robert Cooper, "Why we still need empires", *http://observer.guardian.co.uk*, 7 April 2002.

5. Bernard Lewis claims to have coined the first term in 1957, later popularized by Samuel Huntingdon in his bestseller in 1996. Lewis also claims to have coined the latter in 1990.

6. Dick Cheney, "Defense Strategy for the 1990s: The Regional Defense Strategy", January 1993, 8.

7. Dennis Bernstein and Jeffrey Blankfort, "AIPAC's Lobbying", *www.monabaker. com*, January 2005.

8. It functioned from September 2002 to June 2003 to plan the invasion of Iraq. One of Feith's policy analysts, Larry Franklin, was later convicted of espionage, see below.

9. James Petras, "Bended Knees: Zionist Power in American Politics", *James Petras website*, 20 December 2009, 12, 14.

10. PNAC, "Rebuilding America's Defenses", 2000, i.

11. Ibid., 60.

12. Ibid., 14.

13. US Department of Defense, *Joint Vision 2020*, 2000.

14. John Gray, *Black Mass: Apolcapytic Religion and the Death of Utopia*, New York: Farrar, Straus & Giroux, 2007, 174.

15. James Ciment, "Life expectancy of Russian men falls to 58, *British Medical Journal*, August 21: 319*7208: 468.

16. David Corn, "Nixon on Tape: Reagan Was 'Shallow' and of 'Limited Mental Capacity'", *motherjones.com*, 15 November 2007.

17. The result was far from what Thatcher expected. Her ideal was a return to

Victorian liberal values but instead of the Victorian virtues of stability and thrift, the result was a largely proletarian society, characterized by shiftlessness ("flexible labor market"), low inflation and high personal debt, where the state now promotes only the interests of the corporate individuals, and suppresses truly "liberal" social forces defending people, like unions. It is better called market totalitarianism. Her insistence that "there is no such thing as society" culminating in the notorious poll tax tore asunder the social fabric. "As Marx perceived, the actual effect of the unfettered market is to overturn established social relationships and forms of ethical life—including those of bourgeois societies." Gray, *Black Mass: Apocalyptic Religion and the Death of Utopia*, 19.

18   Inaugural Address, 20 January 1981.

19   Anatol Lieven, "The push for war", *London Review of Books*, 3 October 2002.

20   "The real genesis of al-Qaeda violence has more to do with a western tradition of individual and pessimistic revolt for an elusive ideal world than with the Quranic conception of martyrdom." Olivier Roy *Globalised Islam: The Search for a New Ummah*, London: Hurst, 2004, 44. Sayyid Qtub, generally considered the intellectual founder of radical Islam "owes nothing to Islamic theology and a great deal to Lenin. His view of revolutionary violence as a purifying force has more in common with the Jacobins than it does with the twelfth-century Assassins." Gray, *Black Mass: Apocalyptic Religion and the Death of Utorpia*, 69–70.

21   Samuel Huntington, "The Clash of Civilizations?" *Foreign Affairs*, Summer 1993.

22   Stanley Kurtz, "The Future of 'History'", Hoover Institute, *Policy Review* Number 113, January 2002.

23   Samuel Huntington , "If Not Civilizations, What?" *Foreign Affairs*, Nov/Dec 1993.

24   Tariq Ali, *The Clash of Fundamentalisms: Crusades, Jihads and Modernity*, New York: Verso, 273.

25   In "The Clash of Ignorance", *The Nation*, October 2001, Edward Said criticizes Huntington's categorization of civilizations as fixed, ignoring the dynamic interdependence of cultures.

26   Apart from privileged colonies such as the US, Canada, Australia and South Africa which as settler colonies were allowed to move from periphery to an enlarged, more geographically dispersed center.

27   See endnote 52.

28   Stephen Sheehi, *Islamophobia: The Ideological Campaign Against Muslims*, Atlanta, USA: Clarity Press, 2011, Introduction.

29   Ali, *The Clash of Fundamentalisms*, 274–5.

30   American politicians, in the first place Bush II, continue to deny the concept of a US empire: "We have no desire to dominate, no ambitions of empire." State of the Union address, January 2004. The West largely accepts the ruse, as unipolar hegemony is now the norm and is thus invisible to most people.

31   Michael Ignatieff, "The American Empire: The Burden", *New York Times Magazine,* 5 January 2003.

32   Stephen Walt, "What Intervention in Libya Tells us About the Neocon-liberal Alliance", *www.informationclearinghouse*, 21 March 2001. This use of 'liberal' is not to be confused with liberalism as defined in Chapter 1.

33   Engdahl, *A Century of War*, 229–231.

34   Freeman and Kagarlitksy eds, *The Politics of Empire: Globalisation in Crisis*, London: Pluto Press, 6.

35   Michael Hudson, "Financial Bailout: America's Own Kleptocracy: The largest transformation of America's Financial System since the Great Depression", *www.*

michael-hudson.com, September 2008.

36   After the Republicans took control of Congress in 2010, Ron Paul became chair-
        man of the House Domestic Monetary Policy and Technology Subcommittee of
        the House Financial Services (also referred to as the House Banking Committee)
        and continued to push legislation reining in the central bank, despite resistance
        from his own Republican Party. Phil Mattingly and Robert Schmidt, "Monetary
        Policy: Fed Critic Ron Paul's Power Play", *www.businessweek.com,* 2 December
        2010.

37   "Some heavyweight hedge funds have launched large bearish bets against the
        euro in moves that are reminiscent of the trading action at the height of the US
        financial crisis. It is impossible to calculate the precise effect of the elite traders'
        bearish bets, but they have added to the selling pressure on the currency—and
        thus to the pressure on the European Union to stem the Greek debt crisis."
        Susan Pulliam, Kate Kelly, Carrick Mollenkamp, "Hedge Funds Try 'Career Trade'
        Against Euro", *Wall Street Journal,* 26 February 2010.

38   Greece's refusal to allow integration of Macedonia and Kosovo into the EU/ NATO
        structures for its own nationalist reasons is possibly why Greece was chosen for
        destabilization first.

39   Jean-Michel Vernochet, "Euro: The Worst Case Scenario", *www.voltairenet.org,*
        21 July 2010.

40   Jean-Michel Vernochet, "La guerre d'Iran aura-t-elle lieu?" *www.voltairenet.*
        org, 17 July 2010.

41   "OPEC warns oil prices could rocket to $500 per barrel", *www.post1.net,* 21
        August 2008.

42   Henry C K Liu, "The BIS vs national banks", *www.atimes.com,* 14 May 2011.

43   Available at: http://www.imf.org/external/np/ speeches/2010/051110.htm, 11
        May 2010.

44   China and Russia also talk about SDRs, but are more concerned about gaining
        a consensus that they will have direct input into determining an internationally
        acceptable alternative to the dollar.

45   "Bush tells group he sees a 'Third Awakening'", *Washington Post,* 13 September
        2006.

46   Quoted in Jonathan Cook, *Israel and the Clash of Civilisations,* London: Pluto,
        2008, 19. Libyan leader Muammar al-Gaddafi realized the new rules of the
        game could mean US invasion and quickly came to terms with the US. In 1991,
        Libyans had been indicted in connection with the 1988 PanAm (the so-called
        Lockerbie incident) and 1989 UTA air crashes and Abdelbaset Ali Mohmed al-
        Megrahi was convicted in 2001 on circumstantial evidence. Suspicions are that
        the PanAm crash was the work of Iran in retaliation for the US shooting down
        an Iranian civilian airliner the same year. Al-Gaddafi's support of Iran in the
        Iraq-Iran war could well have been a motive in framing a Libyan for the attacks.
        Nonetheless, to end the stand-off, Libya formally accepted "responsibility for
        the actions of its officials" in 2003 concerning the Lockerbie bombing, agreed to
        pay compensation of $2.7 billion to the victims, and threw wide open the doors
        to its weapons program in 2006, thereby ending its isolation. Bush I agreed to
        renew diplomatic relations with Libya in 2006 and UN sanctions were lifted in
        2008 – the only clear-cut neocon victory so far in GGIII, accomplished without
        firing a shot. The US even agreed to pay Libyan families $300 million for casual-
        ties suffered due to the 1986 US airstrikes.

47   Like the Reagan Doctrine coined by Krauthammer.

48   Speech to Congress on the National Security Strategy, September 2002.

49   Concerning Afghanistan, "Obama had to do this surge just to demonstrate, in effect, that it couldn't be done." General Douglas Lute cited in Robert Woodward, *Obama's Wars*, New York: Simon and Schuster, 2010.

50   "The United Nations and the war in Afghanistan", *www.humanist.org.nz,* 8 October 2001. <http://www.humanist.org.nz/docs/ UN_Afghanistan.html>.

51   Robert Fox, "Aid, Afghanistan and unhelpful hearsay", *Guardian*, 18 May 2010. <http://www.guardian.co.uk/commentisfree/2010/may/18/aid-in-afghanistan-military-thinking>.

52   By unleashing the free market from the 1980s on, inequality between the richest and poorest nations increased from 88:1 (1970) to 267:1 (2000). At the height of GGI it was just 22:1. The net effects of opening capital markets in the South to the North has been to drain them: in 1992 debt service payments by developing countries were $179b and financial inflows $128b. By 2000 the figures were $330b and $86b. Doing the opposite of the IMF advice—maintaining strict national capital controls—as did Malaysia in 1997 was the best solution, just as Russia's 1997 debt default was the only way out of its free market abyss, Argentina's refusal to pay its debt except from proceeds following recovery, and Iceland's refusal to bail out its banks. Statistics from Freeman and Kagarlitksy, eds, *The Politics of Empire: Globalisation in Crisis*, 9,11.

53   Rasmussen quote in "NATO chief wants to 'reach out' to China, India", *Deutsche Presse-Agentur*, 7 October 2010. <http://sify. com/news/ nato-chief- wants-to- reach-out- to-china- india-news- international- kkhwEeafgia. html>.

54   See Appendix: Critique of 'New NATO' literature.

55   Courtesy of <http://web.stratfor.com/images/europe/map/NATO_v2_800. jpg?fn=9117341898>.

56   Diana Johnstone, "NATO'S True Role in US Grand Strategy", *Counterpunch*, 18 November 2010.

57   Rasmussen quote in David Brunnstrom, "NATO says must stay capable of Afghan-size missions", *Reuters*, 7 October 2010.

58   David Graham, "German president defends military action", *Reuters*, 28 May 2010. Unlike Rasmussen, he was vilified for his honesty and forced to resign.

59   Fifteen ex-Soviet and seven Yugoslav republics.

60   Robert Cooper, "Why we still need empires", *Guardian*, 7 April 2002.

61   Daniel Martin, "Nation states are dead: EU chief says the belief that countries can stand alone is a 'lie and an illusion'", *Daily Mail*, 11 November 2010.

62   Eric Hobsbawm, "America's Imperial Delusion", *Guardian*, 15 June 2003.

63   Kofi Annan was UN general secretary 1997–2006. The term came into use during negotiations over Kosovo when Annan approved "collective international pressure ... on the parties to come to the negotiating table with the possible threat of use of force". "Annan: Unscom allegations have damaged UN", *BBC News*, 1 February 1999.

64   Freeman and Kagarlitksy eds, *The Politics of Empire: Globalisation in Crisis*, 27.

65   Engdahl, *A Century of Conflict,* 240.

66   Quoted in Richard Labeviere, *Dollars for Terror: The US and Islam*, New York: Algora Publishing, 1999, 5–6.

67   Quoted in George Monbiot, "Oil, Afghanistan and America's pipe dream", *www. dawn.com,* 25 October 2001.

68   Interview in Paris with Jean-Charles Brisard, co-author with Guillaume Dasquie, *Forbidden Truth: US-Taliban Secret Oil Diplomacy, Saudi Arabia and the Failed*

Search for bin Laden, New York: Nation Books, 2002. available at <http://www.serendipity.li/wot/bl_tft.htm>.

69   In 2003, Khalilzad became the US ambassador to Afghanistan and in 2005 ambassador to Iraq.

70   Reported on *BBC News*, 18 September 2001.

71   "Twenty years on, shockwaves of Kuwait invasion are still felt in Middle East" *www.dw-world.de*, 2 August 2010, <http://www.dw-world.de/dw/article/0,,5850911,00.html>.

72   In a "60 Minutes" interview 11 January 2004.

73   Available at <http://www.americanrhetoric.com/ speeches/stateof the union2004.htm>.

74   Gray, *Black Mass: Apocalyptic Religion and the Death of Utopia,* 153.

75   Ibid., 154.

76   This was confirmed during Egypt's revolution in January 2011, when both the US and Israel publically supported Hosni Mubarak until the last moment.

77   George Wright, "Wolfowitz: Iraq war was about oil" *Guardian*, 4 June 2003, <www.iraqwararchive.org/data/jun04/UK/guardian03.pdf>.

78   The original codename for the invasion was Operation Iraqi Liberation or OIL, later changed to Operation Iraqi Freedom.

79   Krassimir Petrov, "The Proposed Iranian Oil Bourse", *Christmartenson.com*, 29 October 2008.

80   Ari Shavit, "White Man's Burden", *Haaretz*, 3 April 2003.

81   The invasion was launched at the start of Purim, the Jewish festival celebrating the pre-emptive slaughter of the Persians in Babylonia/ Baghdad.

82   Ralph Peters, "Blood borders: How a better Middle East would look", *Armed Forces Journal,* June 2006. Bernard Lewis proposed a similar readjustment of borders in "Crescent of Crisis", *Time*, January 1979. See Andrew Gavin Marshall, "Creating an 'Arc of Crisis': The Destabilization of the Middle East and Central Asia", *www.globalresearch.ca*, 7 December 2008.

83   Peters, Ralph, "Blood borders: How a better Middle East would look". <http://web.archive.org/web/20061117135836/www.armedforcesjournal.com/xml/2006/06/images/afj.peters_map_before.JPG>, <http://web.archive.org/web/20061117135843/www.armedforcesjournal.com/xml/2006/06/images/afj.peters_map_after.JPG> .

84   *Coping with Crumbling States: A Western and Israeli Balance of Power Strategy for the Levant,* Institute for Advanced Strategic and Political Studies, December 1996. Available at <http://www.israeleconomy.org/strat2.htm>.

85   Pepe Escobar, "Exit strategy: Civil war", *Asia Times*, 10 June 2005.

86   The first four commands are located in the US, the last two in Germany. There are also four Unified Combatant Commands organized according to function, including troops, space operations, information, surveillance, intelligence and missile defense. map available at <http://www.defense.gov/specials/unifiedcommand/>.

87   See Chalmers Johnson, *Nemesis: The Last Days of the American Republic*, New York: Metropolitan Books, 2007.

88   Peace Pledge Union <http://www.ppu.org.uk/>.

89   Johnson, *Nemesis: The Last Days of the American Republic,* 143.

90   Stockholm International Peace Research Institute, 11 April 2011, <http://www.sipri.org/research/armaments/milex/factsheet2010>.

91   Defense Science Board Task Force Report on Sea Basing, US Defense Depart-

	ment: Washington, August 2003. <http://seasteading.org/stay-in-touch/blog/3/2009/05/11/defense-science-board-task-force-report-sea-basing>.
92	Keir Lieber and Daryl Press, "The Rise of US Nuclear Primacy", *Foreign Affairs*, March/April 2006.
93	Rick Rozoff, "Pentagon Plans For Global Military Supremacy: US, NATO Could Deploy Mobile Missiles Launchers To Europe", *www.globalresearch.ca*, 22 August 2009.
94	Thomas Reed, *At the Abyss: An Insider's History of the Cold War*, New York: Presidio Press, 2004.
95	David Hoffman, "Cold War hotted up when sabotaged Soviet pipeline went off with a bang", *Sydney Morning Herald*, 28 February 2004.
96	Quoted in Rick Rozoff, "US Cyber Command: Waging War In The World's Fifth Battlespace", *www.globalresearch.ca*, 27 May 2010.
97	Dennis Ross, *Statecraft and How to Restore America's Standing in the World*, New York: Farrar, Straus and Giroux, 2007, quoted in Freedland, "Bush's Amazing Achievement", *New York Review of Books*, 2007.
98	The nuclear station in Ukraine which experienced a meltdown in 1986, a devastating blow to Gorbachev's *perestroika*
99	Center for Defense Information. Available at <http://www.infoplease.com/ipa/A0904490.html>.
100	Richard Grimmett, "US Arms Sales to Pakistan", *www.fas.org*, Washington DC: Congressional Research Service, 24 August 2009. <http://www.fas.org/sgp/crs/weapons/RS22757.pdf>.
101	Bill Emmott, *Rivals: How the Power Struggle between China, India and Japan will Shape our World*, Chicago, USA: Houghton Mifflin Harcourt, 2008, 4.
102	See the author's "All roads lead to the Caucasus", *ericwalberg.com*, 9 March 2010.
103	Rick Rozoff, "India: US Completes Global Military Structure", *rickrozoff.wordpress.com*, 10 September 2010.
104	William Blum, *Rogue State: A Guide to the World's Only Superpower*, 2nd ed., New York: Common Courage Press, 2005, 187.
105	See Richard Sale, "Saddam Was key in early CIA plot", *UPI*, 11 April 2003. Available at <http://www.informationclearinghouse.info/article2849.htm>.
106	"Like the Iran-Iraq war", *Goliath Business News*, 30 April 2007.
107	The operations are discussed by officials sympathetically in Michael Hirsh and John Barry, "'The Salvador Option': The Pentagon May Put Special-Forces-led Assassination or Kidnapping Teams in Iraq", *Newsweek*, 9 January 2005.
108	Dirk Adriaensens, "Beyond the WikiLeaks Files: Dismantling the Iraqi State", *truthout.org*, 5 November 2010.
109	Seymour Hersh, "Annals of National Security: Preparing the Battlefield", *New Yorker*, 7 January 2009.
110	Both the US and al-Qaeda funded Chechen guerrilla leaders Shamil Basayev and Omar ibn al-Khattab from the mid-1990s. According to Yossef Bodansky, then-director of the US Congressional Task Force on Terrorism and Unconventional Warfare, Washington was actively involved in "yet another anti-Russian jihad, seeking to support and empower the most virulent anti-Western Islamist forces ... [culminating in] Washington's tacit encouragement of both Muslim allies (mainly Turkey, Jordan and Saudi Arabia) and US private security companies to assist the Chechens and their Islamist allies to surge

in the spring of 2000 and sustain the ensuing jihad for a long time." The US saw the sponsorship of "Islamist jihad in the Caucasus" as a way to "deprive Russia of a viable pipeline route through spiraling violence and terrorism". Quoted in Nafeez Mosaddeq Ahmed, "Our terrorists", *New Internationalist*, 426, 25 October 2010.

111   Joe Stephens and David Ottaway, "From US, the ABC's of Jihad", *Washington Post*, 23 March 2002.

112   Blum, *Rogue State: A Guide to the World's Only Superpower,* 180.

113   Corine Hegland, "Peace Work", *National Journal*, 26 April 2008. <http://www. usip.org/files/ national_journal.pdf>.

114   Bill Robinson, «The Crisis of Global Capitalism: How it looks from Latin America", in Freeman and Kagarlitsky eds, *The Politics of Empire: Globalisation in Crisis*, 173.

115   Walden Bello and Marylou Malig, "The Crisis of the Globalist Project and the New Economics of George W. Bush", in Freeman and Kagarlitsky eds, *The Politics of Empire: Globalisation in Crisis,* 93.

116   James Petras and H Veltmeyer, *Empire with Imperialism: Global Dynamics of Neoliberal Capitalism,* London: Zed, 2005, 184.

117   Michel Chossudovsky, "'Manufacturing Dissent': the Anti-globalization Movement is Funded by the Corporate Elites", *www.globalresearch.ca*, 20 September 2010.

118   A Canadian United Church-sponsored NGO Kairos that helped Palestinian refugees was defunded by the Canadian International Development Agency in 2009 after 35 years when the Zionist NGO-Monitor group claimed (falsely) that Kairos was advocating the Boycott, Disinvestment and Sanctions (BDS) campaign against Israel.

119   The radical youth group *Otpor* (resistance), which received NED funding, attacked and partially burned the parliament and a protester rammed the republican TV building; hence, the Bulldozer Revolution. It established the Center for Applied Non-Violent Action and Strategies (CANVAS) in 2003 to train other youth groups eager to overthrow autocratic governments. CANVAS participates in workshops financed by the Organisation for Security and Cooperation in Europe, the United Nations Development Program, and Freedom House.

120   Jenny Booth, "Bush hails Georgia as a 'beacon of liberty'", *The Times,* 10 May 2005.

121   Courtesy of Thomas Bloomberg at Wikimedia Commons <http://en. wikipedia. org/wiki/File:Baku_pipelines.svg>.

122   Nicholas Blanford, "Is Hezbollah right that Israel assassinated Lebanon›s Rafik Hariri?", *Christian Science Monitor*, 10 August 2010.

123   ukit, "Iran's Fear Of A George Soros-Funded 'Velvet Revolution'", *www. dailykos.com*, 14 June 2009.

124   Courtney Comstock, "George Soros Taking Heat Over Ties To Pro-Iranian Group", *www.businessinsider.com*, 18 November 2009.

125   In 2002, *Otpor* members founded the Center for Applied Nonviolent Action and Strategies, which has conducted workshops for pro-democracy activists in Egypt, Palestine, Western Sahara, Azerbaijan and the US.

126   This began on 25 January 2011, a national holiday commemorating the 1952 revolution, National Police Day, to protest what, under US patronage, had become a virtual police state, See the author's "Egypt/Turkey-Israel: 'A clean

break'", *ericwalberg.com*, 24 February 2011.

127   See <http://en.wikipedia.org/wiki/Alliance_of_Youth_Movements>.

128   WikiLeaks in November 2010 revealed that virtually all the Middle East regime leaders support a US attack on Iran. Bush II claims in his memoirs *Decision Points* that Egyptian President Hosni Mubarak urged him to invade Iraq, assuring him Hussein had WMDs, though Mubarak issued an official denial. "Bush: Mubarak Informed US that Iraq Had Biological Weapons", *www.voanews.com*, 11 November 2010.

129   See the author's "Egypt: Peering into the revolution's crystal ball", *ericwalberg. com*, 10 March 2011.

130   See especially Peter Dale Scott, *Drugs Oil and War: The United States in Afghanistan, Colombia, and Indochina*, New York: Rowman and Littlefield, 2003, and Alexander Cockburn and Jeffery St Clair, *White Out: The CIA, Drugs and the Press*, London: Verso, 1999.

131   See US Department of Justice Inspector General, "Report of Drug Trafficking by CIA", *www.scribd.com*, December 1997. <http://www.scribd.com/doc/29071814/>.

132   Alfred McCoy, "Drug Fallout: the CIA's Forty Year Complicity in the Narcotics Trade", *The Progressive*, 1 August 1997.

133   Scott, *Drugs Oil and War: The United States in Afghanistan, Colombia, and Indochina*, 29.

134   McCoy, "Drug Fallout: the CIA's Forty Year Complicity in the Narcotics Trade".

135   McCoy's testimony before the Special Seminar (13 February 1997) focusing on allegations linking CIA secret operations and drug trafficking organized by US Congressman John Conyers, *www.daily.pk*, 27 May 2010.

136   Quoted in Charles Smith, "Bush Will Not Stop Afghan Opium Trade", *NewsMax. com*, 28 March 2002.

137   Michel Chossudovsky, "Heroin is "Good for Your Health": Occupation Forces support Afghan Narcotics Trade", *www.globalresearch.ca*, 29 April 2007.

138   Jeremy Hammond, "The Afghan Drug Trade and the Elephant in the Room", *www.foreignpolicyjournal.com*, 9 April 2011.

139   William Engdahl, "America's Phoney War in Afghanistan", *www.information-clearinghouse.info*, 21 October 2009, and Jeremy Hammond, "The Afghan Drug Trade and the Elephant in the Room".

140   Peter Dale Scott, "Continuity of Government: Is the State of Emergency Superseding our Constitution?" *www.globalresearch.ca*, 24 November 2010.

141   An October 2010 poll in Berlin among former East Germans revealed that 57 per cent defend the overall record of the former East Germany and 49 per cent agreed that "the GDR had more good sides than bad sides. There were some problems, but life was good there." Available at <http://21stcenturymanifesto. wordpress.com/2010/10/28/life-was-better-in-east-germany-opinion-poll/>. Only 30 per cent of Ukrainians approve of the change to democracy vs 72 per cent in 1991, 60 per cent of Bulgarians believe the old system was better, according to a 2009 US Pew Research Center poll. Anna Mudeva, "In Eastern Europe, people pine for socialism", *www.reuters.com*, 8 November 2009.

142   60 per cent of Americans feel the country is on the wrong track in 2010, albeit down from 89 per cent in 2008 during the closing days of Bush II rule. CBS News/New York Times Poll, 21–26 October 2010. Available at <http://www. pollingreport.com/right.htm>.

143   Ronald Asmus, *Opening NATO's Door: How the Alliance Remade Itself for a*

New Era, New York: Columbia University Press, 2004, xvi.

144   Ibid., 11–12.

145   R Asmus, R Kugler, S Larrabee, "Building a new NATO", *Foreign Affairs,* Washington: CFR, September 1993.

146   Asmus, *Opening NATO's Door: How the Alliance Remade Itself for a New Era,* 122.

147   Ibid., 153.

148   Ibid., 125.

149   Ibid., 198.

150   Ibid., 291.

151   Robert Kagan, *Of Paradise and Power: America and Europe in the New World Order,* New York: Alfred Knopf, 2003, 57.

152   William Pfaff, "The NATO Nuisance", Tribune Media Services, 28 April 2010. Available at <http://original.antiwar.com/pfaff/2010/04/27/the-nato-nuisance/>.

153   NATO consists of more than 300 committees—all requiring decisions by consensus, and 13,000 personnel scattered across western Europe at NATO's many military bases. When France rejoining the integrated military structure in April, it had to send 900 military staff to the various NATO commands.

154   By expanding NATO instead of dissolving it, the result was not to unite Europe, but merely to move the dividing line east, Russian Foreign Minister Sergei Lavrov said in 2009 at the Munich Conference on Security "NATO or PATO?" The expansion was in violation of Baker's public pledge to Gorbachev: "The Americans promised that NATO wouldn't move beyond the boundaries of Germany after the Cold War but now half of central and Eastern Europe are members, so what happened to their promises? It shows they cannot be trusted." Mikhail Gorbachev as reported in the *Daily Telegraph*, 7 May 2008.

CHAPTER FOUR

GGIII: ISRAEL— EMPIRE-AND-A-HALF

The Israeli embassy is practically dictating to the congress through influential Jewish people in the country.
Secretary of State John Foster Dulles (1957)[1]

The Israelis control the policy in the congress and the senate.
Senator Fullbright, Chair of Senate Foreign Relations Committee, on CBS "Face the Nation" (1973)

Every time we do something, you tell me Americans will do this and will do that. I want to tell you something very clear, don't worry about American pressure on Israel; we, the Jewish people control America, and the Americans know it.
Prime Minister Ariel Sharon (2001)[2]

The colonial enterprise that Zionism is has corrupted everything it touched, beginning with the United Nations and including the mainstream media, what passes for democracy in the Western world (America especially) and Judaism itself.
Open letter to British Conservative Party leader David Cameron, Alanhart.net, (2007)

Judaism and Zionism—goals

Hannah Arendt states in *The Origins of Totalitarianism* (1951) that the key to understanding "the rise and fall of the Jews" is "the relationship between Jews and the state". Historically, in response to the hostile attitudes and actions of their neighbors, Jews frequently sought the protection of the state. As Ginsberg argues in *The Fatal Embrace: Jews and the State*, for their own purposes, rulers often were happy to accommodate the Jews in exchange for their services, resulting in "the rise to great power by Jewish elites, but creating conditions for their subsequent fall".[3]

They made alliances "responsible for the construction of some of the most powerful states of the Mediterranean and European worlds, including the Hapsburg, Hohenzollern, and Ottoman empires ... [though] in Wilhelmian Germany and Hapsburg Austria-Hungary, the regimes provided access to a small number of very wealthy Jews while subjecting the remainder to various forms of exclusion."[4] This led to the paradoxical situation where some Jews were ministers or viziers while the majority of them were oppressed and rebels, a foretaste of the twentieth century GGs.

In 13th–15th cc Spain, "royal power was sustained by Jewish money, industry, and intelligence." It was thus very much in the interests of this Jewish elite to "centralize royal authority at the expense of the nobility" and support "efforts of these monarchs to expand the boundaries of the Castilian state".[5] Thus, the Spanish empire—again dramatically presaging the role of Jews in the British and now American empires. The underlying logic of the Jewish embrace of the state is simple: wield financial resources at the national level and encourage the expansion of the nation state abroad in pursuit of profit—the logic of imperialism.

But there is another logic at work among the various Jewish diasporas which goes beyond this Jewish promotion of the imperial power of a nation such as Spain, Britain or France. Jewish diasporas throughout history have sought to maintain links with each other both as insurance against the threat to any one community, but also to cooperate in financial and trade activities in good times. The bonds tying these diasporas together vied with the bonds tying Jews in any one diaspora to their (Christian/ Muslim) rulers, both a useful and at the same time threatening feature for the local ruler. He could benefit in economic terms from access to a unique worldwide financial and trade network, but had to keep in mind that his Jewish financiers had their own agenda as well, which could well conflict with the needs of his empire.

In the 19th–20th cc the leading powers were first Britain, then the US, both with their Jewish financial elite. Jews also rose to prominence in the Soviet Union. However, by the time Israel was founded in 1948, the US possessed unmistakable advantages over the Soviet Union in its ability to impose its world order (Britain was clearly out of the running), and Jewish influence and the ability to act freely in coordination with Jews abroad was seriously restricted by Stalin. In any case, the Soviet Union was not an empire operating on finance capital and did not respond to Jewish elite influence as traditional empires did.

Given the historical precedents, it was logical in the post-WWII period for world Jewry to put its eggs in the US imperial basket, where it could strive to shape politics, economics and culture according to a Jewish, now Zionist agenda.[6] There was no such leeway under Stalin's Soviet Union, where Jews were expected to assimilate, where their prominence and power was strictly limited. Even though they still held privileged positions throughout Soviet society, they were expected to think and act as equals with other minorities.

It follows from this that when Jews achieved their own state, those who approved of this state would use their embedded influence in their host empire(s) to promote their own empire, and as a corollary even undermine or abandon a host if it interferes with the goals of the Jewish state. This latter corollary, of course, presupposes the firm commitment of world Jewry to the cause of the Jewish state, which was not always the case.

Ginsberg wrote his provocative *Fatal Embrace* in 1993 following the attempt by Bush I in 1991 to force Israel to stop building settlements on occupied land, denying Israel its request for $10 billion in loan guarantees in 1991 and again in 1992. Bush was determined to use the US empire's window of opportunity to wrestle Israel into finally making peace with the Palestinians, making his "new world order" a permanent reality, going as far as to appeal to Americans on TV to reject the pressures of the Israeli lobby, which had turned Congress and the Senate against him. Bush's approval ratings prior to his tussle with the Israeli lobby had approached 90 per cent—a presidential record—and a majority of Americans even backed withdrawing all aid to Israel after Bush's TV appeal, yet he was defeated in his 1992 re-election bid.

This instance of 'the monarch turning against the Jews' reminded Ginsberg of times in the past when Jews reached dizzying heights of power only to find their position of power threatened. King Ferdinand expelled them from Spain in 1492 even as the empire was reaching its zenith. They fled to Holland and then came to Britain with the invading William, becoming the backbone of the Dutch and British empires, and had the last laugh at Spain as its empire eventually declined without them, as they were now in the service of Spain's enemies.

Benjamin Disraeli, a descendant of Jewish refugees from Spain and Portugal, served twice as British prime minister between 1868–80.[7] Disraeli helped fashion an imperialist program that bound together "the aristocracy, the military and administrative establishments with segments of the financial community, the press and the middle class" in a coalition that would strengthen the British imperial state and allow it to expand into India, the Middle East and Africa during the heyday of GGI.

The empire was a boon to the growing British middle class as well as the elite, providing career opportunities in "the work of building and administering the empire".[8] Disraeli ensured financial and local Egyptian support from Lionel Walter Rothschild and Henry Oppenheim for taking control of the Suez Canal in 1878, leading Hobson to allude in his *Imperialism* to "men of a single and peculiar race, who have behind them centuries of financial experience" and who formed "the central ganglion of international capitalism".[9] Disraeli critic Goldwyn Smith, a professor at Oxford, charged that his government's foreign policies were motivated more by Jewish than British interests. "No Jew could be a true Englishman or patriot."[10] This, before the creation of Israel and the tradition of *sayanim*.[11]

Jews were the backbone of US imperialism too. Jewish bankers such as Joseph Seligman were to a large extent shut out of the lucrative railway investment opportunities in the rapidly expanding US in the nineteenth century, and were forced to turn to much riskier Latin American investments.[12] Seligman organized the financing of the Panama Canal Company through stock issues and mobilized public opinion and the imperial enthusiast president Teddy Roosevelt, using as lobbyist former secretary of the navy Richard Thompson and others to argue for his Panama route. He even helped organize Colombian rebels to secede when the Colombian government refused to cooperate, coordinating the immediate recognition of the new Panama government by Roosevelt.

The parallel role of Disraeli and Rothschild in Suez, and Seligman in Panama, and their ability to raise huge sums and manipulate politicians in both the center and periphery was vital to the expansion of both empires. This important role that Jews have played in imperialism, culminating in the creation of a Jewish state tied to a host empire, suggests the descriptive phrase 'empire-and-a-half'.

GGI
The rule of thumb of Jewish involvement in the political process as described by Ginsburg is:

- for absolutists states, provide finance and advice to the monarch;

- for liberal regimes, in addition to the financial role, to "actively participate in politics, political mobilization and opinion formation".[13]

In GGI, this meant the support of imperialist foreign policies in all the countries where Jews came to play a prominent role, from Spain and Holland to England and America, both as political actors and as bankers. At the same time, as intellectuals in post-Napoleonic Europe, where Jews were granted new civil rights, they became prominent as liberals and communists.

In GGI&II, Jews and Zionists played a strong supportive role to the empire—in GGI as loyal ally to the various imperial teams; in GGII, both as US citizens and, as embodied in Israel, as a "strategic ally" of the US, as prophesied by Mackinder. An independent, even leading role by Jews on the world stage, with specific strategies and goals, was being charted formally for the first time in the Zionist project at the First Zionist Congress in 1899, with Lionel Walter Rothschild the chief funder and inspiration for the creation of a Jewish state in Palestine.

The Israel factor has been implicit in all of the Great Games. The professed goal of Zionism during GGI was to create a modest Jewish state in the Middle East based on a negotiated accommodation with the Palestinian Arabs. The underlying goal was from the start to create a Greater Israel incorporating all the so-called Biblical lands, including Sinai, by displacing the natives, as indicated in Zionist discourse from Theodor Herzel and Zeev Jabotinsky[14] on—the Jewish version of Manifest Destiny.[15]

GGII&III

Diaspora Jewish elites embracing their local monarch was one thing, but when a Jewish state entered the picture, the GGI dynamic changed. Jews were playing their previous role—requiring/ providing imperial support—plus a new one, independent of the imperial sponsors of yore. In geopolitical terms, Mackinder's citadel is a heartland country curiously emulating the original geopolitical German heartland of GGI&II in its quest for *Lebensraum,* in alliance with the now world rimland US.

But it is a tiny heartland, and reliant, as Jews have been throughout recent history, on a special relationship with the empire. Once Israel was a fact it needed US backing for its policies, just as diaspora Jews had needed the protection of the monarch. This required both the efforts of US Jews petitioning their political leaders, and active politicking by Israel itself, to make it appear not just valuable in the Middle East to the strategic interests of the empire, but irreplaceable.

In GGI the pre-Israel Arab states/colonies resented colonial Britain and France but had a favorable view of the US. To convince the US that Israel would serve to ensure Middle East oil supplies—the chief underlying goal of US empire in the Middle East—while leaving itself room to pursue its own agenda of expansion, it was necessary for Israel to continue to antagonize the local Arabs, rather than make concessions to obtain peace. Without hostile neighbors, it would be of no use to the US as reliable Middle East gendarme keeping unreliable, anti-American Arab states in line.

This was a most unusual and risky strategy for a weak, heartland country surrounded by enemies. Germany, though never a benign neighbor, dominated its neighbors by sheer might. However, for Israel, this strategy worked because of the *perception* of broad Jewish power, promoted by the Jewish elite in the US, who were able to convince the US leaders of their own domestic power despite their small numbers.

This need for hostile neighbors has been reiterated time and again through Israel's history; for example, future Israeli prime minister and would-be peacemaker Yitzhak Rabin as a general in 1991 bemoaned that "Israel was doomed to live forever in war, or under the threat of war with the entire Arab world."[16] That Israelis implicitly accept this as the normal state of affairs was confirmed by a 2010 poll by *Time*: "Asked ... to name the 'most urgent problem' facing Israel, just 8 per cent of Israeli Jews cited the conflict with Palestinians ... Israeli Arabs placed peace first, but among Jews here, the issue that President Obama calls 'critical for the world' just doesn't seem—critical."[17]

Hostility and war are more than just a strategy for Israel, but its *raison d'etre*, along with *Lebensraum*, the underlying goal of the Zionists in GGII&III. While Jewish elites traditionally benefited from wars between states in the past, they had no particular interest in being involved directly in such a perpetual war, being able to prosper during peacetime as well, and appreciating the stability of their host nations. This state of perpetual war is a new strategy made necessary by the colonial nature of Israel itself.[18]

Ensuring US support for Israel in GGII meant supporting the empire's other GGII goal: to fight communism. This also required considerable effort—to suppress its own Jewish-American communist roots.

Jews were prominent in both the US political elite and in the communist opposition during the GGI endgame and the early stages of GGII. From the 1930s on, there was strong support by US Jews for the progressive Democrat Franklin Roosevelt and his New Deal, with his push for centralization of power to create a stable, capitalist welfare state.[19] In the face of strong isolationism in the 1930s, they lobbied hard for US entry into WWII on Britain's and later communist Russia's side.

Jewish support for the New Deal and WWII, GGI's endgame, was consistent with both traditional Jewish political roles: support of centralization and imperial expansion and, in liberal regimes, political mobilization and opinion formation. Ginsberg acknowledges, "There was a sense in which the New Deal was a Jew Deal."[20] This was a dilemma as the Cold War got under way, and remarkably, the later purging of left wing Jews, most famously the electrocution of the Rosenbergs, was orchestrated purely as an anticommunist move, with no public mention of Jews and Judaism. The judge and prosecution in the Rosenberg trial were both Jews. Attempts to link Jews and communism, especially by McCarthy and his supporters in the early 1950s, were quickly suppressed, despite the predominance of Jews in the communist movement.

At precisely the same time, and just as remarkably, Israel was quickly abandoning its intimate ties with the Soviet Union. Initially the Zionists played both sides against the other in the budding Cold War. Soviet support was essential both for official recognition by the UN and for military support, given the US embargo intended to stop the exploding civil war in Palestine. Without Soviet arms, intended by Stalin to ensure Israel would be *its* "strategic ally", it would have been overwhelmed by the local Arabs it was intent on displacing. Most of the Jews who came to Palestine in the 1920–40s were socialist or communist and lived on communes (kibbutzim).[21] Menachem Begin was an NKVD agent, recruited as part of the Polish army which the Soviet secret police set up in Russia as a rival to the free Polish army operating from London. He served with the Soviet-created Polish army in Transjordan and then Palestine in 1942–43.[22]

Despite Arab Muslim suspicions of the atheist Soviet Union and Stalin's initial support for Israel, the frontline states Egypt and Syria and the Palestinians were forced to seek support from the only world power willing to provide it—the Soviet Union—making them allies of the new US enemy. In 1955, Moscow began providing military assistance to Syria and Egypt. This followed from Israel's new unconditional allegiance to the US, and confirmed Israel's role as a 'bulwark against communism' in the Middle East. "Without Israel, there was little chance that any of the Arab regimes would turn away from their dependence on the West."[23]

As the 1950s progressed, the US moved ever closer to Israel, but its support would often be covert so as not to antagonize the Arabs. The shift toward Israel was not as rapid as it might have been because Eisenhower was popular as a wartime hero and could politically afford to buck the new energetic Israel lobby. Eisenhower's threat of UN Security Council sanctions in 1956 brought about Israel's withdrawal from Sinai.

For Israel, victory in the 1967 war was a vital turning point in its relationship with the US and the world. Its own regional GGII was now won, long before the US GGII against the Soviet Union was. 1967 gave it all of Palestine, destroyed the Arab dream of defeating Israel in the field, and eventually knocked Israel's main foe—Egypt—out of the game. By decisively defeating the forces of Arab nationalism, Israel proved its value to the United States—if indeed the Arab nationalists' defeat was in the US imperial interest. After all, whatever threat the Arab nationalists posed to western interests had been initially caused by Israel in 1948. Israel's 1967 victory "imparted fresh momentum to forces, ascendant since the late 1950s, that were pushing for a stronger US commitment to Israel as a strategic asset."[24] The specifically Zionist logic was entrenched at this point at the heart of US strategic thinking.

1967 changed the thinking of Jews, both in Israel and abroad, encouraging a more aggressive game plan, which came to fruition only in the 1980s, in conjunction with US domestic political developments and the sudden rapid decline of the Soviet Union,[25] and evolved into a radically new game—GGIII.

The traditional roles of Jews as both financiers of the imperial state and in political mobilization and opinion formation are present in all three GGs, with the "political mobilization" focused more and more exclusively around support for America's new 'half' empire—Greater Israel—from GGII on. The creation of Israel meant that it is "virtually impossible for a secular Jew anywhere not to be Zionist",[26] trumping traditional leftist leanings, sapping the energies that once fueled Jewish support for liberal and communist causes. 1967 reinforced this dynamic and led some radical leftist Jews and others with strong sympathy for Israel to shift sharply to the right, founding the neocon movement described in Chapter 3. It encouraged the rapid colonization of the Occupied Territories, and an end to the original UN plan (agreed to by both the US and Israel in 1948) of partition and "two states for two peoples", now a "'five states for two peoples' plan: one contiguous state, surrounded by settlement blocs, for Israel, and four isolated enclaves for the Palestinians."[27]

Ideology

The religion of Judaism was born in the Middle East and has always been insular, not a proselytizing religion. By the seventh century AD Jews had established communities in Central Asia, Europe and North Africa, though wherever they were, they continued to see themselves as a diaspora and did not integrate into local societies, living in (often walled) ghettoes. Over time, the ghetto mentality of Jews transformed a religion into a embryonic nationality in Europe which used a German dialect, Yiddish, written in Hebrew script. Jews in Spain, North Africa and the Middle East were more assimilated with their neighbors, and spoke a Spanish, Berber or Arabic dialect. Hebrew was considered a language for religious purposes only.

The tradition Jewish prayer "Next year may we meet in Jerusalem", the biblical promise of return to the land of Israel and the rebuilding of Solomon's temple, are fundamental to Jewish folklore and religion, and were traditionally used metaphorically, either to mean the endtimes or "when God wills". In orthodox Judaism the Promised Land belongs to God, a gift to the faithful, conditional on obedience. However, these metaphors were used concretely by the secular Zionists in the nineteenth century to justify the colonial project of Jews 'returning' to the Middle East. Zionism, the founding ideology of Israel, was the product of nineteenth century secular European nationalism, rather than religious tradition. Founder of Israel Ben Gurion dismissed Judaism as "the historical misfortune of the Jewish people and an obstacle to its transformation into a normal state."[28]

Zionism is thus a negation of Judaism, rather than its continuation. Orthodox religious Jews (Haredim) were initially anti-Zionist or apolitical. But increasingly, in Israel, they have been seduced by the trappings of state power, and are supporters of the National Religious Party (renamed Jewish Home). About half of Israel's orthodox Jews now recognize the secular Israeli state and thus implicitly equate Zionism and Judaism. The most famous orthodox leader, Rabbi Abraham Kook, justified the modern state as being in line with Old Testament Jewish kingdoms, "the work of God himself", reinterpreting the Torah admonition against precipitating the arrival of the Messiah.[29]

Stalin had essentially established the modern Jewish nationality as one of many Soviet nationalities with their own homelands. The Jewish homeland was arbitrarily decided to be Birobidjan in Siberia. This secular Soviet Zionism (or rather anti-Zionism) denied the biblical heritage of the Jews as meaningful, felt it was harmless until the creation of Israel, which on the contrary reaffirmed the biblical heritage among Jews everywhere. The geopolitical atavism so zealously encouraged by the Zionists acted as a poison for Soviet Jews. The most productive and well-educated Soviet minority was suddenly perceived as a possible traitor class, giving rise to anti-Jewish resentment and mistrust, and in the end helping to shatter the Soviet Union itself.

This was recapitulated throughout the world. For all Jews, Zionism established a political quasi-religious ideology and allegiance which suddenly put them at odds with their host countries. Rabkin documents how Zionists made it a practice to "cultivate the myth of a world Jewish plot"[30] to incite anti-Jewish sentiment in Russia, Britain and Germany (and later, Egypt, Iraq and other Middle East countries with large, assimilated Jewish populations) precisely to encourage emigration to Palestine.

Israel as the Jewish state has from the beginning both sacralized the holocaust and national symbols such as the flag, and secularized religious symbols, undermining *bona fide* Jewish religious beliefs, fusing religious and secular in a new Jewish identity, even in the diaspora. Prophets such as Moses became national heroes, the Hebrew religious term *bituhon* (trust in God) became "security of the state of Israel", *keren kayemet* (permanent fund) became the Jewish National Fund.[31]

More important than religion or even ethnicity for Israel in geopolitical terms has been the ideology of the "special relationship" with the US which became integral to American politics by the 1960s, an inevitable result of Israel's creation and its early need to make an unbreakable bond with the leading empire. The special relationship grew naturally from its deep roots in American exceptionalism, the celebration of the arrival of the Puritans in the seventeenth century seeking their own Promised Land, oblivious to the American natives they would displace, and the immigration of 2 million eastern European Jewish immigrants in the late 19th–early 20th centuries. The idea that European and American Jews wanted to 'return' to the original Promised Land of the Old Testament appeals to Americans both Jewish and non-Jewish. Israel became both the physical and spiritual embodiment recapitulating the sweep of western civilization. Hence, Christian Zionists, enthusiastic supporters of a colonial project in a non-colonial era, Bush II's rhetoric, including a "Crusade" to be waged against Muslim terrorists, used in his White House press conference on 16 September 2001, which touched Christians subliminally however insulting and disturbing it was to Muslims, and the widespread acceptance of a Judeo-Christian civilizational construct.[32]

On the surface, the special relationship has been fashioned as a subliminal bond between two 'chosen peoples', Israel representing America in the Middle East, watching over the local Arab regimes, and making sure the oil flowed.

The underlying special relationship, however, was the 'embrace' of the US state by the Zionists, both in the diaspora and now *in situ* in the Middle East, the need to control US foreign policy, especially there, to further the Zionist goals, and to do whatever that required, be it fighting communism, providing arms to Iran or the Contras and drones to NATO troops in Afghanistan, conducting false-flag operations, or turning its Arab neighbors against the US. Elite Jews had always nurtured special relationships with whatever strong host states there be to safeguard Jews living in their host countries—as well as, indeed and maybe foremost, to pursue their own interests. Now this special relationship would take on unpredictable dimensions as the empire became an empire-and-a-half.

It also disturbed the relationship between diaspora Jewish communities. Before the creation of Israel, there was greater solidarity between Jewish diasporas. This solidarity broke down most famously in the 1930s–40s when Zionists cooperated with the Nazis in order to get the Nazis to expel German and later Hungarian Jews to Palestine and in the 1940s–1950s when Israeli agents carried out terrorist acts, including attacks on Jewish diasporas, in North Africa, Egypt and Iraq, to frighten Arab Jews into fleeing to Israel and to stoke anti-Jewish sentiment just to make sure they left for their new 'homeland'. Zionist leaders were in effect ethnically cleansing Jewish diasporas to build up Israel (see endnote 91).

Rules of the game and Strategies

Israel's rules of the game[33] are a variation on the GGI&II rules:
1. free trade with the outside world and controlled trade for the Occupied Territories,
2. war and occupation, and
3. exceptionalism, ensured by the special relationship with the US, the 'fatal embrace', a secular version of a historically cherished notion of being "chosen"

With this in mind, Israel and diaspora supporters of Israel, both Jewish and non-Jewish, employ a full array of financial and military-political policies, soft and hard.

Financial Strategies
GGI—Money and Finance
'Money makes the world go round.' The mutual embrace of the Jewish financial elites and western states from the Middle Ages on is an important form of parapolitics, the pursuit of politics by covert means. Jewish prominence in finance in all the games has meant that throughout, while only a tiny percentage of a host nation's population is Jewish, an outsize percentage belongs to the super-rich. In Britain on the eve of WWI Jews constituted 1 per cent of the population and 23 per cent of the millionaires, and in GGIII in the US, 2 per cent of the population and 50 per cent of the billionaires.[34]

However, the charge that the Rothschilds and a few other elite Jewish families exercise complete control over the world overly simplifies politics and economics, attributes superhuman powers to humans, a fetishism that Marx would be the first to criticize. Karl Marx (1818–1883), grandson of the rabbi of Trier,[35] famously criticized nineteenth century Jews in the context of the triumph of capitalism:

> What is the secular basis of Judaism? Practical need, self-interest. What is the worldly religion of the Jew? Huckstering. What is his worldly God? Money. The Jew has emancipated himself in the Jewish fashion not only by acquiring money power but through money's having become (with him or without him) the world power and the Jewish spirit's having become the practical spirit of the Christian peoples.[36]

With the decline of Christianity, for proponents of western civilization, "we are all Jews". And, as Vice President Joe Biden put it, "You don't have to be Jewish to be a Zionist." The secular Zionist project is now largely embraced by western ruling elites, and it came about largely because of the financial power of the Rothschilds, the principal promoters of a Jewish state in Palestine from the nineteenth century on.

Money, though it facilitates exchange and acts as a store of value, is in itself sterile. It produces nothing. Money can only promote economic activity as a catalyst. On the surface, money accumulating interest appears to be productive:

M -> M1 (M is a quantity of gold or silver) **M1 > M**

but the underlying formula is:

M -> { P + work -> P1 } -> M1 (P represents productive capital (machinery, etc.), P1 commodities) the value of **P1 > P** and hence **M1 > M**.

Until 1971, most money was backed by gold or silver. The freeing of the dollar from any anchor in the real world in 1971 would be seen by Marx as the perfection of money fetishism, as now the formula becomes

M -> M1 (M is a worthless piece of paper) **M1 > M**

The parasitical nature of finance capital, claiming magically to produce value, was recognized by all the montheisms and condemned, though the Hebrew Bible allows interest[37] to be charged to strangers but not "to thy brother" (*Deuteronomy* 23:19). This exception became the foundation in the Middle Ages for Jewish lending to non-Jews, and with the rise of banking, Jewish dominance in the role of state financier. Christianity also outlawed it; hence, Jews became the usurers of the middle ages. With the rise of capitalism, it was accepted by Christianity too.[38] It is the sense behind the statement of founder and spiritual leader of the Shas Party (a key member of the current Likud coalition government) and former Sephardi Chief Rabbi of Israel Ovadia Yosef in a Sabbath sermon: "*Goyim* were born only to serve us. Without that, they have no place in the world; only to serve the People of Israel."[39] The *goyim* (gentiles) are the workers in the above formula, the Jews the owners of M, M1. Islam is the only monotheism that still forbids usury and interest.[40]

In his study of the rise of capitalism in the late medieval period, Werner Sombart described the "struggle between two—Jewish and Christian—outlooks, between two radically differing—nay, opposite— views of economic life", the former intent on maximizing profit, the latter on just prices, "fair wages and fair profits", on observing "commercial etiquette". "To make profit was looked upon by most people throughout the period as improper, as 'unchristian', economic life still tied together by "religious and ethical bonds". The Jews, living in ghettoes, at times expelled, for example from Spain in 1493, were divorced from the customs of their Christian communities, 'freed' of the Christian ethical strictures. Thus, it was logical that

> It was not an individual here and there who offended against the prevailing economic order, but the whole body of Jews. Jewish commercial conduct reflected the accepted point of view among Jewish traders. Hence Jews were never conscious of doing wrong, of being guilty of commercial immorality; their policy was in accordance with a system, which for them was the proper one. They were in the right; it was the other outlook that was wrong and stupid. ... Not his usury differentiated him from the Christian, not that he sought gain, not that he amassed wealth; only that he did all this openly, not thinking it wrong.[41]

Sombart was inspired in his research by Max Weber's *The Protestant Ethic and the Spirit of Capitalism* (1905), but asks "whether all that Weber ascribes to Puritanism might not with equal justice be referred to Judaism, and probably in a greater degree; nay, it might well be suggested that that which is called Puritanism is in reality Judaism."[42] For Marx the happy ending is the negation of this: "Emancipation from huckstering and money, consequently from practical, real Judaism, would be the self-emancipation of our time."

The most famous Jewish financier in history was Mayer Rothschild (1744–1812), who famously quipped, "Give me control of a nation's money and I care not who makes the laws." He founded the dynasty that still acts as *eminence grise* in the shadowy world of banking today. His most famous son was Nathan, who handled 40 per cent of all loans floated in London by Austria, Russia and France from 1818–32. "The Vienna and Paris branches of the family raised money and sold bonds for the Hapsburgs, Bourbons, Orleanists, and Bonapartes. By mid-century the entire European state system was dependent upon the international financial network dominated by the Rothschilds."[43] In the 1860–70s, the Jewish Baron Gerson von Bleichroeder was a principal figure in the creation of a united German state. Bismarck entrusted him with negotiating the indemnity to be paid by France after its defeat in the Franco-Prussian War in 1871 (on the French side, negotiations were conducted by the Rothschilds).[44] Rothschild money financed Garibaldi in his campaign to unify Italy. Though on the face of it, it was supporting the noble cause of Italian unification, it also served the interests of finance capital and imperialism by strengthening a new (grateful) nation state.

The Rothschilds set up or strongly influenced the creation of central banks everywhere, the US Federal Reserve being the most important, one of the few central banks completely in private hands, owned by its board members.[45] These central banks control the supply of money, and the US Federal Reserve thus effectively controls the supply of the world's money. Its GGIII governors Paul Volker (1979–87), Alan Greenspan (1987–2009) and Ben Shalom Bernanke have all been Jewish.[46]

For the leading Jewish financiers such as Rothschild, Greenspan and Bernanke there has never been any anti-Semitism. Jews lived separately in the Middle Ages and there was little day-to-day interaction between them and local peasants. The pogroms which occurred in the Middle Ages were incited by the authorities to deflect attention from their own failings or in response to a calamity such as the Black Plague. The rise of overt anti-Jewish sentiment, what came to be called anti-Semitism, was a nineteenth century phenomenon, a reaction to the formal integration of Jews into European society following the Napoleonic wars, a working class and bourgeois reaction to the philo-Semitism of British ruling circles and the rising economic power of Jews, who were translating financial power into political, economic and cultural power. It was not the Rothschilds who suffered, but the non-elite Jews, who became scapegoats for this resentment.

The importance of the Rothschilds and Jewish financiers in general to the Zionists is impossible to overestimate. Nathan Rothschild and his son Lionel Walter were committed Zionists, the latter responsible for the Balfour Declaration, which was a letter addressed to him by the British foreign minister, Alfred Balfour.[47] This promise of a Jewish state in Palestine was a direct result of Zionist lobbying of both the British and Germans as WWI dragged on. Jewish bankers were financing both sides in WWI. Rothschild and the Jewish Conjoint Foreign Committee (JCFC) lobbied the British government intensely during WWI to push for a commitment to a post-war Jewish state. As British fortunes ebbed, the JCFC assured Lord Robert Cecil that American Zionists would lobby for US entry into the war if the British were to promise a Jewish state in Palestine after the war.[48]

The perception in the British government was that these elite Jews could make or break the British war effort,[49] that if the British refused, the Zionists would turn to their Germany cousins to broker a deal for control of a post-war Palestine, and bring their American cousins into the war on the German side, ensuring British defeat. US President Wilson had just won re-election on the explicit promise to keep the US out of the war but shared this fear. His Zionist Supreme Court appointee, Louis Brandeis, assured him that the British had agreed to issue such a statement, and that US Jewish financiers would throw their support behind Britain and not Germany, and that Wilson should joining the winning team. Wilson reversed himself and urged Congress to declare war in April. The Balfour Declaration was issued to Rothschild by the British government in November, and the war was over 12 months later. This masterful use of parapolitics,[50] employing the perception of unrivalled power based on financial prominence, was a decisive replay of the age-old win-win for Jews in European wars of the past,[51] now in the promotion of their own state.

GGIII—Oligarchs and Mafia

The Russian Jewish oligarchs who came to prominence in the 1990s following the collapse of the Soviet Union (seven of the nine oligarchs were Jewish) used the chaos of the Yeltsin years and the privatization process to amass huge fortunes, assisted by US advisers. They include Boris Berezovsky (media and oil), Mikhail Friedman (oil), Vladimir Gusinsky (banking and media), Mikhail Khodorkovsky (banking and oil), Alexander Smolensky (banking and media), Roman Abramovitch (oil, aluminum, insurance) and Viktor Vekselberg (aluminium).

Harvard professor David Lipton and Jeffery Sachs of the Harvard Institute of International Development led an advisory team including Andrei Shleifer (close friend of then-Deputy Treasury Secretary Larry Summers) to Russian Prime Minister Yegor Gaidar (Lipton, Sachs, Schleifer, Summers and Gaidar are all Jewish) that proposed "shock therapy", which included mass privatization, lifting price controls leading to hyperinflation, and making the ruble convertible. This wiped out ordinary Russians' savings and created the billionaire oligarchs who quickly transferred "over $200 billion dollars out of the country, mainly to banks in New York, Tel Aviv, London and Switzerland"[52] before the collapse of the ruble in 1998. Living standards of ex-Soviet citizens plummeted as seven billionaires who were Jewish swallowed up much of Soviet industrial property and spirited their capital to Britain, the US and Israel.

By 2000, the attempt to gain greater political power in opposition to Russian President Vladimir Putin, first by Berezovsky and then by Khodorkovsky, ended in the exile of the former in 2001 and the jailing of the latter in 2005. The whirlwind 1990–2005 period in the ex-Soviet Union confirms Ginsberg's thesis concerning Jewish elites allying with the nation state, but always vulnerable to the threat that the national leader can turn against them as popular resentment increases. Berezovsky and Khodorkovsky strayed from the fatal-embrace script; they were not playing by the rules of the game, but instead had designs on seizing power themselves, and suffered the wrath of the ruler for their troubles.

The underground world of money laundering, drug and arms trafficking also expanded rapidly in the post-Soviet period. The so-called Russian mafia, claimed by Friedman to be the largest in the world, is in fact largely Jewish—the Kosher Nostra. It put down roots in the US thanks to the GGII war against communism, with the passing of the 1974 Jackson-Vanik amendment tying US-Soviet trade to the emigration of Jews.[53]

Overall, oligarch and Kosher Nostra interests are congruent with the empire-and-a-half—expansion of US-Israeli access to world resources and markets. When the ex-Soviet Union and eastern Europe were opening up by the late 1980s, Kosher Nostra players were able to return, renew their contacts, and join the above-board oligarchs to play an important role in economics and politics in the ex-Soviet republics, given their knowledge of both systems, various languages, and multiple passports (Israeli, Russian and/or other ex-Soviet ones). The government in Moscow estimates that, apart from the oligarchs, the mafia controls 40 per cent of private business, 60 per cent of state-owned companies and 80 per cent of Russian banks.[54] The most important figure in the Kosher Nostra today is Semion Mogilevich. Basing his first operations in Israel, Mogilevich also acquired Hungarian citizenship in 1991, in addition to Israeli, Russian and Ukrainian citizenships. He has agreements with all the major intelligence agencies, thereby avoiding any imminent prosecutions.[55]

Because Israel acts as a refuge for Jews fleeing persecution, including such as Mogilevich, Israeli banks have a reputation for money laundering and for getting special treatment in the banking world. In 2004–05 the New York Branch of Israel's third largest bank, Israel Discount, processed $35.4 billion "that exhibited characteristics and patterns commonly associated with money laundering",[56] yet the US Treasury did not declare the bank a primary money-laundering concern under Section 311 of the Patriot Act as it did with the small Banco Delta Asia, where only $20 million worth of laundering had been alleged. In 2009 senior employees of Israel's largest bank, Hapoalim, were indicted on suspicions of money laundering and fraud connected with Israeli-Russian businessman Arcadi Gaydamak.

At least partially thanks to the Kosher Nostra and Russian oligarchs, Israel has more billionaires per capita than any other country. Now, as immigration dries up, Israel is burnishing its image as a tax haven to entice offshore funds, offering new residents a ten-year tax exemption. This is in defiance of the Organization for Economic and Community Development, which Israel succeeded in joining in 2010.[57]

The world financial establishment—Israeli, non-Israeli, Jewish and non-Jewish—continues to benefit from wars, now conducted solely by the US-Israeli empire-and-a-half. Even the current world financial crisis and the possibility that an invasion of Iran that could plunge the world economy into a depression can serve the needs of the world's financial elite. As long as the current imperial order exists, with money controlled by central banks, the too-big-to-fail banks are always able to pass their losses on to taxpayers through government bailouts. Goldman Sachs' profits have soared since the US financial meltdown of 2008 and the EU picked up the tab for the Euro-meltdown.

The Mega Group of the 50 richest and most powerful Jews in the US and Canada was founded in 1991 by Leslie Wexler, Charles Bronfman and others as an informal but very powerful financial and economic group to add greater clout to the Israel lobby.[58] However, there is no one group, be it Bilderberg, CFR, or Mega that controls all the financial levers. It is enough that the perception of omnipotence endures. **M1 > M** is the secret formula by which this perception endures.

Just as Kissinger epitomizes the US empire in GGII and Reagan in GGIII, American-Israeli financier Marc Rich, who dabbled in Middle East intrigue through his extensive, shadowy banking connections, epitomizes the Israeli empire-and-a-half. He is a commodities trader indicted in the United States on federal charges of tax evasion and of illegally making oil deals with Iran during the Iranian hostage crisis. He was identified as a colleague of Samir Najmeddin, an arms dealer for

Saddam Hussein.[59] Rich was pardoned by President Clinton in 2001. Just how conscious such a private individual is of his role in the greater political game is impossible to say.

The importance of the financial world and its use as parapolitics to the game strategy in GGIII, touched on here and in Chapter 3, like the importance of the Rothschilds to the strategies of GGI&II, cannot be overestimated. The *Protocols of the Elders of Zion* was initially viewed and continues to be seen by many as the program of an emancipated nineteenth century Jewish financial elite using Freemasonry as a vehicle to achieve world power.[60] The worth of the *Protocols* is not assessed here. It is enough to trace the development of the politics of Zionism from attributable sources and to observe the moves it gives rise to.

Maxim Ghilan argued in 2002 that the Israeli-neocon plan for remaking the Middle East was motivated not just by the goal of Greater Israel, but by financial capital intent on undermining the financial power of the Arab oil states. Because of the massive dollar holdings of Saudi Arabia and Kuwait, Israeli financiers feared the parapolitical use of this accumulated wealth to influence US politics away from support for Israel. Ghilan sees the real "clash of civilizations" between the "Judeo-Christian" and Islamic worlds as being waged in the world of international finance.[61]

GGIII Military-political Strategies
Doctrines
With the dismantling of Soviet anti-imperialist/anti-Zionist foreign policy in the 1980s by Mikhail Gorbachev (see endnote 25) and the collapse of the Soviet Union in 1991, Israel was freed of its main foe outside the Middle East, the one superpower that provided firm support to the Arab and Palestinian cause. This presented a radically new playing field for both the US and Israel. The seemingly coincidental ascendancy of the neocons in Washington further strengthened the special relationship on the surface, but the underlying goals and hence strategies of the two imperial powers were beginning to diverge more seriously even as loud avowals of eternal friendship were mouthed on Capitol Hill and in the media.

Israeli military strategy in GGIII was honed in the early 1980s, after the elimination of Egypt as a military threat. Two names are identified with it. Ariel Sharon announced publicly in 1981, shortly before invading Lebanon, that Israel no longer thought in terms of peace with its neighbors, but instead sought to widen its sphere of influence to the whole region "to include countries like Turkey, Iran, Pakistan, and areas like the Persian Gulf and Africa, and in particular the countries of

North and Central Africa".[62] This view of Israel as a regional superpower/ bully became known as the Sharon Doctrine.

But this was really nothing new. Sharon's invasion of Lebanon in 1982 followed traditional GGI direct invasion and co-opting of local elites, carrying out the earlier plan by chief of staff Moshe Dayan in 1954 to "create a Christian regime which will ally itself with Israel".[63] This was in the create-a-strongman tradition, relying on a dependent local proxy to evict the Palestinian leadership and fighters, to reduce Syrian influence, annex desired land and create a non-Muslim ethnic state alongside Israel. But already this strongman policy was losing its appeal. It didn't work for Israel in Lebanon. There was always the risk of a strongman turning against his patron or being overthrown.[64]

The more extreme version of the new Israeli game plan to make Israel the regional hegemon was Israeli scholar Oded Yinon's "A Strategy for Israel in the 1980s". Yinon was nicknamed "sower of discord" for his proposal to divide-and-conquer to create weak, dependent statelets with some pretense of democracy, similar to the US strategy in Central America, which would fight among themselves and, if worse came to worse and a populist leader emerged, he could be sabotaged easily—the Salvador Option. This would be used by the US in the dismemberment of Yugoslavia in the 1990s and in the wars against Iraq and Afghanistan following 9/11. Hizbullah leader Hassan Nasrallah described the Israeli policy based on Yinon in 2007 as intended to create "a region that has been partitioned into ethnic and confessional states that are in agreement with each other. This is the new Middle East."[65]

Yinon was using as a model the Ottoman millet system where separate legal courts governed the various religious communities using their own Muslim *sharia*, Christian Canon or Jewish *halakha* laws. It called for Lebanon to be divided into Sunni, Alawi, Christian and Druze states. The Shia of Lebanon and Syria would flee to southern Iraq, now a Shia state, with the rest of Iraq divided into Sunni and Kurd states. The Saudi kingdom and Egypt would also be divided, leaving Israel the undisputed master (along the lines of Peters, see Figure 3.2). "Genuine coexistence and peace will reign over the land only when Arabs understand that without Jewish rule between Jordan and the sea they will have neither existence nor security."[66]

Yinon's plan resembles the strategy of Nazi and Soviet mass deportations of Jews, Chechens, Crimean Tatars and others during WWII, and was inspired by Zeev Jabotinsky, who wrote in 1939: "There is no choice: The Arabs must make room for the Jews in Eretz Israel. It was possible to transfer the Baltic peoples, it is also possible to move the Palestinian Arabs."[67] Yinon correctly observed that the existing

Middle East states set up by Britain following WWI&II were unstable and consisted of sizable minorities which could be easily incited to rebel. All the Gulf states are "built upon a delicate house of sand in which there is only oil".

Some combination of Sharon/Yinon would be supplemented with new alliances farther afield to encircle hostile Arab neighbors by building strategic relationships with Europe, Russia, Turkey, African nations such as Ethiopia, and India, to realize Ben Gurion's goal to encircle Israel's hostile Arab neighbors.[68]

Hard Power
Wars
In addition to Israel's own invasions of Lebanon in 2006 and Gaza in 2008, it had long advocated the dismemberment of Iraq, beginning with links between Jewish officials in Palestine and the Kurds in Iraq started in the 1920s. Israel was the primary source of arms and military training for the Kurds in Iraq from the 1950s on. "In 1972 this support had taken a security dimension: providing the Kurds with weapons through Turkey and Iran and receiving Kurdish groups and guerillas for training in Israel and in Turkey and Iran. We achieved in Iraq more than we expected and planned."[69]

Following on Yinon's strategy in 1982, Richard Perle's 1996 "A Clean Break" states: "Israel can shape its strategic environment, in cooperation with Turkey and Jordan, by weakening, containing, and even rolling back Syria. This effort can focus on removing Saddam Hussein from power in Iraq—an important Israeli strategic objective in its own right." Perle, Paul Wolfowitz, David Frum (the coiner of Bush II's description of Iraq as part of an "axis of evil"), Norman Podhoretz, Philip Zelikow (co-author of the National Security Strategy of September 2002 advocating the invasion of Iraq), Cheney's chief of staff Lewis "Scooter" Libby (drafter of Colin Powell's 5 February 2003 UN speech), and the Pentagon's Office of Special Plans director Douglas Feith were all lobbying Bush II from day one to invade Iraq; they are all Jewish, outspoken Zionists and neocons.[70]

Israeli internal security minister, Avi Dichter, said at the Israeli National Security Research Center shortly after the invasion of Iraq in 2003:

> Weakening and isolating Iraq is no less important than weakening and isolating Egypt. Weakening and isolating Egypt is done by diplomatic methods while everything is done to achieve a complete and comprehensive isolation to Iraq. Iraq has vanished as a military force and as a united country. Our

strategic option is to keep it divided. Our strategic goal is not to allow this country to take its regional and Arabic role back. ... The top goal for Israel is to support and provide the Kurds with weapons and training and to make them our partners in security in order to establish a Kurdish independent state in the northern part of Iraq where it can control Kirkuk's and Kurdistan's oil. ... Iraq, the country which was united, suddenly became divided geographically, and its people is [sic] divided, it has now a civil war which led to the death of hundreds of thousands of the Iraqis.[71]

Israel thereby replaces the Ottoman Turks of yore as the local imperial power in the entire region. The Arab nations (prepared by British imperial divide-and-conquer and local-strongman policies) would thereby be kept divided, weak, dependent now on Israel to ensure safe access to oil. An Israeli-style peace would break out throughout the region: Sharon and his cohorts "envision a domino effect, with the fall of Saddam Hussein followed by that of Israel's other enemies: Arafat, Hassan Nasrallah, Bashar Assad, the ayatollah in Iran and maybe even Muhammar Gadaffi."[72]

By presenting the US with facts-on-the-ground and using its US lobby, Israel would keep itself at the heart of American plans for the Middle East no matter how "maddening", as Kissinger put it. Abdel Jawwad concludes, "Sequential wars with the Arab world have given Israel opportunities to exhaust the Arab world."[73]

A further Israeli objective in promoting the invasion of Iraq, deriving from its determination to play regional hegemon, is to see Iraq's oilfields divided up and sold to dozens of private operators, and in the process to break up the Saudi-dominated oil cartel, OPEC. Observers argue that this is the underlying motive of both the US and Israel in the occupation of Iraq, even though this is not in the interest of Big Oil.[74] The invasion as a prelude to weakening OPEC is primarily an Israeli objective, advocated as early as 2002 by Ariel Cohen of the Heritage Foundation.[75] Politically it is useful to Israel to undermine Saudi Arabia's influence and its ability to fund Islamic extremists and Palestinian resistance, paving the way for future ethnic cleansing of Palestinians from both Occupied Territories and from inside Israel.[76] This is Ghilan's point (see endnote 61).

According to Jeff Blankfort, Israel-first strategists in Washington and Tel Aviv, devising reasons for the US to invade Iraq, may or may not have consciously articulated another important motive for the invasion of Iraq and Afghanistan:

Israel also wanted to see the US as an occupying force in the Middle East, just like it is, so the US could then use Israeli 'expertise' in occupying Palestine to occupy Iraq. And many of the same techniques that Israel has used to occupy both Lebanon in the past and to occupy the Occupied Territories in West Bank and Gaza were used by the United States in Iraq. Also, if the United States was occupying an Arab country, it would be less prone to criticize Israel for doing the same thing. And we saw there has been far less criticism by the US government since 2003 than before in terms of what it was doing in the Occupied Territories.[77]

The invasion of Iraq was always intended as a prelude to the invasion of Iran. US approval of Israeli plans for the region is demonstrated at the December 2003 Herzliya conference, Israel's main national policy platform, attended by 42 US officials, including Deputy Defense Secretary Gordon England, Under-secretary of State for Political Affairs Nicholas Burns and former CIA director James Woolsey.[78] Half the Israeli cabinet and Prime Minister Ehud Olmert focused on the new threat from the Shia "arc of extremism", now that Sunni extremism was supposedly vanquished with the invasions of Afghanistan and Iraq. The new enemy was Iran, which possibly was trying to produce nuclear bombs, undermining hegemon Israeli's nuclear status in the Middle East, and by implication that of the US.

The Israeli logic, which is hard to fault, is that with Iraq now occupied, unstable and its inevitably pro-Iranian Shia majority asserting control, Iran has been strengthened, and that the same war plan against Iran is necessary to defeat the chief remaining regional anti-Israeli regime, which is now gathering support from not only Shia, but also from Sunni opponents to the US-Israeli project throughout the Arab world. Ben Eliezer told the gathering: "They are twins, Iran and Iraq."[79] The strategy developed at Herzliya was to first eliminate the direct Shia threat embodied in the Lebanese Hizbullah; hence, the 2006 invasion of southern Lebanon.[80] This was intended to intimidate Syria and isolate Iran, freeing Israel and the US to attack Iran after the requisite provocation was engineered.

Arms production
The "special relationship" is really only a mutually beneficial relationship for Israel and the US military industrial complex, rather than for the US government. Financed by US aid and loans, Israel buys US arms, inducing

its neighbors to do the same in an unending arms race, keeping the Arab enemy dependent on the US, even as Israel proceeds quietly with its own, increasingly anti-US agenda.

Even here, the special relationship is losing its shine, as Israel is increasingly a competitor to US arms producers. By 2006 Israeli arms exports were $3.4 billion, making Israel the 4th largest arms dealer in the world, ahead of Britain.[81] The high-tech arms industry is a new GGIII form of the age-old fatal embrace of GGI. Not only do Jewish elites within their host countries have outsize political clout due to their financial power, but Israeli does as well around the world through its monopoly on sophisticated weapons and willingness (or refusal) to export them.

Israel now wields political power not only as a regional hegemon, but in many countries otherwise immune to Zionist pressures, such as India, China, and Turkey. Its drones, perfected in attacks on Palestinians in Gaza, are purchased by Germans, Russians, Turks— on the approval of the Israeli government. Germany both provides submarines to the IDF which deploy nuclear weapons, and imports Israeli drones for its NATO operations in Afghanistan. Russia's decision to supply Syria with P-800 missiles incensed Israel, which claimed they could be stolen by Hizbullah (they would of course interfere with any future plans to attack Syria), and Israeli officials threatened to sell "strategic, tie-breaking weapons" to "areas of strategic importance" to Russia in retaliation.[82]

Arms sales played an important role in overcoming both India and China's anti-Israeli stance. In GGII India supported the Palestinians and only recognized Israel to 1992, though there had been contacts between intelligence officials in third countries.[83] In light of Arab support for Pakistan in Kashmir, without the Soviet Union as a balance in world affairs, India naturally drifted towards the US and Israel.[84] Mustafa El-Feki predicts that soon India will "assume the role of a policeman in the Indian Ocean and the outskirts of the Gulf, with US blessing and with the aim of encircling so-called Islamic violence. This would be in harmony with Israel's agenda, and it may pave the way to a scheme of joint control over the Greater Middle East."[85] In 2003, during the visit to India by Sharon (the first by an Israeli prime minister), his deputy Yosef Lapid told journalists that an "unwritten, abstract" axis had been created between Israel, India and the US. Israel's sales to China angered even Bush II who insisted it cancel its planned sale to China in 2002 of the Phalcon radar system incorporating US.

An important role Israel plays in its ongoing invasions is to test new military hardware of use to the US in its own wars. Israel field-tested US bunker-busting bombs against Hizbullah, intended for a possible invasion of Iran. Israeli business booms on the back of the Middle East chaos it inspires, and acts as model for an increasingly terror-stricken world, "a living example of how to enjoy relative safety amid constant war".[86] America and many other countries' high-security gated communities are in effect the traditional Jewish ghetto of the Middle Ages, perfected in Israel, now necessary for not only US elites but for Iraqi ones too, as the cities become increasingly dangerous. Senior US commanders in Iraq, David Petraeus and James Amos, advised by four Israeli officers in Fort Leavenworth, planned and executed the sealing off of occupied areas in Baghdad using special ID cards based on Israeli experience with the "separation wall".[87]

Israeli security company ICTS controls security in many US airports including the four airports involved in the 9/11 highjackings, Charles de Gaulle (the 2001 "shoe bomber") and Schipol (the 2009 "crotch bomber") airports. Israel security firms work closely with the US on new security measures, including full-body scanning at airports introduced in 2010. From 2001–08 "security product" sales to the US more than quadrupled.

An important move by Israel to extend its influence beyond the Middle East into strategic geopolitical territory in opposition to both the US and Russia, but in league with its neocon allies in the US, has been active military support for President Saakashvili in Georgia. Randy Scheunemann, advisor to neocon Republican Senator John McCain, was advising Saakashvili prior to his war against Russia in August 2008, which turned out to be a fiasco for US-Russian relations. Military advisers from Israeli security firms were training the country's armed forces and were involved in the Georgian invasion of South Ossetia. Georgian Defense Minister Davit Kezerashvili and Minister of Reintegration Temur Yakobashvili are both Israeli citizens who returned to Georgia to enter politics.

Nuclear weapons

Israel's nuclear program was already underway in the 1950s with French support after their collaboration in the invasion of Egypt in 1956 — outside of US and IAEA control. No attempt was made to develop civilian nuclear energy, only bombs, which it is believed to have produced by the late 1960s. President Kennedy tried to force Israel to end its nuclear ambitions without success.[88] A secret protocol between Israel and Nixon negotiated by Kissinger required America to keep Israel's nuclear weapons secret while actively preventing attempts to sanction Israel for failure to sign the NPT. The Israeli drive to develop nuclear weapons was the key strategy behind its long term goal of establishing itself as the regional hegemon, responsible only to itself, the professed goal being self-defense, the underlying goal being nuclear blackmail of any country that stands in the way of its agenda.

After 1967, France ended its cooperation to mollify its Arab allies but it was too late. Commenting on the creative political use of its nuclear weapons, head of the French Atomic Energy Agency Francis Perrin explains, "We thought the Israeli bomb was aimed against the Americans, not to launch against America, but to say 'if you don't want to help us in a critical situation we will require you to help us, otherwise we will use our nuclear bomb.'"[89] This became a particularly alarming issue during the 1973 war with Egypt. Martin van Creveld, an Israeli professor of military history warned: "We have the capability to take the world down with us. And I can assure you that this will happen before Israel goes under."[90]

Terrorism/ mercenaries/ mafia

Throughout history, terrorism has been used by empires to cow the newly conquered, less often by those enslaved to intimidate their masters. The use of imperial terror in GGI, embodied in piracy and privateering, had been largely abandoned as an imperial strategy of surplus expropriation by the nineteenth century. Rhodes and friends hoped to build a British empire that operated quite legally, with the agreement of the periphery (after the Germans were put in their place), but the "war against terror" was used even then to condone violations of the personal freedoms enshrined in the official GGI ideology of liberalism, especially when the communist reaction to imperialism set in.

The extent of Israeli and Israeli-inspired terrorism is impossible to determine. Mossad is the most feared intelligence agency, responsible for countless targeted assassinations and black-ops both in the Middle East and around the world since its founding in 1949, documented by ex-agent Ostrovsky in *By Way of Deception*. The ability of Israel, both through its armed forces and secret police, to function outside international law is legendary; for instance, the bombings in Arab countries in the 1950s to provoke the largely non-Zionist Arab Jews to emigrate,[91] the Entebbe raid to rescue Israeli hostages in Uganda in 1976 conducted by the IDF and Mossad, the bombing of Iraq's nuclear power facilities in 1981. Most recently, Mossad was linked to the cyber attack which paralyzed computers at Iran's nuclear reactors in September 2010, the blast at the Iranian Revolutionary Guard's top security Imam Ali military base in October 2010 that killed 18, as well as abductions and assassinations of Iranian scientists.[92]

Among openly functioning Jewish terrorist organizations in the West, the Jewish Defense League is the most well known, operating in Europe, North America and South Africa. Founded at the height of GGII by Rabbi Meir Kahane[93] in New York City in 1968, the JDL's purpose is purportedly to protect Jews from local manifestations of anti-Semitism, but instead it became a loud proponent of anticommunism and Islamophobia, bombing Soviet and Arab properties in the US, and targeting for assassination alleged "enemies of the Jewish people", ranging from Arab-American political activists to neo-Nazis.[94] In "Terrorism 2000/2001", the FBI referred to the JDL as a "violent extremist Jewish organization", though it still operates openly. This marks a new strategy for Israel, a hands-off openly international terrorist Israeli-first organization, a luxury the US itself can't afford in pursuit of its imperial goals.

The use of terror as the current enemy of the empire-and-a-half is a Zionist strategy, a logical outcome of the Israeli strategy of permanent war, imposed on the US to ensure the continuation in GGIII of the special relationship. The terror act that marks the beginning of the GGIII "war on terror" was the 1983 bombing and killing of 213 US and French marines in Lebanon which, like 9/11, Israel knew about and failed to inform the US.[95] Neither the 1983 bombing nor 9/11 were interpreted as acts of revenge for US complicity in Israel's own reign of terror—which both were[96]—but as yet a further attack on "our common values", as Prime Minister Sharon said about 9/11, declaring, 'I believe together we can defeat these forces of evil.'"[97] "The Americans will know how it feels to have a terrorist attack."[98] Israel achieved a new chess 'queen' of its own in GGIII by getting America to adopt its strategy of permanent war and terror, making it the new GGIII ideology.

The terror inflicted on the empire by its enemies (whether real or black-op), so the argument goes, requires the empire to reply in kind, which implies the use of collective punishment as a strategy. Because we are all perceived as complicit by our enemies, who supposedly are happy to kill us indiscriminately in revenge, we are justified to retaliate in kind.

9/11 came to symbolize a kind of collective punishment enacted by America's foes, a re-enactment of WWII German bombings of England and Russia, which were an attempt to create terror among the civilian population leading to defeat and were the excuse for a vengeful response of collective punishment in return; namely, the 1945 bombing of Dresden, which had no military significance. The same logic is used today to justify hourly bombings of Afghanistan and the widespread killing of civilians and destruction of homes in Iraq, Afghanistan and Palestine.[99]

A further corollary when all morality is abandoned is that we should rely on the best and most experienced people in the use of terror. First are professional soldiers for hire (mercenaries)—Cheney's Haliburton and KBR "contractors" blend into Dyncorps (founded in 1951 as Land-Air) and Xe (founded in 1997 as Blackwater) private security contractors and mercenaries in the GGII&III wars. Mercenaries are growing in importance as a factor in fighting the imperial wars, just as they were used in the past where standing armies were too expensive to maintain and conscription politically unfeasible. It is estimated that there are up to 75,000 mercenaries in Afghanistan and more in Iraq.

Along with North Korea, Israel is the most militarized nation in the world, with universal conscription and service to the age of 50, so it is no surprise it is in the forefront of mercenary activity, on both sides of conflicts:

> Former Israeli army troops, with counter-terror experience, are aiding Colombian army and police units in the field. This is nothing new, and has never been much of a secret, at least in Colombia. For one thing, Israel has sold over a hundred million dollars worth of military equipment to Colombia in the past few years. The gear and weapons often comes with technical experts, often former Israeli military, to show how to get the most out of the stuff. Israelis have been popular in Colombia for years as bodyguards and security experts. ... Earlier this year, the government issued international arrest warrants for three Israeli men who had provided special operations training for drug gang killers. ... The drug gangs need trained assassins to remove rivals and government officials that get in the way.[100]

Then there are the pirates—today's mafias. The premier one, born in the ex-Soviet Union and with a safe haven in Israel, is the Kosher Nostra, now welcomed into Israeli government circles to share its expertise. According to a US State Department cable published in November 2010 by WikiLeaks, officials from H.A.Sh Security, an Israeli firm involved in "security technologies" production with India's giant Micro-Technologies, tried to enter the US. The chairman of H.A.Sh Security is retired Major General Dan Ronen, who led the invasion of Lebanon in 2006. Many such members of "OC [organized crime] slip through the consular cracks", according to the State Department cable.[101]

Israeli organized crime operates in New York, Miami, Las Vegas, Canada, Israel and Egypt, especially in cocaine and ecstasy trafficking, and credit card and computer fraud. Their ready access to advanced communications technologies, as witnessed by the FBI and other US enforcement agencies, means they are almost impossible to stop. A 1997 Los Angeles federal and state investigation failed because the Israeli drug dealers were monitoring the police communications. A CIA investigation later concluded, "The organization has apparent extensive access to database systems to identify pertinent personal and biographical information."[102]

Piracy and terrorism in GGI was ad hoc but in GGIII has been given a new lease on life. In a complex web, international (especially Israeli) banks, working with international mafia, ensure the appropriation of a significant part of the world's surplus through the provision of security services and laundering of proceeds from drug, arms and other smuggling.

These are the new terrorists, operating according to the traditional mafia strategy to terrorize victims and then demand protection money, now in the context of the Israeli-inspired war on terror. Thus Israel incites, abets and possibly even perpetrates terrorism attributed to Muslim fanatics, and then sells the world drones, full-body scanners and operates security at dozens of world airports, both protecting against and at the same time facilitating terrorism and collective punishment, encouraging the use of ever more sophisticated security technology, in a vicious circle.

The connection between senior Israel military, officials and "OC"[103] in a society that is totally militarized, especially in the field of communications security technology now used around the world, increases Israel's ability to pursue plans outside of US control, and together with the extensive array of soft power at its disposal, to forestall any attempts to pressure Israel into following a US agenda.

Soft power
Politicide and co-opting the PLO
The original idea of benign British imperial strategists in GGI was that Jewish settlers in Palestine would bring economic development which would benefit the local Arabs, providing the "civilizing benefits" of imperialism. However, the real goal of Israeli/ Zionist soft power was to pursue what Israeli sociologist Baruch Kimmerling calls politicide, the gradual but systematic annihilation of the Palestinians as an independent political and social entity.[104] This has been done through many strategies, beginning with the denial that there are Palestinians at

all, and arguing that Palestine was "a land without a people for a people without a land", a term made famous by Golda Meir.[105]

Through arrests, murder and deportations it was possible to keep the Palestinians divided and leaderless until finally Palestinians united around Yasser Arafat and the PLO in 1964, though they were driven from Jordan and then Lebanon under Israeli pressure and invasion. Convinced by President Clinton that the PLO was ready to be co-opted as a friendly regime which would control the Palestinians, Israel allowed the leadership back to Gaza as part of the Oslo Accords in 1994, returning hesitantly to Sharon's and the traditional imperial policy of grooming a local strongman. Arafat's role would be to enforce Israel's security in the West Bank and Gaza. Sharon himself, Barak and the entire Israeli military establishment were opposed to this risky plan, and with the assassination of Rabin in 1995 the Israeli political establishment too turned against the process, as it had backfired, allowing Arafat an international platform to encourage Palestinian nationalism. The pretence by Barak to negotiate in 2000 likewise collapsed; Arafat was virtually a prisoner in Ramallah and possibly poisoned by Israel in 2004, replaced by the weak Mahmoud Abbas.

Both Abbas and his technocrat prime minister, Salam Fayyad, now ruling the West Bank are unpopular but bow to the demands of US and Israel and thus have their support. After Hamas was elected in Gaza, Israel returned to Yinon's divide-and-conquer policy, now between the two Palestinian camps, Fatah and Hamas. In February 2010, Fayyad spoke before Israel's security establishment at the annual Herzliya Conference, where he was compared by Shimon Peres to David Ben Gurion. His plan to "build" a state (not to declare one unilaterally) is in line with Netanyahu's notion of "economic peace" which proposes that development precede independence[106] (even as Israel prevents that very development). It implicitly accords with Israel's plans for South African-style Bantustans controlled by a comprador Palestinian leadership enforcing law and order in cooperation with Israel and the US, as is already the case in the West Bank, and has been endorsed by the Quartet (the US, EU, UN, and Russian Federation) and supported by international donors.[107]

Use of Islamists

In 1978, Begin formally licensed Muslim Brotherhood leader Ahmed Yassin's Islamic Association in Gaza. Religious elements and wealthy businessmen in Saudi Arabia and Kuwait helped finance Yassin, and Israelis collaborated by allowing funds to flow.[108] It was the Israeli right— Begin, Shamir and Sharon—who pursued this policy most vigorously.

"Supporting the radical…Muslim fundamentalism sat well with Mossad's… plan for the region."[109]

During most of 1980s, the Muslim Brotherhood in the region did not support resistance to Israeli occupation, its political energy going into fighting the PLO. It seemed unlikely that the Brotherhood would find a secure foothold among Palestinians, a significant number of whom were Christian, and who were the most modern and well educated community in the Arab world, with a militant diaspora connected around the world to a popular cause. Israel arrested Yassin in 1984 for stockpiling weapons and sentenced him to 13 years but then released him after one year and in 1987 registered his Religious Center, which morphed into Hamas in the Occupied Territories, hoping that it would weaken the PLO (Israel assassinated the wheelchair-ridden, quadriplegic and nearly blind sheik by helicopter gunship in 2004). According to Charles Freeman, former US ambassador to Saudi Arabia, "Israel started Hamas. It was a project of Shin Bet, the Israeli domestic intelligence agency,"[110] though, of course, that did not mean that Israel controlled it.

While the PLO built a reputation of active resistance with its guerrilla attacks beginning in 1965, the Brotherhood remained passive, and its membership among Palestinians was weak. It was only in the first Intifada 1987–93 that Hamas took up arms against Israel, replacing Fatah in Palestinians' eyes as the backbone of resistance, which persuaded 'moderate' Israelis like Rabin, Peres and Barak to enter negotiations culminating in the Oslo Accords. But whenever the now pliable PLO and Israelis moved towards an accord, Hamas would unleash a wave of attacks, playing into the hands of Israeli hardliners. From 1993 onwards, Likud and Hamas would reinforce each others' opposition to peace talks. Even as Hamas backed the second Intifada of 2000–05 and won elections in Gaza in 2006, its fight with the PLO and occasional, mostly victimless rocket fire into Israel were useful to Israel to justify the invasion of Gaza in 2008.

Not surprisingly, this experience of Israel in supporting Islamists, as is the case with the US, has been in the long run negative, leading to the emergence of new forms of resistance which are more determined and harder to eradicate or deal with than the more secular representatives of the region.

Spies/ assets/ *sayanim*/ gatekeepers

The age-old strategy to infiltrate the enemy (or in this case, ally) to subvert it from within took on a new dimension with the creation of Israel. For the first time in history, a citizen of another country, in this case a Jew living outside Israel, had grounds for an automatic allegiance to another country. From 1948 on, all Jews were considered by Israel as potential citizens, with the automatic right to immediate citizenship of Israel.[111] Suddenly Jews employed by US government organizations, especially those who formally embraced Israeli citizenship, became a possible—unmonitored—security risk, just as was the case in the Arab world, in the Soviet Union and all countries where Jews lived.

It is impossible to know how many American Jews have acted in some capacity as agents of Israel. With only one exception, those that have been caught have been acquitted, given suspended sentences, or, if holders of Israeli passports, merely deported to Israel. AIPAC officials Steve Rosen and Keith Weissman, who were accused of spying along with Department of Defense official Lawrence Franklin in 2004, were ultimately acquitted in April 2009 when prosecutors determined that they could not make their case without doing significant damage to national security (Franklin was sentenced to 13 years reduced to 10 months house arrest). A month after the Rosen and Weissman case was dismissed, Ben-Ami Kadish was caught redhanded and admitted to passing US defense secrets to Israel while working as an engineer at Picatinny Arsenal in New Jersey, but was only forced to pay a fine and continues to receive his Defense Department pension.[112]

Israeli agent Jonathan Pollard was arrested and given a life sentence in 1987 for his extensive spying. He is the only such agent actually serving a sentence, and is treated as a hero in Israel.[113] "Pollard's activities were completely illegal but not unusual. ... Israeli espionage activities were, for the most part, ignored by the US."[114] But Pollard and Franklin are the tip of the iceberg. The US is in fact riddled with undeclared agents who are virtually immune from suspicion, blending in with average Americans.

Take, for instance, Dr Lani Kass, who is the senior special assistant to the Chief of Staff of the US Air Force General Norton Schwartz, and who was born in Israel and a major in the IDF. She has a PhD in Sovietology but advises Air Force generals on cyberwarfare, terrorism, and the Middle East. She left Israel and began working for the US Defense Department in 1981, when Pollard was active. She was a leading participant in Project CHECKMATE, a "highly confidential strategic planning group tasked with 'fighting the next war' as tensions rise with Iran" that was established by the US Air Force in June 2007." In a speech at Mountain Home Air Force Base in Idaho in 2007, she said radical Muslims hate the western world because Europe took their dominant political position away and they want it back and that the long war against the Islamists will end "when they learn to love their children more than they hate us," a comment originally attributed to Israeli Prime Minister Golda Meir.[115]

It is hard to conceive that Kass is not serving Israel's interests in the first place, even without pay from Israel or without sending microfilms or other hard evidence of spying. She may be a *sayan* (helper), a Jew living outside Israel who volunteers to provide assistance to Mossad (in her case, more likely Israeli military intelligence). Typical assistance of *sayanim* includes facilitating medical care, providing money, logistics, and even overt intelligence gathering. Estimates put the number of *sayanim* in the thousands. The existence of this large body of volunteers is one reason why Mossad operates with fewer case officers than fellow intelligence agencies. A *sayan* can operate as an accomplice but still not be legally at risk of prosecution under US law due to a lack of the requisite intent regarding the broader goals of any illegal activity. When not aiding an ongoing operation, *sayanim* gather and report intelligence useful to Israel. *Le Figaro* in 2007 revealed that in 1978, Israeli Prime Minister Menachem Begin ordered the infiltration of the French ruling Gaullist party *Union pour un Mouvement Populaire,* and recruited French President Nicolas Sarkozy as a *sayan* in 1983.[116]

Kass is most certainly an asset, someone who provides information and supports the foreign power's goals in his/her work, without necessarily the intent to commit a crime. This volunteer corps of *sayanim*, assets and agents is deeply imbedded in western legislative bodies, particularly in the US. Though *sayanim* "must be 100 per cent Jewish,...the Mossad does not seem to care how devastating [their role] could be to the status of the Jewish people in the diaspora if it was known. The answer you get if you ask is: 'So what's the worst that could happen to those Jews? They'd all come to Israel. Great!'"[117]

Gatekeepers are pro-Zionist public figures, both left and right, even including Israel critics, whose role is to limit the debate about Israel in the public discourse; gatekeeping is the role that the Israel lobby and Jewish-dominated leftist and peace groups play. Blankfort explains that for leftist groups, this is often unconscious "tribalism", that rather than admitting that Israel is a vital accomplice in CIA arms and covert operations, it is

> a lot easier to blame US foreign policy, US imperialism. For example, when Israel was heavily involved in supporting the Contras in Nicaragua, supporting and arming the Salvadoran government, arming the government in Guatemala, the solidarity groups in those particular arenas were predominantly Jewish,

but they refused to take critical positions on Israel arming Salvador, Israel arming [the] Nicaragua [Contras], and Israel arming Guatemala. And when I organized a demonstration in 1985, opposing Israel's roles as a US surrogate in South Africa and Central America, those organizations would not endorse the demonstration. ... It's like the monkey: see no evil, hear no evil, speak no evil. This is how the solidarity movement has been when it comes to this cabal.[118]

Blankfort documents the same phenomenon with members of Congress, happy to condemn the Nicaraguan Contras and South African apartheid, but refusing to condemn or even mention Israel's active support of both, let alone Israel's own illegal activities and apartheid regime.

This gatekeeping is beginning to lose control over peace groups, an example being Code Pink's "Move Over AIPAC" conference which at this writing is scheduled to coincide with the annual AIPAC conference in Washington 21-24 May 2011. It was endorsed by over a hundred peace groups, including American Jews for a Just Peace, International Jewish Anti-Zionist Network, Israel Committee Against House Demolitions, Jews Say No, and Jewish Voice for Peace.

Israel lobby
Maintaining the special relationship through thick and thin requires a strong lobby of American Zionists, originally Jews, now including Christian Zionists, but more generally, many non-Jews who have identified unlimited personal wealth and power, the "secular basis of Judaism" as their *Weltanschauung*, the "practical spirit" of nineteenth century capitalism identified by Marx.

The Zionist lobby in the US was not as comparably significant a factor in US politics prior to WWI. Brandeis, President Wilson's Supreme Court choice in 1916 and president of the Zionist Organization of America (ZOA), was an important exception. He was instrumental in securing the Balfour Declaration in 1917 (see above), a landmark for the Zionists, whose support grew rapidly following the Balfour Declaration, the major supporting organizations being B'nai B'rith (founded in 1843), ZOA (founded in 1897) and the American Jewish Committee (AJC, founded in 1906). The impetus that increased their political power to a new level was the pressing need to ensure US government support for the creation of Israel after WWII.

At that crucial moment, because Britain was restricting emigration of Jews to its Palestine Mandate, the Zionists turned against their British sponsors, despite the fact that Britain had allowed 200,000 Jews to immigrate to the UK from 1933–44 and had been the guarantor of Jewish claims to a presence in Palestine from 1917 on. The assassination of Lord Moyne in Cairo in 1944 and the bombing of the King David Hotel in Jerusalem in 1946 by Jewish terrorists were virtual declarations of war against the British.

As part of their preparations for the founding of a Jewish state in Palestine, in 1946, the US Jewish lobby, led by the ZOA and AJC, pressured the US government to force Britain to allow 100,000 Jews to go to Palestine from Europe, rather than to the US.[119] They used the negotiation of a massive postwar US loan to Britain as a blackmail tool, much as Brandeis in 1917 was able to get President Wilson to extract the promise of a Jewish state from a desperate Britain. The British were forced to increase immigration to Palestine, despite fierce native Arab opposition, defeat of the Nazis, the closure of the concentration camps, and the elimination of the threat to Jews in Europe.

The US Senate vote on the loan was far from certain, and it was only the lobbying of US Zionists that ensured passage in the Senate (46-34). British Foreign Secretary Ernest Bevin fumed that the Americans "did not want too many Jews in New York". British diplomat Howard Crossman says that Israel's future president, Chaim Weizmann, told him that it was a question of choosing "between the greater and lesser injustice", to be "unjust to Arabs or Jews".[120]

This 'success' led to the British losing all control over developments in Palestine and handing responsibility over to the UN. It also pushed the Zionists firmly into the sphere of US presidential politics, getting both Democratic and Republican presidential candidates, Truman and Dewey, to promise to support partition and the recognition of Israel, presaging what by GGIII would become total Zionist control of US Middle East policy, Democrat and Republican.[121]

The lobby came into its own only after 1956, when Eisenhower insisted that Israel withdraw from Sinai. Israel lobbyists found they had access to only two "minor Congressional offices" at that crucial moment and set about crafting a network of political action committees (PACs). By the 1980s, when asked how many Congressional offices they had access to, an Israeli embassy official said, "Almost all of them."[122]

There are now at least 52 major American Jewish organizations actively engaged in promoting Israel's agenda in the US, coordinated by the Presidents of the Major American Jewish Organizations (PMAJO).[123] The grassroots membership ranges from more than 200,000 activists in the Jewish Federations of North America (JFNA) to the approximately 100,000 wealthy power brokers in the American Israel Public Affairs

Committee (AIPAC), influencing Congressional votes, nomination of candidates, and defeating incumbents who do not unconditionally support the Israeli line.[124] There are scores of think tanks, established by grants from wealthy Zionists, including the Hudson Institute (founded by Herman Kahn in 1961), the Washington Institute for Near East Policy (founded by AIPAC in 1985), and the Brookings Institute's Saban Institute for Middle East Policy (founded by Haim Saban in 2002).[125] Scores of Zionist-funded PACs intervene in all national and regional elections, controlling nominations and influencing election outcomes.

Petras argues that even scholarly publishing houses, such as Yale University Press, have been taken over by Zionists, and calls this complex network and its activities the Zionist Power Configuration.[126] He argues that fewer than half of the 5.1 million US Jews support these Zionist organizations but they are highly organized, and while the Jewish population is relatively tiny, the percentage of Jews who vote is not. In any case, until recently no one dared lobby against Israel, leaving the field open to the Israel-firsters.

While all their activity is dedicated first and foremost to ensuring that US Middle East policy serves Israel's colonial expansion in Palestine and war aims in the Middle East, what B'nai B'rth calls a "focus on Israel and its place in the world", many groups specialize in different spheres of activity. For example, the "Friends of the Israel Defense Force" is primarily concerned "to look after the IDF", essentially providing financial resources and recruiting US volunteers for a foreign army. Hillel is the student lobby at 500 colleges and universities. Taglit-Birthright sent over a quarter-million Jews age 18–26 to Israel from 2000–10 for 10-day trips to Israel, involving indoctrination in the company of Israeli soldiers, where they are urged to become dual citizens and encouraged to serve in the Israeli armed forces.[127]

Local Zionist organizations recruit local politicians, celebrities, publishers, preachers and minority leaders for all-expenses-paid tours to Israel on the understanding they will write or give interviews when they return to the US. Local leaders mobilize activists to attack anti-Zionist Jews in public and private, to demand they be excluded from media roundtables on the Middle East, threaten local editorial staff publishing articles critical of Israel, monitor meetings and speakers to detect anti-Zionist criticism, which they label "the new anti-Semitism", and lobby to deny critics tenure at universities. Most synagogues conduct regular fundraising for Israel, including the financing of settlements and parks built on former Palestinian villages. Books critical of Zionism or Israel are prevented from being used, kept out of libraries, or at best ignored in the mainstream media.

To understand US submission to Israeli policies it is necessary to note the Zionist presence in important policy positions, including the Departments of Treasury and State, the Pentagon, the National Security Council, the White House and as chairs of key congressional committees. "It is irrelevant, we are told, that all but a handful of neocons happen to be Jewish and not only Jewish but very pro-Israel and that the whole movement was Jewish and Zionist from the start."[128] Israelis call Zionist Jews in key administration posts, especially State and Treasury, "warm Jews", who consult not only with AIPAC and other domestic lobbies, but also with the Israeli state. Morris Amitay, former executive director of AIPAC, the most powerful lobby in Washington, explains: "There are a lot of guys at the working level up here [on Capitol Hill]...who happen to be Jewish, who are willing ... to look at certain issues in terms of their Jewishness ... These are all guys who are in a position to make the decision in these areas for those senators ...You can get an awful lot done just at the staff level."[129]

In 2004, AIPAC successfully pressured the Bush II administration to create the office of Under-secretary for Terrorism and Financial Intelligence and to appoint "warm Jew" Stuart Levey to head it. His office became the major foreign policy venue for setting US, EU and even UN policy toward Iran, "elaborating the Iran sanctions policies which Washington imposed on the EU and the Security Council", investigating trade and investment policies of the major world manufacturing, banking, shipping, petroleum and trading corporations. He pressures US pension funds, investment houses, oil companies and economic institutions to divest from any companies dealing with Iran's civilian economy and threatens sanctions against companies in Europe, Asia, the Middle East and North America which refuse to sever relations with Iran. He "coordinates his campaign with Zionist leaders in Congress", constantly exerting pressure against Iran, clearly hoping to provoke an incident that can be used to pressure the US to invade.[130]

The Republicans and Democrats now vie for which party is most pro-Israel. Obama's initial attempts to pressure Israel made him a target in mid-term elections in 2010, prompting Congressman Gary Ackerman to exhort Jewish voters that "Israel's best bet for addressing any concerns about Obama's policy" was for the Democrats to retain power, citing "the forceful criticisms they conveyed to the White House when they thought that Obama was leaning too hard on Israel". Ackerman, who chaired the sub-committee on the Middle East and South Asia of the House Committee on Foreign Affairs, said that if Israel wanted "positive influence on the White House" it needed what he called the "first-class team" of Howard Berman, Barney Frank, Henry Waxman, Sander Levin and himself to continue chairing key House committees, because "we are all pro-Israel and we all have major, major, major influence in the executive branch".[131] The Republicans won a majority in Congress 2010, and the new House Majority Leader Eric Cantor told Netanyahu in a private meeting that the new Republican majority in Congress would work to serve and protect Israel's interests, that "the Republican majority understands the special relationship between Israel and the United States, and that the security of each nation is reliant upon the other."[132]

Christian Zionists, numbering some 20 million, are strongest in the southern Bible Belt states where there are few Jews and instead a tradition of anti-Jewish prejudice. These states are used to bring up the most pro-Israeli bills in Congress, and Senators and House members from those states are well rewarded by donations from pro-Israel Jewish donors and PACs in spite of legislation that tries to prevent non-local funding.[133]

The Israel lobby is supported by Jewish American billionaires, a sizable fraction of the American ruling class (50 per cent of US billionaires). The *Mother Jones* 400 list of the leading individual donors for the 2000 election showed that 8 of the top 10 were Jews, and at least 125 of the top 250. They support a pro-Israeli orientation in American Middle East policy, and the non-Zionist or 'soft' Zionist elite, represented by the Zionist *bête noire* Brzezinski, can't mobilize an effective response.

After the disaster of Bush II, Brzezinski's protégé Obama was elected president—clearly to try to undo some of the damage done to the empire by the neocons (See Chapter 3). The Zionists set about co-opting him, even calling him the "first Jewish president"[134] and apart from Obama's failed attempt to bring some balance to his cabinet with Charles Freeman and his speech at Cairo University in June 2009 calling for a "new beginning between the United States and Muslims",[135] have not been disappointed. He had little choice but to continue Bush II's policies in the Middle East given the strength of the lobby and the facts on the ground.

New groups are created to address new issues. Even under Bush I, when Pollard was convicted of treason and Bush tried to stop Israel's settlements, Israeli lobbyists worked with his administration to establish the Committee for Peace and Security in the Gulf, chaired by Richard Perle.[136] PNAC came along in 1997, and neocon William Kristol joined forces with rightwing Christian evangelical Gary Bauer to establish a new group in 2010, the Emergency Committee for Israel's Leadership, to target candidates in key Senate and Congressional races, along with the entire Obama administration. Its initial victims were Congressman

Joe Sestak and Mary Jo Kilroy whom it portrayed as "openly hostile" to Israel. Sestak did not sign an AIPAC-sponsored letter calling on Obama to comply with Israel's continued settlement agenda and criticized the 2007 blockade of Gaza. This targeting has resulted in the defeat of many congressmen (senators are more careful and toe the line), the most famous being Paul Findley in 1982 (the campaign led by Rahm Emanuel), and the latest—Sestak and Kilroy in 2010.

The first of such letters, initiating what would become a popular lobby technique, was signed by 76 senators addressed to President Ford in 1974–75 warning him of fallout from a "reassessment of relations with Israel" at a time when Israel was refusing to negotiate in good faith with Egypt for the return of Sinai. Ford backed down. Then Bush I got one in 1990 from 94 senators over his attempt to stop the settlements. The latest two in April 2010, signed by 363 members of Congress and 76 Senators emphasized the "unbreakable bond" with Israel.

The spy scandal involving AIPAC beginning in 2004 revealed that the organization is deeply involved in spying as well as lobbying— with the knowledge of the FBI. Though acquitted, Steve Rosen launched a $20 million defamation lawsuit against AIPAC in 2010 threatening to expose documents showing that his activities of passing on classified material to Israeli sources is standard AIPAC procedure. Rosen said, "AIPAC approved of the receipt of classified information,"[137] and regularly traffics in sensitive government information, especially material related to the Middle East.

With criticism of the Israel lobby surfacing by 2007, a new 'soft' Zionist lobby was created, J Street PAC 2008, "the first and only federal Political Action Committee" for those "who believe a new direction in American policy will advance US interests in the Middle East and promote real peace and security for Israel and the region".[138] Roundly denounced by AIPAC, it has nonetheless proved to be a gatekeeper, supported by the non-Likud Israeli political center, including Kadima.

Israel itself has responded to mounting criticism by creating new groups such as the Israeli NGO Monitor with affiliates around the world to monitor "activities of humanitarian NGOs in the framework of the Arab-Israeli conflict". It has successfully lobbied governments to defund NGOs which criticize Israel and encourages governments to recognize the "new anti-Semitism". In November 2010, the Canadian Parliamentary Coalition to Combat Anti-Semitism called on all political parties to endorse expanding the definition of anti-Semitism to include criticism of Israel, declaring such criticism "hate speech" in reaction to Israeli Apartheid Week events at Canadian universities.[139]

There are powerful lobbies in all major western powers. The World Jewish Congress founded in Switzerland in 1936 acts as "the diplomatic arm of the Jewish people", with headquarters and a tax-exempt Foundation in New York and offices in Brussels, Jerusalem, Paris, Moscow, Buenos Aires and Geneva. Its 2009 Plenary Assembly in Jerusalem was attended by representatives from 62 countries. As well as the World Zionist Organization (founded in 1897), the associated World Zionist Congress, and the Anti-Defamation League (founded in 1913), there are holocaust-related organizations such as the Elie Wiesel Foundation for Humanity (founded in 1986) which raise funds for Israel and lobby world governments to support Israeli policy. The Friends of Israel Initiative is an umbrella organization set up in 2010 to coordinate existing European Friends of Israel (EFI) groups. EFI and associated lobby groups throughout the EU target the major parties on Middle East policy.

Media manipulation
Jewish dominance of Hollywood is well known, and prominent Hollywood Jews such as Ben Stein even boast "Do Jews run Hollywood? You bet they do... & what of it?"[140] Jewish humorists Bryan Fogel and Sam Wolfson confirm Jewish dominance in Hollywood, noting that of the ten major studios, nine were created by Jews (Walt Disney was a gentile), and as of 2006 all ten studios were run by Jews.[141] "Yes, we do control the movie studios. All Jews please report to the World Conspiracy Headquarters immediately (don't forget to bring your pass code)." In a more serious vein, playwright David Mamet noted, "For those who have not been paying attention, this group [Ashkenazi Jews] constitutes, and has constituted since its earliest days, the bulk of America's movie directors and studio heads." For American TV network control, Fogel and Wolfson claim the figure is 75 per cent, while for print media, they found that seven of ten major publications are run by Jews. "Conclusion: Jews have lots of opinions that they love to write about and charge you money to read! Cool."[142]

Among Jews prominent in the finance and economic elite in the US there are no publicly proclaimed anti-Zionists, resulting in an implicit bias towards Israel in US media. Reinforcing this bias, the (tax exempt) Israel Project was set up in 2002 as a propaganda arm of Israel with 18 members of Congress on its board of directors, which buys commercial time to air pro-Israeli advertising on CNN, MSNBC, Fox News and other cable networks. It also provides "media fellowships" for US students, and conducts focus-group public opinion research. A member of one such group said she was "called in for what seemed an unusual assignment: to help test-market language that could be used to sell military action against Iran to the American public."[143]

At a conference in 2009, Zionist media magnate Haim Saban described his pro-Israeli formula, outlining "three ways to be influential in American politics...make donations to political parties, establish think tanks, and control media outlets."[144] The extensive activities by Zionists to promote Israel in the US media by the early 1960s was confirmed by the release in 2010 of declassified files from the 1962–63 Senate investigation revealing Israel's clandestine programs for "cultivation of editors," the "stimulation and placement of suitable articles in the major consumer magazines" as well as controlling US reporting about sensitive subjects such as the Dimona nuclear weapons facility.[145] While the national Zionist organizations procured the journalists and academic writers and editors, it was the local affiliates who carried the message and implemented the line.

After the investigation, the Justice Department under Robert Kennedy ordered the American Zionist Council (founded in 1949) to register as a foreign agent in late 1962. It transferred responsibilities to AIPAC, which was set up especially for this purpose in 1963, granted tax-exempt status in 1968, and has never been required to register as an Israeli agent. Though eventually AIPAC would be caught in a serious spy scandal in 2004, by then, Zionist influence in the Justice Department was able to defuse the scandal and leave the aggressive pro-Israeli lobby intact, without so much as a slap on the wrist.

But this focus by Jewish elites on media is nothing new. Reuters news agency was established by a German Jew, Paul Reuter, in 1851 and came to specialize in swashbuckling, sensational British imperial news, enthusiastically supporting empire, in line with the interests of Jewish financial capital at the time. Jewish interests controlled much of German media until the rise of Hitler. By the 1870s, while 1 per cent of Germany's population, Jews controlled 13 out of 21 daily newspapers and had strong presence in four others.[146]

The focus of Jewish elites on the media and manipulating it to serve their ends is a corollary of the 'fatal embrace' of Jews and the state, an outgrowth of Jewish culture, an instinctual attempt to protect group interests in the face of the host country's population whose interests are not the same, and at times can be hostile. This need to control public opinion became a science in the early twentieth century—public relations—founded by Edward Bernays, cousin of Sigmund Freud, and friend of presidents Roosevelt and Kennedy.

Public relations is generally associated with advertising and sales, but it has always been an important factor in politics. Bernays wrote *Public Relations* (1945) but he also wrote *Propaganda* (1928). He engineered the public relations effort behind the US-backed coup in Guatemala in 1953–4.[147] Though he was not a committed Zionist, his friend Chaim Weizmann offered him the job of Israeli foreign minister in 1948. He never visited Israel, but when asked if he would take on Israel as a client, he said "Sure!" and offered the following advice: Israel should

> establish much closer relationships with the democratic countries of the world and get those countries to make much more visible in the public mind how much they support Israel and how much they believe in freedom of religion, just as the democratic countries believe in freedom of the press, freedom of assembly, freedom of petition. Israel should appoint an international public relations committee, made up of all the best public relations people in the democratic countries of the world England, France, Germany, Italy, even Spain.[148]

The opposite of advertising is "dynamic silence", invented by the AJC's Rabbi S.A. Fineberg in 1947.[149] Through local Jewish businesses threatening to stop advertising, the AJC pressured newspapers and radio stations across the country to refrain from publicizing anticommunist circuit speaker Gerald Smith, who identified Jews as sympathetic to communism and criticized their control of Hollywood.[150] The one US senator who dared to vote against Israel on resolutions (Robert Byrd senator 1959–2010) received the same treatment. Because he was too well-loved and well-established to attack, he was just ignored by AIPAC and the media.

This technique has been supplemented by one of forcing public critics of Jewish power to apologize on threat of destroying their careers. In September 2010 when CNN commentator Rick Sanchez complained publicly that CNN and the media are largely run by Jews and elitists, he was fired and a few days later made a grovelling public apology. When Oliver Stone told the *Sunday Times* about the same time that "public opinion was focused on the Holocaust because of 'Jewish domination of the media'", he too quickly retracted under the threat of having his film career destroyed: [151] "In trying to make a broader historical point about the range of atrocities the Germans committed against many people, I made a clumsy association about the Holocaust, for which I am sorry and I regret. Jews obviously do not control media or any other industry."[152] Earlier outbursts by Mel Gibson and Marlon

Brando caused them similar career problems and required humiliating public apologies.

But nothing quite compares to the backtracking in March 2011 by Judge Richard Goldstone, head of the UN Fact-Finding Mission investigating the Israeli operation Cast Lead in Gaza of 2009-2010, who tried to discredit his own report, popularly known as the Goldstone Report, in an op-ed in the *Washington Post* after more a year of intense pressure. His solo retraction without consulting the other three members of the mission was actually illegal, discrediting only himself, as the others issued this statement: "There is no justification for any demand or expectation for reconsideration of the report as nothing of substance has appeared that would in any way change the context, findings or conclusions of that report with respect to any of the parties to the Gaza conflict."[153]

Cultural wars

Culture has always been a vital tool of the ruling elite to secure the economic and political system as a whole. With the creation of Israel in GGII, it took on a special meaning. Imperial state support was no longer just for a small Jewish financial elite within the empire, but for an aggressive Jewish state fighting wars and increasingly determining US policy in the strategic Middle East.

The Zionist project required broad popular support, in order to ensure the US special relationship with this problematic state would not evaporate. Without unquestioning support nurtured through education and entertainment—culture—Israel would be seen immediately for what it is and would be rejected as a colonial, racist state. It would be forced to make a just peace with its neighbors based on international law. Jews would no longer have automatic dual nationality and would have to assimilate in their host countries or move to a non-Zionist Israel. Zionism would suffer the same fate as other colonial doctrines and Judaism would once again be associated with a religious tradition rather than a political ideology.

There can be no culture without an economic base. It is only because of enduring Jewish prominence in the world of finance and hence the economy as a whole, and then via a commanding presence in the media world, that Jews have been able to achieve a considerable degree of hegemony in the world of culture. This cultural hegemony was relatively benign, at least in the US, until the creation of Israel.

The Hollywood film industry was the heart of American culture in the twentieth century, largely the creation of 'liberal' media-savvy

Jews. Before the creation of Israel, the Hollywood cultural message was generally one of social justice within the system, fighting for the rights of the underdog and minorities. With the creation of Israel and the onset of the Cold War, Hollywood and US culture lost much of its anti-capitalist, occasionally socialist message, though the rights of minorities continue to be an important Hollywood theme.

Interestingly, to date, Israel rarely appears in US culture directly. Instead, especially after 1967 war, the topic of the WWII persecution of Jews—the Holocaust—became a major focus of Hollywood, as part of what Norman Finkelstein, as a son of Holocaust survivors, dubbed the "Holocaust Industry",[154] an indirect justification of Israel, assuring unconditional US support. There have been over 40 US and Canadian feature films about the Holocaust produced in the past two decades, but none about the tragedy that the invasion of Palestine caused for the Palestinians, especially in 1948 and from 1967 to the present, supposedly justified by the Holocaust.

From the 1980s on Jewish organizations have promoted Holocaust commemoration and education, with Holocaust Studies now a required part of most western school curricula, laws specifically prohibiting questioning of the official Israeli-sanctioned version of WWII history concerning the Jews, and Holocaust Museums in at least 20 US cities and another 30 in other countries.

Though Muslims played no role whatsoever in the persecution of Jews in Europe under the Nazis, this Holocaust industry is a central part of the campaign to vilify Islam. David Horowitz has organized "Islamofascism Awareness Week" (IFAW)[155] on close to 100 college campuses since 2007, identifying Islam with Nazism. Ironically, Michigan State University Young Americans for Freedom invited a *bona fide* fascist—Nick Griffin, the head of the British National Party—to speak on how Europe is becoming "Eurabia". IFAW is now an annual event, with seminars on jihad and Islamic totalitarianism.

A significant new development in this cultural war is the phenomenal growth of the ultra-orthodox Chabad-Lubavitch community. The most famous leader of Chabad was Rabbi Menachem Mendel Schneerson (1902–94), the "Lubavitcher Rebbe" who is worshipped as the messiah by his followers. The movement began an outreach programme in the US in the 1950s in reaction to the assimilation of American Jews, founding a collective of Jewish religious cultural centers across the US. In GGIII it has blossomed into a movement with 4,000 full-time emissary families directing 3,300 institutions and a workforce that numbers in the tens of thousands dedicated to the welfare of the Jewish people worldwide.

This includes control of the synagogues (with affiliated cultural centers) in the ex-Soviet Union through the Federation of Jewish Communities, promoting emigration to Israel and undoubtedly acting as a cover for Israeli intelligence gathering and possibly subversive activity. The role of the Chabad movement is particularly important in Russia and ex-Soviet Central Asia, as unlike Jews from Arab countries that were induced to emigrate to Israel in the 1950–60s, Jews in the ex-Soviet Union are able to emigrate to Israel and then return to conduct business—and espionage—in a Jewish-friendly environment, holding two passports. Ironically, the desire of many Soviets to emigrate from the 1970s on meant that many actual émigrés to Israel—at least 30 per cent of the 1 million—came on the basis of forged documents or as the spouse of a Jew and have no racial or religious claim to being Jewish.[156]

The Lubavitchers actively lobby all levels of the US governments and were able to get Congress and President Carter to declare 18 April 1978 Education and Sharing Day (ESD) in honour of Schneerson, for his efforts for "education and sharing" for Jews and non-Jews alike. Since then each year in April, the US president proclaims ESD on a day close to Schneerson's birthday (11 Nissan). In the 1991 bill declaring ESD, the Noahide laws—a version of Judaism for non-Jews—were described as the "ethical values and principles" that are "the basis of civilized society and upon which our great Nation was founded".[157] In 2009 Obama proclaimed 5 April 2009 Education and Sharing Day and said: "Few have better understood or more successfully promoted these ideas than Rabbi Menachem Mendel Schneerson, the Lubavitcher Rebbe, who emphasized the importance of education and good character. ... On this day, we raise his call anew." In a further move, in 2006 Bush II announced that May would henceforth be celebrated as Jewish American Heritage Month, and Obama held the first JAHM White House reception in 2010 "to highlight and celebrate the range and depth of Jewish American heritage and contributions to American culture."

Hundreds of Chabad Houses now span the world, purportedly for education and worship, but used primarily by Israelis, since the Chabad movement now recognizes Israel—unlike strict orthodox Jews—as a Jewish state in the tradition of the ancient Israelite kingdoms. *Sayanim* can use Chabad Houses as safe houses, where there would be no record of a person's stay. Senior Israeli government and military officials visit and stay there alongside Israeli backpackers. The Chabad House in Mumbai was at the center of a still unsolved terrorist event in 2009 where up to 200 people were killed, including Chabad emissary Rabbi Gavriel and five other Chabad visitors.

The success of Jewish cultural hegemony in the West is epitomized in the wide acceptance of the cultural construct "Judeo-Christian heritage", a concept useful to a largely Christian empire where Jews play a powerful role, but one which is rejected by serious scholars, both Christian and Jewish. Talmudic scholar Jacob Neusner was quoted in *Newsweek*: "Theologically and historically, there is no such thing as the Judeo-Christian tradition. It's a secular myth favored by people who are not really believers themselves."[158] The concept was popularized in the 1940s as a reaction to Nazism and was used by the imperial elite in promoting anticommunism, and now the empire-and-a-half in its "clash of civilizations" targeting Islam.

Penetrating US imperial strategic thinking
Just as it is difficult to pin down Judaism (is it a religion, an ethnicity, a race, in its Zionist guise—a political ideology?), so it is difficult to describe what exactly Israel is (Is it a modern nation, a postmodern one, an empire colonizing Palestine, a US colony?). In as much as it is a colony, what is its mother country? Israel is not just an independent offspring of a mother country, as was the case in GGI, say, when Britain created its colonies. Alam answers this poser as follows: "By winning over the Jews in the western diaspora, and galvanizing them to use their wealth, intellect, and activism to promote Zionist causes, the Zionists succeeded in substituting the West for the missing natural mother country."[159]

Indeed, without the unswerving support of the West and the Jewish diaspora, Israel would quickly have collapsed. And though it is defiantly following its own policies in many countries around the world these days, operating both above-board as a modern state and in the shadows through its mercenaries and mafia, its most important role is still within the GGIII establishment in the US, on the left and the right, both in and out of power, its 'mother country', which it dare not abandon completely.

But Alam's hypothesis suggests something more. World Jewry itself is in a sense the "missing natural mother country", and given the leverage it has in the West through its 'fatal embrace', and given the leverage the US has in a world of predominantly postmodern nations, that gives the Zionist project far-reaching power, with the 'mother country' in a sense "the world", as diaspora leaders publicly assert.[160]

Zionism became the ruling ideology of the neocon GGIII precisely because the 'embrace' was not just an informal understanding between emperor and banker (which can be discarded), but is now formalized in the Jewish state which, arising out of the fatal embrace of yore, has secured itself a place at the heart of the GGIII empire's financial and military-political strategies albeit still necessarily through the special relationship. For what is Zionism but a specifically Jewish form of imperialism? A colonial venture based on tribal legends and employing the skills honed over the centuries which fit so well with the economic system now ruling the world.

But given the political, economic and cultural power of Jewish elites in the empire, Israel as the embodiment of world Jewry implies that it is now more like the 'mother country' in its relationship with the US than its 'colony', that it is the US that now functions as *Israel's* colony at least in Middle East politics—the 'tail wags the dog'—reversing the usual center-periphery logic of imperialism (see Appendix). The most telling proof of this reversal was the US invasion of Iraq.

True, Israel's creation was made possible by the support of the US, from Wilson's support in 1917, Truman's support in 1948 and the support of every president since, but just as the US outgrew its colonial status with Britain and took over the position of center, so Israel in GGIII has outgrown its colonial status with the US, relying on its powerful Jewish diaspora to direct US policies on its behalf. Hence, Sharon's alleged outburst at an Israeli cabinet meeting shortly after 9/11: "Every time we do something, you [Shimon Peres] tell me America will do this and will do that ... I want to tell you something very clear: Don't worry about American pressure on Israel. We, the Jewish people, control America, and the Americans know it."[161] Through the powerful role Zionists play in shaping the western "Judeo-Christian" culture, the West has even adopted the Israeli ideology of permanent war and terror, and come to accept Israeli-style collective punishment against Muslims as a legitimate strategy in the joint "war against terror".

Israel's ability to mobilize world Jewry in its cause means there is a continuum between Israel, the Israel lobby, and politicians such as Rahm Emanuel, David Miliband, and NATO's 2010 Strategic Doctrine chair Madeleine Albright, despite Israel not even being a member of NATO. At a NATO-Israel Relations seminar in Herzliya on 24 October 2006, Israeli Foreign Minister Tzipi Livni declared: "The alliance between NATO and Israel is only natural....Israel and NATO share a common strategic vision. In many ways, Israel is the front line defending our common way of life."[162]

Ex-Israeli Gilad Atzmon charges,

> There is also a continuum politically on the left between Israel and Zionism and the Jewish left in the Palestine solidarity movement who try to control the discourse, to insist on secular, socialist solutions, who try to prevent boycott campaigns, to keep Hamas

supporters and other Muslims from playing a leading role in western Palestinian support groups," so-called gatekeepers. Dissent, like assent, is manufactured. "Both left and right, they are 'the enemy within'.[163]

Imperialism is a system; the players are mostly unconscious of their roles, playing a game they believe in, be it GGI, II or III, operating according to implicit rules. Where Jews are more or less assimilated in their host countries, even to a large extent invisible, and largely in thrall to Zionism, this means that the West is implicitly supportive of the Zionists' goals. Jewish elites in the West do not necessarily make or change the rules consciously to serve Israel, but simply operate implicitly according to the old saw "Is it good for the Jews?"[164] The old/new goals—greater wealth and greater security—now include Greater Israel.

Such non-Jewish public political figures as Obama, Condoleezza Rice or Bush II do not separate out what's 'good for the Jews' from what's 'good for the US', and they would similarly deny that they think in terms of what's 'good for the empire'. They and their Jewish colleagues are for the most part willing handmaidens to the empire-and-a-half. Only a small backroom elite, such as Rhodes and Mackinder in GGI, Cheney or Sharon in GGIII, consciously determine the rules and manipulate events to meet goals of greater empire. No doubt Bush II sincerely believes he was fighting the good fight in his 'Crusade' against terror, though the reality is something very different.

Control of world resources

The Israeli part of the empire-and-a-half is ultimately beholden to the fate of the US empire. But in GGIII, it is energetically pursuing its own regional and world agenda—some kind of world hegemony, some form of empire, based on finance capital, the assertion of Jewish economic and cultural clout. The concept of a Jewish/ Israeli empire-state, anointing a supposed race as superior, is surely the highest form of political fetishism.[165]

This belief is implicit in the Talmudic version of Judaism. Schneerson claims, "The body of a Jewish person is of a totally different quality from the body of members of all other nations of the world. Bodies of the Gentiles are in vain. An even greater difference is in regard to the soul ... A non-Jewish soul comes from three satanic spheres, while the Jewish soul stems from holiness."[166] Similar claims have been made by Jewish public figures such as Menachem Begin and Ehud Barak.[167] But a belief in racial superiority is not necessary as long as the group remains distinct and economically privileged, and has the world in thrall culturally, with its own state, freed of the fatal embrace of former host states.

Remarkably, Israel has achieved so far something Nazi Germany tried and failed to achieve: to occupy other people's lands on dubious historical grounds, and as a heartland, to enforce itself as a regional hegemon through military superiority. This, despite the fact the Nazis had a large territory and population and a much greater ethnic cohesion than tiny Israel, with its stolen land and disparate tribes of Ashkenazi, Sephardic and Russian origins, with little in common.

However, Israel's plan and strategies to govern the Middle East directly or indirectly as outlined above have seriously hampered its economic control of the region. Though it has successfully expanded to control the entire Palestine Mandate and thus all its resources (especially labor and water), it still must rely on Russia to supply oil and on a very reluctant Egypt to supply gas. Its plans to break up OPEC and import its energy needs from an accommodating Iraq (or at least an independent Kurdistan) have yet to succeed. The dependence on Egypt may change with natural gas finds off the coast of Palestine,[168] though rightfully they belong to Palestine and Lebanon, and the growing movement to boycott, divestment and sanctions (BDS) in the West will seriously affect Israel's ability to exploit them.

Israel has robust economic relations with the US, Canada, the EU, the ex-Soviet Union and Asia, but again its settlement policy is increasingly confronting official EU sanctions and the BDS movement is affecting its exports.[169] Very simply, Israel cannot develop itself as regional economic hegemon until it negotiates a meaningful peace with its neighbors. As this runs counter to the entire strategic planning of Zionists from even before the creation of Israel, Israel is effectively besieged and will remain so in the foreseeable future.

Israel from the start looked for ways to benefit from the decolonization of the British empire, but was largely shut out throughout GGII because of its image as a colonial pariah among third world countries not in thrall to the new US hegemon. In GGIII, this has changed, and it is developing trade relations, especially in arms, with India and China. It has growing ties with many African countries, especially Nile basin countries Ethiopia, Kenya, with the long term interest in access to Nile water,[170] as well as Darfur.

But its main activity in Africa is in the diamond trade, Israel's largest export industry,[171] involving the Democratic Republic of Congo and Sierra Leone, source of "blood diamonds"[172] and the worst atrocities of the post-WWII period, presided over by competing Euro-American-

Canadian Jewish and Israeli interests. This is a chilling example of what the world can expect from an enduring empire-and-a-half.

Israeli-American Dan Gertler and Brooklyn-born Rabbi Chaim Yaakov Leibovitch are two of the principals behind the Congolese diamond mining company, Emaxon Finance Corporation. Together with Chabad-nik Uzbek-Israeli Lev Leviev, they control the diamond market in Congo and Sierra Leone. In 2003, the Congolese diamond state-owned Societe Miniere De Bakwanga signed an exclusive contract with Emaxon Finance International, involving Israeli's Foreign Defense Assistance and Defense Export Organization and high-level Israeli defense and intelligence officials. Dan Gertler facilitated this as he is close to Israeli politicians, especially Israeli Foreign Minister Avigdor Lieberman, and to billionaire diamond magnate Beny Steinmetz, friend of Olmert and one of the biggest clients of Gertler's largest rival, de Beers. His activities involve Israeli arms dealers in operations reminiscent of the Iran-Contra arms smuggling, where rival political factions attain illegal arms in exchange for illegal goods (here diamonds). The UN also documented diamond sales by Sierra Leone rebels to Lazare Kaplan International (CEO Jewish American Maurice Templeman). The Israeli network of organized crime syndicates, offshore subsidiaries, interlocking directorships and affiliated mercenaries, using Israeli operatives and businessmen with multiple nationalities, has been involved in some of the world's worst violations of human rights in Africa. The genocide going on in the Congo is directly due to the fight among rival Israeli corporate interests for control of resources, draped in *faux* Judaic religious garb, with the local government a helpless pawn and the country ravaged by private militias.[173]

The appropriation of surplus from the periphery is the ultimate goal of imperialism. "Blood diamonds" from Africa and growing high-tech arms sales to many countries are Israel's main direct sources of surplus. Given its virtual state of war in its immediate neighborhood, the process of surplus extraction is limited to its exploitation of low-wage Palestinian and 300,000 third world workers working as "virtual slave labor".[174]

However, through its control of the Occupied Territories, it has developed a novel technique to extract tribute from the EU in the latter's attempts to help the Palestinians prepare for their state. Since the Oslo Accords, the EU has provided aid to build Palestinian infrastructure in preparation for their state, at the same time providing extra funds to Israel to make this palatable to the Israeli public. In addition, Israel has extracted millions of euros in import duties and transport fees from the Palestinians—only Israeli ports, trucks, drivers are permitted. Billions of euros worth of projects in Gaza have been half built after long delays and then *bombed* by Israel, in a continuing cycle. As a result, after 12 years of aid, the Palestinian economy lies in ruins, Israel has become a lender of foreign capital, while most of the EU donor countries are in debt.[175]

Israel also extracts more than $3 billion annually from the US, with total direct US aid to Israel since 1948 amounting to well over $140 billion,[176] this tribute further confirming its role as 'center' to its US 'periphery'.

Though more than 25 million Soviets died in WWII and the country was devastated by the Nazis, the allied agreement to provide the Soviet Union with reparations was cancelled in 1953. However, Israel and the World Jewish Congress (WJC), on behalf of European Jewish victims of Nazism, have received billions. The 1952 Reparations Agreement between Israel and West Germany initially paid Israel 3 billion marks over the next fourteen years and the WJC—450 million marks. The payments played a vital role in Israel's survival—87.5 per cent of the state income in 1956. Later, Swiss banks and German banks, such companies as Deutsche Bank, Siemens, BMW, Volkswagen and Opel, and the ex-socialist Hungarian government were also required to pay additional reparations to the state of Israel on behalf of Jews who suffered under Nazism. In 2009, Israeli Finance Minister Yuval Steinitz demanded a further 1 billion euros from Germany as well as a discount on the purchase of two German-built warships.[177]

The ability to mobilize world Jewry and use both the Israel lobby and the suffering of Jews in WWII to extract surplus from the center is just as remarkable as the ability of Israel to carry out a Middle Eastern version of the Nazi agenda of *Lebensraum* while securing itself a prominent place among the world's nations. The flow of surplus value from the imperial center to Israel, the extensive support that Israel receives from wealthy diaspora Jews, and the wealth of Jewish oligarchs and the Kosher Nostra brought to the Jewish financial safe haven compensate for Israel's inability to extract surplus in the traditional imperial fashion from its own colony.

GGIII Endgame

Israel's behind-the-scenes role in the major GGIII wars in Afghanistan and Iraq recaps the US role in earlier games:

- In GGI, the wars took place far from the US, and the US emerged relatively unscathed compared to its allies, which were weakened and indebted to the US.

- In GGII, the US mostly used proxies and subversion to dispose of undesirable regimes, and was generously rewarded by the Soviet collapse and the opening up of the entire Eurasian heartland.

- The GGIII wars cost Israel nothing; on the contrary, its sales of weapons have increased dramatically. But they have burdened the US with huge expenditures and troop commitments while putting the US at the center of the fighting. As the US destroys itself through overreach, fighting Israel's wars (in the case of Afghanistan, a neocon war inspired by Israeli strategy), Israel, like the US in GGI&II, is free to expand its relations around the world.

Some commentators suggest that this is a deliberate strategy by Israel to wear out the US waging wars on its behalf,[178] just as in GGI&II, the US used wars and proxies to weaken the competing empires and then the Soviet Union. Using zero-sum logic, by weakening the US part of the empire-and-a-half, Israel strengthens itself, the 'half empire', at least relatively.

Whether intentional or not, the result has been both the weakening of Israel's Arab and Muslim enemies and a sharp decline in the US economy and its authority abroad. The world financial crisis since 2008 has resulted in a general breakdown of the neocolonial financial world order, with countries such as Venezuela, Bolivia and Iran opting out of much of the US-imposed post-WWII set up, and the rising economic powerhouse, China, taking an independent path, increasingly using bilateral instead of multilateral relations to expand trade. It is not clear that this is a desirable outcome for Israel, as it too is dependent on the dollar as world reserve currency.

The result in the occupied lands is also unsettling for the 'half' empire. Namely, the spawning of new types of resistance—the Taliban, Hizbullah, Hamas, al-Qaeda and others—that were not present in GGI&II. During those games, resistance to imperialism was primarily by communists and nationalists, both within the center and institutionalized in the Soviet Union, forces which responded to traditional strategies and were eventually defanged with the collapse of the Soviet Union. The new forms of resistance don't respond to traditional US/ Israeli imperial force, though both the US and Israel have tried to use them, and even supported and infiltrated them initially to try to make sure they served imperial aims.

These resistance groups have no interest in the colonial constructs imposed on the Middle East by the imperial powers in GGI&II

or even the walled ghettoes built in GGIII.[179] They continue to resist and gather strength, biding their time. Though Hizbullah participates in the political rituals of the state, it grew out of local needs, like the Taliban, and both are genuine movements not dependent on the state institutions or infrastructure for their existence. They are parallel organizations to the state, militias that cannot be intimidated or bullied by the state or outside forces. Neither the US invasion of Afghanistan nor Israel's invasion of Lebanon in 2006 were able to destroy them, though the result was to destroy the countries' infrastructure.[180]

While al-Qaeda and the Taliban are more a problem for the US than Israel, Israel is more concerned about Hizbullah, the resilience of Hamas and the Palestinians, who live in concentration camp conditions, refusing to give up their last bits of land, and the now sizable Palestinian diaspora, which rivals that of the Jews themselves, and continues to demand the right to return.

The result of Israel's attempted politicide of the Palestinians has been to encourage a greater Islamic fundamentalism among desperate Palestinians and reinforce the popularity of the Shia Hizbullah even among Sunnis, portending a reversal of the Sunni-Shia discord Israel and the US encouraged as part of their neocon Yinon-inspired strategies. Israeli observers such as Caroline Glick recognize the new danger: "the willingness of Muslim secularists to form strategic relations with jihadists and the willingness of Shia to form strategic partnerships with Sunnis was unimaginable 20 years ago."[181]

At some point, the best simulation models break down. Sharon and Yinon's plans to win GGIII with the US in tow, even translated into mathematical game theory strategies for the IDF by Nobel laureate Robert Aumann, no longer make sense when the real enemy—the offspring of Israeli terrorism[182]—exists at the sub-state level in both 'host' countries (the US and Israel) and those of the 'enemies', in defiance of the entire system of nation states operating according to the principle of balance of power and market capitalism.

There are three possible scenarios for Israel deriving from the GGIII game:

1. Sharon's five-states-for-two-peoples Bantustan plan (which Rabin almost secured in the Oslo Peace talks before he was assassinated in 1995 for his non-Zionist apostasy).
2. A "final solution" of expelling or killing all Palestinian Arabs. This is the preferred solution for the 130,000 (and growing rapidly) religious Zionist settlers who see their lives as colonizers of Palestine not simply as a GGI colonial game, but in terms of life

and death, a "mystical reunion between the people of Israel and the land of Israel,"[183] where the Arabs, like the Jews in Nazi Germany, are alien and must be expelled. It is projected they will soon outnumber the secular settlers, and are now joining the police and army as part of their mission.

3. A non-Jewish one-state democracy. If the religious settler population growth weakens and international pressure mounts, Israel will be forced to comply with international law. This would, in the short term, create a condition of civil war between the secular and non-Zionist religious Jews and the newly Zionist followers of Schneerson and Kook.

But given the foreseeable failure of Israel as a safe haven for diaspora Jews, the prospects for the third possibility becoming the desirable solution from the point of view of those very diaspora Jews are improving. Britain's unofficial leader of the Jewish business elite, Mick Davis, said: "Israel is harming diaspora Jews." He warned that Israel was on the road to becoming an "apartheid state" and that "the government of Israel has to recognize that their actions directly impact on me as a Jew living in London."[184]

When combined with the growing number of outspoken non-Zionist Jews in both the diaspora and Israel itself, such as Gilad Atzmon, Noam Chomsky, Norman Finkelstein, Naomi Klein, Gideon Levy, Ilan Pappe and Israel Shamir, these critics of Israel apartheid are now leading, as Jews have always done in their traditional role of "political mobilization and opinion formation", a powerful movement to delegitimize the Zionists' plans.[185]

As for the US empire's endgame, this will depend on its other 'half'. If the Israeli endgame is ugly, this could hasten the US collapse. The imperial project of colonizing Palestine has meant unending war. The US empire is also now faced with the consequences of its fatal embrace by twentieth century Jewish elites and their 'half' empire. In the past, the emperor could push the Jews out and start afresh. This is no longer possible. The empires mimic each other—Israel is a microcosm of the US; the US is Israel writ large. Without Israel at its core, the US empire quite possibly could have lasted a long time—it had many advantages over its tiny, resource-poor British parent. But unless the US frees itself from Israel's clutches and forces it to make peace with its neighbors, the US is doomed along with its offspring.

***

Appendix:
The Israel lobby and 'Dog wags the tail' debates

Two heated debates broke into the mainstream media by 2006 as the GGIII game neocon plan and Israel's role in it came under fire, the first concerning the outsize role of the Israel lobby in shaping US policies in the Middle East, and deriving from that, a debate about the very nature of the US-Israel special relationship, referred to as the 'dog wags the tail' vs the 'tail wags the dog' debate.

The Israel lobby debate

Why, from the moment of its birth, has Israel faced unremitting hostility from all its neighbors? True, after more than 3 decades and as many wars it succeeded in officially making peace with two of them, Egypt and Jordan, but it is peace in name only. Could it be that Israel has no intention, and never had any intention, of establishing peaceful relations with its neighbors? That it thrives on war and aims only at the peace of the grave for its opponents? That it is the cause of the animosity towards the US in the Middle East?

This simple truth has been obscured by the Israel lobby, especially following each modest attempt by a US president to rein in Israel—Eisenhower in 1956, Ford/Carter following the 1973 war, Bush I in 1991, Obama in 2009. However, even as its influence reached a zenith under the Bush II neocons, the devastation wrought to the US economy and its foreign relations finally led to an open debate about the lobby in 2006–09.

John Mearsheimer and Stephen Walt opened up the mainstream debate with the publication of their article in the *London Review of Books* (it was commissioned and then turned down by the *Atlantic Monthly*) and the subsequent publication of *The Israel Lobby and US Foreign Policy* (2007), and have faced the wrath of the Israeli lobby ever since.[186] They assert that "No lobby has managed to divert US foreign policy as far from what the American national interest would otherwise suggest, while simultaneously convincing Americans that US and Israeli interests are essentially identical."[187]

The lobby has been able to deflect many instances of US anger with Israeli actions, all the while using the excuse that whatever mistakes or problems there are, Israel is the strategic ally of the US in the Middle East. The *USS Liberty* incident is the most egregious one that just won't go away.[188] Israel bombed the naval intelligence ship on the fourth day of the 1967 war in international waters, killing 34 and wounding 174 US sailors. President Johnson covered up the incident, accepting the excuse that it was an accident. For 40 years, survivors have been forbidden to tell their story under oath, but the story has leaked out. The *USS Liberty* was secretly listening in on the Israelis who were intent on continuing the war to seize the Golan Heights and East Jerusalem in defiance of promises to the US. Israeli defense minister Moshe Dayan wanted to prevent the *Liberty* from relaying its actions to the US government which would have forced a UN ceasefire before Israel had seized its most important objectives.[189] President Johnson did nothing about the incident, an important lesson for Israel and the lobby —that it would not be confronted publicly by the US over its violations of international law even if Americans were targeted.

The importance of the lobby in maintaining this state of affairs, as described in this chapter has been noted by Jews and non-Jews, pro- and anti-Israel, alike:

- Uri Avnery: "Israel's governments have mobilized the collective power of US Jewry—which dominates Congress and the media to a large degree—against them. Faced by this vigorous opposition, all the presidents, great and small, football players and movie stars—folded one after another."[190]

- Edward Said describes "the power of Zionist organizations in American politics, whose role throughout the 'peace process' has never been sufficiently addressed—a neglect that is absolutely astonishing, given the policy of the PLO has been in essence to throw our fate as a people into the lap of the United States, without any strategic awareness of how American policy is dominated by a small minority whose views about the Middle East are in some ways more extreme than those of Likud itself."[191]

- As a tribute to the lobby, on a trip to the US to criticize the proposed freeze to renewed settlement building in November 2010 while Obama was touring the far east, Netanyahu said, "I am confident that the friends of Israel led by the United States will not let that happen."[192]

However, the importance of the Israel lobby continues to be downplayed by even the anti-Zionist left. Joseph Massad insists "it exonerates the US government from all the responsibility and guilt that it deserves for its policies in the Arab world ... it is the very centrality of Israel to US strategy in the Middle East that accounts, in part, for the strength of the pro-Israel lobby and not the other way around."[193] Chomsky concurs that targeting the lobby "leaves the US government untouched"; Stephen Zunes—that Mearsheimer and Walt are "absolving from responsibility the foreign policy establishment that they have served so loyally all these years."[194] Yes, Mearsheimer and Walt are imperialists. They would not deny this, though they might wince at the use of the term.

None of the mainstream critics of the lobby dares to point to the continuity between the Israel lobby and the fatal embrace by Jewish elites of past empires. Among revisionist critics in Israel, only Israel Shamir does so when he identifies the chief warmonger as Mearsheimer's "Israel Lobby", Petras's "Zionist Power Configuration", or his own eponymous "Masters of Discourse". It is this contemporary manifestation of an historical and ongoing practice of elite Jewish power—the lobby with its fatal grip on the US government—that is the real enemy, not the Iraqis or Iranians.[195]

Dog wags the tail, vs tail wags the dog

Israel is a "reliable client" of the US and "since 1971 Israel has had no alternative to serving as a US base in the region and complying with US demands," says Chomsky.[196] It is certainly the case that US and Israeli interests have on the surface coincided throughout much of Israel's history. After initially posing as a friend to both the Soviet Union and the US at the time of its founding, Israel quickly sided with the US and loudly claimed the status of "the only democracy in the Middle East", at the same time doing Washington's dirty work as go-between with less illustrious examples of democracy, such as apartheid South Africa, China, the Nicaraguan Contras, even arch-enemy Iran, though in each case, there were specific Israeli objectives involved, distinct from US ones.

No one can deny that Israel has its own agenda. Chomsky admits its "commitment to expansion".[197] He also states that the majority in the US essentially approve of the Saudi plan, want aid to go to Israel and Palestine equally and feel that Oslo was a sham,[198] and that "the US is basically a status quo power opposed to destablization of the sort to which Israel is increasingly committed."[199]

The argument that the dog wags the tail, that Israel is a vital and reliable strategic US ally has been debunked by many, including Obama's nominee for chair of the National Intelligence Council (NIC), Charles Freeman, who was forced to withdraw after his subjection to a campaign of slander led by AIPAC functionary, Steve Rosen, facing "libelous distortions of my record ... efforts to smear me and destroy my credibility ... by unscrupulous people with a passionate attachment to the views of a political faction in a foreign country".[200] In "Israel is useless to US power projection" and in a debate at the Nixon Center, he gives reasons why Israel is not a strategic ally of America:

- Israeli bases are not available for US use and there are no US bases.

- None of Israel's neighbors will facilitate overflight for military aircraft even transiting over Israeli territory; it is hence useless for strategic logistics or power projection.

- US relations with Israel weaken US influence in the Middle East and jeopardize Middle East energy supplies rather than securing them.

- Israel does not fund aid programs in third countries to complement and support US foreign or military policy as other allies and strategic partners do.

- Israel's experience in sophisticated means of torture, pacification, interrogation, assassination, and use of drones has encouraged the US to abandon its values and inspire US operations in Fallujah, Abu Ghraib, Somalia, Yemen, and Waziristan.

- The claim that Israel acts as a US proxy in the Middle East is belied by the fact that prominent American apologists for Israel were the most energetic promoters of the US invasion of Iraq and now Iran, explicitly to protect Israel and to preserve its nuclear monopoly in the Middle East, fully coordinated with the government of Israel.

Freeman reverses the question, asking tongue-in-cheek whether the US is a strategic asset for Israel, whether the tail wags the dog, listing points supporting this:

- American taxpayers fund 25 per cent of Israel's defense budget and half of its military research projects, with Israeli companies uniquely treated like American companies for purposes of US defense procurement.

- Identifiable US government subsidies to Israel total over $140 billion since 1949, leaving aside relief payments to Egypt, Jordan, Lebanon, and support for Palestinians in refugee camps and the Occupied Territories which are a direct result of Israeli actions, despite the fact that per capita income in Israel is now about $37,000—on a par with the UK.

• The American government works hard to shield Israel from the international political and legal consequences of its policies and actions in the Occupied Territories, against its neighbors, or in the case of the Israeli attack on the Freedom Flotilla in international waters. The nearly 40 vetoes the US has cast to protect Israel in the UN Security Council are the tip of iceberg. Where Israel has no diplomatic relations, US diplomats routinely make its case for it. Freeman was personally thanked by Israel for his interventions on Israel's behalf in Africa as a diplomat.[201]

Freeman says that while all this is openly acknowledged, it is considered taboo to ask what advantage the US gets from its support of Israel because it is a question of loyalty to American ideals, something not to be questioned, like patriotism, reflecting the dominance of Zionism in American life and its centrality to American politics.

People in the Middle East understand that the tail increasingly wags the dog only too well. Asked what motivates Israeli policies and US support for them, a plurality of 47 per cent of a poll of Arabs in Egypt, Jordan, Lebanon, Saudi Arabia and the UAE said they believed "Israel decides on its own interests and influences the US", compared to 24 per cent who took that position two years ago. As opposed to the 47 per cent who see Israel in control, only 20 per cent said they believed "Israel is a tool of American foreign policy" while 33 per cent agreed that the "US and Israel have mutual interests."[202]

Anatole Lieven concludes, in agreement with the GGII model here, that Israel was a strategic ally during the Cold War but is now "a very serious strategic liability".[203] "This is not a case of the tail wagging the dog, but of the tail wagging the unfortunate dog around the room and banging its head against the ceiling." He compares the US-Israel relation to Russia-Serbia prior to WWI, where Russia was drawn into Serbian intrigues against the Austro-Hungarian empire leading to war. "A great power guarantee encouraged parts of the Serbian leadership to behave with criminal irresponsibility." Whereas in GGII, Israel abetted the US in its Cold War and was therefore forgiven its Middle East crimes, "Israel and the US have traded places," the US fearing terrorism and Israel the (local) superpower.[204]

Norm Finkelstein says the Mearsheimer/Walt thesis about the importance of the lobby "misses the big picture", as all other countries in region could "fall out of US control tomorrow".[205] However, not only Finkelstein, but all the 'dog wags the tail' partisans miss the main detail in the GGIII "big picture": the US *no longer* controls Israel (if it ever did). Former State Department staffer Stephen Green Goes even further: "Israel, and friends of Israel in America, have determined the broad outlines of US policy in the region. It has been left to American presidents to implement that policy, with varying degrees of enthusiasm, and to deal with the tactical issues."[206]

The reason mainstream critics of the lobby and the purported special relationship took so long to come forward is the fact that they believe that Israel once was serving US interests during GGII. They believe the US represented the 'good guys' in GGII, vs the communist 'bad guys', that it served the cause of world peace. But in GGII it was not the Soviet Union and countries fighting to throw off the imperial yoke that were the enemy of world peace, but imperialism, with the US and Israel the main imperial protagonists.

Carter is a particularly tragic figure here: even as he signed SALT I and pushed for detente with both the Soviet Union and China, he is responsible for unleashing the project to massively fund Islamists in Afghanistan in 1979, intent on destroying the Soviet Union. This was similar to his policies in Latin America, where the US backed paramilitary death squads in Nicaragua, Salvador and Colombia to arm the empire's local supporters against progressive political movements.

It would have been in the rational long term interests of a well-meaning 'liberal' imperialist such as Carter (i.e., genuinely pursuing détente) to cooperate with the Soviet Union to contain the Islamists and create a stable Afghanistan, even within the 'Soviet orbit'. Instead, by waging war *against* the Soviets *in alliance* with the Islamists the US acted irrationally then, just as it did throughout GGII, leaving itself open to deception by the Zionists promoting their special relationship with the empire.

ENDNOTES

1   Donald Neff, *Fallen Pillars*, Washington: Institute for Palestine Studies, 2002, 99.

2   Available at <en.wikiquote.org/wiki/Talk:Ariel_Sharon>. See endnote 161 for the debate about this quote.

3   Ginsberg, *The Fatal Embrace: Jews and the State,* Chicago: University of Chicago Press, 1993, ix. Benjamin Ginsberg is a libertarian political scientist and professor at John Hopkins University since 1992, best known for his critique of corporate control of American politics.

4   Ibid., 9–10.

5   Ibid., 14.

6   Though many Jews continued to support the Soviet Union or as Trotskyists to wish a plague on both houses, the drift to the right accelerated with the creation of Israel.

7 Disraeli (1804–1881) had made himself indispensable to the Tory Party by developing techniques of party management and electioneering that ensured the conservatives would not be shut out of power when voting qualifications were relaxed. Although he converted to Anglicanism at the age of 12, Disraeli defended his Jewishness in parliament: "Yes, I am a Jew, and when the ancestors of the Right Honourable Gentleman were brutal savages in an unknown island, mine were priests in the Temple of Solomon." See Josef Joffe, "The Lost Art of the Insult", *Time*, 6 July 2003.

8 Ginsberg, *The Fatal Embrace: Jews and the State*, 23.

9 J.A. Hobson, *Imperialism: A Study*, 3d ed., London: Allen and Unwin, [1902] 1938, 56–7.

10 Ginsberg, *The Fatal Embrace: Jews and the State*, 24.

11 *Sayanim* (sing. *Sayan*) refer to "diaspora Jews who provide assistance to the Mossad". This entry on the English language Wikipedia was deleted in 2010 but is still available at other Wikipedias, including the Dutch site <http://nl.wikipedia.org/wiki/Sayanim>. See Gatekeeping below.

12 This presaged the enthusiasm of Jewish bankers such as Milken and Boesky for the risky innovation "junk bonds" in GGII&III.

13 Ginsberg, *The Fatal Embrace: Jews and the State*, 19.

14 Theodor Herzel (1860–1904) is the founder of political Zionism. Zeev Jabontinsky (1880–1940) is the most renowned Zionist revolutionary and inspiration of the Jewish Defense League. See below.

15 The idea of population transfer accompanied the Zionist movement from its very beginnings, first appearing in Theodore Herzl's diary. There was little dispute among Zionists about the desirability or morality of forced transfer. In the late 1930s, Ben-Gurion wrote: "What is inconceivable in normal times is possible in revolutionary times; and if at this time the opportunity is missed and what is possible in such great hours is not carried out – a whole world is lost." The 'revolutionary times' would come with the first Arab-Israeli war in 1948, when the Zionists were able to expel 750,000 Palestinians (more than 80 per cent of the indigenous population), and thus achieve an overwhelmingly Jewish state, though not including all the land the Zionist leaders wanted. According to Ilan Pappe, the mindset of Israelis has always been "Palestine is by sacred and irrefutable right the political, cultural and religious possession of the Jewish people represented by the Zionist movement and later the state of Israel." Any concession made to Palestinians is at best temporary or "an act of ultimate and unprecedented international generosity". "Any Palestinian, or for that matter international, dissatisfaction with every deal offered by Israel since 1948, has therefore been seen as insulting ingratitude in the face of an accommodating and enlightened policy," explaining the "righteous fury" that Israelis show. See Ilan Pappe, "What drives Israel?" *www.heraldscotland.com*, 6 June 2010.

16 Israel Shahak, *Open Secrets: Israel Nuclear and Foreign Policies*, London: Pluto Press, 1993, 46.

17 Karl Vick, "Why Israel Doesn't Care About Peace", *Time*, 2 September 2010.

18 It was posited by Orwell in *1984* as the GGII endgame, where the West has adopted the worst features of the Soviet Union, which Orwell dismissed as just another empire, and the world is held in thrall by a state of permanent war between competing *faux* communist empires. It was written before the creation of Israel, which he opposed. See John Rodden, *George Orwell: the politics of literary reputation*, New Jersey: Transaction Publishers, 2002, 318.

19   Ginsberg, *The Fatal Embrace: Jews and the State*, 97.

20   Ibid., 115. Ginsberg is a libertarian political scientist and professor at Johns Hopkins University since 1992, best known for his critique of corporate control of American politics.

21   Ben Gurion published a eulogy to Lenin following his death in 1923, where he compared himself to Lenin. Reprinted in *Midstream*, October 1996, in an article by Eli Tzur.

22   See, for instance, *www.mail-archive.com*, 11 April 2006. <http://www.mail-archive.com/osint@yahoogroups.com/msg20338.html>.

23   M Shahid Alam, *Israeli Exceptionalism: The Destabilizing Logic of Zionism*, New York: Palgrave Macmillan 2009, 171.

24   Ibid., 206.

25   With the advent of Gorbachev in 1985 and his "new thinking," relations between the Soviet Union and Israel improved dramatically. Gorbachev tried to undo the legacy of Soviet-era anti-Zionism by opening the doors to the emigration of Soviet Jews in 1988 and preparing to renew full diplomatic relations with Israel. At the same time Gorbachev promised Arafat during a state visit that year that the Soviet Union would recognize an independent Palestinian state if proclaimed, naively hoping that Israel would show gratitude for his generosity by negotiating a genuine peace with the Palestinians. Arafat declared independence in November 1988 and got Soviet recognition the next year, while Israel was busy setting up consular offices in Moscow. Hundreds of thousands of Russian Jews got instant Israeli citizenship and emigrated, many of them settling illegally in the Occupied Territories, nominally part of a Soviet-recognized Palestinian state. By the end of 1991 when full diplomatic relations with Israel were restored, over 325,000 Soviet Jews had emigrated. Gorbachev's hope to bring a quick peace to the Middle East were dashed as he was ousted from power, leaving the PLO abandoned and Israel stronger than ever. Just as the Zionists had hoodwinked Stalin into recognizing Israel, they once again hoodwinked a Soviet leader into re-recognizing it. Instead of increasing Soviet/Russian influence by this dual recognition, all influence was lost, the Palestinians were hurt by the Soviet betrayal, while the Israelis welcomed a million new Jewish immigrants.

26   Yakov Rabkin, *A Threat from Within: A History of Jewish Opposition to Zionism*, London: Zed, 2006, 48.

27   Sharon as reported in *Haaretz*, 18 June 2007, quoted in Jonathan Cook, *Israel and the Clash of Civilizations: Iraq, Iran and the Plan to Remake the Middle East*, London: Pluto, 2008, 131.

28   Rabkin, *A Threat from Within: A History of Jewish Opposition to Zionism*, 56.

29   Ibid., 158.

30   Ibid., 34.

31   Ibid., 57.

32   Bulliet argues that the correct terminology would be Islamo-Christian vs Judaic, as there is a direct continuity between Christianity and Islam, which have more in common with each other than either has with Judaism. See Richard Bulliet, *The Case for Islamo-Christian Civilization*, New York: Columbia University Press, 2006.

33   MI6 director (1999–2004) Sir Richard Dearlove said in a conference marking 60 years of British-Israeli diplomatic relations that he had "no doubt that Israel plays by a different set of rules than the rules that we observe in the UK. The UK didn't always feel safe to share intelligence with Israel." *Haaretz*, 31 March 2011. <http://www.haaretz.com/news/diplomacy-defense/u-k-didn-t-always-feel-safe-to-share-

intelligence-with-israel-1.353348>.

34   Ginsberg, *The Fatal Embrace: Jews and the State*, 22; Israel Shamir, *Pardes: An etude in Cabbala*, USA: BookSurge, 2005.

35   Marx's father converted to Lutheranism shortly before Karl's birth.

36   Karl Marx, *On The Jewish Question*, 1844. available at <http://www.marxists.org/archive/marx/works/1844/jewish-question/index.htm>.

37   Interest and usury have the same meaning. The term usury derives from medieval Latin *usuria* (interest) referring to the monetary charge imposed on loans. Usury is now understood as only excessive interest charges, but the underlying argument that money in itself is sterile is true whatever the rate of interest proposed.

38   As late as the reign of Pope Leo XIII (1878-1903) usury and speculation were condemned by the Catholic Church as harmful forms of lending and investment.

39   Jonah Mandel, "Yosef: Gentiles exist only to serve Jews", *Jerusalem Post,* 18 November 2010.

40   The word "riba" means excess, and in *sharia* law is forbidden in transacting loans, as it implies surplus value without counterpart. "That they took *riba*, though they were forbidden and that they devoured men's substance wrongfully." *Quran* 4:161.

41   Werner Sombart, *The Jews and Modern Capitalism*, Glencoe, USA: The Free Press, [Leipzig, 1911] 1951, 119–20, 129, 133.

42   Sombart, *The Jews and Modern Capitalism*, 192.

43   Ginsberg, *The Fatal Embrace: Jews and the State*, 18.

44   Ibid.,18.

45   The ten major shareholders of the Federal Reserve Bank System are the London and Berlin branches of the Rothschild's banking dynasty, the Paris-based Lazard Brothers, Israel Seiff (Italy), Kuhn-Loeb Company (Germany), Warburg (Hamburg and Amsterdam), Lehman Brothers (New York), Goldman and Sachs (New York), Rockefeller (New York). All of these corporate 'families' are Jewish with the exception of the Rockefellers. The balance of stock is owned by major commercial member banks. In Peter Kershaw, *Economic Solutions,* Englewood, USA: Quality Press, 1994. Quoted at <http://www.meguiar.addr.com/frb.htm>. This line-up has no doubt changed since the collapse of Lehman Brothers in 2008.

46   According to Wikipedia, Volker is Lutheran, but according to Ynet News he was "born to a Jewish family in 1927… After leaving the Fed, he went into private practice, becoming chairman of the prominent New York investment banking firm, J. Rothschild, Wolfensohn & Co." Roni Sofer, "Former Fed chair, who headed committee tasked with securing Swiss restitution funds for Holocaust survivors, shortlisted for two of new administration›s top financial positions", *www.ynet.co.il*, 9 November 2008. <http://www.ynet.co.il/english/articles/0,7340,L-3619625,00.html, www.ynet.co.il>. Peter Myers exposed this contradiction, adding that "There are similar conflicting statements about the head of the World Bank, Robert Zoellick. He succeeded James Wolfensohn and Paul Wolfowitz, both Jewish. A Jewish site says Zoellick is Jewish <http://www.jewishsightseeing.com/2007-sdjw/2007-05%20sdjw/2007-05-30/2007_05_30.htm> but Wikipedia lists him as Christian. Clearly, Marranism is alive and well. We thought it only occurred in Catholic countries, and under the Inquisition, but here it is in Protestant America." <http://mailstar.net/index.html>.

47   The Rothschild stamp is everywhere in Israel. Between 1890 and 1924 Edmond Rothschild funded many settlements in Palestine through the Jewish National Fund. Later his son, James, established Yad Hanadiv, the family charity fund which sponsored the construction of the Knesset building and the Israeli Supreme Court.

Jacob Rothschild is now head of Yad Hanadiv, an Honorary Fellow of Jerusalem and president of Institute for Jewish Policy Research. Daniel Rothschild is head of the Interdisciplinary Center Herzliya in Israel, which sponsors the Herzliya Conference, where Israeli foreign policy is formulated.

48   Robert John, *Behind the Balfour Declaration*, Costa Mesa, CA: IHR, 1988, 55–6.

49   Tom Segev, *One Palestine*, New York: Complete Metropolitan Books, 2000, 36. This fear of world Jewry's power in the aftermath of WWI motivated Churchill to write a full page article "Zionism vs Bolshevism: the struggle for the soul of the Jewish people" in the *Illustrated Sunday Herald*, 8 February 1920, where he blamed the Jews for "every subversive movement during the Nineteenth Century".

50   Alfred Lindemann, *Esau's Tears*, Cambridge: Cambridge University Press, 1997, 417. This strategy is admitted by the ADL's Abe Foxman who boasts how he bullies foreign governments to acquiesce to his demands, claiming influence in top US government circles, at the same time as he denies accusation of excessive Jewish power. See Yoav Shamir, "Defamation", 2009. <http://www.defamation-thefilm.com/html/about_yoav_shamir.html>.

51   Such as the 30 Years War in the seventeenth century, where all states in "central Europe and Scandinavia make use of resources and talents of Jews to compete with their rivals." Ginsberg, *The Fatal Embrace: Jews and the State*, 17.

52   Petras, James, "Capitalism versus socialism: The great debate revisited", *www.globalresearch.ca*, 28 June 2004.

53   Robert Friedman, *Red Mafiya: How the Russian Mob Has Invaded America*, Berkeley CA: Little Brown, 2002, 245–247.

54   "The rise and rise of the Russian mafia", *BBC News,* 21 November 1998.

55   Mogilevich was arrested in Moscow in 2008 but released six months later when the Russian Interior Ministry said the charges against him "are not of a particularly grave nature." A few months later he was put on the FBI's Ten Most Wanted list.

56   Gavan MacCormack, *Client State*, London: Versim, 2007, 110.

57   The new resident is not required to submit any tax reports and the finance minister has authority to double the 10-year tax free period to 20 years, if the persons makes a "significant investment" in Israel. See Bob Bauman, "The State of Israel a Tax Haven?" *www.globalpolicy.org*, 1 March 2011.

58   Israel Shamir, "Kugel Eaters" in *Masters of Discourse*, USA: BookSurge, 2008, 529.

59   "BCCI: The Dirtiest Bank of All", *Time*, 29 July 1991.

60   In 1905, Sergei Nilus published the text, claiming he had received it in 1901 from a member of the secret Jewish Freemasonic conspiracy intent on world domination. Since then, the charge of a Jewish-Masonic conspiracy has frequently been made. See <http://en.wikipedia.org/wiki/Judeo-Masonic_conspiracy_theory>.

61   Cook, *Israel and the Clash of Civilisations: Iraq, Iran and the Plan to Remake the Middle East*, 122.

62   Quoted in Cook, *Israel and the Clash of Civilisations: Iraq, Iran and the Plan to Remake the Middle East*, 102.

63   Ibid., 101.

64   Israel's invasion of Lebanon did not destroy the PLO, its proposed Christian strongman Bashir Jumayyil was killed shortly after becoming president, and the (Israeli) death toll turned the Israeli pubic against the war. Elsewhere in the region Libya's al-Gaddafi was initially backed by the US but turned against it. More recently Egypt's Hosni Mubarak was a faithful ally of US-Israel but was overthrown, while Libya, on the other hand, came under attack by the US and NATO.

65   Seymour Hersh, "The Redirection: Is the Administration's new policy benefiting

our enemies in the war on terrorism?" *New Yorker,* 5 March 2007.

66   Oded Yinon, "A Strategy for Israel in the 1980s", *Kivunim,* WZO, 1982.

67   "Zeev Jabotinsky-A Brief Biography & Quotes", *www.palestine remembered.com,* 23 October 2001.

68   Abdel Jawwad, "Israel: the ultimate winner", *Al-Ahram Weekly,* 17–23 April 2003.

69   Avi Dichter, "Israel: We Destroyed Iraq. Iraq must Stay Divided and Isolated", *Jouhaina News,* 26 May 2010.

70   Maidhc O Cathail, "Who's To Blame For The Iraq War?" *Countercurrents.org,* 16 March 2010.

71   Avi Dichter, "Israel: We Destroyed Iraq. Iraq must Stay Divided and Isolated".

72   *Haaretz* correspondent Aluf Benn writing on the eve of the invasion of Iraq in 2003, in Cook, *Israel and the Clash of Civilisations: Iraq, Iran and the Plan to Remake the Middle East,* 35.

73   Abdel Jawwad, "Israel: the ultimate winner".

74   Cook, *Israel and the Clash of Civilisations: Iraq, Iran and the Plan to Remake the Middle East,* 118–20.

75   Ariel Cohen and Gerald O'Driscoll, "The Road to Economic Prosperity for a Post-Saddam Iraq", *www.heritage.org,* 25 September 2002.

76   Cook, *Israel and the Clash of Civilisations: Iraq, Iran and the Plan to Remake the Middle East,* xiv.

77   Jeff Blankfort, interview by Kathleen Wells, *www.race-talk.org,* 4 November 2010.

78   Cook, *Israel and the Clash of Civilisations: Iraq, Iran and the Plan to Remake the Middle East,* 37.

79   Quoted in Cook, *Israel and the Clash of Civilisations: Iraq, Iran and the Plan to Remake the Middle East,* 43.

80   According to Seymour Hersh, Cheney, Elliott Abrams and David Wurmser were directly involved in the Lebanon invasion plans. Seymour Hersh, "Watching Lebanon", *New Yorker,* 21 August 2006.

81   "Israel becomes world's 4th largest arms exporter, defense officials say", *www. ynetnews.com,* 11 December 2007.

82   Itamar Eichner, "Israeli official: We'll sell arms to Russia's enemies", *www.ynetnews. com,* 19 September 2010.

83   In 1962 during the border war with China, and after the India-Pakistan war of 1971, providing India with mortars and ammunition.

84   Russia still provides up to 70 per cent of India's arms, though Israel Aerospace Industries Ltd signed a $2.5 billion deal in 2008 with India to develop an anti-aircraft system and missiles for the country, the biggest defense contract in Israel's history, to replace the Soviet system. Tearing up its policy of an arms embargo following India's nuclear bomb tests in 1998, Obama signed a $5 billion dollar arms deal in November 2010 during his state visit to India, putting the US ahead of Russia in India's arms imports. in "India, US to ink huge military deal", *Global Times,* 13 June 2010.

85   Mustafa El-Feki, "An Indo-Arab blunder?" *Al-Ahram Weekly,* 23 February 2005.

86   Naomi Klein quoted in Cook, *Israel and the Clash of Civilisations: Iraq, Iran and the Plan to Remake the Middle East,* 125.

87   Robert Fisk quoted in Cook, *Israel and the Clash of Civilisations: Iraq, Iran and the Plan to Remake the Middle East,* 139.

88   See Michael Karpin, *The Bomb in the Basement: How Israel Went Nuclear and What That Means for the World,* New York: Simon & Schuster, 2006.

89   Cook, *Israel and the Clash of Civilisations: Iraq, Iran and the Plan to Remake the*

Middle East, 97.

90   Dutch weekly magazine *Elsevier,* 27 April 2002, 52–3 . Interestingly, by 2010, the same Creveld was writing: "Should Israeli rule over [the Palestinians] continue, then the country will definitely turn into what it is already fast becoming: namely, an apartheid state that can only maintain its control by means of repressive secret police actions. To save itself from such a fate, Israel should rid itself of the West Bank, most of Arab Jerusalem specifically included, it should do so by agreement with the Palestinian Authority. ... Or else I would strongly advise my children and grandson to seek some other, less purblind and less stiff-necked country to live in." Martin van Creveld, "Israel Doesn't Need the West Bank To Be Secure", *www. forward.com,* 15 December 2010.

91   The 1950-1951 Baghdad Bombings, widely attributed to Israel, targeted Jews to encourage them to leave Iraq. The most infamous destabilizing terrorist act that was exposed was the so-called Lavon affair in Egypt in 1954, when local Egyptian Jews were used by Israeli agents to plant bombs in the US and British information centers in Alexandria with other bombings planned, both to force Egyptian Jews to flee 'anti-Semitism' and to create a schism between Egypt and the US. "To prevent an alliance between the West and the Arab world, especially with the most important Arab country—Egypt .... an alliance between the West and Nasser's prestigious leadership in the third world, and in the Middle East, would inevitably lead to a peace agreement forced on Israel," wrote Israeli Prime Minister Moshe Sharett at the time (quoted in Harms, *Straight Power Concepts in the Middle East: US Foreign Policy, Israel, and World History,* London: Pluto, 2010, 81.) The operation was exposed but the damage was still done. Egypt's Jews were now seen as potential traitors and Nasser turned to the more reliable SU for assistance, effectively cementing the US-Israeli special relationship. Similar terrorist acts were carried out throughout Arab countries, especially Iraq. Pre-Israel Zionist operatives also scuttled a Moroccan and other Jewish refugee ships during WWII, killing hundreds of refugees, attributing the act to Arabs. The intent was to use this as anti-Arab propaganda to force Britain to allow free immigration to Palestine. See Naeim Giladi, *Ben-Gurion's Scandals,* Durango, USA: Dandelion 2003.

92   Concerning the most recent terrorism against Iran, see "Mossad behind Iranian military base blast", *www.ynetnews.com,* 25 October 2010.

93   Patron of Baruch Goldstein, who emigrated to Israel in 1983 and murdered 29 Palestinians at prayer in the 1994 Cave of the Patriarchs Massacre in the West Bank city of Hebron.

94   Just as Israel used official US anticommunism in GGII to buttress its special relationship with the US, the JDL used it to make its terrorist activities acceptable on a mass level, quickly growing to a national organization with over 15,000 members. One of the JDL's five principles, "Love of Jewry", states that, "In the end... the Jew can look to no one but another Jew for help and that the true solution to the Jewish problem is the liquidation of the Exile and the return of all Jews to Eretz Yisroel—the land of Israel."

95   Victor Ostrovsky and Claire Hoy, *By Way of Deception,* New York: St Martin's Press, 1990, 321.

96   Assuming 9/11 was carried out by Islamic extremists

97   Maidhc Cathail, "Myth-Debunking Snopes Obscures Israel's Role in 9/11", *maidhcocathail.wordpress.com,* 21 July 2010.

98   "The Moshe-Dayan-Method of Intimidation", *notsylvia.word press.com,* 24 July 2009.

99   Jeff Halper explains that when Israel wishes to make a point in Gaza, it sends fighter jets every three minutes at low levels for up to 48 hours. The first flotilla to Gaza in 2008 was asked to bring thousands of hearing aids for children. Scott Stockdale, "People liberating Egypt, next Gaza, says Jeff Halper", *www.thecanadiancharger. com*, 16 February 2011.

100   "Israeli Mercenaries in South America", *www.strategypage.com*, 15 August 2007. Being on both sides recapitulates the GGI Jewish financing of both sides in European wars. See endnote 44.

101   A 15 May 2009 cable "Israel, A Promised Land for Organized Crime?" from the US embassy in Tel Aviv refers to leading mafia figures trying to get visas to attend a "security-related convention" in Las Vegas. "Zvika Ben Shabat, Yaacov Avitan, and Tzuri Roka requested visas ... many known OC [Organized crime] figures hold valid tourist visas to the United States and travel freely." Zvika Ben Shabat is president of H.A.Sh Security Group, a joint venture with an Indian firm building a "command and control center" in Mumbai, scene of the Chabad House bombing. They export security technologies for identification and monitoring of cell phones, vehicles, structures, computers, infrastructures and WIFI technologies to Europe and Africa. See Yossi Melman, "Why are so many Israelis arrested over illegal arms deals worldwide?" *Haaretz*, 1 July 2010.

102   Carl Cameron, Fox News report 17 December 2001, in Justin Raimondo, "WikiLeaks Exposes Israeli Mafia's Growing Influence", *www.informationclearinghouse.info*, 6 December 2010.

103   See below for evidence of how top politicians have relations with leading figures involved in shady operations in Congo.

104   Baruch Kimmerling, Politicide: Sharon's War Against the Palestinians, London: Verso, 2003.

105   Golda Meir, *Sunday Times*, 15 June 1969. The term was coined by Lord Shaftsbury in 1839. See Yves Engler, *Canada and Israel: Building Apartheid*, Vancouver: Fernwood Publishing, 2010, 12.

106   The Fayyad Plan is to build national Palestinian institutions so as to create a *de facto* state over a period of two years, ending in August 2011.

107   Nathan Thrall, "Our Man in Palestine", *New York Review of Books*, 14 October 2010.

108   Dreyfuss, *Devil's Game: How the United States Helped Unleash Fundamentalist Islam*, New York: Owl Books, 2006,197.

109   Ostrovsky, *By Way of Deception*, 48.

110   Dreyfuss, *Devil's Game: How the United States Helped Unleash Fundamentalist Islam*, 191, 208.

111   The Law of Return was formally issued by the Knesset in 1950, but as soon as Israel became independent in 1948, all those claiming Jewish heritage were welcomed and granted citizenship.

112   Philip Giraldi, "Israeli Mossad Spying in America", *www.intifada-palestine.com*, 23 August 2010.

113   His birthday is celebrated officially in Israel, where his 9000th day in prison was commemorated with a light show on the walls of the old city of Jerusalem, and a constant stream of appeals to every US president to free him. There have been several petitions by congressmen to Obama and an appeal by Henry Kissinger to pardon him.

114   Ginsberg, *The Fatal Embrace: Jews and the State*, 215.

115   Philip Giraldi, "Dr Strangelove, Made in Israel", *original.antiwar.com*, 15 April 2010.

116   Gamal Nkrumah, "Furl the flag", *Al-Ahram Weekly*, 25–31 October 2007.

117   Ostrovsky, *By Way of Deception*, 88.

118   Jeff Blankfort, interview by Kathleen Wells.

119   In *Journey to Nowhere*, London: Granta, 2008, Eva Figes criticizes this move to force Jewish refugees to go to Palestine rather than the US, calling the founding of Israel "a catastrophic mistake", the result of a conspiracy between Truman and land-grabbing Zionists desperate for settlers.

120   Peter Clarke, *The Last Thousand Days of the British Empire*, London: Bloomsbury, 2008, 423.

121   See Edwin Wright, "Zionist Jews Worked 'To Capture the US Government'", *www.rense.com*, 19 September 2004.

122   Quoted in Debbie Menon, "Can Obama escape the dominating influence of AIPAC and the American Jewish/Zionist Israeli lobby?" *payvand.com*, 2 December 2009.

123   Available at <http://www.conferenceofpresidents.org/>.

124   Blankfort estimates that the Israel lobby has been responsible for at least 60 per cent of contributions to the Democrats since the founding of Israel. Blankfort, interview by Kathleen Wells.

125   The Brookings Institute was reasonably evenhanded on the Middle East, which prompted Saban to donate $13 million to set up his institute there to correct this. The same year he donated $12.3 million to the Democratic Party.

126   James Petras, "The State and Local Bases of Zionist Power in America", *www.atlanticfreepress.com*, 1 September 2010.

127   *Boston Globe*, 26 August 2010, in James Petras, "The State and Local Bases of Zionist Power in America".

128   Jeff Blankfort, "Chomsky – Blankfort discussion goes on and on", discussion, *shamireaders*, 2010. <http://groups.yahoo.com/group/ shamireaders/ message/1856>.

129   Mitchell Bard, "Israeli Lobby Power", Midstream, January 1987, quoted in Morris Solomon, "The Agenda and Political Techniques of the American Israel Public Affairs Committee", Washington, D.C.: National Defense College, 1993, 19. <http://info.publicintelligence.net/AIPAC.pdf>.

130   See James Petras, "The State and Local Bases of Zionist Power in America". Stuart Levey outlined his strategy in his article "Iran's New Deceptions at Sea Must be Punished", *Financial Times*, 16 August 2010. He was succeeded by his deputy David Cohen in February 2011.

131   Nathan Guttman, "Some Israelis Hoping for A GOP Win, But Will History Repeat Itself?" *Jewish Daily Forward*, 27 October 2010.

132   Press release from Cantor's office 10 November, available at "Cantor Pledges GOP Allegiance To Israel", *www.therightperspective.org*, 15 November 2010.

133   See Jeff Blankfort, "The Debate that never Happened: Blankfort vs. Plitnick on the Israel Lobby", *peacepalestinedocuments*, July 2005.

134   Natasha Mozgovaya, "Some Chicago Jews say Obama is actually the 'first Jewish president'", *Haaretz*, 13 November 2008. Obama's non-Jewish vice president, Joe Biden, proclaimed "You don't have to be Jewish to be a Zionist," during the election campaign, both emphasizing that it was now more devotion to Israel's agenda than ethnic identity that secured one's place in the political pecking order.

135   Available at <http://www.msnbc.msn.com/id/31102929/ns/politics-white_house/>.

136   Ginsberg, *The Fatal Embrace: Jews and the State*, 208.

137 Jeff Stein, "Ex-AIPAC official got at least $670,000 from donors", *Washington Post*, 19 November 2010.

138 *jstreet.org/*There is no J Street in Washington, which is built on a grid starting with A Street.

139 Mordecai Briemberg and Brian Campbell, "Anti-Semitism and free speech: In Parliament this weekend", *rabble.ca*, 4 November 2010.

140 Ben Stein, "Do Jews run Hollywood? You bet they do... & what of it?" *EOnline. com*, 13 March 2002. <http://loveforlife.com.au/content/09/07/05/do-jews-run-hollywood-you-bet-they-do—-and-what-it-ben-stein-reproduced-eonlinecom>.

141 Jewish directors include Turner Broadcasting System's chairman and CEO Philip Kent, TimeWarner CEO Jeffrey Bewkes, FOX NewsCorp CEO Peter Chernin, Chairman of the Board of the National Amusements theatre chain Sumner Redstone, Paramount CEO Brad Grey, Walt Disney/ABC's CEO Robert Iger, CBS CEO Leslie Moonves and NBC Universal CEO Jeff Zucker.

142 Bryan Fogel and Sam Wolfson, *Jewtopia: The Chosen Book for the Chosen People*, New York: Grand Central Publishing, 2006. Petras, Blankfort and Shamir document Zionist media control in their writings.

143 "Focus Grouping War with Iran", *Mother Jones*, 19 November 2007.

144 Connie Bruck, "The Influencer", *New Yorker*, 10 May 2010.

145 "The nuclear reactor story inspired comment from many sources: editorial writers, columnists, science writers and cartoonists. Most of the press seemed finally to accept the thesis that the reactor was being built for peaceful purposes and not for bombs... Some columnists felt that the US should have awaited more information before 'ventilating its suspicions'. Drew Pearson's syndicated column justified Israel's secrecy; William Laurence in *The New York Times* stressed Israel's peaceful intent, in contrast to Arthur Krock who wanted the reactor placed under international safeguards. Arab protagonists in this country—including those in the State Department who raised all the fuss initially—used the occasion to try to cast doubt on Israel's friendship toward the US." The congressional documents were made available through a freedom of information request in 2010 and are available at <http://www.irmep.org/11-121960AZC.pdf>.

146 Ginsberg, *The Fatal Embrace: Jews and the State*, 25.

147 See Stephen Schlesinger and Stephen Kinzer, *Bitter Fruit: The Story of the American Coup in Guatemala*, New York: David Rockefeller Center for Latin American Studies, revised edition, 2005, 79-97.

148 "The public be swayed: Edward Bernays, the 'father of public relations,' is still giving advice on his 100th birthday" *The Jerusalem Report*, 13 February 1992. <http://www.jeffjacoby.com/5708/the-public-be-swayed>. In his autobiography, he relates how he advised Golda Meir to rewrite her speech at the UN "stressing a common denominator of interests" and "common goals" rather than Israeli goals. Edward Bernays, *The Biography of an Ideal: Memoirs of Public Relations Counsel*, New York: Simon and Shuster, 1965, 704.

149 See *<www.wikinfo.org/index.php/Dynamic_silence>* and Jeffrey Kaplan, "The Politics of Rage: Militias and the Future of the Far Right", *www.religion-online.org*, *Christian Century*, 19-26 June l996. <http://www.religion-online.org/showarticle. asp?title=226>.

150 Ginsberg, *The Fatal Embrace: Jews and the State*, 124.

151 Referring to Oliver Stone, Saban told *The Wrap* in an email, "This guy should be helped in joining Mel Gibson into the land of retirement, where he can preach his

anti-Americanism and anti-Semitism in the wilderness where he belongs." Saban, a major stakeholder in Univision and chairman of Saban Capital Group, said he is spreading the word among his Hollywood friends to avoid working with Stone. *www.thewrap.com*, 28 July 2010.

152 *Wall Street Journal*, 26 July 2010. <http://blogs.wsj.com/speakeasy/2010/07/26/oliver-stone-sorry-about-holocaust-comments/>.

153 Hina Jilani, Christine Chinkin and Desmond Travers, "Goldstone report: Statement issued by members of UN mission on Gaza war, May-September 2009", *Guardian*, 14 April 2011.

154 Norman Finkelstein, *The Holocaust Industry: Reflections on the Exploitation of Jewish Suffering*, New York: Verso, 2000.

155 Citing the fact that some Muslim leaders in the Middle East supported the Axis powers during WWII, ignoring the fact that they did so as part of their struggle to free themselves from British/French occupation. The 2007 coining of the name Islamo-Fascism Awareness Week suggests it was a direct response to the success of Israeli Apartheid Week (IAW), which began in Toronto in 2005 and quickly spread to campuses in the US and Europe.

156 Knesset member Avraham Ravitz estimated that there were a half-million non-Jewish Russians. Donna Rosenthal, *The Israelis: ordinary people in an extraordinary land*, New York: Simon and Schuster, 2003, 141.

157 Bill Text 102nd Congress (1991-1992) <http://thomas.loc.gov/cgi-bin/query/z?c102:H.J.RES.104.ENR>.

158 "Losing Our Moral Umbrella", *Newsweek*, 6 December 1992.

159 M Shahid Alam, "Zionist Dialectics Past and Future", *www.foreignpolicyjournal.com*, 21 September 2010.

160 "Jerusalem belongs to all Jews, and they must play a role in its future and Israeli policy in general, said US and European Jewish leaders, including former presidential adviser, Elliott Abrams; Malcolm Hoenlein of the Conference of Presidents of the Major American Jewish Organizations; former US ambassador to Israel, Daniel Kurtzer; head of the Anti-Defamation League Abraham Foxman; senior vice president of B'nai B'rith International, Daniel Mariaschin; French leader Pierre Besnainou, in a conference in Jerusalem in November 2010 organized by the Jewish People Policy Planning Institute." 'World Jews must play role in future Mideast peace talks', *Haaretz*, 21 October 2010.

161 On 3 October 2001, Information Association of Palestine News cited Israel Radio (Kol Yisrael) reporting on the Israeli cabinet weekly session. See Mohamed Khodr, "Sharon to Peres: We Control America", *www.mediamonitors.net*, 20 November 2001. CAMERA (Committee for Accuracy in Middle East Reporting in America), a pro-Israeli site, reported 20 May 2002 that Kol Yisrael political correspondent Yoni Ben-Menachem later denied having made this statement. *www.camera.org*, 20 May 2002. The quote however is widely accepted as accurate. See James Petras, *The Power of Israel in the United States,* Georgia, USA: Clarity Press, 2006; William Hughes, "You're Ariel Sharon and Life is Good", *www.counterpunch*, 3 December 2002; "Washington Post urges dismissal of AIPAC espionage case", *mondoweiss. net*, 14 March 2009.

162 Quoted in Diana Johnstone, "NATO'S True Role in US Grand Strategy", *Counterpunch,* 18 November 2010.

163 Gilad Atzmon, "Connecting the Zionist Dots", *www.giladatzmon.net*, 2010.

164 See for instance <http://goodforthejews.net/>.

165 As orthodox pro-Zionist religion takes hold in Israel, the belief in Jewish racial

superiority is growing. More than half of Jewish children in Israel attend religious primary schools where "they are taught that Jews sit above nature, which comprises four categories: inanimate, vegetable, animal and speakers— or non-Jews, who are considered no more than talking animals." Jonathan Cook, "Israel's racist rabbis: wave of edicts urge 'Hate the gentile'", *www.redress.cc*, 10 December 2010. That Ashkenazi Jews are genetically intellectually superior as a group is the conclusion of more than one scholarly study, based on IQ statistics, low intermarriage, historic restrictions on professions such as money-lending, banking and tax collecting that "favour higher intelligence", and even genetic mutations. See, for example, Gregory Cochran, Jason Hardy and Henry Harpending, "Natural History of Ashkenazi Intelligence", University of Utah, 2005. <http://homepage.mac.com/harpend/.Public/ AshkenaziIQ.jbiosocsci. pdf>.

166 Quoted in Shahak and Mazvinsky, *Jewish Fundamentalism in Israel*, London: Pluto Press, 1999. Available at <http://answers.yahoo.com/question/index?qid =20100220144332AAjCV8G>.

167 Menachem Begin in the Knesset called Palestinians "beasts walking on two legs"; then-IDF chief of staff Rafael Eitan called Arabs "roaches in a glass jar"; Ehud Barak called them "crocodiles"; Israeli tourism minister Rehavem Zeevi called Arafat a "scorpion". Robert Fisk, "When Journalists Refuse to Tell the Truth About Israel", *The Independent*, 17 April 2001. In an attempt at damage control, CAMERA argues the quotes refer only to suicide bombers and dismisses Fisk "known for his virulent anti-Israel sentiment". "Exposing False Zionist Quotes II (Quote Busters II)", *www.camera.org*, 4 October 2004. See endnote 161 for CAMERA's dismissal of Sharon's purported 9/11 statement.

168 Gal Luft, "Discovery of Natural Gas in Israel is a World-class Game Changer", *www.thecuttingedgenews.com*, 14 June 2010.

169 In August 2010 the Chilean parliament decided to adopt the boycott of Israeli products made in the settlements, following similar moves in Norway and Sweden. Nehemia Shtrasler "Anti-Israel economic boycotts are gaining speed", *www.haaretz.com*, 5 September 2010.

170 Ronald Bleier, "Will Nile water go to Israel? North Sinai pipelines and the politics of scarcity", *Middle East Policy*, Volume 5, Number 3, Washington: Middle East Policy Council, 1 September 1997.

171 "Diamond News", The Israeli Diamond Industry, 22 December 2008. <http:// www.israelidiamond.co.il/English/NEWS.aspx?boneID=918&objID=4408&Sear chS=israel%20industry>.

172 Hollywood made a movie "Blood Diamond" (2006) decrying the violence behind the trade, airbrushing out any hint of Israeli/Jewish responsibility.

173 Information on Israeli activities in Africa from Keith Harmon Snow, "Gertler's Bling Bang Torah Gang: Israel and the Ongoing Holocaust in Congo (Part 1)", *dissidentvoice.org*, 9 February 2008.

174 To keep Palestinians unemployed and encourage them to abandon Greater Israel, migrant workers, a majority illegal, are shipped in, mostly from Asia and Africa, according to Michael Ellman & Smain Laacher, "Migrant Workers in Israel – A Contemporary Form of Slavery" London: Euro-Mediterranean Human Rights Network & International Federation for Human Rights, 2002. <http://www.fidh. org/IMG/pdf/il1806a.pdf>.

175 A talk by Shir Hever in Toronto August 2010 and documented in Shir Hever, *The Political Economy of Israel's Occupation: Repression Beyond Exploitation*,

London: Pluto Books, 2010.

176   In 2003 dollars See <http://www.ifamericansknew.org/stats/usaid.html, 2010> and Charles Freeman, "Israel: Strategic Ally or Liability?" Nixon Center Debate, July 2010, subsequently removed from the Nixon Center website. Available at <http://www.intifada-palestine.com/2010/07/chas-freeman-"israel-asset-or-liability"/>.

177   "Israel seeks discount on two German warships", *Reuters*, 25 November 2009.

178   Gordon Duff, "In Motion: The Plot to Destroy the United States", *www.veteranstoday.com*, 11 November 2010.

179   Cook, *Israel and the Clash of Civilisations: Iraq, Iran and the Plan to Remake the Middle East,* Chapter 4.

180   There are critics such as Sibel Edmonds in "The Three-Decade US-Mujahideen Partnership Still Going Strong", www.informationclearinghouse.info, 14 October 2010, who insist the US still assists the Taliban even as it fights them in Afghanistan. While this may be in Israel's interests, it is unlikely that the US is still pursuing this policy. While it helped create al-Qaeda and initially supported the Taliban, it is now trying to put the genie back in the bottle.

181   Caroline Glick, "James Baker's disciples", *Jerusalem Post*, 6 July 2007.

182   Two top al-Qaeda spokesmen, taking the place of Osama bin Laden, were revealed on Youtube as American-born Jews, but the videos were removed immediately and the news removed from the press. 'Crotch bomber' Abdul Mohammad's computer showed a trail of emails to Israel and he passed through airports without a passport or visa in Ghana, Nigeria and the Netherlands where airport security personnel are largely either Israeli or employees of Israeli companies. Are they part of a new ultra-Zionist movement anxious to promote *faux* terrorist attacks or genuine rebels against Zionism? See Gordon Duff, "Dazed and confused: Why Jews are joining al-Qaeda", *www.veteranstoday.com*, 29 June 2010.

183   Gadi Taub, "In Israel, Settling for Less", *New York Times,* 29 August 2010.

184   Isi Leibler, "The de-Zionization of Anglo Jewry", *Jerusalem Post,* 25 November 2010.

185   Soft Zionists such as Rabbi Michael Lerner, editor of *Tikkun*, still call for a two-state solution based on 1967 borders, despite the fact this is no longer practicable. He embraced the Egyptian revolution of 2011 as a long term plus for Israel, despite the likelihood of an Egyptian government hostile to Israel, since it will force Israel to end the occupation of the West Bank and the blockade of Gaza, which is the only way to ensure the security of Israel. Michael Lerner, "Jewish prayers for Egypt's uprising", *Al-Jazeera*, 1 February 2011.

186   Walton had to resign as dean of John F. Kennedy School of Government at Harvard.

187   John Mearsheimer and Stephen Walt, "The Israel Lobby", *London Review of Books*, Volume 28 Number 6, 23 March 2006.

188   *USS Liberty* Memorial website *<http://www.gtr5.com/>*

189   Napalm was used to try to make sure that there would be no survivors. Alan Hart, "Why, Really, Was The *USS Liberty* Attacked By Israel?" *Alanhart.net*, 19 June 2010.

190   *Haaretz*, 6 March 1991. Quoted by Jeffrey Blankfort, "AIPAC Hijacks the Roadmap", *www.counterpunch*, 27 May 2003.

191   Edward Said, "America's Last Taboo", *New Left Review* 6, November-December

2000.

192 James Gundun, "The mice will play", *Al-Ahram Weekly*, 25 November 2010.

193 Quoted in Harms, *Straight Power Concepts in the Middle East: US Foreign Policy, Israel, and World History*, 2010, 172.

194 Stephen Zunes, "The Israel Lobby: How Powerful is it Really?" *Mother Jones*, 18 May 2006.

195 Israel Shamir, "Fear Not", *www.israelshamir.net,* 2010.

196 Chomsky, *Hegemony or Survival*, New York: Holt, 2003, 24.

197 Ibid., 165.

198 Ibid., 170.

199 In Noam Chomsky, *The Fateful Triangle*, New York: South End Press, 1999, quoted in Cook, *Israel and the Clash of Civilisations: Iraq, Iran and the Plan to Remake the Middle East*, 113.

200 "Charles Freeman's Statement in Wake of Withdrawal From Intelligence Post", *Wall Street Journal*, 10 March 2009.

201 Charles Freeman, "Israel is useless to US power projection", *mondoweiss.net*, 30 April 2010, and "Israel: Strategic Asset or Liability?"

202 "Iran gains as Arabs' Obama hopes sink", *www.zogby.com,* 6 December 2010.

203 Anatol Lieven, *America right or wrong: an anatomy of American nationalism*, Oxford: Oxford University Press, 2004, 186.

204 Ibid., 187.

205 Norman Finkelstein, "Are American Jews Beginning to Distance Themselves from Israel?" *Counterpunch*, 1 May 2006.

206 Quoted in Jeff Blankfort, "The Israel Lobby and the Left: Uneasy Questions", *www. leftcurve.org*, 2003, from Stephen Green, *Taking Sides: America's Secret Relations with Militant Israel*, US: Amana, 1987.

CHAPTER FIVE

GGIII:
MANY PLAYERS
MANY GAMES

*The United Kingdom, Western Europe (and by extension you Americans
too) are now back in the thick of playing the Great Game.
This time we aim to win!*
Prince Andrew to the US ambassador to Kyrgyzstan[1]

When everyone is dead the Great Game is finished. Not before.
Hurree Chander Mookerjee to Kim in Rudyard Kipling's *Kim* (1901)

Major players

The US and Israel

The **US** has been the main protagonist in GGIII, its main objective to
unite under its hegemony the Middle East and Central Asia—the
strategic Eurasian heartland, the fabled Silk Road, with its trade routes
and energy resources. To ensure this, it has carried out unprecedented
invasions, transformed NATO into its world military extension, and
moved to surround Russia, China and Iran to prevent them from
challenging US power there. This has been justified with an ideology
of terror-as-the-enemy, leading to the endgame of permanent war, a
strategy crafted over the past two decades by it and Israel, its other
'half', sometimes in tandem, sometimes in conflict. A 'smart' policy
of Middle East peace and a benign imperial new world order, Bush I's
project in 1991, was scuttled by the powerful Israel lobby defending an
increasingly willful Israel.

Given the 'dumb' neocon policy that followed, the GGIII wars
have nonetheless achieved their main goal at least in the short term,
whether or not they are judged successful in strictly military terms. The

current imperial order is still being governed, however precariously, by US global military hegemony. The deployment of coalition troops and advanced weapons systems by the US, NATO and its partners is occurring simultaneously in all major regions of the world. The new US-NATO missile defense shield is projected to cover the globe.

There has been a slew of 'Great Game' literature since the collapse of the Soviet Union (See Appendix I). GGIII is better referred to as GGIIIs. Just as the world is divided up according to US command structures, so there are military alliances and games in all corners of the globe, all following similar strategies, with the aim everywhere—for the US as chief player—of world hegemony, involving a host of players in the South China Sea, the Pacific and Indian Oceans, the Black Sea, the Persian Gulf, the Mediterranean and Caribbean Seas, the Arctic and off the coast of Africa. Georgia was armed and rearmed in defiance of Russia. Even without overt war, its many war games are warnings to Russia, China, Iran, Venezuela, Cuba and any other possible defector from the imperial order, as it moves the shows of force to geopolitical hotspots as the need arises.

Brzezinski lists "at least five key geostrategic players (France, Germany, Russia, China and India as the players—he calls Britain a "very loyal ally, a vital military base" but "a retired geostrategic player") and five "geopolitical pivots" (Ukraine, Azerbaijan, South Korea, Turkey and Iran, defined as countries with "sensitive positions" and "vulnerable conditions for the behavior of geostrategic players".)[2]

We could also consider the most important countries according to their status in the game, without the arrogant categories of players and pivots; instead, making the distinction between truly independent actors and US puppets. This means considering first the remaining modern states besides the US and Israel which qualify as key players, such as Russia, China, Pakistan, India, Turkey and Iran. There is also a collection of postmodern states, such as Canada, Australia, the ex-socialist bloc and EU states, Central Asia and much of the Middle East, composed of smaller, weaker states where nationalism is abating and which are willing (or rather their elites are willing) to acquiesce to US and/or Israeli hegemony. There are also premodern or failed states which have not survived the colonial/neocolonial games as functional states, such as Somalia, Afghanistan, Kyrgyzstan, and possibly now Iraq, which are geostrategic.

However, there is no fixed relation between states. The imperial hierarchy of center/periphery adjusts to historical developments: colonies like Canada and Australia (originally, the US for that matter) join the center under special circumstances, former imperial centers such as Spain, Turkey, possibly even Russia today, can lose their ability to extract surplus from the periphery and even slide into bankruptcy. Other ex-colonies (Cuba, Venezuela, Brazil, Bolivia, even such newcomers as Kazakhstan), through strong governments and astute use of their natural resources, are able to defy the US imperial reach, however precariously. China holds a special place in GGIII, having experienced imperialism (both as center and periphery), communism, and neocolonialism (both periphery and center). Israel is unique as a colony-empire, a law unto itself.

Alliances and international organizations such as the UN, the Shanghai Cooperation Organization (SCO), Collective Security Treaty Organization (CSTO), the informal economic bloc Brazil Russia India China (BRIC), the Non-Aligned Movement (NAM) and the major Arab/Muslim and Jewish international organizations are considered in Appendix II.

The Middle East

Despite the continuation of its special relationship with the US, **Israel** is playing an increasingly independent role in GGIII around the world, with its government, corporations and Kosher Nostra working with whatever states and non-state actors are willing to condone its deadly games, selling arms (for example, to China, Russia, India, Sri Lanka), smuggling drugs (to Europe and the US)[3], buying blood diamonds (from Africa), conducting covert operations to subvert governments (for example, in Syria, Iraq, Iran), assassinating opponents, forging passports, spying and eavesdropping, harboring 'Jewish' fugitives, sometimes in support of the US in its game strategies and objectives, sometimes not, depending on its own interests. Its diaspora community and Chabad network, found in virtually every corner of the globe, facilitate its game plan, keeping ahead of US plans and technology through its American *sayanim*, operatives, spies and powerful lobby.

In keeping with Jewish survival strategy throughout history, Israel's plans are more subtle than those of the current ruling US empire, as it cannot hope to subdue the world directly, but rather primarily by shaping or subverting its host empire's aims and strategies, to achieve its geopolitical "place in the sun" both through its diaspora and through its own use of statecraft and subversion, untroubled by world reaction. Already with the decline of the US in European affairs, Israel is making inroads, and is now a member of the Organization for Economic Cooperation and Development and implicitly the EU.[4] "The United States has stopped being a factor in European affairs ... For countries like Romania, Israel offers a more interesting relationship than the United States."[5]

Palestine is, despite its helplessness, in a sense the most powerful player of all in the GGs, its tragic fate a constant reminder of the injustice and horrors of GGI colonialism for all around the world to witness every day. And yet it has never really existed as a legitimate modern state, let alone a postmodern state, which is the best it could hope for if Israel were to grant it nominal sovereignty. Israel's strategy of politicide is intended to make it at best a failed state, if the 'interim' Palestinian Authority (PA) Prime Minister Fayyad declares independence (with tacit Israeli approval) in 2011. The Palestinian people continue to defy plans for Greater Israel, still calling for the right of return, though both the PLO successors, the PA and Hamas, have come to accept the 1948 Zionist-imposed borders as the boundaries for a separate Palestinian state, however unjust.[6]

2009–2011 saw a flurry of official recognitions of a Palestinian state with 1967 borders by Venezuela, Chile, Ecuador, Bolivia, Brazil, Argentina, Uruguay, Paraguay, Guyana and Suriname. Russia reaffirmed the still-born 1988 Soviet recognition of Palestine. France, Spain, Portugal, Ireland and the US recognized Palestinian general delegations in 2010–11. The UK and Denmark upgraded their Palestinian general delegations to missions in 2011. In fact more countries recognize Palestine than they do Israel.

Given Israel's four decades of illegal settlements, such a Palestinian state is no longer feasible, and Palestinians increasingly call for a one-state solution which would bring Jews and Arabs together in a unified state. Palestine will remain at the center of the world's concerns, both of GGIII players of geopolitical games and, as a catalyst, of people who don't care to partake in these 'games' but are concerned with social justice.

Syria continues to defy the US and Israel, still awaiting the return of the Golan Heights before it contemplates signing any peace treaty with Israel. By bridging the Sunni-Shia divide, it is now Israel's major remaining neighbor which continues to pose meaningful resistance, earning the Baathist regime of Bashir al-Assad the wrath of Saudi Arabia and the US as a result. It has improved relations with both Turkey and Russia, signing a nuclear power deal in 2010 and agreeing to allow Russia to use a former Soviet naval base at Tartus (which, significantly is where the Syrian version of the 2011 so-called Arab spring broke out with most fervor). The US and Israel tried to use the 2005 assassination of **Lebanon**'s former prime minister, Rafik al-Harari, to undermine the Syrian regime, but after 5 years of a UN-sponsored investigation, the original testimonies implicating Syria were proved false, and relations between Syria and Lebanon remain good. New non-state GGIII player, Hizbullah, based in Lebanon, managed to defeat the Israelis in their invasion of 2006 and Israel hesitates to replay this dangerous move.

The most important of the players in the Middle East should include Saudi Arabia (27 million) and **Egypt** (90 million), but both regimes had become intimately tied to the US by the start of GGIII, the latter, along with Jordan, the only Arab countries to have diplomatic relations with Israel. While Saudi Arabia continues to serve US interests in the region, Egypt's revolution of January 2011 suddenly thrust Egypt back into GGIII, much as the ascendancy of Nasser in 1952 in reaction to British domination made it a key player in countering Greater Israel.

Egypt's revolution took the world by surprise, an unlikely offspring of the color revolutions of the 1990s, which the US all along had encouraged[7] but which it nonetheless tried to quell, standing by its favorite Middle East dictator until the country was brought to a standstill and the army stepped in, forcing the stubborn 82-year-old Hosni Mubarak to step down. Ironically, this new face for Egypt is one that any US president should embrace. It could force Israel to finally negotiate a reasonable peace with Palestine, giving backbone to other Arab governments to push Israel out of serious fear for their own survival, undercutting the US Israel lobby. It could be the US president's best ally. An openly operating Muslim Brotherhood could contribute in a host of ways to solving Egypt's horrendous poverty and social degradation, giving Muslims a new confidence and pride. Sectarian problems, also ironically, would fade as Muslims take control of their lives after decades of neocolonial humiliation.

But this requires the US extricating itself from the 'fatal embrace' of Israel while Israel would have to bring to an end its settler-colony project, its 'half' empire. If Israel had to do that, then its major players would all "go home", their dreams of world empire dashed, rather than join in less ambitious games in a small peaceful playing. Egypt, as a vital pivot in the US game of world hegemony, could play a key role in bringing this about as it proceeds to undo the damage of more than three decades of its unholy alliance with Israel, and its domestic policy of neoliberalism, the underlying causes of the revolution.

As with Israel, **Saudi Arabia** has its own (albeit much more modest) agenda, which generally follows US requirements but occasionally falls outside US needs. The monarchy, beholden to the US for legitimacy, hosts *de facto* US bases despite official denials.[8] It officially coordinates its foreign policies with Washington and is a foe of all the US foes in the region, in particular Iran[9] and Syria. It served as a conduit for relations between Washington and Kabul during the Taliban reign and now claims to be acting as mediator between the Taliban and the US. With US connivance, Saudi and Egyptian polite resistance to

Israel and tepid support for the Palestinians have acted as a safety valve and control mechanism to contain popular Arab support for Palestine.

However, the substantial private wealth of many Saudi princes and such families as the bin Ladens continues to finance jihadists outside of US interests, and the Saudi government is actively working to undermine America's fledgling Iraq government. As revealed by WikiLeaks in November 2010, it is not Iran or Israel, but Saudi Arabia that the US now sees as the biggest threat to the Shia-dominated Iraqi government. US Ambassador Christopher Hill warned, "Iraqi contacts assess that the Saudi goal (and that of most other Sunni Arab states, to varying degrees) is to enhance Sunni influence, dilute Shia dominance and promote the formation of a weak and fractured Iraqi government."[10]

Though both the Saudi and Egyptian governments quietly approved of the 2003 US invasion of **Iraq**, US and Saudi leaders now realize their mistake: they both wanted to weaken Iraq, but not too much. A weak dismembered Iraq would be prey to Iranian control of Shia areas, and as Iraqi Shia are the majority, the next military coup in Iraq would probably result in a Shia dictatorship, making Iraq an ally of Iran. As such, Saudi Arabia is not in favor of US withdrawal, as either of the two likely scenarios—civil war or a new strongman—would threaten the Saudi regime. In an oblique threat to the US, in December 2006, King Abdullah warned Cheney that the kingdom would give money and arms to Iraq's Sunni militias if the US withdrew, echoing Saudi Ambassador to the US Prince Turki al-Faisal's comment that "Since America came into Iraq uninvited, it should not leave Iraq uninvited."[11] The US funded 'nice' Sunni militias (the so-called Awakening movement), recruited from the insurgency, and was able to secure a plurality for secularist and neocon favorite Ayad Allawi in the 2010 elections.[12] However, now the Shia forces are still dominant, both those that tolerate the US occupation and those in opposition to it, and as the US is reducing its troop levels, members of the Sunni militias are rejoining the insurgency, making a long civil war likely, though it will not necessarily be sectarian as much as a war of liberation, both by the Kurds for their long-sought state and by the Sunni-Shia against continued US presence.

US-Saudi destabilization of the Iran-Iraq 'Shia arc' replays the GGII endgame against the Soviet Union in Afghanistan, this time with clandestine operations being carried out by the US, Saudis and Israelis—all jealous of Iran's increasing influence in the Middle East. Even with US bases in Iraq, Iran will be the most powerful player in the Persian Gulf. It is in the interests of both Saudi Arabia and Iran that a united Iraq remain weak, or that Iraq fall apart, curiously in line with Yinon, but this would leave Iran as the regional hegemon, rather than Israel. This situation starkly shows the underlying commonality of interests between the US, Israel and Saudi Arabia with respect to Iran-Iraq. The US-Israeli special relationship endures here and is in fact a trilateral relationship.[13] Unless, of course, the situation of Saudi Arabia were to change radically, at this point still an unlikely prospect.

Other than as unofficial recruiting grounds for Islamists, **Tunisia, Algeria, Morocco** and **Libya** have not been players in GGIII, all 'strongman' regimes effectively accepting US hegemony in the region. Algeria's Islamists, recruited during the 1980s by the US, returned to ride a wave of Islamic revival, but were denied their election victory in the 1991 by the military backed by the US, leading to civil war resulting in 160,000 deaths. A low-level insurgency continues, with a local "Al-Qaeda Organization in the Islamic Maghreb" still active.

Though none of these countries can strive to be major players, the situation in north Africa is now worrisome for the US and Israel following the 14 January 2011 overthrow of Tunisia's Zine el-Abidine Ben Ali, president for 23 years, and the 11 February overthrow of Egypt's Hosni Mubarak. These successful revolutions prompted a wave of popular protests across the Arab world which will be difficult for Washington and Tel Aviv to deal with. They were at least partially due to western NGO pro-democracy activity and use of the internet.[14] The US reluctantly withdrew support of first the Tunisian and then the Egyptian regimes, embracing the protesters only when the writing was on the wall (after Ben Ali had fled to Saudi Arabia and after the Egyptian army had given Mubarak his marching orders).

Libya was a different matter, as al-Gaddafi's welcome to the fold under Bush I (see Chapter 3 endnote 46) was quickly withdrawn as the eccentric pan-African/ Arab leader refused to step down when faced with an uprising. It began as Mubarak was fleeing the presidential palace in Cairo, and was both popular and unseemly quickly supported by the West. It appears that western operatives moved in secretly and immediately to work with the rebels. Al-Gaddafi's attempt to reassert control prompted the PNAC neocons to call for US-NATO intervention—a no-fly-zone a la Iraq and Yugoslavia in the 1990s based on R2P,[15] which the compliant Arab League agreed to.[16] Obama openly called for the CIA to move in to support the rebels.[17]

Whatever the real story is on western subversion in Libya, such overt intervention, involving an alliance of neocons and liberal humanitarian interventionists is much more problematic, given the disasters of Bush II in Afghanistan and Iraq. According to CFR analyst Charles Kupchan, a full-scale invasion would have to be "with the full support of the Arab League and African Union, if not the UN." World reaction was immediate and negative and the invasion was soon bogged down and quickly turning into another Afghanistan/ Iraq. Already GGIII is slipping out of the grasp of the neocon players.

The uprisings in the Arab world continue to reverberate across North Africa, creating the possibility that these faithful non-players could re-enter the game as allies of a new anti-Israel coalition led by Egypt and Turkey. This new wave of democratic fervor in the Middle East is not the plaything of the US; on the contrary, it is strongly motivated by the humiliation of the governments' collusion with the US and Israel, uniting Islamists and secularists. The neocon GGIII appears to have entered its endgame there.

With unification in 1990, **Yemen** quickly unraveled and is a failed state now. The northern elite, under the US-backed military dictator Ali Abdullah Saleh, attempted to quell insurgencies by the once socialist south and by the Houthi in the north on the border with Saudi Arabia. False-flag operations abound[18] and Saudi and US planes bombed the border area in 2010.

Figure 5.1 map Yemen

Despite the complex tribal nature of Yemen, the strength of Islamists in the opposition, and the north-south divide, inspired by revolutions in Tunisia and Egypt, youth and opposition parties in the capital Sanaa mobilized as a united force. But Saleh had time to mobilize his (tribal) supporters too, after he saw what happened to Ben Ali in Tunisia and Mubarak in Egypt, and refused to resign, bringing the country to a standstill for more than two months. It is unlikely now that any national government will be able to regain control over the divided country, as its tribal heritage asserts itself.

Geopolitically strategic but now off-limits given the new assertion of independence in the Middle East, it remains a dilemma for the US, concerned not so much to stem the very real insurgencies and help create a viable state that can deal with them, but in search of "Al-Qaeda in the Arabian Peninsula". However, al-Qaeda itself is becoming more and more irrelevant, as potential recruits opt instead for participation in the political process. On the strategic Horn of Africa, plagued by pirates from **Somalia**, another failed state, and the US-French base in former French colony **Djibouti** across the strait, Yemen is a tempting prize, a geopolitical pivot wrongly overlooked by Brzezinski, but one already slipping from the US grasp as the empire overreaches itself.

The **UAE** and **Bahrain** have proved loyal oil and gas rich allies of the US in its wars in Afghanistan and Iraq, providing both air and naval support (Bahrain has a formal US base with 1500 personnel) and buying large quantities of US arms. They do not defy the US in its plans to attack Iran, despite the horrendous fallout this would have for them. Large demonstrations in (predominantly Shia) Bahrain calling for an end to the (Sunni) monarchy were checked with the help of Saudi troops supported by the US unwilling to watch another pro-US Sunni regime fall into Shia hands and risk losing its base. These tiny kingdoms are very useful tiny "pivots" and so far remain under US control.

Qatar, home of Al-Jazeera, is the odd-man-out, trying to appear neutral. Though Sunni and close culturally to Saudi Arabia, Emir Hamad bin Khalifa al-Thani signed a defense agreement with Iran in 2010 and supports Iran in its insistence that its nuclear program is peaceful. It has developed into the world's largest exporter of liquified natural gas (LNG). Its relative openness and subtle political maneuvers were belied when it became a loud supporter of both the Saudi occupation of Bahrain and the Libya no-fly-zone, providing planes and offering to sell Libyan oil for the rebels in Benghazi. This latter very risky move by a pivot can only be seen as a move by the US itself, and has resulted in a deterioration in its relations with Iran.

Iran is courting and courted by China, Russia, India, Pakistan and Turkey in defiance of the US and Europe. The key player for Iran at this point is Russia, which is playing its own complex game. Iran and Russia have geopolitical commonalities and common interests:

- Iran is encircled by US allies Turkey, Iraq, Saudi Arabia, Bahrain, Pakistan and Afghanistan, and by US naval power in the Persian

Gulf and the Indian Ocean. Russia is similarly contained by US allies in the west and south and with a newly hawkish Canada, in the north as well.

- In terms of exploitation of the Caspian Sea oil reserves, Iran and Russia share the same strategy opposed to the new Caspian states Kazakhstan, Turkmenistan and Azerbaijan. Iran and Russia also face the threat of militant Sunni Islam.

- They both have good relations with Armenia in the Caucasus.

- Iran has become the third-largest importer of Russian weapons, after China and India.

- Moscow finished construction of a nuclear reactor at Bushehr (started by the German Siemens firm in 1975 under the Shah, but damaged during the Iraq-Iran war in the 1980s). However, the Russian delays in commissioning the plant and its political maneuvering in 2010 (agreeing to UN sanctions and cancelling the S300 missile sales) make it clear it is using its relations with Iran to further its own agenda with the US and Europe. It fears Iranian competition not only in supplying Europe's energy needs, but in Iranian cultural influence in the Caucasus and among its Muslim populations.

On many fronts, Iran holds the key to readjusting the playing field and establishing rules of GGIII that can lead away from the deadly game being played by the empire-and-a-half, including in Afghanistan, Iraq, and with implications for nuclear disarmament, EU-US relations, but above all, for the continued role of the dollar as world reserve currency. It has been trying since 2008 to trade all its oil in any currency but dollars, and the euro, yuan and ruble would be the perfect alternatives, if not for US financial sanctions and its financial power to leverage the same all over the world. This lonely call became a chorus by 2010, most notably from other oil exporters such as Russia,[19] Venezuela, Norway, the Emirates, as well as Beijing.[20] This is a primary reason (second only to the incessant US domestic Zionist pressure since 2007[21]) behind the US drive to overthrow the Iranian regime under its assertive President Mahmoud Ahmadinejad since 2005, keep Russia onside and threaten China. The end of the petrodollar means

the end of the dollar as the world's reserve currency; the end of the world paying for America's massive budget deficits; and the end of an Anglo-American finance stranglehold over the world that has lasted since the second part of the 19th century.[22]

The desire by both the US and Israel to overthrow the Iranian government is now the only common goal left in the empire-and-a-half, but it is a common goal only because Israel is in the driver's seat. Israel resents Iran as an existential threat not to Israel itself (unless attacked), but to Greater Israel and regional domination, serving as both an example, a third way for Islamic countries, and a rival as Middle East hegemon.

A rational US policy to accommodate Iran would save the dollar, or at least give the US a chance to prepare for an orderly transition to a new international currency. If Russia, China and Iran defuse the current nuclear crisis between the US and Iran peacefully, with a nod to Turkey and a resolve to make Israel join the Nuclear Non-Proliferation Treaty, this could pave the way for a new Eurasian playing field. If and when the US withdraws from Afghanistan, Pakistan and India will be drawn in as well.

This would set off a chain of events that could change the whole nature of GGIII leading to a Russia-India-China axis (RIC summits have already been held yearly since 2001), leaving Pakistan, Azerbaijan, Armenia and Israel to sort out their regional conflicts outside of a new, very different great game. US interests would be considered but without US *diktat,* forcing, or rather allowing the US to put its own house in order. Iran would finally be accepted as the legitimate regional player that it is. If the US cannot bring itself to make a graceful exit from its self-imposed crisis in the region, this will only accelerate its decline.

With the gradual return of Turkish culture to Islam after the death of its westernizing founder, Kemal Ataturk, in 1938,[23] and Israel's increasing aggressiveness since 2000, **Turkey** has become an independent voice in GGIII, pushing its relations with the US and Israel to the limit. Turkey is heir to the Ottoman Caliphate, which governed a largely peaceful Middle East for half a millennium, before the imperial intrigues of GGI. It is now playing an active, independent role in the Middle East, criticizing Israel and US wars, and supporting Iran.

Relations with Russia have changed radically in GGIII; the powerful neighbors have the 2001 Eurasia Cooperation Action Plan and the 2009 Caucasus Stability and Cooperation Platform, providing a new focus for security in the region, excluding the US and Israel. Russia is Turkey's number one trade partner, providing 80 per cent of its gas, with trade to triple by 2015, using the Turkish lira and the Russian ruble. They introduced a visa-free regime in 2010.[24] Russia's AtomStroiExport started construction of Turkey's first nuclear plant in 2009, and Russia secured Turkey's cooperation in Gazprom's South Stream gas pipeline to Europe, which it is co-funding with Italy's ENI (see Chapter 2), probably meaning the end of the West's rival Nabucco pipeline.[25]

Figure 5.2 map pipeline[26]

Turkey has a free trade agreement with Lebanon and plans to extend this to Syria and Jordan. Turkish Prime Minister Recep Erdogan warned Israel on a visit to Lebanon that Turkey would defend Lebanon in the event of an Israeli invasion: "If you invade Lebanon and Gaza using the most modern tanks and you destroy schools and hospitals, don't expect us to be silent about it. We will not be silent, but will support what is right."[27]

Turkey is now very much a key player in this new Great Game, only it has changed sides. It is admired throughout the Middle East. Two-thirds of Middle East respondents in a poll considered Turkey the ideal model for the Middle East.[28] The new Egypt in cooperation with the new Turkey could mean the end of Israel as the regional empire, replaced by a Turkish-Arab 'postmodern caliphate'.

Central Asia

In the GGII endgame, **Pakistan** appeared to have benefited from a huge

Figure 5.3 map Afpak

geopolitical windfall, strengthening its position against India and setting the stage to be the key geopolitical player in **Afghanistan**. From the start, Pakistan fashioned the Afghan wars (1979 war of liberation, 1992 civil war, 2001 war of liberation) to meet its own goal of greater regional power vis-à-vis India. An Islamic regime in Afghanistan allied with Pakistan would also lessen the threat of a Pashtunistan secession or a war with Afghanistan over the arbitrary border devised by the British in the nineteenth century precisely to leave a legacy of local tribal conflict. Neither of Pakistan's aims were intended by the US, which naively assumed that once the Soviets were driven out of Afghanistan, everything would return to normal, that Pakistan would not seek to change the balance of power in the region, that all the thousands of Islamists would return home, content to have defeated communism, that a grateful independent Afghanistan would welcome US regional plans for pipelines and exploitation of Afghanistan's resources.

But Pakistan's protégés, the Taliban, were not the plaything of either the Pakistani government or the US. There was absolutely no sign that the new Afghan government was interested in being used by the US infidel—considered far worse than the Russian one, being more powerful and more decadent—to support its empire. The US got fed up and invaded to teach the unruly 'students' a lesson, but has run aground in Afghanistan in GGIII, the nexus of both GGI and GGII rivalry.

Pakistan's military dictator Pervez Musharaf (2001–08) was forced to accede to US invasion plans of Afghanistan in 2001 or face a US invasion of Pakistan, and understandably acquiesced. Washington again naively assumed that throwing billions of dollars annually at the Pakistani government ($20 billion from 2001–11) would be enough incentive for it to drop its own geopolitical designs. But, also understandably, though accepting *de facto* US occupation and the flood of dollars, the Pakistani government at the same time has worked to undermine the US occupation of Afghanistan through continued support for the Taliban. According to documents exposed by WikiLeaks in 2010, ISI functionaries regularly meet with the Taliban in secret strategy sessions to organize networks of militant groups that fight against American soldiers in Afghanistan, and even hatch plots to assassinate Afghan leaders. The ISI provides aid to insurgents in Waziristan and Baluchistan. "A network of Pakistani assets and collaborators runs from the Pakistani tribal belt along the Afghan border, through southern Afghanistan, and all the way to the capital Kabul."[29]

Pakistan is now counting on the US being forced to withdraw after negotiations with the predominantly Pashtun Taliban, a strategy already approved by Karzai, despite the continued resistance of his predominantly Tajik Northern Alliance colleagues. This crisis within the US-imposed Afghan government was made clear at a Loya Jirga meeting in June 2010, when Karzai announced a review of all Taliban suspects being held in the country's prisons and the release of many suspected militants. He fired his interior minister, Hanif Atmar, and general director for National Security, Amrullah Saleh, US favorites (the latter a CIA agent since the 1990s), because they opposed the release and negotiations. Bruce Riedel, Obama's Afpak adviser, said, "Karzai's decision to sack Saleh and Atmar has worried me more than any other development, because it means that Karzai is already planning for a post-American Afghanistan." On yet another front, the neocon GGIII is unraveling.

William Dalrymple calls the war in Afghanistan "a complex local and regional conflict ... primarily a Pashtun rebellion against a Tajik, Uzbek and Hazara-dominated regime, which has only a fig leaf of Pashtun window-dressing in the person of Karzai." The West is caught in a north-south, secular-religious, urban-rural conflict where the Taliban are "the authentic voice of rural Pashtun conservatism, whose wishes are ignored by the government in Kabul and who are largely excluded from power. Externally the war has now turned, like Kashmir, into an Indo-Pak proxy war in which NATO is really a bit player,"[30] and Pakistan will not tolerate an Indian presence in Afghanistan.

But it may be too late for the Pakistani military, with the Taliban evolving into an independent, decentralized insurgency that no one controls, and Pakistan itself descending into civil war. The assassination of bin Laden in May 2011 indicated that the US was preparing to change gears in Afghanistan, as this was a "Mission accomplished" moment for Obama and could justify scaling back the US presence there

An exit strategy for the US at this point would be to let all the regional governments take over in stabilizing the current Afghan regime. This, however, would require the US mend fences with Iran. Iran is eager and willing to do just this and has been since it provided the US with valuable assistance in routing the Taliban after 9/11.[31] Iran supports the Karzai regime, which is dominated by the Persian-speaking Tajiks, and strongly opposes making any deals with the Taliban. In a meeting in New Delhi in August 2010, Iran's Deputy Foreign Minister Mohammed Ali Fathollahi said, "Empowering the military forces of Afghanistan and also the police of Afghanistan are points on which countries of the region should help, and Iran voices its readiness to help in this regard."[32]

The advantage of this option is that peace would break out in the region without US occupation of Afghanistan and subversion of Iran, and the US would still have quite a bit of influence in post-pullout Afghanistan. Both India and Russia would be solid supporters of such a scenario and the latter would ensure the support of the 'stans' on Afghanistan's northern borders. Pakistan and the Saudis would have no choice but to acquiesce.

This would dash Pakistan's goal of becoming regional hegemon and end its destructive strategic alliance with the US. But peace with both Afghanistan and India could be a win-win for it too if it is accompanied by de-escalation of border wars and mutually profitable cooperation with India, Iran and China, including the completion of the Iran-Pakistan-India (IPI) Peace Pipeline.

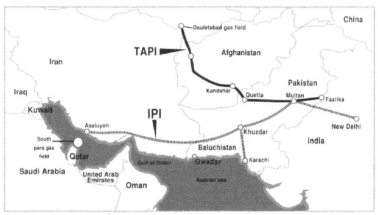

Figure 5.4 map pipelines IPI & TAPI

The **ex-Soviet Central Asia**n countries (Uzbekistan, Kazakhstan, Tajikistan, Kyrgyzstan and Turkmenistan—the 'stans', plus Azerbaijan) are too weak, with underdeveloped political institutions, and too poor, despite considerable resource wealth, to qualify as important actors in their own right. They are strategically important as geopolitical pivots to the major players, their territories lying at the very heart of the Silk Road playing field, and require considerable care and careful use of pressures. Geopolitically fated to be in Russia's orbit they can't easily aspire to a comfortable postmodern niche like the Balkans and the Baltic ex-Soviet republics that enthusiastically embraced anonymity in the EU. Initial flirtation with the US in GGIII soon gave way to realism, and to offset US influence, all governments are closing ranks with their immediate, less intrusive neighbors, Russia and China. Still, they see their NATO Partnerships for Peace and US presence generally "as a useful counterweight to Russia and China."[33]

The 'stans' leave the game strategies up to the major players— the US, Russia and China. They all recognize Israel, which promotes its agenda there through soft power—high level government contacts, NGO activity, the Chabad synagogues, dual citizenship, the various drug and money-laundering mafias based in Israel. They are treated individually in Appendix III.

Russia

In GGI Russia was an unsuccessful imperial rival to the British and rising American empires. In GGII, the Soviet Union's economic relations with the imperial camp were as a raw material exporter and consumer goods importer, the traditional exploitee of imperialism, but politically it was treated as an equal in terms of world influence, given the powerful role socialist ideology played in opposition to imperialism around the world. By ceding its role as leader of the anti-imperial opposition in 1991, Russia was reduced to a second-rate power. Though still the largest country in the world with extensive raw materials, especially oil, and a well-educated population, it could no longer be considered the head of a rival anti-imperial system in opposition to the US empire, nor is it (yet) a secure part of the imperial center.

After the US "briefcase invasion" ended in the collapse of the ruble and default on the debt in 1999, a newly sobered post-Yeltsin government returned to quasi-Soviet policies of state development, re-nationalizing much of the oil industry, seizing some of the ill-gotten gains of the oligarchs, and—after a brief respite following 9/11— vigorously protesting NATO expansion in eastern Europe and the ex-Soviet Union. This raised the hopes of anti-imperialists that Russia was being forced by objective conditions to continue to oppose the US imperial project.

But the end of the Soviet Union meant that much of the economy passed into the hands of the mafia and much wealth was traded for dollars and transferred abroad. The new political leaders in Russia inevitably reflect this new constellation of forces, making it a dubious ally of anti-imperialists. The Russian communists are still a force but much reduced and unlikely to gain significant political power in the near future.

The ability of the US and Israel to undermine the still unstable new political formations of the ex-Soviet Union, including Russia, is great, and weighs heavily on those formulating policy. The Russian Federation itself could further disintegrate with western support of Chechens and others demanding independence. US support for Islamists in the GGII endgame continues to haunt the region even as US power ebbs. Following the uprisings in the Arab world in early 2011, Russian President Dmitri Medvedev suggested that the revolts in the Arab world were sparked by outside forces scheming to undermine Russia. "I won't call any names but a whole range of countries, even those we have friendly relations with, have nevertheless been involved in terrorism in the [Russian] Caucasus."[34]

In the ideological vacuum created by the collapse of communism, two ideologies have arisen—Atlantism and Eurasianism, both with roots in the nineteenth century, the latter, a geopolitics in the vein of Haushofer but as a reaction to the decadence of the West, articulated persuasively by Nikolai Trubetskoi and Lev Gumilev in the mid-1920s.[35] The ideological *diktat* of communism suppressed these musings on the assumption that communism would do away with geopolitics, eventually make such arguments redundant. The differences in the new political elites between Atlantists and Eurasians are over whether to accede to the western agenda or pursue a new multi-polar strategy in alliance with China, Iran and other countries not in the western orbit.

As GGIII got underway, Russian military leaders in particular were enamored with Eurasian Alexander Dugin's aggressive proposals to renew Russian hegemony over its near abroad and distance itself from the West (see Appendix I), but so far there is no clear Russian strategy to confront the US empire, with Atlantism under President Yeltsin giving way to Eurasianism under Putin. Atlantism is now making a resurgence under Medvedev in response to Obama's call for pressing the "reset button" on relations with Russia. A less aggressive policy under Obama saw NATO's move eastward halt, prompting Russia to allow US supplies to transit Russia to Afghanistan, train Afghan police and military, and contribute helicopters to NATO. Russia supported new US-sponsored UN sanctions against Iran over its nuclear program in 2010. The Institute of Contemporary Development, a leading Russian think tank chaired by Medvedev, drew up a report outlining positive scenarios of relations between Moscow and NATO, including Russia's accession to the alliance. Russia faces three options:

1. If NATO succeeds in cowing the Afghans and continues to threaten Russia with encirclement, the Atlantists could push to accede to the US empire. This is the future Brzezinski predicted, with Russia's only real geostrategic option "an increasingly organic connection with a transatlantic Europe".[36] Russia would benefit in terms of trade and investment, but as a junior partner, a postmodern nation like Poland, or at best Turkey after it "shed its imperial ambitions and embarked on the road of modernization, Europeanization, and democratization."[37] But history since 1997 has not been kind to this vision: Turkey has already veered far from its postmodern role, reacting to the major lacunae in the Brzezinski analysis—the US and Israeli imperialisms which hang over the Middle East and Central Asia like a storm cloud. Greater openness to the US and EU would lead to the dismantling of the Russian Federation into possibly dozens of postmodern statelets after civil war. The popularity of Putin from 2000–08 derives largely from his rejection of western interference, his embrace of the Eurasian vision and his reassertion of Russia as a rival to the US.

2. Alternately if the US empire continues to falter, Russia could build up its BRIC and SCO ties, and join with Germany and France to lead the EU as the countervailing power to the US empire. This is the neo-Atlantist geopolitical logic that produced the Deauville Summit in October 2010 between France, Germany and Russia, a policy midway between Atlantists and Eurasians. Advocates of this strategy would like to see NATO replaced by a Euro-Russian security treaty, which would by definition exclude the US and include Russia. It would prevent member states from taking actions which threaten other members, effectively excluding Ukraine and Georgia from NATO, and eventually lead to the exclusion of US missile bases in Europe. NATO would wither or be transformed into "a full-fledged strategic partnership between Russia and NATO".[38] North America would be forced to ally with a new, independent Europe, where Russia is now the dominant power. In Washington's worst-case scenario, if its Afghan gambit implodes, not only will it have to take Russia seriously, but so will Europe, giving the Russian neo-Atlantists the opportunity to integrate with Europe without becoming just another postmodern state in the empire-and-a-half.

3. Or it could fully embrace the Eurasian option, turning to China, Iran and others opposed to US hegemony, the option that Washington fears most, as this would push the US out of Eurasia. Given Russia's weakened state, it would have to acknowledge China as senior partner in any such anti-hegemonic coalition, making Russia a "buffer" between what Brzezinski calls "an expanding Europe and an expansionist China".[39]

Perhaps the Russians (and Chinese) are tolerating US meddling in Central Asia in line with the age-old strategy of playing off your enemies against each other—in this case, the Americans and the Taliban. This strategy was used by the US in the 1930s–40s, when American capitalism helped develop both fascist Germany and the Soviet Union, increasing the likelihood of a destructive war between them—conveniently far away, and with the result that American business could help pick up the pieces after the inevitable war. It can just as well be used against the Americans today.

Russia's role in the Middle East and relationship with Israel are complex. Gorbachev's initiative to extend relations to both Israel and the PLO as representing an embryonic Palestinian state on Occupied Territories in the 1988 arguably contributed to Bush I's resolve to confront Israel over settlements in 1991–92, providing impetus for the Madrid Conference in October 1991, co-sponsored by the US and the Soviet Union, and the subsequent Oslo Accords in 1993. But by then Russia was out of the picture.

Russia's relations with the Middle East since the collapse of the Soviet Union have been low key. It maintains relations with Hamas, and, as a member of the so-called quartet of Middle East negotiators (along with the EU, the US and the UN), insists that Israel freeze expansion of settlements in the Occupied Territories as a condition of further talks. It appears to be trying to regain some of the goodwill that existed between the Soviet Union and Arab states, supporting the UN Goldstone Report which accused Israel of war crimes in its 2008 invasion of Gaza. It embarked on a diplomatic offensive with Arab states in 2008, offering Syria and Egypt nuclear power stations, and is re-establishing a military presence in the Mediterranean at the Syrian port, Tartus.[40] With its 16 million Muslims (about 12 per cent of the population), it has expressed interest in joining the Organization of Islamic Conference.

However, the importance of Jewish financial and economic interests—both the oligarchs and the Kosher Nostra—in post-Soviet Russia ensures that Israel gets a sympathetic hearing from Russian leaders. Israeli Foreign Minister Avigdor Lieberman is a Russian Jew who emigrated in 1978. Another factor in Russian geopolitical thinking in the Middle East is the Muslim insurgency in the Caucasus. Israel is able to take advantage of the persistence of Muslim unrest and dreams of independence in the Caucasus within Russia to prevent Moscow from taking any strong position to pressure Israel. Georgia harbors Chechen rebels and Georgia's president, Mikheil Saakashvili, uses Israeli and US military advisers. An Israeli footprint in the Chechnya issue was hinted at during the scandal surrounding the murder of Russian FSB defector Alexander Litvinenko in London in 2008.[41] While the nature and extent of Mossad activity in the Caucasus is impossible to know for sure, there is no doubt that abetting terrorists is a useful way for Israel to apply pressure on the Russian government, and that Russian security forces do their best to keep track of it.

China
America's ultimate geopolitical enemy is China, for both the neocons[42] and the 'liberal' faction of the empire,[43] as 2010 amply witnessed, with the US trying to force China to revalue its currency while at the same time conducting military exercises in the South China Sea with Vietnam and in the Yellow Sea with Korea, indirectly supporting Vietnam's claims to the disputed Spratly and Paracel islands.[44] So far in GGIII, NATO has moved to China's borders in

Afghanistan, Kyrgyzstan and Tajikistan, and is turning ASEAN into an Asian NATO, with Singapore, Malaysia and Thailand even sending troops to Afghanistan.[45]

Brzezinski is one of the few US strategists who does not see China as a serious threat to the US global empire, if for the wrong reasons: "An effort by China to seek global primacy would inevitably be viewed by others as an attempt to impose a national hegemony. To put it very simply, anyone can become an American, but only a Chinese can be Chinese—and that places an additional and significant barrier in the way of any essentially national global hegemony."[46] He is confident that the US empire will endure and can contain China, which will always suffer from the 'yellow peril' syndrome. It is "the very multinational and exceptional character of American society" that makes it easy for the US "to universalize its hegemony without letting it appear to be a strictly national one."

But Brzezinski makes clear in *The Grand Chessboard* that the US will "brook no rival for hegemony in Eurasia", and with Russia already a pale shadow of the Soviet Union, this could only mean China.

China's sheer economic presence and subtle use of soft power in promoting itself as an alternative to the US, qualities which so appeal to Brzezinski, make it a formidable rival in GGIII. Already EU trade with China is greater than with the US. As Brzezinski clumsily noted, it can't infiltrate and subvert non-Chinese societies easily and must rely on above-board economic power and mutual benefit, unlike the US and Israel, which rely on financial manipulation, subversion, black-ops and cultural hegemony to pursue their imperial goals. This is actually a plus for countries which are used to being victims of subversion, as practiced to such devastating effect in GGI&II&III.

China's greater role in GGIII represents a positive development in many ways, undermining the US dollar's role as reserve currency, which has provided a free ride for the US for 40 years, working against the militarization of space and—at least so far—the use of cyberwarfare to subvert rivals. Its focus on economic development has been a boon to many African countries, and encouraging economic cooperation is a much better way to deter countries like Iran from pursuing nuclear weapons than isolating and boycotting them. It is building the IPI (Iran-Pakistan-India) Pipeline to carry Iran's natural gas to Pakistan with the intent of the pipeline extending to India and China, in competition with the US-backed TAPI (Turkmenistan-Afghanistan-Pakistan-India) pipeline. China is also upgrading Pakistan's port at Gwadar for use by the Chinese Navy. (See Figure 5.4)

Even if TAPI is built, China will still be in a strategic position to prevent the US from controlling where the gas pumped from Central

Asia ultimately goes to. TAPI would be better called TAPIC. And there is no geostrategic argument for India to pull out of IPI. Pakistan has excellent relations with Iran and the new geopolitical formation in Eurasia around pipelines is bringing all these countries together with the prospect of peaceful economic development, with only the US standing in the way. Both TAPI and IPI face security problems as both pass through Baluchistan, and the Baluchistan Liberation Army has blown up pipelines on several occasions to press its demands for independence or at least better treatment by the Pakistani government. TAPI has the additional problem of transiting Afghanistan. Either pipeline requires peace in AfPak.

While China is now importing oil from Kazakhstan and Russia via new pipelines, it still relies primarily on oil shipped in from Iran and the Middle East. However, Pepe Escobar notes,

> If the energy cooperation between Iran, Pakistan, and China goes forward, it will signal a major defeat for Washington in the New Great Game in Eurasia, with enormous geopolitical and geo-economic repercussions. For the moment, Beijing's strategic priority has been to carefully develop a remarkably diverse set of energy-suppliers—a flow of energy that covers Russia, the South China Sea, Central Asia, the East China Sea, the Middle East, Africa, and South America. If China has so far proven masterly in the way it has played its cards in its Pipelineistan 'war', the US hand—bypass Russia, elbow out China, isolate Iran—may soon be called for what it is: a bluff.[47]

China surpassed Japan as the world's second largest economy in 2010 and is projected to surpass the US by 2027 if not sooner. The US is playing a particularly high-stakes game with China, having mortgaged itself irretrievably to China financially and now asserting itself militarily against it. In a sense, the countries are tied together in an embrace no less fatal than the one that Jewish financiers traditionally made with the reigning political powers. The US government is trying to play Spain's King Ferdinand to its Chinese court financiers, threatening to cancel much of its debt with China (held in treasury bonds) through a devaluation of the dollar. But if China simply moves on in its trade relations and refuses to play ball with the US, it could turn the tables, leaving the US bankrupt, just as Spanish Jews left Spain for the new empires at the end of the fifteenth century, precipitating Spain's decline in the seventeenth century, and the Dutch and British empires took off.

> China is getting the key to world power from Iran by agreeing to buy Iranian oil with the Chinese yuan, and if Iran stands firm and succeeds to become the new pitbull in the Middle East, all the Arab countries will change dollars to yuan in international trade. The West has its pitbull in the Middle East called Israel. The fight is on, and the question is which pit bull can kill the other pit bull.[48]

China also plans to dispense with the dollar in its oil trade with the Persian Gulf states, which will achieve what Saddam Hussein tried to do in 2000.[49]

China is learning to use its wealth to assert parapolitical power, investing overseas, lending to other countries, and using the yuan in cross-border trade, intent on making the yuan a reserve currency with its regional trade partners.[50] When these gradual assertions of financial clout reach a tipping point, China will succeed in undermining the dollar as world reserve currency, marking the beginning of the transition to a new Great Game.

Israel is cultivating China, chiefly as China's second largest source of arms after Russia. China was officially a Cold War foe of Israel during GGII, but when China joined the US-sponsored war in Afghanistan in 1979, Israeli magnate Shaul Eisenberg undertook a secret $10 billion 10-year deal to modernize the Chinese armed forces, "one of the most important [deals] in Israeli history",[51] finally establishing diplomatic relations in 1992. As it does with India and other countries, Israel uses high-tech arms exports to China as a bargaining chip to make sure China doesn't sell specific weapons to Israel's Middle East rivals.

Despite Israel being the West's pitbull in the current game, culturally there is an underlying affinity between Israelis and the Chinese, both claiming cultural if not racial superiority. Although there is no 'Judeo-Chinese' meme equivalent to the purported Judeo-Christian one, Chinese television produced a joint Israeli-Chinese twelve-part documentary "Walk into Israel—the Land of Milk and Honey" in 2010, portraying Jewish culture as a beacon of human thought on a par with Chinese culture.

Sinophiles including Brzezinski[52] welcome the resurgence of China as a benign future world hegemon, based on its millennial existence as a "civilization state" as opposed to the "nation state" of the European Enlightenment.

If Europe provided the narrative and concepts that have informed not just western but world history over the past two centuries, so China may do rather similarly for the next century or so, and thereby furnish the world with an entirely different story and set of concepts: namely the idea of unity rather than fragmentation, that of the civilisation state rather than the nation state, that of the tributary system rather than the Westphalian system, a distinctive Chinese notion of race, and an organising political dynamic of centralisation/ decentralisation rather than modernisation/ conservatism.[53]

Jacques predicts that with the end of colonialism, international relations will move away from nation states and China's Confucian traditions will prove robust, based on the centrality of the state and highly structured civil relations based on tradition.

Japan

Japan remains a passive actor in Eurasia, the Asian link in the Rockefeller-sponsored Trilateral Commission, first headed by Brzezinski in 1973 to coordinate US, European and Japan affairs. Japan was by then the leading economic power and US ally in Asia. It dutifully follows US policy on all major problems. "Like Britain in the case of Europe, Japan prefers not to become engaged in the politics of the Asian mainland," says Brzezinski, and is therefore not a "geostrategic player".[54]

With the historic defeat of the Liberal Democrats in 2009, it appeared to be tentatively asserting itself—trying to evict US bases and create an Asian economic space without the US, but Prime Minister Yukio Hatoyama failed to push the US out and resigned in disgrace. As the US dollar weakens and the US loses its imperial edge, China would like to develop a Japanese-China axis similar to the Franco-German axis which effectively presides over European affairs, with China the dominant partner.

India

India has drifted away from its non-aligned position of GGII Cold War days, aligning now more with the US and Israel on GGIII issues, pursuing neoliberal policies of privatization and free trade. India, like its rival China, does not have the reputation for intrigue and subversion that the US, Israel and its nemesis Pakistan have.

It is now in the US interest to replace the GGII Indian-Pakistani rivalry over Kashmir—once useful when India was an ally of the Soviet Union—with Indian-Chinese rivalry. The border conflict between India and China is a direct result of British colonial map-drawing, when British greed extended its colony's claims deep into Tibet. When a weak, independent India tried to make good these claims in 1962, a war-hardened Chinese army gave India a black eye. Since then, India has spent huge sums on building and maintaining high-altitude air bases and a network of new roads in Indian Tibet, but the poorly demarcated border could be used as a potential source of conflict for the two nations.

In geopolitical terms, India is the southern extension of Eurasia, and aligning its foreign policy with China, Russia and Iran, as opposed to rimland Britain and the US and geopolitical pygmy Israel, would make it part of a strong heartland axis, breaking the hold of the Anglo-American empire, to which it was subjugated in GGI and is now flirting with in GGIII. It is working with China and Russia in BRIC and RIC, and is an associate member of the SCO (see Appendix II), but the underlying Chinese-India border problem of GGII lingers. The US is actively using this to isolate China, including India in its military exercises aimed at China along with ASEAN nations, Japan, and Australia.

It makes much more sense for India to reach a *modus vivendi* with China, as it will never prevail against China militarily. What appears to be India playing hard-to-get in GGIII, trying to work with all the players, is really a matter of opportunistic Indian elites holding out for the most advantageous alliance. But without a clear strategic aim or principled position it risks being shunted aside, and merely used by other equally opportunistic players. Considering the Chinese moves to contain India and to extend its economic power into political and military advantage, while faced with equally determined US and Israelis strategists out for their own regional hegemony, India could easily find itself losing on several fronts—Kashmir, Tibet, energy from Iran. Russia is in no position nor has it any particular interest in supporting India, as it did in Soviet days.

India has the third largest Muslim population after Indonesia and Pakistan, and recognized Israel only in 1992, previously being a strong supporter of the Palestinians. However, Hindu nationalists identify with Israel, much as Chinese nationalists do, all having claims to 'chosen people' status, and Israel-India ties, especially military, have developed rapidly in the past decade. Since Israel is limited in its military use of the Mediterranean, it has enthusiastically developed relations with the Indian Navy in the Indian Ocean. In 2000, Israeli submarines reportedly conducted test launches of cruise missiles capable of carrying nuclear warheads in the Indian Ocean; off the Sri Lanka coast.[55] Israel and India's interests coincide in destabilizing Pakistan.

At the same time India and Iran are jointly constructing power plants and India is involved in the construction of a deep water port in Chabahar, Iran that would be a twin for the Pakistani port of Gwadar being expanded by China, providing another access to the Indian Ocean for landlocked Afghanistan, potentially freeing it from dependence on Pakistan.

Russia, India, Iran and China are the natural Eurasian coalition, with Russian, Central Asian and Iranian oil and gas carried both east to China, south to India and west to Europe via pipelines built and financed without Anglo-American control. This is the only scenario that would push Pakistan to resolve its border dispute in Kashmir and stop destabilizing Afghanistan.[56] At this point, a win-win for all, but the very one impossible for the empire-and-a-half to accept. Good cop Israel can afford to court RIC (minus Iran), leaving the US bad cop to align southeast Asian countries against China, and east European and ex-Soviet countries against Russia—a warning to India to stay on the US team. Neither Israel nor the US can deal with Iran.

Europe

The European nations were built up after WWII with US financial and military means, and integrated into the post-WWII US empire and GGII&III, much like Japan was in the east. But it was a struggle in the early post-war years to prevent their drift towards socialism or a separate accommodation with the Soviet Union.

Germany is the main European power, the source of so much angst for the Anglo-American empire in GGI, divided between East and West in GGII. When GGIII began, British Prime Minister Thatcher was not in favor of a reunited Germany, the fear being that a united Germany would come to dominate Europe and, with a reformed Russia, develop into a strong counterweight to the Anglo-American empire, a world-dominating Eurasian heartland, as indeed Mackinder had feared and Haushofer had hoped. After the Berlin Wall came down in 1989, over Thatcher's protest Germany was unified and became the dominant European power, but on the understanding that it was now a postmodern nation and NATO was the vehicle for its foreign policy. US policy towards Europe since then has been focused on preventing Europe from turning east, which would allow Eurasia to unite and push the US and its rimland schemes for world empire aside.[57]

Attempts to wield the EU into an independent player in GGIII have been undermined at every step, as they were in GGII. The EU attempted to chart an independent energy course—the 1992 Energy Charter Treaty—to develop Russian energy for Europe from the Caspian Sea. The US did not support it and in 1995 initiated the Interstate Oil and Gas Transport to Europe program "to promote the security of energy supplies". In 1996 ex-Secretary of State James Baker, acting as attorney for US-British interests (Amoco-BP) in Azerbaijan, established the Southern Balkan Development Initiative for pipeline cooperation with Bulgaria, Macedonia and Albania. Openly admitting US interests trump any Euro ones even in Europe, he wrote in 1997 that it "was in the strategic interests of the US to build the strongest possible economic, cultural and political ties to Georgia."[58]

Recall Britain's sabotage of Germany's pre-WWI Baghdad railway, which was intended to open an independent trade route to the Persian Gulf in GGI. Just as Britain then outmaneuvered its imperial rival to keep control of Saudi oil, so this US ploy in the Caucasus is intended to maintain US pre-eminence over Europe and Russia in determining Europe's energy future.

The post-9/11 wars and the subsequent neocon hysteria were used by the US to force old Europe into line using anti-Russian new Europe. The 2008 financial crisis precipitated by the US which devastated Europe, and the weakening of the euro were also orchestrated to keep Europe in line. Euro-dominoes are still falling as governments meekly cave in to banker demands. The bankers' darling, Latvia, lost 25 per cent of its GNP in 2009, and its working young were forced abroad to find work. According to Brzezinski, failure to confront the bankers will

> lock in a new kind of international financial class extracting tribute much like Europe's Viking invaders did a thousand years ago in seizing its land and imposing tribute in the form of land. Today, they impose financial charges as a post-modern neoserfdom that threatens to return Europe to its pre-modern state.[59]

After the collapse of the Soviet Union, European protest against US imperialism ebbed. However, there are signs this is changing, especially in Germany. As German chancellor, Gerhard Schroeder made clear overtures to Russia and has since lobbied for closer Euro-Russian ties. He is currently the chairman of the board of Nord Stream AG; the Nord Stream pipeline bringing Russian gas to Germany almost finished in 2010 despite US disapproval (see Figure 5.2). *Die Linke*,[60] critical of Israel and calling for disarmament and an end to NATO, now is the second largest opposition party after the Social Democrats, replacing the Greens. It is a matter of time before old Europe shakes off its US-Israeli-imposed stupor and forges a new European identity with a revived Russia leading to a Eurasian integration, Brzezinski's feared "Russo-German or a Russo-French flirtation".[61] Russia's 2008 European Security Treaty proposal would displace the old Cold War arrangements towards something closer to the pre-WWI Concert of Powers.

Strong Euro-Israeli lobbies achieved Israel's accession to the OECD in 2010, and Israel has a "special relationship" with NATO and the EU, though the extent of Zionist cultural hegemony in Europe is much less than in North America. Israeli politicians can't travel to Spain, Britain and elsewhere for fear of arrest on war crimes charges under the universal jurisdiction laws in those states. Anti-Israeli grassroots organizations in Europe are increasingly a force to contend with. The accession of Turkey to the EU would accelerate the unraveling of the empire-an-a-half's grip on Europe.

Continued economic crises without confronting the underlying cause—the manipulation of the US dollar—could mean the disintegration of Europe and the euro, even as the world struggles to develop a stable international exchange mechanism without the US dollar. In *Losing Control* Paul Rogers posits that change will come—a benign domino effect—when a postmodern European country such as Germany asserts itself and leads the way for other countries, rejecting military force, building a multi-facetted foreign policy of economic assistance, including proactive trade policies, to undermine the logic of insurgents and terrorists.

Such a voluntary move by a postmodern country to give up its privileged position in the present world order would begin a meaningful process of redistributing income internationally, effectively undermining the imperial logic. What is necessary is

- for national governments and NGOs to make sure that any 'aid' reaches poor farmers and third world producers rather than third world elites to allow for a meaningful transfer of surplus to the third world, and eventually for a truly level economic playing field to be negotiated between first and third worlds;

- for national governments to clamp down on huge international corporations and stop speculative currency transactions, thereby controlling the excesses capitalism in its imperialist guise gives rise to;

- for national governments to shake off their postmodern funk and reject the conditionalities imposed by the IMF which enforce the neoliberal political regimen and global financialization, and to regain control over their capital accounts.

Popular forces of resistance

Besides Hizbullah, Taliban and al-Qaeda, popular movements embracing all countries are also players in the world today. Just as the likes of Margaret Thatcher ultimately switched sides when popular resistance against South African apartheid reached a critical mass in the 1980s, the same dynamic is playing itself out today in the growing **BDS** (Boycott, Disinvestment, Sanctions) movement to boycott Israeli apartheid, to delegitimize Israel as a racist state, as a sponsor of terrorism, a state that must be nudged/ pushed/ shamed into joining the comity of nations.

Israeli think tanks have described the global justice movement as a greater threat to Israel than Palestinian violence, have castigated reliance on international law as a dangerous form of "lawfare", and conduct public relations activities to discredit what is sometimes called "the Durban approach", referring to the UN-sponsored World Conference against Racism held in Durban in 2001 which re-identified Zionism as a form of racism.[62] Princeton professor of international law and United Nations Special Rapporteur on Palestinian Human Rights Richard Falk is cautiously optimistic about the prospects of Palestinians achieving a breakthrough in their struggle, given growing world sympathy:

> Despite its huge advantage in resources devoted to this campaign, Israel is definitely losing the legitimacy war. Still, even if the Palestinians win the legitimacy war there is no guarantee that this victory will produce the desired political results. It requires Palestinian patience, resolve, leadership and vision, as well as sufficient pressure to force a change of heart in Israel, and probably in Washington as well. In this instance, it would seem to require an Israeli willingness to abandon the core Zionist project to establish a Jewish state, and that does not appear likely from the vantage point of the present. But always the goals of a legitimacy war appear to be beyond reach until mysteriously attained by the abrupt and totally unexpected surrender by the losing side. Until it collapses the losing side pretends to be unmovable and invincible, a claim that is usually reinforced by

police and military dominance. This is what happened in the Soviet Union and South Africa, earlier to French colonial rule in Indochina and Algeria, and to the United States in Vietnam.[63]

The end of Israel as an apartheid state, if achieved, will expose the underlying contradiction in the empire-and-a-half as a whole. This, changes in Egypt and Turkey, and the possible unraveling of Afghanistan and Iraq, will point the way to a more rational world system.

Conclusion

The GGI plans of Mackinder for a permanent British world empire ran aground on the inherent problems of colonialism—imperial overreach and hubris. GGII was a dramatic showdown with communism, the secular antidote to imperialism, where the US dollar was transformed into the world currency devoid of any real backing, and the other ex-imperial powers were lined up behind the empire. Hudson's post-WWII "super-imperialism" had managed to defeat the enemy. However, imperial hubris struck again in GGIII, and, combined with blowback and the emergence of Israel as a new imperial power at the heart of the US empire, has resulted in a bad case of "deep politics", a political process out of control spawning new and unexpected nightmares which are experienced by all, conquerors and victims alike.

The current crisis in US-Israeli relations centers around their diverging concerns. The US government, representing the two often conflictual interests of Big Oil and the banking establishment, is most concerned to maintain the present world financial order which allows it free access to the world's resources, while the world's Zionist elite is intent on consolidating Greater Israel as a specifically Jewish haven, with an expanding role in world affairs. Ultimately, Israel depends on the present world financial order every bit as much as the US does, confronting Zionists with a contradiction as the US imperial order stumbles.

The Israel lobby at the heart of the empire-and-a-half is a watchdog preventing rational, non-Zionist US imperial strategists from enforcing a Middle East peace requiring Israel to renounce its status as a colonial regime. Hints of such a rational imperial strategy have surfaced repeatedly during GGII&III. Eisenhower was able to stare down the albeit still fledgling Israel lobby in 1956. Kennedy was determined to prevent Israel from producing nuclear bombs but was assassinated. In 1979 Carter was able to impose a cold peace between Israel and its main Arab enemy, Egypt, though at great financial cost to the US.

With the smell of victory over communism still in the air, Bush I attempted to define GGIII as a US game with Israel playing by newly rational US imperial rules, but instead of Bush I's postmodern imperialism—a peaceful conquest of a willing world—GGIII became a replay of the GGI endgame, a violent conquest through wars and domestic repression. The current wars in the Middle East and Central Asia could easily spread. Israel continues to threaten Lebanon and Iran, and to pursue its Greater Israel through ethnic cleansing. The wars in Afghanistan and Iraq could be joined by one between Pakistan and India, an invasion of Iran or North Korea, or a war against China, using the full array of GGIII weapons, including financial warfare, direct invasion, use of proxies, terrorism and cyberwarfare. And now, at this writing, further imperial engagement in Africa, not just in Libya by NATO but in Ivory Coast by the French, under the guise of humanitarian intervention, has begun.

Obama's decision to honor Bush I with the 2010 Presidential Medal of Freedom, awarded for "contribution to the security or national interests of the United States, world peace, [or] cultural" was a wistful nod to Bush I's efforts to put GGIII on the road to a more benign imperialism. The same week, in a reflection of his efforts in a contrary direction, Bush II was warned by London Mayor Boris Johnson not to come to Britain to promote his memoirs as "He might never see Texas again."[64] Obama had inherited not Bush I's dream of a thousand-year postmodern imperialism, but Bush II's replay of the plan for a thousand-year Reich.

The US is and always has been an empire despite repeated denials over the past two centuries. But ordinary Americans do not have the imperial mentality that the British had in GGI, the sense of entitlement that allowed Britain to undertake unilateral imperial wars of conquest without any compunction. Americans (except for US-born Zionist immigrants to Israel) are not colonizing US neocolonies as the British did British colonies in the 17th–19th cc, commencing with North America. The American revolution was *against* British imperialism, even if it was intended to clear the way by US elites for a US imperialism. British citizens pursued colonial wars with enthusiasm, while Americans have been tricked into supporting US wars, from the Philippines and WWI through the Cold War to the war on terrorism today.

Convicted spy Jonathan Pollard is an important symbol of the ambivalence of US leaders about the direction of US empire. As long as he remains in prison, he represents a toe-hold for a rational US imperial strategy in GGIII.[65] The solidarity movement in support of a just peace in the Middle East, and enduring Arab hostility if such a peace is not reached, mean that Israel is and will remain a strategic liability to the US, belying the much-vaunted special relationship.

US imperial strategy, even if more rational without the 'half', is still a problem which must be faced for those concerned with social justice. At present, the enemy so necessary to justify the empire is defined as Islamic terrorism. Leaving aside the fact that the US itself fostered this problem, its response—a war on terror—is not intended to end terror (an impossibility) but to use it as justification for 'reforming' Islam in the process, occupying strategic areas of the Eurasian heartland, both to ensure access to its resources, but also to pursue containment of the real rivals for US world hegemony—China and Russia.

Islam has remained remarkably unchanged since the days of the Prophet. This was the intent of the *Quran*—to correct errors in the Abrahamic tradition which had crept into the Torah and New Testament. While orthodox Jews have been able to rationalize Israel as an "act of God", especially after 1967,[66] and both Jews and Christians have adapted easily to the radical secularism of life under capitalism, this willingness to abandon their ancient beliefs is not so easy for Muslims. While the West surged ahead in economic affairs under capitalism, Muslim countries, where the *Quran* and the Five Pillars of the faith[67] play a central role in the lives of the people, have found it much more difficult to adapt to this amoral economic system.

To what extent can Islam be 'reformed' to meet the needs of twenty-first century society? The Judaic prophets, followed by Jesus and Muhammad, and the nineteenth century secular prophet of revolution Marx, rejected usury and interest, as representing ill-gotten gain, with good reason. Marx condemned this mode of extraction of surplus as the highest form of fetishism, based on private property and exploitation of labor. They all rejected this exploitation on a moral basis as unjust, insisting that morality be embedded in the economy, a principle which was abandoned when capitalism took hold. While Judaism and Christianity adapted, Islam did not.

Interest, and today's money based on US military might alone, are the root cause not only of the current world financial crisis, but, as a corollary to Rothschild's dictum about money and politics, and Clausewitz's dictum about politics and war, the primary instrument facilitating (and benefiting from) the wars in the Middle East and Central Asia, and the world political crisis.

The unyielding anti-imperialist nature of Islam, its rejection of the fundamental principles of capitalism concerning money, its refusal to be sidelined from economic and hence political life, as are Christianity and Judaism, is anathema to both the US and Israel. These features of Islam unite its Abrahamic cousins in their goal of subduing the main source of resistance today to the empire-and-a-half.[68]

Islam has an important role to play in world affairs, as the many players in GGIII continue to jockey for economic and political power. Without its insight into the root causes of the world's economic problems, we will inevitably be faced with a return to GGI-style war as the postmodern imperial order breaks down.

Appendix I: Review of new Great Game literature

With the collapse of the Soviet Union, there came a rush of "new Great Game" literature dealing with the obvious political maneuverings of the US in Central Asia in search of the Mackinder/ Brzezinski Holy Grail, almost exclusively focused on oil. Apart from Dugin (1997), the collapse of the Soviet Union is seen as merely an opportunity for "brash new, Wild West-style entrepreneurs" and securing long-term US energy needs. Most, like Johnson (2007) and Engdahl (2004) argue that the US-British strategy is dominated now by oil security.[69]

The classic work in this field is *The Grand Chessboard* by Brzezinski (1997), which inspires his protégé Obama's "geostrategy"[70] in Eurasia. "The defeat and collapse of the Soviet Union was the final step in the rapid ascendance of a Western Hemisphere power, the United States, as the sole and, indeed, the first truly global power. ... For America, the chief geopolitical prize is Eurasia"[71] Brzezinski marvels that throughout history, world affairs were dominated by Eurasian power but that "for the first time ever, a non-Eurasian power [the US] has emerged not only as the key arbiter of Eurasian power relations but also as the world's paramount power."[72] Fortunately for America, Eurasia is too big to be politically one. For Brzezinski, history began in the fifteenth century; however, he rightly identifies "the Eurasian chessboard" as "the setting for 'the game'".[73]

His vision of the future is of a world in thrall to US cultural imperialism[74] with post-Soviet Russia a postmodern state much like his native Poland, a willing handmaiden of a US world order, with only China to be cajoled into acquiescence. The era of direct invasions ended with the Soviet occupation of Afghanistan. The much more sophisticated US would be able to co-opt local elites and feed them on Hollywood blockbusters to establish the necessary control over Eurasia.

He condemns the neocon wars,[75] but his hubris blinds him to his own vital role in preparing the stage for precisely today's nightmare. He remains unapologetic about his policy of supporting Islamists against the Soviet Union (thereby facilitating the anti-imperialist Islamic awakening), ignores Israel completely in his analysis and policy prescriptions, and desists from calling the US an empire, referring to a "common global community" a "trilateral relationship among the world's richest and democratic states of Europe, America, and East Asia (notably Japan)". Even without the neocon nightmare, he is pessimistic about the future of this "community" unless the US discards its consumerism and overcomes its "spiritual emptiness",[76] apparently oblivious to his own argument that US mass culture is an essential tool in the imperial project.

The term "new Great Game" has become prevalent throughout the literature about the region, appearing in book titles, academic journals, news articles, and government reports. The mainstream literature simply compares the British-Russian nineteenth century stand-off with the twenty-first century situation, granting that the playing field is complicated by transnational energy corporations with their own agendas and the brash new entrepreneurs who have taken control after the collapse of the Soviet Union.

Kleveman argues, "Regional powers such as China, Iran, Turkey, and Pakistan have entered the arena, and transnational corporations (whose budgets far exceed those of many Central Asian countries) are also pursuing their own interests and strategies."[77]

Mullerson, a 'liberal' imperialist, argues that the pre-WWI great game and the current one have "as their components respective *missions civilatrices"*. There are many games now and players change teams depending on what game is being played. China and Russia are watching how the West and the Muslim world exhaust each other in the war over terrorism,[78] yet Washington cooperates with China and Russia on "terrorism" and drug trafficking. The games are not always zero-sum competitions. Russia and China too are competitors in Central Asia for markets, resources, political influence but on a world level are allies, counterposed to US hegemony. Europe is a faithful member of the US team and plays no independent role in either Central Asia or the Middle East.

Mullerson dismisses religion as a legitimizing factor in general and in Central Asia in particular. He argues that Islamic parties there such as the Islamic Renaissance Party (Tajik), which was part of United Tajik Opposition that fought Tajik authorities in a 5-year civil war, the Islamic Movement of Uzbekistan (renamed the Islamic Party of Turkestan), and Huzb ut-Tahrir are really political parties advocating "religious totalitarianism" and using terrorism. He cites Thomas Friedman and Bernard Lewis, approving their view that these ideologies must be wiped out to end terrorism.[79] The West must carry on with its *mission civilatrice*. "The road to democracy, as the Western experience amply demonstrates, is long and hard, full of pitfalls and obstacles."[80]

A Johns Hopkins paper "The Key to Success in Afghanistan: A Modern Silk Road Strategy" tries "to visualize the kind of Afghanistan that might come into existence after US troops begin pulling out in 2011. The basic idea is that instead of being a lawless frontier, post-war Afghanistan should turn into a transit route for Eurasia, providing trade corridors north and south, east and west," requiring more roads, railways and pipelines, making "Afghanistan a hub rather than a barrier".[81]

Critique: The new Great Game literature is weak on important counts. Even where imperialism is alluded to, there is no acknowledgment that the politics of Central Asia is part of a larger game which centers on the wars in Iraq and Afghanistan, with Israel a major player. The Hopkins study makes no criticism of the invasion and the right of the US to decide on how Afghanistan should be developed, and ignores the geopolitical aim to bypass Russia, Iran and China. It finds inspiration not from the ancient silk route but from the conquest and subjugation of America itself which culminated in building the transcontinental railroad in 1869 to promote capitalism regardless of the wishes of the natives.

Only in relation to Russia is the overt imperial nature of US moves in Eurasia discussed openly and opposed in mainstream and popular writings. The Eurasian geopolitical theorist, Alexander Dugin, has provided a radical reinterpretation of the 19th–20th century geopolitics of Mackinder and Haushofer in the context of post-Soviet collapse Russia, aimed at opposing US imperialism. In *The Foundations of Geopolitics: The Geopolitical Future of Russia* (1997), he declares that "the battle for the world rule of [ethnic] Russians" has not ended and Russia remains "the staging area of a new anti-bourgeois, anti-American revolution". The Eurasian Empire will be constructed "on the fundamental principle of the common enemy: the rejection of Atlantism and strategic control by the US, and the refusal to allow liberal values to dominate us. ... Military operations play a relatively little role." Russia's natural resources and its strategic position at the heart of Eurasia should be used to oppose US plans and to promote a new Russian-European alliance without US hegemony, based on a Russo-German axis, excluding Britain since it is part of the Anglo-American axis. He advocates rapprochement with Japan and encouraging China to assert its hegemony in southeast Asia rather than Siberia. His focus is Russian resurgence and he does not incorporate Israel into his analysis, though he promotes the idea of a "continental Russian-Islamic alliance", based on a Russia-Iran understanding, dismissing al-Qaeda and "international terrorism" as instruments of the West.[82]

US sponsorship of new postmodern players is a move in itself in the new Great Game, which is not acknowledged in the mainstream literature. The new states were created by undermining the Soviet Union, instigating the subsequent color revolutions and invading Afghanistan and Iraq—all important moves by the imperial hegemon to reshape the entire Eurasian region to create a new playing field and a new game.

In GGI&II too, British colonies and protectorates were shaped consciously by the colonial office to play quasi-independent roles in some future informal empire (depending on the type of colony, i.e., a privileged settler one like Canada or one like India, as explained in Chapter 2). Over time, these players developed in ways sometimes unforeseen, such as Afghanistan, Iran and Iraq.

Moscow-based Institute of Oriental Studies analyst Knyazev argues that the US strategy is to create its own secular 'postmodern caliphate' to encompass the Middle East and "Greater Central Asia [which] calls for the dilution of borders between the five post-Soviet states and their merger with Afghanistan and Pakistan" which he dubbed a "geopolitical marasmus".[83] However, such an ambitious project of adjusting borders and state-creation is hardly within the scope of current US geopolitical capabilities, nor is Israel any help in bringing together Muslim nations throughout the region into a subservient commonwealth.

The qualitative difference between GGs I, II and III is not clearly seen in the literature. Edwards sees in the original Great Game (my GGI) the "forerunner of the Cold War struggle" and the current game "the last remnant of the struggle between USA and Russia",[84] conflating my GGII&III. Mullerson refers to a Great Game II,[85] which picks up where Kipling laid off, ignoring imperialism as the underlying system, the subsequent Cold War, and the role of Israel.

Mullerson downplays historical parallels as "more interesting than useful and more superficial than profound"[86] reflecting his lack of appreciation of the underlying continuity of these imperial games. He acknowledges that Washington is expanding its influence in region but denies it has any long term interests in staying,[87] and he condemns Dugin's Russian Orthodoxy-inspired messianism (not unlike US manifest destiny) preordained to clash with West, as a reversion to Genghis Khan, Tamerlane and Czarism.[88]

Mullerson notes the interesting irony that as sole superpower, the US has now lost its Cold War legitimacy as the leader of the anticommunist bloc, suffering the burden of providing world order and security (he is an Estonian immigrant to Britain). Therefore, today it "needs more military power than would have been necessary ... since today it would be necessary to carry out the hegemonic burden on a global scale."[89] But he could just as easily argue that after collapse of the enemy the victor should need less military force. He thereby implicitly acknowledges that the current new world order the US is enforcing is not a voluntary association of free nations, that security and peace are defined by the US (i.e., by accepting US hegemony, you have freedom from subversion by the US). While he dismisses the Russian geopoliticians and their pursuit of Russian empire, is there really much difference between the peace and security of Genghis Khan and that of the US today?

His support of secularism and respect for Friedman and Bernard Lewis shows his ignorance of the long history of imperial use and promotion of Islamist "totalitarian ideologies", and the fact that the US engineered the collapse of the Soviet Union using Islamists, allowing the Wahhabis to penetrate Central Asia and the Middle East, while supporting oppressive secular regimes. His proposal to snuff out these movements just adds fuel to a fire that the US has been stoking irrationally for decades.

An interesting description of post-Soviet Central Asia is provided by Rob Johnson who sees it experiencing "the recreation of a pre-communist Khanate", with increasing unrest as a result of the break-up of the Soviet Union: the 1988 Armenian/ Azeri war and riots in Ashgabat, conflict between Uzbeks and Meskhetian Turks in Ferghana in 1989, between Uzbeks and Kyrgyz in Osh and between Tajiks and Armenians in Dushanbe in 1990, the Chechnya separatist uprising of 1991–2000, the Abkhaz and South Ossetian separatists in Georgia from 1990 on, civil war in Tajikistan 1992–97, the Uzbek uprising in 2005, the riots in Kyrgyzstan in 2010. US interference in the form of "democracy support" and pursuit of its geopolitical strategies is merely adding oil to the flames.[90]

The closest in the mainstream media to an accurate understanding of the source of terrorism and the need for the US and Israel to pull in their claws are so-called paleoconservatives, who have long criticized US imperial adventures. Voices crying in the rightwing wilderness include Pat Buchanan, Ron Paul and Eric Margolis (2009), who while agreeing that it's all about oil, call for the complete US withdrawal from Iraq and Afghanistan, and for Israel to make a just peace by granting the Palestinians a state.

The best analysts of the Great Game strategies, the GGIII wars and the role of Israel include M.K. Bhadrakumar, Pepe Escobar, Peter Myers, James Petras, Rick Rozoff, Israel Shamir, and others cited in the main body of this work.

Appendix II: GGIII Alliances

Will we still be talking about a **United Nations** in 10 years time? Will it collapse along with its main founder, the US? One possible reform if the empire-and-a-half's game sputters and other players gain some say in how the world is run is to expand the Security Council to include some combination of Germany, India, Brazil, Japan, Egypt, Nigeria and South Africa. Even if the existing five members keep their veto, an expanded council would make it more difficult to allow another US-led imperial venture like the invasion of Iraq, which the council effectively condoned. Another possible direction for reinvigorating it politically is the creation of a UN parliamentary assembly composed of elected parliamentarians from around the world, evolving into a world parliament.

As for development alternatives, there are now 40,000 internationally recognized NGOs, some of them actually legitimate and effective, dealing with the environment, development, and disarmament, with the UN acting as an umbrella. The **WSF** (World Social Forum), a rival convention to the elitist World Economic Forum, set up in 2001 is attended by representatives from more than 1,000 NGOs.

By definition unstable and ever-shifting, alliances cannot be considered serious players in their own right. One that held out promise in GGII was the 85-nation **NAM** (Non-Aligned Movement), founded in 1961 in Belgrade, which provided a powerful anti-imperial voice. At its Colombo meeting in 1976 it called for a "fundamental reorganization of the international trade system in order to improve terms of trade... a worldwide reorganization of industrial production which would incorporate improved access by the developing nations to industrial products and technology transfer."[91] But this GGII challenge by the young third world alliance was easily deflected and NAM ebbed with the collapse of the Soviet Union, attracting little attention today.

NATO, the most enduring and most powerful of alliances in all the Great Games, is in trouble after assuming the role of frontman for US imperial power in GGIII with its expansion and out-of-region mission in Afghanistan and now Libya. "If Afghanistan falls, I'm not sure how far behind NATO will be," said Biden in 2008.[92] Even if it survives, it will be much harder in the future to mobilize troops for such baldly imperial occupations, as shown in the contentious NATO Libyan adventure, denounced around the world and unpopular among both Americans and Europeans from the start.

In GGII the US organized many such regional Cold War

alliances. The only enduring one is **ASEAN** (the Association of Southeast Asian Nations), created at US prompting in 1967 during the height of the Vietnam war, which the US is trying to turn into an Asian NATO, and expanded to include even Vietnam itself in 1995, all in the effort to contain the latest enemy, China.

However, it has an independent competitor in the region. **SAARC** (the South Asian Association for Regional Cooperation), founded in 1985 by Bangladesh, Bhutan, India, the Maldives, Nepal, Pakistan and Sri Lanka, with Afghanistan joining in 2005 and Mauritius in 2008, and with the US, China and South Korea as observers (Iran pending). It is dedicated to economic, technological, social, and cultural development emphasizing collective self-reliance. The members provide social, economic and infrastructure development funds.

The **SCO** (Shanghai Cooperation Organisation), founded in 1996 and reorganized in 2001, is nominally a security organization set up by China and Russia as a regional counterbalance to NATO, and includes Kazakhstan, Uzbekistan, Kyrgyzstan and Tajikistan, and four observers—India, Iran, Pakistan and Mongolia. So far it has not taken on any substantive role in GGIII, and until India and China resolve their border disputes and Iran calms regional fears about its nuclear intentions, it will remain toothless. With the collapse of the Soviet Union and NATO's self-proclaimed status as world policeman in the past two decades, Russia and China were more or less forced to form their own 'NATO'. Now, it is being courted by NATO itself. The SCO Special Conference on Afghanistan, held in Moscow in 2009, was attended by top US and NATO officials, as well as UN and OSCE heads. The Joint Action Plan underlined the SCO's importance "for practical interaction between Afghanistan and its neighboring states in combating terrorism, drug trafficking and organized crime". The Plan reads like a roadmap for bringing Afghanistan into the SCO fold, a move which India's envoy approved of, showing how at sea western strategists are about what to do with the failed attempt to wrestle Afghanistan into submission. Ironically, as the attempt to surround Russia sputters, it is Afghanistan that is now surrounded by SCO members and observers, notably Iran, anxious to contain drug trafficking.

Can NATO and the SCO become allies in Afghanistan, or are they fated to be enemies? It appears that Russia genuinely wants the US to succeed in bringing Afghanistan to heel. Russia's Ambassador to NATO, Dmitri Rogozin, said recently, "We want to prevent the virus of extremism from crossing the borders of Afghanistan and take over other states in the region such as Pakistan. If NATO failed, it would be Russia and her partners that would have to fight against the extremists in Afghanistan." Rogozin proposed using the NATO-Russia Council to establish a security order stretching "from Vancouver to Vladivostok. Perhaps NATO could develop into **PATO**, a Pacific-Atlantic alliance."[93] Medvedev's agreement at the 2010 NATO summit to work with it on missile defense is a continuation of this Atlantist strategy, which will inevitably weaken the SCO. Though remaining the main protagonists, neither Russia nor China has a coherent policy to counter US hegemony apart from their insistence on a new global reserve currency and resistance to US encirclement and interference in their regional affairs.

CFR analyst Evan Feigenbaum, until recently the State Department's deputy assistant secretary for South and Central Asia, said the 2009 SCO conference "offers an opportunity for the US to try to turn what are ostensibly common interests [in Afghanistan] into complementary polices," but added, "We really don't understand what the SCO is... Is it a security group? Is it a trade bloc? Is it a group of non-democratic countries that have created a kind of safe zone where the US and Europeans don't talk to them about human rights and democracy?"[94] Indeed, there is little uniting the suspicious and uneasy SCO members other than fear and perhaps loathing of the US and Taliban, and a desire to staunch the drug smuggling which the US is failing so spectacularly to deal with. If NATO were to disband or at least retract its claws, the SCO might well collapse. Expanding it to include, say, Iran, let alone Pakistan and India, would paralyze it unless the tentative **RIC** (Russia, India, China) alliance takes hold.

Similar to the SCO is the **CSTO** (Collective Security Treaty Organization) formed in 2002, including Uzbekistan, Kazakhstan, Tajikistan, Kyrgyzstan, Armenia and Belarus, a Russian attempt to bring some military coordination in its near abroad to compete with NATO's Partners for Peace. But they have little in common and the CSTO so far has proved ineffectual, refusing Kyrgyzstan's request for assistance during the break down of order in June 2010.[95]

In 2009 the **BRIC** nations (Brazil, Russia, India and China) held their first summit in Yekaterinburg Siberia. The BRIC countries comprise 15 per cent of the world economy, 40 per cent of global currency reserves and half the world's population. Brazil, India and China also weathered the financial crisis better than the world as a whole. Medvedev said, "The artificially maintained unipolar system is based on one big center of consumption, financed by a growing deficit and ... one formerly strong reserve currency." "The security of some states cannot be ensured at the expense of others, including the expansion of military-political alliances or the creation of global or regional missile defense systems," the joint Chinese-Russian statement says. BRIC, RIC, the SCO are the most likely vehicles to spearhead the coming change in the international system

The most enduring of the GGII groupings of countries in the Middle East and Central Asia are the **Arab League** of heads of state formed in 1945 in Cairo (6 founding members, now 22 plus 4 observers) and the **OIC** (Organization of Islamic Conference) set up in 1969, prompted by the 1967 war and occupation of Al-Quds (Jerusalem). All Arab League members are also members of the OIC. Neither has played an important role in either GGII or GGIII, effectively acknowledging US-Israeli hegemony in the Middle East. The **GCC**, (the Gulf Cooperation Council) was set up in 1981 as a political and economic union of the six Arab states of the Persian Gulf—Bahrain, Kuwait, Oman, Qatar, Saudi Arabia and the United Arab Emirates. Yemen hopes to join by 2016. It has a relationship with NATO similar to the Mediterranean Dialogue (see Chapter 3) and the intent is for the GCC to coordinate with NATO in the region. Given the present dependence of the members on the US, it plays no independent role.

In contrast, there are many powerful international Jewish and Zionist organizations (see Chapter 4), especially the **WJC** (World Jewish Congress) and the **WZO** (World Zionist Organization), and hundreds of Jewish and non-Jewish and foundations and NGOs lobbying world governments to support Israeli policy.

Appendix III: The ex-Soviet Central Asian republics in GGIII

Kazakhstan participates agreeably in all the line-ups—the SCO, the Commonwealth of Independent States (CIS), the CSTO, the Russia-Belorussia-Kazakhstan customs union, NATO's Partnership for Peace, the Organization for Security and Cooperation in Europe (OSCE—President Nazarbayev was its chair in 2010), and maintains good relations with all players, including Russia, the US, Israel, China and Iran. It has done well since the collapse of the Soviet Union, ruled by a strong dictator intelligent and capable enough to wrest control of oil revenue from Big Oil and use it to build infrastructure and provide an adequate standard of living to most citizens. Oil is sent to northern Iranian refineries and gas goes via the Korpedzhe-Kurtkui gas pipeline to Iran; since 2004 oil also flows in the Atasu-Alashankou oil pipeline to Xinjiang. China National Petroleum Corp bought PetrKazakhstan 2005. Nazarbayev nonetheless favors Moscow[96] and has advanced the idea of a Eurasian Union that would bring Europe, Russia and potentially China together in a peaceful, balanced relationship along the ancient Silk Road.

Kyrgyzstan tried to follow a pro-western strategy of democratic reform (its first president, Askar Akayev, was a physics professor), but without oil and a strong leader, it succumbed to US intrigues, suffered a color revolution in 2005 and is now a failed state. In 2005, then-prime minister Kulov talked of the need for a "multi-vector" foreign policy. "For instance, in order not to become too dependent on China we need the presence of Russia and America. ... We simply cannot afford to have enemies."[97] Another coup in 2010 was followed by hundreds of ethnic Uzbek deaths and thousands of refugees from Osh in the south. Pleas to Russia for intervention were ignored, the CSTO and SCO failing to rise to the occasion. The OSCE presented itself as a neutral option, though its observers have yet to arrive. This is reminiscent of the Kosovo scenario, with the OSCE mission a possible prelude to NATO occupation (there is a US base there and plans to build a second one near Osh), though 2010 is not 1999: neither the US or NATO are anxious to take on another out-of-region mission at this point, nor are they eager to antagonize Russia.

If unrest persists, the Kosovo scenario becomes a proven, ready option. Just as ethnic Albanians turned to separatism and violence in Kosovo with US support, Uzbeks in southern Kyrgyzstan could do the same with or without Hizb ut-Tahrir and other Islamists (see endnote 101) or covert destabilization. The collapse of Kyrgyzstan into clan and ethnic warfare could engulf the whole region in similar clashes, given the already angry stand-off between Uzbekistan, Kyrgyzstan and Tajikistan over water,[98] and the indefensible and illogical borders between all three 'republics'.[99] Osh, incidentally, has its own Chabad rabbi for the dozen Kyrgyz Jews there. This scenario is what frightens Russian geopolitical strategists today.

Uzbekistan, though the logical leader in Central Asia, with the most developed infrastructure and largest population (28 million), has become an isolated backwater under the harsh, arbitrary dictatorship of Islam Karimov. The strategic value of Uzbekistan means that the US is working to end the isolation. The lack of legal opposition and the strong Muslim traditions of Uzbekistan means that Islamists there pose a serious threat to both the US and Russia.

Turkmenistan, though rich in gas, has a small population and is mostly desert. It also maintains good relations with all the players, providing assistance to the US in Afghanistan. Turkmenistan appeared to have committed its entire future gas exports to China, Russia, and Iran in 2010 which would have meant the virtual death of the Trans-Caspian Gas Pipeline plans favored by Washington and the EU, but subsequently announced it was still interested in exporting gas to Europe as well as to China (see Figure 3.6). It remains aloof from the SCO and CSTO, and ongoing pressure by Washington eager to move forward with TAPI suggests that the US still is in the running as it continues to work to consolidate its position in Central Asia. Turkmenistan has been "quietly developing into a major transport hub" for the Northern Distribution Network to deliver supplies to U.S. and NATO forces in Afghanistan.[100]

The 'stans' can't play an independent role; the regimes can only protect themselves from subversion and from their own impoverished populations. Local politics are thus conservative, with Islam and communism the chief forces of opposition. When the US withdraws from Afghanistan, the resulting power vacuum will strengthen Islamist forces. Having built up the mujahideen in the 1980s to counter the Soviet Union, and allowed Saudi Arabia to introduce its Wahhabi version of Islam into a culture dominated by Sufi traditions, the US now leaves Russia with an Islamist threat. **Tajikistan** went through a civil war between Islamists and secularists in the 1990s, finally ending in 1997 with Islamists given some political power, though September 2010 saw clashes where 25 government troops were killed by United Tajik Opposition militants connected with the Islamic Movement of Uzbekistan.[101]

Israel and Zionists have been active in the manipulation of the emerging states in the ex-socialist bloc through color revolutions, spearheaded by Soros and the NED, the extensive Chabad network in the ex-Soviet Union and the Kosher Nostra. The latter particularly benefited from the extension of the US-Israeli empire where criminal figures function openly in the security organs and governments. With or without color revolutions, the strongest financial figures who have emerged from the chaos of the collapse of socialism are mafia, and they can succeed politically with or without elections through bribes and intimidation.

Israel has had especially close ties with the Karimov regime in Uzbekistan since establishing diplomatic relations in 1992. Islam Karimov made a state visit to Israel in 1998, a coup for both Israel and Karimov, who is shunned by most foreign states for his record of torture. In September 2000, Karimov appealed to Israel for aid in combating the rise of Islamic violence in the region. Prominent US Jewish leader Leon Levy hailed Karimov's regime as a "democracy for all the Islamic countries". Former Israeli minister of diaspora affairs, Natan Sharansky, defended the regime against critics who would "slander and defame the courageous struggle that Uzbekistan is waging against terrorism". Of the 200,000 Bukharan and Russian Jews who emigrated from Uzbekistan since independence, half live in Brooklyn, the unofficial headquarters of the Kosher Nostra, and half in Israel. Most ex-Soviet citizens retain their citizenship of origin, but the case of Uzbekistan is special because of the huge Jewish émigré population, providing a large pool of potential *sayanim*, agents, blackmarket operatives, and "joint venture" investors. It is widely accepted that Karimov has links with Uzbek mafias operating out of Israel.

Lev Leviev, who emigrated from Uzbekistan to Israel in 1971, now DeBeers' main rival in diamonds and chairman of Africa-Israel Investments, has extensive investments in eastern Europe and the former Soviet Union. He received the personal blessing of Schneerson for his philanthropic activities in promoting the Chabad movement in the ex-SU, and lauded Karimov during the latter's state visit to Israel in 1998, referring to Karimov's having grown up in the same Jewish neighborhood as Leviev's father and grandfather: "As you have been a friend to us, we will be a loyal friend to you."[102]

A key new player from Central Asia deeply involved in energy schemes is Kazakhstan-born Alexander Mashkevich, close friend of the Kazakhstan president and member of Jewish lobby groups working for Israel's interests in Central Asia and Africa. The richest Israeli citizen outside Israel, reportedly worth $5 billion, he controls the major share of the Kazakh Caspian oil fields. Mashkevich is a major shareholder in Eurasian National Resources Corporation, based in London, one of the world's leading natural resources groups. He currently serves as president of the Euro-Asian Jewish Congress one of the five regional branches of the World Jewish Congress. He has close contacts with Israeli government leaders and acts as go-between on delicate matters.[103]

Able to call on powerful Jews from the ex-Soviet Union, both market and blackmarket, Israel has extended its reach throughout Central Asia more easily and directly than the US, which is inevitably seen in terms of the rivalry with Russia and China. Jews holding passports from US, Israeli and ex-Soviet countries have the advantage in pressing Israeli concerns, especially in the Muslim 'stans', where Jews were and still are well integrated. The new, weak states and their governments are easily manipulated. For these new Israelis with their business interests in the ex-Soviet Union, the fate of Israel as a safe haven for their budding empires is essential, and they are good candidates to act as *sayanim*.

Azerbaijan falls between the regional slots, but can be mentioned here as Israel's latest Muslim friend in ex-Soviet Central Asia, having stepped in to re-equip the Azerbaijani forces immediately after the Nagorno-Karbakh war. Israeli firms guard Baku's international airport, "monitor and help protect Azerbaijan's energy infrastructure, and even provide security for Azerbaijan's president."[104] Azerbaijani Prime Minister

Ilham Aliyev has condemned Hamas and criticized Turkish support for Palestinian self-determination.[105] A WikiLeaks cable in 2009 notes that "Baku balances its cordial relations with [Israel] with its perceived responsibilities in to [sic] the OIC. Therefore Azerbaijan does not maintain an embassy in Israel." The Israeli-Azerbaijani relationship "also affects US policy insofar as Azerbaijan tries, often successfully, to convince the US pro-Israel lobby to advocate on its behalf... Israel's main goal is to preserve Azerbaijan as an ally against Iran, a platform for reconnaissance of that country and as a market for military hardware."[106]

ENDNOTES

1   "US embassy cables: Prince Andrew rails against France, the SFO and the Guardian", *Guardian*, 29 November 2010.

2   Brzezinski, *The Grand Chessboard,* 43. He leaves out Israel, presumably seeing it as part of the US empire project.

3   Nathan Guttman, "Israelis at center of ecstasy drug trade", *Haaretz*, 4 June 2003. See Chapter 4 note 79.

4   The EU-Israel Association Agreement entered into force in June 2000.

5   George Friedman, "Geopolitical Journey, Part 8: Returning Home", *www.stratfor. com*, 8 December 2010.

6   "Israel informed the 15 members of the United Nations Security Council last week, as well as several other prominent European Union countries, that if the Palestinian Authority persists in its efforts to gain recognition in September as a state within the 1967 borders, Israel would respond with a series of unilateral steps of its own." Barak Ravidm, "Israel threatens unilateral steps if UN recognizes Palestinian state", *Haaretz*, 29 March 2011.

7   Under the auspices of Freedom House's New Generation program, Egyptian visiting fellows from many civil society groups came to the US for training in 2008, including meetings with US Secretary of State Condoleezza Rice, White House National Security Adviser Stephen Hadley and congressmen. In May 2009, Secretary of State Hillary Clinton met a delegation of Egyptian dissidents, just prior to Obama's visit to Egypt. Sixteen activists met with Clinton and Acting Assistant Secretary of State for Near Eastern Affairs Jeffrey Feltman in Washington as part of a two-month fellowship. According to a WikiLeaks cable, "President Mubarak is deeply skeptical of the US role in democracy promotion. Nonetheless, (US government) programs are helping to establish democratic institutions and strengthen individual voices for change in Egypt." NED grants to Egypt in 2009 went to over 30 opposition groups, including the American Center for International Labor Solidarity, the Arab Society for Human Rights, the Egyptian Union of Liberal Youth, the Project on Middle East Democracy and the Youth Forum. See <http://www.ned.org/where-we-work/middle-east-and-northern-africa/Egypt>.

8   It provided bases and funding to invade Iraq in 1990 and condoned the 2003 invasion without direct participation. Since the Gulf War, the US has had a continued "presence" of 5,000 troops stationed there (10,000 during the 2003 invasion of Iraq).

9   King Abdullah of Saudi Arabia repeatedly urged the US to attack Iran—"Cut the

head off the snake"—to destroy its nuclear programme, according to November 2010 WikiLeaks. King Abdullah told the US ambassador, quoted in Andrew Gavin Marshall, "WikiLeaks and the Worldwide Information War Power, Propaganda, and the Global Political Awakening", *www.globalresearch.ca,* 6 December 2010.

10   Simon Tisdall, "WikiLeaks cables: Saudi Arabia rated a bigger threat to Iraqi stability than Iran", *Guardian,* 7 December 2010.

11   Suzanne Goldenberg, "If US leaves Iraq we will arm Sunni militias, Saudis say", *Guardian,* 14 December 2006. Sunni resistance includes ex-Baathists but also "Al-Qaeda in Iraq".

12   With only US election observers, Allawi's coalition won the most seats but still failed to oust the Shia from power.

13   CFR senior fellow Vali Nasr's comment "The last time Iran was a threat, the Saudis were able to mobilize the worst kinds of Islamic radicals. Once you get them out of the box, you can't put them back" shows the dilemma the 'liberal' imperial faction faces after the neocon policy of invasion and dismemberment of Iraq. Neither strongmen nor weak vassal states, neither US Middle East ally Israel nor Saudi Arabia provide a reasonable way forward. Nasr quoted in Morten Valbjorn and Andre Bank, "Signs of a new Arab cold war", *Middle East Report,* Number 242, Spring 2007.

14   NED grants to Tunisian NGOs in 2009 went to Al-Jahedh Forum for Free Thought, the Association for the Promotion of Education, and the Mohamed Ali Center for Research, Studies and Training. See <http://www.ned.org/where-we-work/middle-east-and-northern-africa/Tunisia>.

15   Jim Lobe, "US: Neo-Con Hawks Take Flight over Libya", Washington: Institute for Policy Studies, 27 February 2011. The Foreign Policy Initiative (FPI), founded in 2009 and widely seen as the successor to PNAC, issued an appeal to Obama on 25 February 2011 urging direct US intervention in Libya. Among the letter's signers were Bush II officials such as Paul Wolfowitz, Elliott Abrams, Cheney's former deputy national security adviser, John Hannah, as well as FPI's four directors: *Weekly Standard* editor William Kristol; Brookings Institution fellow Robert Kagan; former Iraq Coalition Provisional Authority spokesman Dan Senor; and former Undersecretary of Defense for Policy and Ambassador to Turkey, Eric Edelman. Peter Myers points out: "Whereas the Iraq and Afghan wars were brought about through agitation by Israel and the Zionist lobby in the US, this is not the case with the Libya war. It's more like the dismemberment of Yugoslavia, with the US siding with Islamists (Kosovo, the Saudi monarchy, and a would-be Emirate in Benghazi) against Socialists of the neo-Stalinist camp (i.e., critics of Stalin who nevertheless somewhat followed his path)." Peter Myers, "Petras vs Chomsky on 'Oil' motive in the Libya war; neither notices Soros' role", 3 April 2011<*www.mailstar.net/oneworld.html*>.

16   11 out of 22 AL members were summoned for an emergency session; nine voted for the no-fly-zone, including the five GCC states and Saudi Arabia, with Syria and Algeria against. See Pepe Escobar, "Exposed: The US-Saudi Libya deal", *www.atimes.com,* 2 April 2011.

17   "Libya: Barack Obama 'signed order for CIA to help rebels'", *Telegraph,* 16 April 2011.

18   For example, two FedEx letter bombs supposedly sent from Yemen addressed to Chicago synagogues 'discovered' in October 2010 were widely seen as a pretext for direct US-Saudi intervention. "Why was Saudi Arabia the first to tell the world about the packages? Does this mean al-Qaeda is infiltrated by Saudi intelligence?"

Nabil Al-Bukairi in Nasser Arrabyee, "Why Yemen?" *Al-Ahram Weekly* 2 November 2010.

19   "Vladimir Putin said it is 'quite possible' that Russia will one day join the eurozone and create a currency that would eclipse the US dollar as the global reserve standard." in Louise Armitstead, "Putin: Russia will Join the Euro One Day" *Telegraph*, 26 November 2010.

20   "Iran, India to use Chinese Yuan for oil payments", *www.worldoil.com*, 6 January 2011.

21   The empire-and-a-half are united around Iran precisely because of the danger it poses to dollar hegemony. On the US domestic scene, see James Petras, *Zionism, Militarism and the Decline of US Power*, Atlanta, USA: Clarity Press, 2008.

22   Pepe Escobar, "New Great Game Revisited Part I", *www.atimes.com*, 25 July 2009.

23   Necmettin Erbakan, head of the Islamic Welfare Party, became prime minister briefly in 1996 before the party was outlawed, but in 2003 Welfare's successor, the Justice and Development Party, swept the elections and has made Islam an integral part of Turkish cultural life again.

24   As Turkey has with Albania, Jordan, Lebanon, Libya and Syria.

25   The other arm of Gazprom's pincer move around Ukraine is Nord Stream for which Germany gave its final approval in 2009.

26   South Stream and Nabucco pipelines at <http://news.bbc.co.uk/1/hi/world/europe/8039587.stm>.

27   "In Beirut for 48 hours Recep Tayyip Erdogan", *www.zawya.com*, 29 November 2010. <http://www.zawya.com/story.cfm/sidZAWYA20101206073738/In%20Beirut%20for%2048%20hours%20Recep%20Tayyip%20Erdogan/>.

28   Almost the same number saw Turkey "as a successful synthesis of Islam and democracy". Turkish Economic and Social Studies Foundation, "Mideast people see Turkey as model" *www.middle-east-online.com*, 3 February 2011.

29   Mark Mazzetti, Jane Perlez, Eric Schmitt, Andrew Lehren, "Pakistan Aids Insurgency in Afghanistan, Reports Assert", *The New York Times*, 25 July 2010.

30   William Dalrymple, "This is no NATO game but Pakistan's proxy war with its brother in the south", *Guardian*, 1 July 2010.

31   "Context of 'Late Fall-Early Winter 2001: Iranians Offer Assistance to US in War with Taliban'", *www.historycommons.org*, n.d..

32   "National News Executive Summary" http://list.plcom.on.ca, P&L Communications Inc, 7 August 2010.

33   Rob Johnson, *Oil, Islam and conflict: Central Asia since 1945*, London: Reaktion, 2007, 41.

34   Vladimir Radyuhin, "Russia warns the West against interference", *The Hindu*, 11 March 2011.

35   See for instance Nikolai Trubetskoi, *Europe and Man*, Moscow, 1920.

36   Brzezinski, *The Grand Chessboard*, 118.

37   Ibid., 119.

38   President Medvedev at the 2010 NATO summit, on agreeing to cooperate with NATO on missile defence.

39   Brzezinski, *The Grand Chessboard*, 117.

40   The Russians are setting up air defenses around the Syrian naval bases in Latakia and Tartus that will also provide an air umbrella for the entire Syrian coast and parts of the hinterland, using the base in Tartus which the Soviets occupied from 1971–91. See author's "Russia/ America: Rediscovering Realpolitik", *ericwalberg.com*, 19 May 2010.

41   Litvinenko converted to Islam on his deathbed, attended by exiled Chechen rebel leader Akhmed Zakayev and oligarch-in-exile Berezovsky, who is also Israeli.

42   Bill Kristol regularly attacked Bush II for his "appeasement" of Beijing. The PNAC successor, the Foreign Policy Institute, focuses on "challenges" posed by "rising and resurgent powers" China and Russia.

43   "The United States will seek to contain China and ultimately weaken it to the point where it is no longer capable of dominating Asia. In essence, the United States is likely to behave toward China much the way it behaved toward the Soviet Union during the Cold War." John Mearsheimer, in Mearsheimer and Brzezinski, "Clash of the Titans", *Foreign Policy*, Issue 146, Jan/Feb 2005.

44   After claims that China harassed ExxonMobil ships prospecting for oil near the Paracels Islands off the coast of Vietnam, Secretary of Defense Gates says the US has a "longstanding policy that it takes no position on conflicting sovereignty claims in the South China Sea" but objects "to any effort to intimidate US corporations or those of any nation engaged in legitimate economic activity". Vietnam's détente with the US is clearly a tit-for-tat: the US government will support US corporations' economic activity requiring Vietnamese sovereignty. Jonathan Adams, "South China Sea: The coming war?" *www.globalpost.com*, 27 June 2010.

45   The new 'enemy' was confirmed by MGM's 2010 remake of "Red Dawn", with the Soviet Russians replaced by the Chinese (abetted by the Russians), and with the US president deploying troops in Taiwan and welcoming Georgia into NATO. The hero is an Afghanistan war veteran who switches from fighting Islamists to fighting the Chinese invading via Alaska. Ironically the film's release was held up for lack of funding due to the post-2008 economic crisis, and, in a case of 'economics trumps politics', after it was finished in 2011 the producer digitally removed the images of Chinese flag and Chinese military symbols, and altered the dialogue in the movies, changing the invaders into North Koreans, with an eye on the Chinese market.

46   Brzezinski, *The Grand Chessboard,* 210.

47   Pepe Escobar, "Pipelineistan's New Silk Road", *www.tomdispatch.com*, 12 October 2010.

48   Ibid.

49   Merlin Flower, "China could displace US Dollar dominance", *www.oil-price.net*, 14 October 2009.

50   "Ausweitung der Yuan-Menge China attackiert den Dollar", *www.spiegel.de*, 2 March 2011.

51   Ostrovsky, *By Way of Deception*, 27.

52   See Mearsheimer and Brzezinski, "Clash of the Titans".

53   Martin Jacques, "A new sun rises in the east", *New Statesman,* 25 June 2009.

54   Brzezinski, *The Grand Chessboard,* 45.

55   "Huge New US-India Arms Deal To Contain China", *www.globalresearch.ca*, 13 July 2010.

56   Pakistan has been a destabilizing force in Afghanistan, out for its own geopolitical ends all along. The scenario that Iran wants is Karzai without the US. Pakistan would have to go along if the US overcomes its aversion to Iran and this scenario succeeds.

57   The eagerness of France and Britain in the NATO operation against Libya which started in March 2011—and the willingness of Russia to go along—was due to its implications for NATO in Europe. It shifted NATO south to police north Africa, taking pressure off Russia and giving pre-eminence to France and Britain over Germany. The EU will be drawn south as well, which will leave Germany and Russia

on the sidelines. This could actually accelerate Russian-EU integration if NATO is preoccupied elsewhere and not involved in Georgia and the Caucasus.

58   James Baker, "America's Vital Interest in the 'New Silk Road'", *The New York Times*, 21 July 1997.

59   Brzezinski, *The Grand Chessboard*, 117.

60   A coalition of dissident Social Democrats and the Party of Democratic Socialism— the successor of the Socialist Unity Party of Germany, which merged in 2007.

61   Brzezinski, *The Grand Chessboard*, 117.

62   The US and Israel withdrew from the conference even though the final Declaration and Program of Action did not contain the text that the US and Israel objected to. A separately held NGO Forum also produced a Declaration and Program of its own, asserting the Zionism-racism connection.

63   Richard Falk, "The Palestinians are winning the legitimacy war: will it matter?" *Transnational Institute* April 2010. See also Francis Boyle, *The Palestinian Right of Return Under International Law*, Atlanta, USA: Clarity Press, 2011.

64   Boris Johnson, "George W. Bush can't fight for freedom and authorise torture", *Telegraph*, 26 November 2010.

65   The government argument at the time was that because there are "potentially many American Jews who might consider spying for Israel, Pollard must receive an especially harsh sentence." Ginsberg, *Fatal Embrace: Jews and the State*, 216.

66   See Gadi Taub, "In Israel, Settling for Less", *The New York Times*, 29 August 2010, and such polemics as Donna Rosenthal, *The Israelis: Ordinary People in an Extraordinary Land*, New York: Free Press, 2004.

67   Shahada (profession of belief), salah (5-times daily prayer), sawm (fasting during the month of Ramadan), zakat (charitable donations of 2.5 per cent of one's wealth every year), hajj (pilgrimage)

68   Luigi Pasinetti at Cambridge University in the 1970s argued that a long run real positive interest rate is impossible except in the presence of per capita productivity increase. This is a conclusion that you can reach from purely economic argument or from all three monotheisms.

69   Engdahl mentions "peak oil" worries, citing a Submission to the Cabinet Office on Energy Policy in Britain coincidentally published on 9/11 2001 which targeted Iraq as the most likely long term source of cheap oil. Engdahl, *A Century of War*, 259.

70   "the strategic management of geopolitical interests" in Brzezinski, *The Grand Chessboard*, xiv.

71   Ibid., xiii.

72   Ibid., 30.

73   Ibid., 35.

74   "Zbigniew Brzezinski Calls Iraq War a Historic, Strategic and Moral Calamity & Says Stop the Trappings of Colonial Tutelage", *www.thewashingtonnote.com*, 31 January 2007.

75   The logic that Brzezinski operated on is wittily captured by Thomas Friedman's quip, "No two countries with a McDonald's restaurant have ever gone to war." Thomas Friedman, *The Lexus and the Olive Tree*, New York: Anchor Books, 2000, 253.

76   Zbigniew Brzezinski, *Out of Control: Global Turmoil on the Eve of the 21st century*, London: Collier, 1993, 221–2.

77   Lutz Kleveman, *The New Great Game: Blood and Oil in Central Asia*, New York: Grove Press, 2004, 3.

78   Rein Mullerson, *Central Asia: A Chessboard and Player in the New Great Game*,

New York: Columbia University Press, 2007, 98.

79   Thomas Friedman, "The Real War", *International Herald Tribune,* 25 November 2001.

80   Bernard Lewis, "What Went Wrong?" *Atlantic Monthly,* 6 January 2002, 289, quoted in Mullerson, *Central Asia,* 112.

81   John Hopkins University, "The Key to Success in Afghanistan: A Modern Silk Road Strategy", 2010.

82   Alexander Dugin, *The Foundations of Geopolitics: The Geopolitical Future of Russia,* Moscow: Arktogeya, 1997.

83   Vladimir Radyuhin, "Russia warns the West against interference", *The Hindu,* 11 March 2011.

84   Matthew Edwards, "The New Great Game and the new great gamers: disciples of Kipling and Mackinder", March 2003.

85   Mullerson, *Central Asia,* 36.

86   Ibid., 38.

87   Ibid., 91.

88   Ibid., 76.

89   Ibid., 111.

90   Johnson, *Oil, Islam and Conflict: Central Asia since 1945,* 33–4.

91   Engdahl, *"A Century of War,* 156.

92   Joe Biden, Conversation with Katie Couric, *Foreign Affairs,* Washington: CFR, 25 February 2008.

93   Interview in *Le Monde,* quoted in Pepe Escobar, "Globocop versus the TermiNATO", *www.atimes.com,* 4 April 2009.

94   Robert McMahon interview with A. Feigenbaum, "The SCO Role in Afghanistan", *Foreign Affairs,* Washington: CFR, 26 March 2009.

95   Given that the borders are arbitrary and that these are really just pseudo-states, Russia, as the backbone of the CSTO, might reasonably have responded to a member's crisis. Russia and used the opportunity to establish itself as a benign regional hegemon.

96   A quarter of the population are Russian and Russian remains the *lingua franca.*

97   Mullerson, *Central Asia,* 94.

98   See Konstantin Parshin "Uzbekistan vs. Tajikistan: Competition over Water Resources Intensifying", *www.eurasianet.org,* 8 December 2010.

99   See M.K. Bhadrakumar, "Kosovo on the Central Asian steppes", *Asia Times,* 7 August 2010.

100   Deirdre Tynan, "Turkmenistan: Ashgabat Playing Key US/NATO Support Role In Afghan War", *www.eurasianet.org,* 10 January 2011.

101   The most significant Islamic groups active in Central Asia include the Islamic Revival Party of Tajikistan, the United Tajik Opposition, the Islamic Renaissance Party, Hizb ut-Tahrir, the more militant Islamic Movement of Uzbekistan, the Islamic Jihad Union, the Movement for the Islamic Revival of Uzbekistan, the East Turkistan Islamic Movement and the Islamic Movement of Turkistan. See Ben West, "The Tajikistan Attacks and Islamist Militancy in Central Asia", *www.stratfor,* 23 September 2010.

102   During his only official visit to the US in 2002, Leviev and Kissinger arranged for Karimov to get the Beer Hagolah Institute's award for international leadership in recognition of Karimov's support of the Uzbek Jewish community and of the war on terror. Chabad boasts three centers in Uzbekistan (Tashkent, Samarkand, Bukhara), each with its Chabad emissary and rabbi. There is a Chabad rabbi in Andijan, the

site of the massacre of a thousand Muslims in 2005.

103   In 2002, then-Foreign Minister Shimon Peres and Defense Minister Binyamin Ben-Eliezer asked him to have Nazarbayev (as Muslim leader of Kazakhstan) intervene with Iran concerning Israeli soldiers captured by Hizbullah.

104   Ilya Bourtman, "Israel and Azerbaijan's Furtive Embrace," *Middle East Quarterly*, Volume 13, Number 3, Summer 2006.

105   Jimmy Johnson, "Palestinian rights don't factor into Israel-Azerbaijan relations", *electronicintifada.net*, 28 March 2011.

106   <http://213.251.145.96/cable/2009/01/09BAKU20.html>.

BIBLIOGRAPHY

Ahmed, Nafeez Mosaddeq, "Our terrorists", *New Internationalist*, 426, 25 October 2010.

Ahrari, Mohammed, and Beal, James, *The New Great Game in Muslim Central Asia*, Darby, USA: Diane Publishers, 1996.

Alam, M Shahid, *Israeli Exceptionalism: The Destabilizing Logic of Zionism*, New York: Palgrave Macmillan, 2009.

---- "Zionist Dialectics Past and Future", *www.foreignpolicyjournal.com*, 21 September 2010.

Ali, Tariq, *The Clash of Fundamentalisms: Crusades, Jihads and Modernity*, New York: Verso, 2002.

Asmus, Ronald, *Opening NATO's Doors*, New York: Columbia University Press, 2002.

---- with Kugler, R., Larrabee, S., "Building a new NATO", *Foreign Affairs*, Washington: CFR, September 1993.

Atwood, Paul, *War and Empire: The American Way of Life*, London: Pluto Press, 2010.

Atzmon, Gilad, "Credit Crunch or rather Zio Punch?" *www.giladatzmon.net*, 16 November 2009.

---- "Connecting the Zionist Dots", *www.giladatzmon.net*, 24 June 2010.

Bacevich, Andrew, *Washington Rules: America's Path to Permanent War*, New York: Metropolitan Books/Henry Holt & Company, 2010.

Bamford, James, *Body of Secrets: Anatomy of the Ultra-Secret National Security Agency from the Cold War Through the Dawn of a New Century*, New York: Doubleday, 2001.

Bhadrakumar, M.K.,"All roads lead out of Afghanistan", *www.atimes.com*, 20 December 2008.

---- "Russia, China, Iran redraw energy map", *www.atimes.com*, 8 January 2010.

---- "Obama's Yemeni odyssey targets China", *www.atimes.com*, 9 January 2010.

---- "Kosovo on the Central Asian steppes", *Asia Times*, 7 August 2010.

Bideleux, Robert and Jeffries, Ian, *A History of Eastern Europe: Crisis and Change*, New York: Routledge, 1998.

Blankfort, Jeff, "AIPAC Hijacks the Roadmap", *Counterpunch*, 27 May 2003.
---- "Damage Control: Noam Chomsky and the Israel-Palestine Conflict", *www.leftcurve. org*, 2005.

---- "The Debate that never Happened: Blankfort vs. Plitnick on the Israel Lobby", *peacepalestinedocuments*, July 2005.

---- Interview by Kathleen Wells, *www.race-talk.org*, 4 November 2010.

William Blum, *Killing Hope: US Military and CIA Interventions Since WWII*, New York: Common Courage Press, 2004.

---- *Rogue State: A Guide to the World's Only Superpower*, 2nd ed., New York: Common Courage Press, 2005.

Bolender, Keith, *Voices from the other side: An oral history of Terrorism against Cuba*, London: Pluto Press, 2010.

Bolton, K.R., "The Red Face of Israel", *www.foreignpolicyjournal.com*, 2 August 2010.

---- "Chinese TV Series Lauds Israel: The Alliance Between China and Zionism", *www.foreignpolicyjournal.com*, 18 August 2010.

Breitman, Richard and Goda, Norman, "Hitler's Shadow: Nazi War Criminals, US Intelligence, and the Cold War", Washington: National Archives, 2010. <http://www.archives.gov/iwg/reports/hitlers-shadow.pdf >.

Brisard Jean-Charles and Dasquie, Guillaume, *Forbidden Truth: US-Taliban Secret Oil Diplomacy, Saudi Arabia and the Failed Search for bin Laden*, New York: Nation Books, 2002.

Bulliet, Richard, *The Case for Islamo-Christian Civilization*, New York: Columbia University Press, 2006.

Brzezinski, Zbigniew, *Out of Control: Global Turmoil on the Eve of the 21st century*, London: Collier, 1993.

---- *The Grand Chessboard: American Primacy and its Geostrategic Imperatives*, New York: HarperCollins, 1997.

---- "Zbigniew Brzezinski Calls Iraq War a Historic, Strategic and Moral Calamity & Says Stop the Trappings of Colonial Tutelage", *www.thewashingtonnote.com*, 31 January 2007.

Cheney, Dick, "Defense Strategy for the 1990s: The Regional Defense Strategy", *www.informationclearinghouse.info*, January 1993.

Chomsky, Noam, *The Fateful Triangle*, New York: South End Press, 1999.

---- *Hegemony or Survival*, New York: Holt, 2003.

---- *The Abuse of Power and the Assault on Democracy*, New York: Metropolitan Books, 2006.

---- Introduction to Keith Bolender, *Voices from the other side: An oral history of Terrorism against Cuba*, London: Pluto Press, 2010.

---- with Edward Herman, *Manufacturing Consent: The Political Economy of the Mass Media*, New York: Pantheon, 2002.

Chossudovsky, Michel, "The Spoils of War: Afghanistan's Multibillion Dollar Heroin Trade", *www.globalresearch.ca*, 5 April 2004.

---- "Heroin is "Good for Your Health": Occupation Forces support Afghan Narcotics Trade", *www.globalresearch.ca*, 29 April 2007.

---- "War without Borders": Obama's "Long War", *www.globalresearch.ca*, 15 May 2010.

---- "The Siege against Gaza: America's Ongoing Support of Israeli Military and Intelligence Operations", *www.globalresearch.ca*, 10 July 2010.

---- "Preparing for World War III, Targeting Iran: Part I Global Warfare", *www.globalresearch.ca*, 1 August 2010.

---- "9/11 Analysis: From Ronald Reagan and the Soviet-Afghan War to George W Bush and September 11, 2001", *www.globalresearch.ca*, 9 September 2010.

---- "Towards a World War III Scenario? The Role of Israel in Triggering an Attack on Iran: Part II The Military Road Map", *www.globalresearch.ca*, 13 September 2010.

---- "'Manufacturing Dissent': the Anti-globalization Movement is Funded by the

Corporate Elites", *www.globalresearch.ca*, 20 September 2010.

Clark, Wesley, *Winning Modern Wars: Iraq, Terrorism, and the American Empire*, Jackson, USA: Public Affairs, 2003.

Clarke, Peter, *The Last Thousand Days of the British Empire*, London: Bloomsbury, 2008.

Cockburn, Alexander and St Clair, Jeffery, *White Out: The CIA, Drugs and the Press*, London: Verso, 1999.

Cook, Jonathan, *Israel and the Clash of Civilisations: Iraq, Iran and the Plan to Remake the Middle East*, London: Pluto, 2008.

Cooley, John, *Unholy Wars: Afghanistan, America and International Terrorism*, London: Pluto, 2002.

Cooper, Robert, "The Post-Modern State" in *Re-Ordering the World: The long-term implications of September 11th*, London: Foreign Policy Centre, 2008.

---- "Why we still need empires", *http://observer.guardian.co.uk*, 7 April 2002.

Cordovez, Diego and Harrison, Selig, *Out of Afghanistan: The Inside Story of the Soviet Withdrawal*, Oxford: Oxford University Press, 1995.

Dalrymple, William, "This is no NATO game but Pakistan's proxy war with its brother in the south" *www.guardian*, 1 July 2010. <http://www.guardian.co.uk/commentisfree/2010/jul/01/afghanistan-pakistan-proxy-war-with-india>.

Davidson, Lawrence, "The Peculiar Claim of Michael Oren: Invisible Israel?" *Counterpunch*, 21 October 2010.

Dichter, Avi, "Israel: We Destroyed Iraq. Iraq must Stay Divided and Isolated", *Jouhaina News*, 26 May 2010.

Dreyfuss, Robert, *Devil's Game: How the United States Helped Unleash Fundamentalist Islam*, New York: Owl Books, 2006. available at <http://godgovernmentglobalization.blogspot.com/2009/07/devils-game.html>.

Dufour, Jules, "The Worldwide Network of US Military Bases", *www.globalresearch.ca*, 1 July 2007.

Dugin, Alexander, *The Foundations of Geopolitics: The Geopolitical Future of Russia*, Moscow: Arktogeya, 1997.

Edmonds, Sibel, "The Three-Decade US-Mujahideen Partnership Still Going Strong", www.informationclearinghouse.info, 14 October 2010.

Edwards, Matthew, "The New Great Game and the new great gamers: disciples of Kipling and Mackinder", *Central Asian Survey* 22 (1): 83–103, March 2003.

Ehreshani, A., "Geopolitics of hydrocarbons in Central and Western Asia" in Akiner, Shirin ed., *The Caspian. Politics, Energy and Security*, London: RoutledgeCurzon, 2004.

El-Azawi, Muhannad, "Partioning Iraq" *Al-Ahram Weekly*, 30 September 2010.

Emmott, Bill, *Rivals: How the Power Struggle between China, India and Japan will Shape our World*, Chicago, USA: Houghton Mifflin Harcourt, 2008.

Engdahl, William, *A Century of War: Anglo-American Oil Politics and the New World Order*, revised ed., London: Pluto, [1992] 2004.

---- "America's Phoney War in Afghanistan", *www.globalresearch.ca*, 21 October 2009.

Engelhardt, Tom, *The American Way of War*, London: Haymarket, 2010.

Escobar, Pepe, "Exit strategy: Civil war", *www.atimes.com*, 10 June 2005.

---- *Globalistan: How the Globalized World is Dissolving into Liquid War*, Ann Arbor, USA: Nimble Books, 2007.

---- "The New Great Game Revisited", *www.atimes.com*, 25 July 2009.

---- "Obama's Massive Power Struggle with the American War Machine", *www.alternet. org*, 24 September 2010.

---- "Pipelineistan's New Silk Road", *www.tomdispatch.com*, 12 October 2010.

Estulin, Daniel, *The True Story of the Bilderberg Group,* Oregon: TrineDay LLC, 2007.

Falk, Richard, "The Palestinians are winning the legitimacy war: will it matter?" *Transnational Institute*, April 2010.

Finkelstein, Norman, *The Holocaust Industry: Reflections on the Exploitation of Jewish Suffering*, New York: Verso, 2000.

---- interview by Jelle Bruinsma, "Are American Jews Beginning to Distance Themselves from Israel?" *Counterpunch,* 1 May 2006.

---- interview by Selcuk Gultasli, *Today's Zaman* (Turkey), 19 January 2009.

Fogel, Bryan and Wolfson, Sam, *Jewtopia: The Chosen Book for the Chosen People*, New York: Grand Central Publishing, 2006.

Freedland, Jonathan, "Bush's Amazing Achievement", *New York Review of Books*, 14 June 2007.

Freeman, A. and Kagarlitksy B. eds, *The Politics of Empire: Globalisation in Crisis,* London: Pluto Press, 2004.

Freeman, Charles, "Charles Freeman's Statement in Wake of Withdrawal From Intelligence Post", *Wall Street Journal*, 10 March 2009.

---- "Israel is useless to US power projection" *http://mondoweiss.net*, 30 April 2010.

---- "Israel: Strategic Ally or Liability?" Nixon Center debate *http://www.nixoncenter. org*, July 2010. Note: The article has been removed from the Nixon Center site and is available at <http://www.intifada-palestine.com/2010/07/chas-freeman-"israel-asset-or-liability"/>.

Friedman, Robert I., *Red Mafiya: How the Russian Mob Has Invaded America*, Berkeley, USA: Little Brown, 2002.

Friedman, Thomas, "Vote France Off the Island", *www.globalpolicy.org*, 9 February 2003.

Gabler, Neal, *An Empire of Their Own: How the Jews Created Hollywood,* New York: Doubleday, 1988.

Ganser, Daniele, *NATO's Secret Armies: Operation GLADIO and Terrorism in Western Europe*, New York: Routledge, 2004.

Phil Gasper, *International Socialist Review*, November-December 2001.

Jeff, Gates, "Can the US Beat Israel at their Game?" *http://criminalstate.com,* 25 April 2010.

---- "Obama's Inner Eisenhower", 28 September 2010.

Ginsberg, Benjamin, *The Fatal Embrace: Jews and the State,* Chicago: University of Chicago Press, 1993.

Giraldi, Philip, "Who Owns General Petraeus?" *original.antiwar.com*, 28 July 2010.
---- "Israeli Mossad Spying in America", *www.intifada-palestine.com*, 23 August 2010 .

Global Research Unit For Political Economy, "The Economics and Politics of the World Social Forum: Lessons for the Struggle against 'Globalisation'", *www.globalresearch.ca*, January 2004 reissued 5 September 2010.

Globalsecurity.org, "Target Iran – Air Strikes", 14 April 2007.

Gordon, Philip, "Give NATO a Role in Post-war Iraq", Brookings Institute, 10 April 2003.

Gray, John, *Black Mass: Apocalyptic Religion and the Death of Utopia*, New York: Farrar, Straus & Giroux, 2007.

Harms, Gregory, *Straight Power Concepts in the Middle East: US Foreign Policy, Israel, and World History*, London: Pluto, 2010.

Harneis,Robert, "Old-fashion imperialism", *Al-Ahram Weekly*, 12 August 2010.

Hart, Alan, *Zionism: The Real Enemy of the Jews Volume One: The False Messiah*, Atlanta, USA: Clarity Press, 2009.

Hersh, Seymour, "Watching Lebanon", *New Yorker*, 21 August 2006.

Hertzberg, Arthur, *The Jews in America*, New York: Columbia University Press, 1986.

Hever, Shir, *The Political Economy of Israel's Occupation: Repression Beyond Exploitation*, London: Pluto Books, 2010.

Hilferding, Rudolph, *Finance Capital (Das Finanzkapital)*, Vienna, 1910.

Hobsbawm, E.J., *Age of Empire: 1875—1914*, London, Weidenfeld & Nicolson, 1987.

Hobson, J.A., *Imperialism: A Study*, 3d ed., London: Allen and Unwin, [1902] 1938.

Hoodbhoy, Pervez, "Afghanistan and the Genesis of the Global Jihad", *Peace Research*, 1 May 2005.

Hudson Michael, *Super Imperialism: Economic Strategy of the American Empire*, London: Pluto Press, [1972] 2003.

---- "Financial Bailout: America's Own Kleptocracy: The largest transformation of America's Financial System since the Great Depression", *www.michael-hudson.com*, September 2008

----"The Ending of America's Financial-Military Empire", *Counterpunch*, 15 June 2009.

---- with Jeffrey Sommers, "The Spectre Haunting Europe: Debt Defaults, Austerity, and Death of the 'Social Europe' Model", *www.globalresearch*, 18 January 2011.

Ignatieff, Michael, *Empire Lite: Nation-building in Bosnia, Kosovo and Afghanistan*, London: Vintage, 2003.

---- "The American Empire: The Burden", *New York Times Magazine*, 5 January 2003.

Institute for Advanced Strategic and Political Studies, *Coping with Crumbling States: A Western and Israeli Balance of Power Strategy for the Levant*, December 1996. Available at <http://www.israeleconomy.org/strat2.htm>.

Ivashov, General Leonid, "In the Interests of Israel": Why Russia will not sell the S-300 Air Defense System to Iran, *www.voltaire.net*, 29 September 2010.

Jacques, Martin, *When China Rules the World: The End of the Western World and the Birth of a New Global Order*, London: Penguin, 2009. excerpted at "A new sun rises in the east", *New Statesman*, 25 June 2009.

John Hopkins University, "The Key to Success in Afghanistan: A Modern Silk Road Strategy", School of Advanced International Studies and the Center for Strategic and International Studies, Central Asia-Caucasus Institute Silk Road Studies Program, 2010. < http://www.silkroadstudies.org/new/docs/silkroadpapers/1005Afghan.pdf>.

Johnson, Chalmers, *Nemesis: The Last Days of the American Republic*, New York: Metropolitan Books, 2007.

---- *Dismantling the Empire – America's Last Best Hope*, New York: Metropolitan Books, 2010.

Johnson, M. Raphael, "The Judeo-Russian Mafia: From the Gulag to Brooklyn to World Dominion", The Barnes Review, May/June 2006. Available at <http://www. iamthewitness.com/books/Raphael.Johnson/The.Judeo-Russian.Mafia.pdf>.

Johnson, Rob, *Oil, Islam and conflict: Central Asia since 1945,* London: Reaktion, 2007.

Johnstone, Diana, *Fools' Crusade: Yugoslavia, NATO and Western Delusions*, Monthly Review Press, 2003.

---- "Nothing to Gain, More to Lose: Serbia Surrenders Kosovo to the UN" *Counterpunch,* 18 September 2010.

---- "NATO'S True Role in US Grand Strategy", *Counterpunch,* 18 November 2010.

Joseph, Edward and O'Hanlon, Michael, "The case for soft partition in Iraq", Washington: Saban Centre for Middle East Policy, Brookings Institute, 30 September 2010.

Kagan, Robert, *Of Paradise and Power: America and Europe in the New World Order,* New York: Alfred Knopf, 2003.

Kamal, Yousuf, *The Principles of the Islamic Economic System*, Cairo: Dar Al-Nashr for Universities, 1996.

Kedourie, Elie, *Nationalism,* London: Hutchinson University Library, [1960] 1985.

Kelly, Kevin, *Out of Control*: *The New Biology of Machines,* London: Fourth Estate, 1994.

Kershaw, Peter, *Economic Solutions,* Englewood CO: Quality Press, 1994.

Kimmerling, Baruch, *Politicide: Sharon's War Against the Palestinians*, London: Verso, 2003.

Kissinger, Henry, *Years of Upheaval*, Boston: Little Brown, 1982.

Kleveman, Lutz, *The New Great Game: Blood and Oil in Central Asia,* New York: Grove Press, 2004.

Labeviere, Richard, *Dollars for Terror: The US and Islam*, New York: Algora Publishing, 1999.

Lendman, Stephen, review of F William Engdahl *Full Spectrum Dominance: Totalitarian Democracy in the New World Order,* Third Millennium, 2009, *www.globalresearch.ca*, 22 June 2009.

---- "Nato's Secret Armies", *www.rebelnews.org*, 16 September 2010.

Lenin, Vladimir, *Imperialism, the Highest Stage of Capitalism*, Peking: Foreign Languages Press, [1917] 1970.

Lieber, Keir, and Press, Daryl, "The Rise of US Nuclear Primacy", *Foreign Affairs,* Washington: CFR, March 2006.

Lieven, Anatol, *America right or wrong: an anatomy of American nationalism,* Oxford: Oxford University Press, 2004.

Lindemann, Alfred, *Esau's Tears*, Cambridge: Cambridge University Press, 1997.

Linfield, Michael, *Freedom under Fire: Civil Liberties in times of War*, New York: South End, 1999.

Louis, William Roger, *The British Empire in the Middle East,* Oxford: Oxford University Press, 1984.

Mackinder, Halford, *Geographical Journal*, Volume 23, 1904.

---- *Democratic Ideals and Reality: a study in the politics of reconstruction,* New York: W.W. Norton, [1919] 1969.

---- "The Round World and the Winning of the Peace", *Foreign Affairs,* Washington: CFR, Volume 21, Number 4, July 1943.

Mahajan, Rahul, *Full Spectrum Dominance*, New York: 7 Stories, 2003.

Mahsud, Enver, *9/11 Unveiled*, USA: Wisdom Fund, 2009.

Marshall, Andrew Gavin, "Creating an "Arc of Crisis": The Destabilization of the Middle

East and Central Asia: The Mumbai Attacks and the 'Strategy of Tension'", *www. globalresearch.ca*, 7 December 2008.

---- "Wikileaks and the Worldwide Information War Power, Propaganda, and the Global Political Awakening", *www.globalresearch.ca*, 6 December 2010.

Margolis, Eric, *American Raj: America and the Muslim World,* Toronto: Key Porter, 2009.

---- "China and India: A War of Giants", *www.ericmargolis.com*, 29 August 2010.

Mccoy, Alfred, *The Politics of Heroin: CIA Complicity in the Global Drug Trade*, revised ed., Chicago, USA: Lawrence Hill, [1991] 2003.

---- "Drug Fallout: the CIA's Forty Year Complicity in the Narcotics Trade", *The Progressive*, 1 August 1997.

Mearsheimer, John, "The Future of Palestine: Righteous Jews vs. the New Afrikaners", *www.thejerusalemfund.org* Transcript No 327, 29 April 2010.

---- with Zbigniew Brzezinski, "Clash of the Titans", *Foreign Policy*, Washington: CFR, Issue 146, Jan/Feb2005. Available at <http://mearsheimer.uchicago.edu/pdfs/A0034.pdf>.

---- and Walt, Stephen, "The Israel Lobby", *London Review of Books*, Volume 28 Number 6, 23 March 23 2006.
Menon, Debbie, "Can Obama escape the dominating influence of AIPAC and the American Jewish/Zionist Israeli lobby?" *http://payvand.com*, 2 December 2009.

Mitchell, Richard, *The Society of the Muslim Brothers*, London: Oxford University Press, 1969.

Monbiot, George, "Oil, Afghanistan and America's pipe dream", *www.dawn.com*, 25 October 2001.

Muller, Jerry, *Capitalism and the Jews*, Princeton: Princeton University Press, 2010.

Mullerson, Rein, *Central Asia: A Chessboard and Player in the New Great Game*, New York: Columbia University Press, 2007.

Myers, Peter "Petras vs Chomsky on 'Oil' motive in the Libya war; neither notices Soros' role", 3 April 2011, <www.mailstar.net/oneworld.html>.

NATO, "NATO Training Mission - Iraq" <http://www.nhq.nato.int/ntmi/articles/2010/ artice3310.html, 2010>.

Nazemroaya, Mahdi Darius, "Geo-Strategic Chessboard: War Between India and China?" *www.globalresearch.ca*, 17 October 2009.

Niazi (Makni), Muhammad Aslam Khan, *The New Great Game: Oil and Gas Politics in Central Eurasia*, New York: Raider Publishing International, 2008.

O Cathail, Maidhc, "Who's To Blame For The Iraq War?" *www.countercurrents.org*, 16 March 2010.

Ostrovsky, Victor and Hoy, Claire, *By Way of Deception*, New York: St Martin's Press, 1990.

Papic, Marko, "NATO's Lack of a Strategic Concept", *www.stratfor*, 12 October 2010.

Pappe, Ilan, "What drives Israel?" *www.heraldscotland.com*, 6 June 2010.

Perkins, John, *Confessions of an Economic Hit Man,* San Francisco: Berret-Koehler, 2004.

---- conversation with Amy Goodman, "Confessions of an Economic Hit Man", *www. informationclearinghouse.info*, 2010.

Peters, Ralph, "Blood borders: How a better Middle East would look", *Armed Forces Journal,* June 2006

Petras, James, "Capitalism versus socialism: The great debate revisited", *www. globalresearch.ca*, 28 June 2004.

---- *The Power of Israel in the United States,* Atlanta, USA: Clarity Press, 2006.

---- "Bended Knees: Zionist Power in American Politics", *James Petras website*, 20 December 2009

---- "The CIA and the Cultural Cold War Revisited" *Monthly Review* Volume 51, November 1999.

---- "The State and Local Bases of Zionist Power in America", *www.atlanticfreepress.com*, 1 September 2010.

----and Veltmeyer, H., *Empire with Imperialism: Global Dynamics of Neoliberal Capitalism,* London: Zed, 2005.

Petrov, Krassimir, "The Proposed Iranian Oil Bourse", *Christmartenson.com*, 29 October 2008.

Project for a New American Century (PNAC) "A Clean Break: A New Strategy for Securing the Realm", *www.iasps.org*, 1996.

---- "Rebuilding America's Defenses: Strategy, Forces and Resources for a New Century", *www.newamericancentury.org*, September 2000.

PRNewswire "Declassified Senate Investigation Files Reveal Clandestine Israeli PR Campaign in America", *www.prnewswire.com*, 23 July 2010.

Quigley, Carroll, *Tragedy and Hope,* Georgetown: University Press, 1996. Available at <http://www.archive.org/stream/TragedyAndHope/TH_djvu.txt>.

Rabinovich, Abraham, *The Yom Kippur War: The Epic Encounter That Transformed the Middle East*, New York: Schocken Books, 2004.

Rabkin,Yakov, *A Threat from Within: A History of Jewish Opposition to Zionism*, London: Zed, 2006.

Rashid, Ahmed, *Taliban: Militant Islam, Oil and Fundamentalism in Central Asia,* New York: Yale Nota Bene, 2000.

Roberts, Frederick Sleigh, *Forty-One Years in India*, London: Richard Bentley and Son, 1896. Available at <http://www.gutenberg.org/ebooks/16528>.

Rogers, Paul, *Losing Control*, London: Pluto Press, 2009.

Rokach, Livia, *Israel's Sacred Terrorism: A Study Based on Moshe Sharett's Personal Diary and Other Documents,* Belmont, Massachusetts: Association of Arab American University Graduates, 1980.

Rozoff, Rick, "Pentagon Plans For Global Military Supremacy: US, NATO Could Deploy Mobile Missiles Launchers To Europe", *www.globalresearch.ca*, 22 August 2009.

--- "US Expands Asian NATO Against China, Russia", *www.globalresearch.ca*, 16 October 2009.

---- "Israel: Global NATO's 29th Member", *www.globalresearch.ca*, 17 January 2010.

---- "US Consolidates Military Network In Asia-Pacific Region", *www.globalresearch.ca*, 29 April 2010.

---- "US Cyber Command: Waging War In The World's Fifth Battlespace", *www.globalresearch.ca*, 27 May 2010.

--- "NATO's Role In The Military Encirclement Of Iran", *www.globalresearch.ca*, 26 June 2010.

---- "Iraq: NATO Assists In Building New Middle East Proxy Army", *www.globalresearch.ca*, 14 August 2010.

---- "India: US Completes Global Military Structure", *http://rickrozoff.wordpress.com*, 10 September 2010.

---- "Securing The 21st Century For NATO", *www.globalresearch.ca*, 26 September 2010.

Said, Edward, *Orientalism*, London: Vintage, 1979

---- "America's Last Taboo" http://newleftreview.org/A2285, *New Left Review* 6, November-December 2000.

---- "The Clash of Ignorance", *The Nation*, October 2001.
Saunders, Frances Stonor, *Who Paid the Piper: The CIA and the Cultural Cold War*, London: Granta Books, 1999.

Schulze, Reinhard, "Mass Culture and Islamic Cultural Production in the 19th Century Middle East", in Stauth, Georg and Zubaida, Sami eds, *Mass Culture, Popular Culture and Social Life in the Middle East*, Boulder, USA: Westview Press, 1987.

Scott, Peter Dale, *Drugs Oil and War: The United States in Afghanistan, Colombia, and Indochina,* New York: Rowman and Littlefield, 2003.

---- "Continuity of Government: Is the State of Emergency Superseding our Constitution?" *www.globalresearch.ca*, 24 November 2010.

Segev, Tom, *One Palestine*, New York: Complete Metropolitan Books, 2000.

Shahak, Israel, *Open Secrets: Israel Nuclear and Foreign Policies*, London: Pluto Press, 1993.

---- and Mezvinsky, Norton, *Jewish Fundamentalism in Israel*, London: Pluto Press, 1999.

Shamir, Israel, "Prince Charming", *www.left.ru*, 2002.

---- *Pardes: An etude in Cabbala,* USA: BookSurge, 2005.

---- "Who Needs Holocaust?" *www.israelshamir.net*, 2006.

---- *Masters of Discourse*, USA: BookSurge, 2008.

---- "Fear Not", *www.israelshamir.net*, August 2010.

Shamir, Yoav, "Defamation", 2009. <http://www.defamation-thefilm.com/html/about_ yoav_shamir.html>.

Sheehi, Stephen, *Islamophobia: The Ideological Campaign Against Muslims*, Atlanta, USA: Clarity, 2011.

Shuckburgh, Evelyn, *Descent to Suez: Diaries 1951–1956*, London: Weidefeld and Nicolson, 1986.

Silber, Steven, "Economics / The Midas Touch", review of Jerry Muller's *Capitalism and the Jews, www.haaretz.com,* 1 July 2010.

Sniegorski, Stephen, *The Transparent Cabal: The Neoconservative Agenda, War in the Middle East, and the National Interest of Israel*, Norfolk, USA: Ihs Press, 2008.

Snow, Keith Harmon, "Gertler's Bling Bang Torah Gang: Israel and the Ongoing Holocaust in Congo (Part 1)", *dissidentvoice.org*, 9 February 2008.

Sombart, Werner, *The Jews and Modern Capitalism*, translated by M. Epstein, Glencoe IL: The Free Press, [Leipzig, 1911] 1951.

Stratchey, John, *The End of Empire*, New York: Praeger, 1959.

Taub,Gadi, "In Israel, Settling for Less", *New York Times,* 29 August 2010.

Tessler, Mark, *A History of the Israeli-Palestinian Conflict*, Bloomington IN: Indiana University Press, 1994.

Thrall, Nathan, "Our Man in Palestine", *New York Review of Books*, 14 October 2010.

Trento, Joseph, *Prelude to Terror: Edwin P Wilson and the Legacy of America's Private Intelligence Network*, New York: Carroll and Graf, 2005.

US Department of Defense, *Joint Vision 2020*, 2000.

Vaïsse, Justin, *Neoconservatism: The Biography of a Movement*, Harvard: Harvard University Press, 2010.

Vernochet, Jean-Michel, "Euro: The Worst Case Scenario", *www.voltairenet.org*, 21 July 2010.

---- "La guerre d'Iran aura-t-elle lieu?", *www.voltairenet.org*, 17 July 2010.

Waddell, Eric, "The Battle for Oil", *www.globalresearch.ca*, 14 December 2004.

Wallerstein, Immanuel interviewed by Jae-Jung Suh, "Capitalism's Demise?", *hnn.us*, 12 January 2009.

Wawro, Geoffrey, *Quicksand – America's Pursuit of Power in the ME*, New York: Penguin Press, 2010.

Woodward, Robert, *Obama's Wars*, New York: Simon and Schuster, 2010.

Wright, Edwin, "Zionist Jews Worked 'To Capture The U.S. Government'", *www.rense.com*, 19 September 2004.

Yinon, Oded, "A Strategy for Israel in the 1980s" *Kivunim*, WZO, 1982.

Zunes, Stephen, "The Israel Lobby: How Powerful is it Really?" *Mother Jones*, 18 May 2006.

Bibliography – Chapter 4 Appendix: Critique of 'New NATO' literature

Asmus, Ronald, *Opening NATO's Door: How the Alliance Remade Itself for a New Era*, New York: CFR-Columbia University Press, 2004.

Gheciu, Alexandra, *NATO in the "New Europe": The Politics of International Socialization after the Cold War*, Stanford, USA: Stanford University Press, 2005.

Gordon, Philip, "Give NATO a Role in Post-war Iraq", Washington: Brookings Institute, 10 April 2003.

Kaplan, Lawrence S., *NATO Divided, NATO United: The Evolution of an Alliance*, Santa Barbara, USA: Praeger, 2004.

Moore, Rebecca R., *NATO's New Mission: Projecting Stability in a Post-Cold War World*, Santa Barbara, USA: Praeger Security International, 2007.

Shalikashvili, General John and Sloan, Stanley R., *NATO, the European Union, and the Atlantic Community: The Transatlantic Bargain Reconsidered*, Rowan and Littlefield, 2002.

Slaughter, Marie-Ann, *A New World Order*, Princeton University Press, 2005.

Sloan, Stanley R., *Permanent Alliance? NATO and the Transatlantic Bargain from Truman to Obama*, New York: Continuum, 2010.

Thies, Wallace, *Why NATO Endures*, Cambridge MA: Cambridge University Press, 2009.

Ventura, Jesse, *American Conspiracy*, New York: Skyhorse, 2010.

Yost, David S., *NATO Transformed: The Alliance's New Roles in International Security*, Washington: US Institute of Peace, 1999.

INDEX